MINING
FRONTIERS
OF THE
FAR WEST,
1848-1880

HISTORIES OF THE AMERICAN FRONTIER

Ray Allen Billington, General Editor

Coeditors:
William Cronon, University of Wisconsin
Howard R. Lamar, Yale University
Martin Ridge, The Huntington Library
David J. Weber, Southern Methodist University

MINING FRONTIERS OF THE FAR WEST, 1848-1880

Rodman Wilson Paul
A Revised, Expanded Edition by Elliott West

UNIVERSITY OF NEW MEXICO PRESS
Albuquerque

Library of Congress Cataloging-in-Publication Data

Paul, Rodman Wilson, 1912–
  Mining frontiers of the Far West, 1848–1880 / Rodman Wilson Paul.
    p.   cm.– (Histories of the American Frontier)
    Includes bibliographical references.
  ISBN 0-8263-2771-0 (pbk. : alk. paper)
  1. Frontier and pioneer life–West (U.S.)   2. Mining camps–West
    (U.S.)–History–19th century   3. Mines and mineral resources–
    West (U.S.)–History–19th century.   4. West (U.S.)–History–
    1848–1860.   5. West (U.S.)–History–1860–1890.   6. West
    (U.S.)–Social conditions–19th century.   I. Title   II. Series.
F591 .P3   2001
978'.02–dc21
                                        2001026718

To Anne—R.W.P.

For my grandmother,
Virginia Page,
who showed me Georgetown—E.W.

CONTENTS

LIST OF MAPS
AND ILLUSTRATIONS

MAPS

ILLUSTRATIONS

THE SONGS

Scattered through the text are fragments from popular contemporary songs. They are intended to serve as illustration in words. In most cases they have been taken from the very popular little songbooks compiled by John A. Stone, who was better known as "Old Put." Two editions of this booklet have been used: *Put's Golden Songster, Containing the Largest and Most Popular Collection of California Songs Ever Published* (San Francisco, 1858), and *Put's Original California Songster, Giving a Few Words What Would Occupy Volumes, Detailing the Hopes, Trials and Joys of the Miner's Life* (4th ed.; San Francisco, 1868).

"Old Put" did not always print songs reported by other contemporaries. For example, the Fraser River song quoted on page 38 is from John S. Hittell, *Mining in the Pacific States of North America* (San Francisco, 1861), p. 30. Sometimes it has been necessary to reconcile conflicting versions, as in the case of the wording of the "The Days of the Forty-Nine," quoted on pages 178–179.

Two modern collections are: Eleanora Black and Sidney Robertson, *The Gold Rush Song Book, Comprising a Group of Twenty-Five Authentic Ballads as They Were Sung by the Men Who Dug for Gold in California during the Period of the Great Gold Rush of 1849* (San Francisco, 1940), and Benjamin A. Botkin, *A Treasury of Western Folklore* (New York, 1951).

FOREWORD TO THE 2001 EDITION

This new edition of Rodman W. Paul's *Mining Frontiers of the Far West,* with supplementary chapters by Elliott West, is a noteworthy event. Paul's book, although initially published in 1963, has never been supplanted in either scope or technical accuracy. It remains the premier book in the field. Paul, limited to a mere 100,000 words, managed to explain and analyze one of the most remarkable events in American history. Aware that not all prospectors "struck it rich," he demonstrates the transition from being a gold seeker to being a wage laborer employed to dig for gold. Paul focused on the business and technical institutions created by the mining frontier's insatiable need for skilled foreign labor, working capital, and scientific knowledge. He also recognized economist Joseph Schumpeter's doctrine of creative destruction: economic development always results in the displacement or destruction of one social system by another.

Elliott West's supplement to Paul's book is essentially the story of displacements. He looks at the lives of the people impacted by the mining frontier: the indigenous people living near the mines and those along the way West, the people of color, and the whites, both native and immigrant. He constructs a social rather than an economic or technical history of the years after the gold strike at Sutter's mill. Following that "historical moment" the eyes of the world turned to the mountain west as a place where riches could be gathered by simply picking gold nuggets out of the earth. Just as Rodman Paul demythologized the economic and technical aspects of mining, Elliott West rewrites the history of life in the mining camps and western industrial towns and his stories accurately recapture the boisterous cacophony of the multicultural and often gendered mining frontier. West sees the precious mineral mining frontier as a mirror of nineteenth-century America. It was a time for gamblers, but it was also an era in which industrial America came to fruition. The combined work of Rodman Paul and Elliott West gives readers a splendid and modern view of what the mining frontier meant to the American people and their economy at the beginning of the twentieth century.

Martin Ridge, The Huntington Library,
for the editors of the *Histories of the American Frontier* series

Coeditors:
William Cronon, University of Wisconsin
Howard R. Lamar, Yale University
David J. Weber, Southern Methodist University

FOREWORD TO THE 1963 EDITION

Hidden mineral resources were the lodestone that drew thousands upon thousands of pioneers westward during the three-century-long march of civilization across the American continent. The discovery of rich silver mines at Zacatecas in 1546 touched off the first of the North American "rushes" and started Spanish colonists on that northward advance that carried them ultimately into what is now the southwestern part of the United States. Almost a century later the noblemen and yeomen who braved the Atlantic's storms to plant the banner of England's virgin queen on Virginia's shores were impelled by the hope that they could stuff their pockets with golden nuggets and precious stones. They found no gold, but Virginia's first frontier was artificially advanced when bog iron was discovered in the forested interior, a discovery that helped assure economic stability for the struggling colony. Iron deposits also enticed New England's Puritans westward, upsetting the orderly pattern of agricultural settlement envisaged by the founding fathers. Generations later, pioneers leaped far ahead of the farming frontier to exploit the gold deposits hidden in what is today Georgia; there in the early nineteenth century occurred a mining rush complete with placers, claim jumping, and lynch law. Within a few years other venturesome Southerners were pushing into northwestern Illinois where they founded the village of Galena in the center of rich lead deposits. The Fever River district, as it was called, boasted a boisterous population and was fully equipped with saloons, dance halls, vigilance committees, and daily mayhem while the site of Chicago was still an onion swamp.

These early westward thrusts of the mining frontier only prepared pioneers for the more formidable—and exciting—tasks that lay ahead. Scarcely hidden in the mountains and streams of the Far West were pockets and lodes of silver and gold in such number and richness as to stagger the imagination of even the most starry-eyed prospector. As these were discovered, one after the other, in the years between 1848 and the late 1870s, a series of rushes occurred that brought the first permanent settlers to much of Western America. They began when workmen building a new sawmill on California's American River were electrified by the glint of yellow metal in the bed of the stream; the "rush of the forty-niners" that followed deposited some 50,000 would-be miners in the Mother Lode country of the Sierra Nevada within a single year. Few of them "struck it rich," for the small number of placer sites were soon appropriated, but those of the newcomers who did not return disgustedly to "the States" stayed to become farmers and tradesmen, laying the basis for California's remarkable growth.

Some among them were too smitten with the gold fever to adjust to such prosaic tasks. With a grub stake and a shovel and washing pan strapped to a mule's back, they set out to find gold and silver wherever it might be hidden in all the vast Far West. Most would-be miners wandered away their lives in the fruitless quest, but the few who made "strikes" not only enriched themselves but the nation. Each new discovery was followed by the inevitable rush—into Nevada and Arizona; over the Inland Empire of Washington, Idaho, and Montana; to the Pikes Peak country and out over the sprawling Rocky Mountains; and on into the Black Hills of South Dakota. Wherever miners went, farmers and shopkeepers and lawyers and all the multitudinous creators of a modern civilization followed them, to endow these future territories with their first permanent population. Yet this frontier of settlement differed markedly from the traditional frontiers of the East. Instead of seeking fertile, well-watered fields, miners were attracted to mountain and desert lands that might normally have waited generations for occupants. And instead of advancing from east to west, the mining frontier moved from west to east in a series of thrusts that left islands of wilderness between the new communities. The bridging of these gaps by improved transportation facilities helped open all the Far West to later-comers who completed its transition to the civilized land that we know today.

Many writers have described aspects of the mining frontier's history, but no serious historian has attempted to view the entire movement as an integral part of the settlement process. This is the task that Professor Rodman Wilson Paul has accomplished so brilliantly in this book. His purpose was twofold. He had to rescue the story of Western mining from the hands of fact-worshipping antiquarians, irresponsible popularizers, retired mining engineers, and imaginative tall-tale-tellers to reveal its true importance as a molding force in the evolution of the American social order. And he had to give cohesion to the story by tracing the interrelationships that existed between events and localities that were widely separated in time and space.

He has solved the first problem by stressing the enduring features of Western mining rather than the colorful but ephemeral phases that have fascinated most writers. The reader who seeks on his pages gripping descriptions of wild West rushes and ramshackle camps or hair-raising accounts of bad men and vigilantes will be sorely disappointed. These glamorous events and unsavory characters are justly ignored; their influence on the emerging Western social order was both slight and momentary. Instead his emphasis is on the permanent phases of Western mining and on the men who made them possible: the ingenious contrivers of new techniques or machinery, the hardheaded San Francisco capitalists whose shrewd investments subsidized the development of the most promising mines, the builders who fashioned the transportation routes needed to link mining camps with markets. These, and these alone, are the significant aspects of frontier history. If we are to understand the present by familiarizing ourselves with the past, we must isolate those aspects of the past that most influence the present. This Professor Paul has done with the story of Western mining, and his book is both fresh and informative as a result.

No less of a contribution is the skillful manner in which he has shown the interrelationship between the widely scattered mining frontiers of the Far West. He has brought order to the story for the first time by recognizing two unifying forces. One was provided by miners themselves; they moved from frontier to frontier as new discoveries were made, bearing with them techniques for the extraction of metals and the creation of societies that were applied over and over again with but slight variation. The startling similarities in the history of different mining districts—that of California's Mother Lode country in contrast with that of the Black Hills, for example—are for the first time understandable in the light of his findings. The second cohesive force isolated by Professor Paul was that of distribution centers and transportation routes. His meticulous study of the role played by San Francisco and St. Louis in Western mining—not to mention the subsidiary distribution centers that emerged along the transportation routes branching from these principal depots—makes clear why certain areas thrived or collapsed with little relationship to the quantities of mineral wealth contained in each. Readers can now understand *all* Western mining, not simply a small segment of the total story.

Scarcely less significant is Professor Paul's emphasis on the technical problems of Western mining. He demonstrates, as has no other historian, a thorough knowledge of both geology and technology; his lucid explanations of engineering techniques as they slowly evolved will prove useful to mere mortals without the skill or patience to master the vast specialized literature on that subject. They also shed light on one of the basic problems faced by historians probing the nature of the American character: the relative influence of environmental and hereditary forces in creating the distinctive civilization of the United States. The willingness of miners to innovate and the strong pull of tradition upon them as they grappled with the problem of extracting and processing metallic ores are both fully appraised. Professor Paul's findings on this subject are as timely today as they were when miners debated the relative merits of arrastras and crushing mills.

This volume is one of eighteen in *Histories of the American Frontier*. It tells a complete story; it may also be read as part of the broader history of westward expansion to be told in connected form in these volumes. Each is being written by a leading authority who brings to his task an intimate knowledge of the period and a demonstrated skill in narrations and interpretation. Each will provide the general reader with a sound but readable account of one phase of the nation's frontiering past, and the specialized student with a documented narrative that is integrated into the general story of the nation's growth. It is the hope of the authors and editor that this first full history of the most American phase of the American past will help the people of the United States to understand themselves, and thus be better equipped to face the global problems of the twentieth-century world.

Ray Allen Billington
Northwestern University
January 1963

PREFACE

Writing this book has been a satisfying experience, comparable to going off at last on a trip that has often been planned but always deferred. For more than twenty years the mining West has been a particular enthusiasm of mine. As inspiration and opportunity have thrust themselves forward, I have made a series of special studies that have been essentially small salients driven into the big central questions of the effect of gold and silver mining on the West, and the nature of that mining itself. Then one day the editor of this new series proposed a volume on the gold and silver frontiers. It was like offering World Series tickets to a baseball fan.

Only one significant restriction was written into the publishing contract. Each of the volumes in this series was to be not more than 100,000 words in length. In writing the present book, this limitation has proved to be, on the whole, a helpful influence. It has compelled a constant and ruthless scrutiny of each possible topic, based on asking oneself whether this or that subject or item was really necessary to the development of the main story. It has, perforce, caused analysis, synthesis, and interpretation to displace narrative as the historian's principal reliance.

On the other hand, readers will readily observe that this book is deliberately selective. There is no pretense to covering every episode or every geographic area embraced within the Far West in the years 1848–1880. Stress is upon those developments that proved to be of more than local and temporary significance. Where I have had to choose between incidents or mining communities that could make almost equally valid claims to consideration, I have fixed upon the ones that best satisfied my own judgment and that could be best studied in the materials available to me, fully realizing that another writer might have made a different choice. For this I offer no apologies save to the aficionados who will protest, with justification, that sometimes I have slighted a town or episode of which they are particularly fond. Some day perhaps I will try a highly detailed history, but it would be a big book with an appeal limited very largely to the small group of enthusiasts who share my own concern for this aspect of pioneer Western history.

What is more, any one who examines the subject closely will be impressed by the very large amount of internal repetition that such a book would involve. As the present volume seeks to demonstrate, the life stories of most mining centers can be classified into several broad categories or patterns. To illustrate each species by tracing the experiences of a few towns would be useful; to narrate the adventures of many towns would involve tedious duplication. There is, therefore, a considerable justification for being determinedly selective in discussing the history of gold and silver in the Far West.

The date with which this volume starts is obvious; a terminal date was much less easy to fix. It was clear that the book should stop before railroads, the cyanide process, electricity, and the internal combustion engine had drastically altered operating conditions. On the whole, the opening of the 1880s seemed to be as good a watershed as could be discovered. Manifestly, "frontiers" are too elusive to be delimited with chronological exactness. I have tried to carry the story in each area far enough past the frontier phase to suggest what came after, thus leaving to another day or to someone else the task of examining the modern history of mining.

Two institutions have made this book possible. The California Institute of Technology, where I teach, has been consistently helpful and sympathetic. Hallett D. Smith, chairman of the Humanities Division and a professor of English, has been a model superior. Throughout he has shown that he understood what I was trying to do, and he persuaded the proper authorities to grant me six months' leave of absence and financial aid when, with research far along, I had reached the critical point of actual composition. When the first draft of the manuscript was completed, Professor Smith read it and made highly constructive suggestions. His Colorado upbringing gave him an instinctive "feel" for the subject matter.

A second colleague, James A. Noble, professor emeritus of Mining Geology, has shown a comparable interest. With a background of many years as chief geologist of the great Homestake gold mine in the Black Hills, Professor Noble was the ideal friend to have as one's informal adviser. Patiently he explained to me a great many things that I didn't understand at all. Repeatedly he put aside his own consulting work to make suggestions or corrections. If this book still contains technical errors, it is because the author still misunderstands—not because James Noble has missed something! The excellent library of the Division of Geological Sciences at Caltech has supplied me with much of the material that has gone into this book. To Robert P. Sharp, chairman of the Division, and Miss Daphne Plane, librarian, go my warmest thanks. Without their hospitality and their library's splendid "runs" of technical journals, reports, and monographs, this book would have lost one of its principal dimensions.

The other institution that has sheltered me during the gestation of this book has been the Henry E. Huntington Library and Art Gallery, in San Marino. For years the Huntington Library has been a friendly and helpful host to me, but in recent years, under the leadership of John E. Pomfret, the director, the library has placed me completely in their debt by making something of a specialty of collecting materials relating to Western mining. The bulk of the research that has gone into this book was done at the Huntington, and the whole first draft was written there during a never-to-be-forgotten winter and spring when I was on leave from Caltech and was the holder of a fellowship granted by the trustees of the Huntington. During that memorable and pleasant period, I could hardly help but write, in the pleasant atmosphere of uninterrupted scholarship that Dr. Pomfret and his staff provided, and with the constant inspiration of trying to keep up with Allan Nevins, whose rate of literary production is rivaled only by the speed with which he marches his troops over the Huntington grounds on "short" walks after lunch each day.

Much of the Huntington material on the mining West came into the library through the experienced efforts of Leslie E. Bliss. Within the library it has been made available to scholars through the courtesy and helpfulness of many other devoted members of the staff, of whom I wish to thank especially Robert O. Dougan, Lyle H. Wright, Miss Constance Lodge, Carey S. Bliss, Edwin Carpenter, Miss Mary Isabel Fry, and Mrs. Nancy English.

Over a period of years the Bancroft library, Berkeley, has helped me many times. Dr. George P. Hammond, director, and Dr. John Barr Tompkins gave me particular assistance during a recent brief period of concentrated research. The California State Library, Sacramento, and the California Historical Society, San Francisco, have also supplied items that have gone into this book.

In securing information for the chapter on the Black Hills, I have received valuable aid from James Noble; from Miss Katherine M. Thornby, the daughter of a Black Hills pioneer and now connected with the Adams Memorial Hall Museum, Deadwood; from Mr. Donald P. Howe of the Homestake Mining Company, Lead; and from Mr. Albert F. Gushurst of Colorado, son of a Black Hills pioneer who occupies a prominent place in this narrative. Mr. John P. Farquhar has helped greatly with information concerning his grandfather, Senator John P. Jones of Nevada.

The completed manuscript went first to the editor of this series, Professor Ray A. Billington of Northwestern University. Professor Billington handled the prospective book with admirable promptness, care, and discernment. At many places the text has benefited from his revisions and refinements.

Within the Humanities Division's offices at Caltech particular thanks go to Mrs. Virginia Kotkin, who with tact and charm has seen to it that the day's work got done in Pasadena, even when the writer's thoughts were off in Colorado, the Black Hills, or some other remote place. Mrs. Mary Ellis Arnett and Miss Barbara Wilhite have been unfailingly good-natured in meeting a series of crises, both large and small.

At times the discussion in this book runs parallel to what I have said previously in *California Gold: the Beginning of Mining in the Far West* (Harvard University Press, Cambridge, Mass., 1947) and an article that appeared in the *Mississippi Valley Historical Review* for June 1960. I wish to thank the Harvard University Press and the Mississippi Valley Historical Association for permission to repeat this material.

Any one who has tried to complete a book in the midst of a large and active family will understand that one's wife and children suffer when the alleged head of the household is busy frequently and preoccupied constantly. To Anne and the children, apologies and amends, somewhat indicated by the dedication.

Rodman Wilson Paul
Pasadena, California
January 1963

Gold and Silver Regions as Frontiers

*G*old is where you find it," the forty-niners used to say, and this rephrasing of a passage from the Book of Job became the motto for a generation of prospectors and miners. From Sutter's Mill in 1848 to the Black Hills and Tombstone thirty years later, men sought gold and silver in the rugged mountains, deep canyons, and high plateaus that dominate the Far West. Few obstacles could check them, even though so many had reason to know the sardonic truth of another version of that same maxim: "Gold is where I ain't!"

A few succeeded abundantly, and became the well-advertised Midases of their day, flamboyantly displaying their new wealth on Nob Hill, or Fifth Avenue, or the Rue de la Paix. Others achieved relatively modest returns for the risks run and the time and labor invested. Many failed—that is, returned home "broke," died of illness or accident, or became perpetual penniless wanderers, always hopeful, ever seeking, yet never reaching that rich mass of gold or silver of which they dreamed.

Much that this mining civilization initiated had only a temporary existence. Nearly everything it attempted was done wastefully. Yet out

1

of its turbulent, transitory efforts enough remained to lay the foundations for at least five of our Far Western states. In the Far West prospectors and miners, and the merchants who supplied them, served as the "cutting edge" of the frontier, like the Scotch-Irish farmers of those earlier "Wests" on either side of the Appalachians, or the footloose subsistence farmers who pioneered the Mississippi Valley.

When Frederick Jackson Turner wrote his classic essay on "The Significance of the Frontier in American History," he prefaced it with a quotation from the census of 1890, in which the superintendent of that survey remarked that there was no longer a discernible line of settlement. The last great areas of free land—the Far West and Great Plains— had now been broken up by "isolated bodies of settlement." Turner pointed to the gold rushes to California, Colorado, Montana, Idaho, and the Black Hills as examples of the forces that had, in the brief time since mid-century, cut up the Far West and Great Plains into a patchwork of scattered settlements, and destroyed forever the distinction between the "Indian country" west of the Missouri River and the "civilized" regions to the east of that boundary.[1]

In this, as in so many of his writings, Turner was suggestive rather than specific. He certainly recognized that mining booms were an explosive force, and that no region was ever the same after prospectors and miners had poured through it. But did he recognize how thoroughly a mining boom disrupted the regular advance that he thought he had discerned in earlier "Wests"? That procession of first fur hunters, then pioneer farmers, then substantial farmers, and finally town builders? If that procession ever existed in fact, then it was only in the forested, well-watered lands to the east of the 100th meridian. Westward the natural conditions and natural opportunities were quite different. The beaver hunters (and government explorers) did indeed make the first journeys across the Great Plains and into the remote regions that stretched out to the Pacific. They discovered the best routes for travel and built forts that later became important way stations. A few farmers followed them, to establish islands of husbandry at Great Salt Lake, in the Willamette Valley of Oregon, and in the valleys of central California. There were already Spanish-speaking farmers and ranchers in the Rio Grande Valley of New Mexico and the coastal strip of California.

But over most of the Far West prospectors and miners were the pioneers, just as presently cattlemen were to pioneer the Great Plains. To supply the miners' wants merchants, packers, teamsters, stagecoach lines, and express companies quickly brought their services to each new camp—arriving coincidentally with the speculators and promoters, but well after the saloon keepers and gamblers.

To look after the numerous riding horses and pack animals brought in by the gold seekers, some one usually started a boarding ranch. Presently others realized that if the land would support work animals, it would also support beef cattle. Still others, having been farmers in their boyhood, had the sense to recognize that raising crops for human food and animal feed might be a surer way to wealth than digging for gold or silver. Ultimately cities grew up at points strategically situated on transportation routes, or merely located in the convenient center of a scattering of thriving camps. So, gradually, other activities than mining developed, although for a long time they were dependent on the mines for a market.

The land, too, differed sharply from the Appalachian and Mississippi Valley regions so familiar to Turner. Geographers call it "the cordilleran portion of North America," by which is meant a "huge highland" formed by the Rocky Mountains on the east, the Sierra Nevada and Cascade ranges on the west, and the "chain of high plateaus" in the middle.[2] The latter include the Columbia and Snake River Plateau in the northwest and the Colorado Plateau of the southwest, but they also include that vast elevated region of desert and mountain known as the Great Basin of Nevada and Utah. Taken as a whole, cordilleran America is a land of great distances, high and difficult mountains, deep canyons, and weary miles of arid plateau. Much of it has a precipitation that is highly seasonal in timing and often seriously deficient in total quantity. The greatest supply of rain and snow water is in the northwest corner, and there, too, usable timber is far more available than in most of the region.

It was in the mountainous rather than the level parts of cordilleran America that minerals were found, because the deposits were formed originally during periods of earth movement, when ascending hot liquids that were carrying mineral constituents dropped their load far beneath what was then the surface of the earth. Where these hot liquids flowed into fissures and cracks in the earth's crust, they formed "veins," presumably so called because superficially the mineralized filling seems to wind and twist through the older rock as veins do through the human body. This appearance is misleading, for beneath their visible outcrop, veins extend downward in what geologists call "tabular" form, meaning in planes or sheets that are at an angle from the horizontal. Individual veins vary greatly in length, thickness, pattern, and depth. In length they range from less than an inch up to several miles, occasionally even longer. In thickness, as many a miner has discovered, sometimes they "pinch" into a dishearteningly narrow width; at other times they "swell" into pleasingly big bulges. They may split up into thin branches and then converge again. They may persist downward to great depths. This disconcertingly irregular conduct does much to explain why a miner finds it such a speculative business to stake his fortune on the course of a vein.

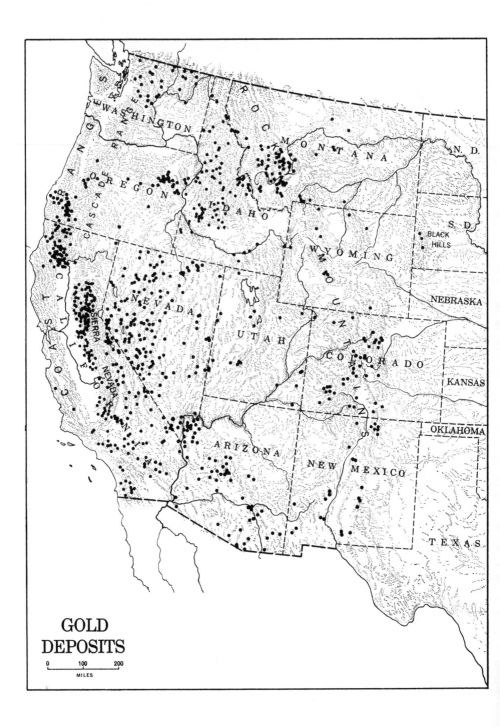

GOLD
DEPOSITS

0   100   200
MILES

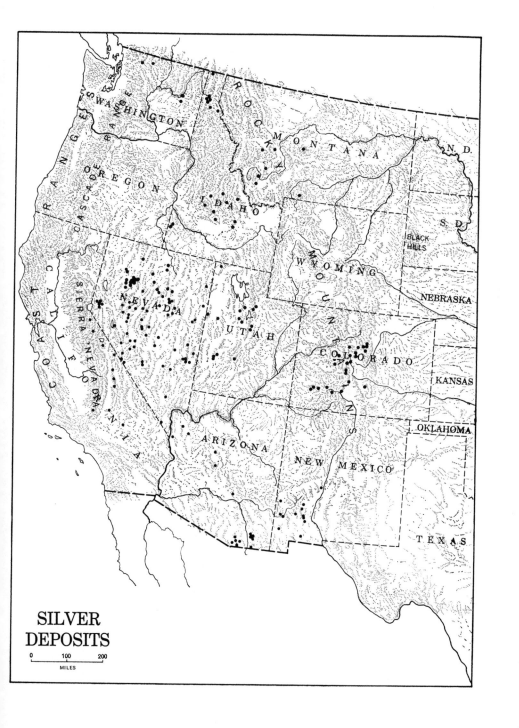

SILVER
DEPOSITS

0   100   200

MILES

When there is enough gold or silver in the rock to make exploitation profitable, then in miners' language the rock is an "ore." Again to define an important mining term, when several veins are found close together, so that they and the intervening rock can be worked as a unit, this is, technically speaking, a "lode," and geologists often use the word in this restricted sense, but in both mining practice and mining law "lode" and "vein" are used virtually interchangeably. If there is any distinction between the two in everyday mining usage, it is that a miner probably would not call a vein a lode unless it carried ore and occupied a fissure of at least moderate dimensions. A very small vein or one filled with barren material would be unlikely to receive the appellation of "lode."

Gold or silver, when found in solid rock, is not always in the form of veins or lodes. Sometimes these precious metals occur as "replacement deposits." This means that the hot ore-bearing solutions rising from below actually penetrated solid rock, perhaps aided by minute cracks, dissolved it, and substituted new minerals for the original matter. In this process, as the old rock was dissolved, the new material slowly replaced the old, atom for atom, very much as if one were to remove clay bricks from a wall, one at a time, while putting a metal brick in each vacancy thus created. Such an occurrence has been especially common with limestone, which can be replaced unit by unit, in a way which perfectly preserves the structure of the original limestone even while completely altering the content of the rock.

In either case, whether deposition has been in the form of veins or replacements, the result is solid rock from which gold or silver can be extracted only by great effort. Fortunately for the mining world, much of the gold discovered by man has been freed from its encasement by erosion over a prolonged period of time. Through being eroded out of the rock, the gold has been reduced to a loose condition that has permitted it to be transported and abraded by existing or prehistoric streams, which have finally deposited it on sandbars, in gravel banks, or in "potholes" in the stream beds. Since gold has a greater specific gravity than most common substances, a stream that was carrying a mixture of eroded material was bound to drop the gold more quickly than ordinary sand and gravel. Such gold has long been called "placer gold" by miners, and the deposits in which it is found are called "placers." Like so many mining terms, the word is of Spanish origin, in tribute to one of the world's great mining peoples. While some placers present complex problems, in most cases it is manifestly easier to extract gold from placers than from veins or replacement deposits, because nature has done so much of the job of separating the valuable from the worthless materials.

Silver, on the other hand, is not ordinarily found in placer deposits, because silver, which combines readily with most acids, forms soluble compounds and is carried off during erosion, thus failing to form placer accumulations. Gold, which is chemically inert, preserves its original form while being eroded, transported, and deposited, and therefore can be captured by placer miners.[3]

In cordilleran America both placer gold and gold and silver in solid rock have been discovered primarily in areas that have been subjected to tectonic activity (that is, mountain building). In areas where no geologic disturbance has taken place, so that the rocks still lie horizontal, mineral deposits are rare or inferior in value. Reflecting this, maps of gold- and silver-mining districts show that most of the latter followed the mountain ranges, while few districts came into being in the plateau and valley lands. Thus large parts of the Columbia and Snake River Plateau and of the Colorado Plateau produced little mining and will play only a secondary role in this story.[4]

Cordilleran America is essentially the area called the Far West. To the original Gold Rush population it was the land beyond the Great Plains, the land that was 600 or 700 miles from the Missouri frontier, in the case of Colorado, or 2000 in the case of California. Since the Great Plains were untenanted save for a few way stations, prior to the completion of the Pacific railroad in 1869 the Far West was as isolated as if it had been an island. To reach Colorado in the rush of 1859, one had to travel for five or six weeks by wagon or at least a week by stagecoach. Overland to California in 1849 took all of the spring and part of the summer, while by sea the trip took four to eight months via Cape Horn, or at least five weeks by the steamers that connected at the Isthmus of Panama.

If the mining West seemed at times to be preoccupied with its own affairs, the reason was simply the remoteness and immensity of that vast, difficult, and lovely land. Here, to return to the words of Turner's famous essay, "American social development" had to begin "over again." An impatient crowd of prospectors, miners, speculators, traders, gamblers, and saloon keepers found no existing institutions in each new region that they entered, and thus had to create, amidst hurry and confusion, just enough economic, social, and political controls to permit each one to seek his fortune as an individual and yet enjoy some of the benefits that came only with organized society. The result was a curious blending of the new and the familiar, of innovation and imitation.

The greatest achievement by far was technological—the art of mining. Gold and silver mining, being utterly alien to the previous experience of most Americans, had to be learned from the beginning, often from foreign teachers, and then adapted, developed, and improved to meet local needs. By the close of the nineteenth century, Americans had advanced so rapidly and had proved so inventive in their new profession that they were regarded as world leaders in the art of extracting precious metals. Their advice, services, and machinery were sought by men in South Africa, Australia, and Siberia, and at times even in Europe.

Their accomplishments as mining businessmen were less unique. Most were small-scale operators who worked as self-employed individuals or as partners in small companies, sometimes with additional help from what few hired hands were available. In either case, the distinguishing characteristic of their efforts was the uncertainty of the outcome. It was as if they were farmers raising crops in a region of widely varying rainfall. A few mining men became notably successful in the difficult art of managing large enterprises under Western conditions, with all that that implied in terms of high cost of capital, labor, and materials, not to mention the undiscriminating demand for speed and "results." The difficulties encountered were perhaps most nearly akin to those met by the early railroad builders.

In financing their larger operations, Western mining men too often did little more than duplicate the contemporary excesses of Eastern finance of the General Grant era. If they never quite produced a Jim Fisk, Daniel Drew, or Jay Gould, nevertheless speculation, misrepresentation, and outright thievery were all too common. This was especially the case after the Comstock Lode of Nevada revealed the possibilities of selling unlimited numbers of shares to investors who had no means of discovering how their corporations were being managed.

When faced by the need to organize their political affairs, the men of the mining West did even worse, at least in the initial phase. Through carelessness, unfamiliarity with one another, and absorption with money-getting, the early mining population allowed local government and the administration of justice to lapse very nearly beyond recovery. Eastern standards of that day were bad enough, but those of the mining West came too often to rest upon little save the rule of naked force.

Their social and esthetic aspirations were to a considerable degree imitative, as the architecture of the more expensive residences and business buildings would suggest. But it was not entirely so. A visitor said of Denver society in 1867: "There was a freedom from 'airs,' and a directness of manner among them that was marked."[5] The enforced simplicity of life, the absence of comforts, and the daily experience of witnessing sharp fluctuations in the material fortunes of individuals, all tended to make democratic thinking a reality in the West beyond the Great Plains. Nor was a sturdy independence the region's only virtue. At its best the mining West had vigor, optimism, generosity, and good humor, as anyone can learn by reading that classic account, Mark Twain's *Roughing It*.

In making generalizations, two qualifications are important. First is the relationship between the West's own, local development and that of the nation as a whole. The first great rush, that to California, began at a time when changes in industry and transportation were just beginning to cause major alterations in the economy and society of the main part of the United States. By 1880, on the other hand, factories, crowded industrial towns, and busy railroads were commonplace on the Northeastern seaboard and in the Middle West. Eastern and Middle Western society, correspondingly, advanced—if that is the right verb—from the noisy, egalitarian Jacksonian democracy of the 1840s to the elegant, class-conscious way of life that marked the height of the Victorian era.

While the mining West was a part of this rapidly evolving nation, the West's own rate of change was not necessarily identical with that of the country as a whole. For some fruits of progress, such as railroads and cheaper manufactured goods, the mining regions had to wait until the states east of the Missouri had taken care of their own needs and were prepared to shower their surplus blessings on the underdeveloped states and territories. The full cycle of change can be illustrated by the role of the railroads in two great "rushes," spaced nearly thirty years apart. In 1849 a few—a very few—Argonauts were able to use the little local Eastern railroads to get started on their journey. One of them, when departing for New York City to board his ship, started his misspelled diary with the entry: "March 6th, 1849. Left Troy Ny. at 7 in the morning in the cars for Ny. Nothing of note occured on the way."[6] By contrast, when the rush to the Black Hills of western South Dakota was taking place in the 1870s, the gold seeker could take the "cars" through Chicago to Cheyenne, Wyoming, or the little waystation of Sidney, and have left only the relatively short distance of 260 miles by stagecoach to Deadwood, in the "diggings"—through ticket, Chicago to Deadwood, $49.25.[7] No factor was more influential in bringing to an end the frontier phase of the mining West than this revolution in transportation.

The West as a mining frontier thus began when the nation was just emerging from a preindustrial, prerailroad era, and closed in a day of urban, industrial, railroad dominance that often saw the West lagging. But that is not the whole of the problem. There is the question of change within the mining West. Because of the nature of mining, which removes natural resources but cannot restore them, mining towns and regions have rarely been stable. Change has often been toward exhaustion of mineral deposits, and hence decadence. Or a district may have come into being under false pretenses in the first place. Consider the life cycle of a typical Western mining community in the nineteenth century.

The cycle started, in most cases, with a real or alleged discovery—it might be either—in an area little known to white men. Quite commonly the area was one of difficult topography or climate. After a very brief period of concealment by the original discoverers, rumors would leak out and quickly become exaggerated. A disorderly crowd would then come rushing in to the new El Dorado. Usually the leaders were a few veterans of previous similar excitements, but the bulk of the population, being quite inexperienced, was bound to suffer disappointment and hardship.

As the crowd came pouring into the new diggings, the early discoverers were apt to sell out to the "tenderfoot," or the man with capital, and push off on prospecting trips into the surrounding, more rugged terrain, thereby greatly increasing the known area. If there was anything worth the effort, flush production would develop rapidly, based on placer deposits and perhaps on the easily worked upper parts of veins. If the boom was based on nothing but exaggerations, it would, of course, collapse as soon as experience demonstrated that the deposits were not rich enough to leave a profit under the prevailing high cost of living.

In either case this initial boom lured into the wilderness the chaotic society that has come to be regarded as characteristic of the Western mining camp in its early stages. With evident distaste, a Colorado mining geologist wrote this description for a prospectors' manual:

> A boom follows. The offscourings of the country pour in with the saloon, dance hall and gambling hell element. A murder or two follows. Lynch law takes a hand. Then a horde of real estate men come in, and lots are sold at fabulous prices, and the town is inflated with a population and everything else usually far above the capacity of the mines to support. A collapse follows, and a steady retreat of hollow-eyed, disappointed adventurers. In time the town and camp assume their lawful proportions and business settles down to its lawful regime.[8]

The period of flush production was bound to be brief, usually no more than half a dozen years, sometimes only half that time, sometimes only a season. As the flush period passed, the former boom area faced either of two fates. It might survive a period of depression and start up once more because of new discoveries made economically valuable by greater capital investment, technological improvements, and greater scientific understanding. Or the area might for a period of years support a constantly shrinking population of small-time operators, who struggled to eke out a living from the dwindling annual output. Whether decline came early or late, the ultimate fate for most was the status of a ghost town, from which relief would come only in the twentieth century, when men learned that it was more profitable to work tourists than ore bodies.

The rise and fall of individual communities makes it unwise to think of the whole mining West as ever constituting a single "frontier" at any one time. If the word "frontier" connotes sparseness of population, richness of untapped natural resources, isolation, hardship, and danger, then the region of the Sierra Nevada of California was a true mining frontier during much of the decade that began in 1848. Thereafter, many of the

Sierra Nevada districts fell into decline or were virtually abandoned, while others underwent an intensive development that carried them well beyond any reasonable definition of "frontier" conditions. In similar fashion, Colorado and Nevada were true frontiers for a number of years beginning in 1859, and the same could be said of Idaho and Montana during the early and middle 1860s. Subsequently, just as they seemed to be maturing, a disheartening decline in mineral yield afflicted all of these states and territories and caused an exodus of population and investment. Vigorous revival carried both Nevada and Colorado to new heights in the 1870s, and Montana and Idaho at a somewhat later date. The mineralized parts of Arizona and New Mexico, by contrast, were little more than the foreshadow of a mining frontier until the 1870s. Prior to that the combination of unchecked Apaches and Navahos, insuperable obstacles to transportation, and climatic extremes brought death or failure to most of those who sought to open a mining frontier. Or again, the gold in the Black Hills of South Dakota, despite nearness to that main route of travel across the Great Plains, the Oregon Trail, was not discovered until late and could not be exploited until the threat of the Indians and the opposition of the army could be dissipated in the middle 1870s.

Therefore it is more accurate to think of the mining West as constituting a series of frontiers, sometimes successive, sometimes widely separated geographically and chronologically, rather than a single entity. In each an improvement in transportation, a growth of towns, stores, and population, and a decreasing danger and hardship, coupled with a rapid engrossing of the known mineral deposits, presently removed the justification for the term "frontier." As already suggested, the gain was not always permanent. Many regions, just as they were outgrowing frontier conditions, received a severe check. Finally, it must be recognized that within each major area there were retarded subregions, such as the mountains in the northwestern corner of California, those in the southwestern corner of Colorado, and the northern part of Idaho. Primitive economic and social conditions and unexploited mining opportunities continued in such vast isolated pockets long after the more famous central districts had grown to maturity.

California
1848-1858

*W*hat crowds are rushing out here for gold! What multitudes are leaving their distant homes for this glittering treasure!" So wrote the Reverend Walter Colton, the Navy chaplain who was serving as alcalde at Monterey. The date was March 11, 1849.[1] When Colton made this notation in his journal, the exclamation must have seemed almost an understatement, and yet by that date California had seen only the preliminary phase of the Gold Rush.

James Marshall's discovery at Sutter's Mill, or Coloma, on the American River, took place on January 24, 1848.[2] John A. Sutter, a Munchausen-like Swiss emigré, had come to California in 1839 and had persuaded the Mexican authorities to grant him a large tract of land in the valley of the Sacramento River, that major stream which forms a natural waterway between San Francisco Bay and the northern half of California's great interior valley—the so-called Central Valley. Nostalgically, Sutter had given the name of New Helvetia to the fortified settlement that he had built near the site of the present city of Sacramento. To gain access to a better supply of lumber, in August 1847 Sutter had signed a contract with James W. Marshall by which the latter was to build a sawmill on the south fork of the American River, a tributary of the Sacramento, about forty-five miles from New Helvetia.

Skilled workmen were scarce in frontier California, and Sutter had rejoiced at obtaining in Marshall the services of an experienced American carpenter and jack-of-all-trades, even though Marshall was notoriously peculiar and difficult. As the year 1848 opened, the mill was nearing completion. Tests had shown that the tailrace was not yet deep enough, and Marshall had decided to cut it further by having his men dig and blast during the daytime, while at night the river was turned into the new ditch to wash away the loose dirt and gravel.

On January 24, while most of his men were still at breakfast, Marshall went out to make his usual early-morning inspection. Scattered along the newly exposed bed of the tailrace were several bits of glittering yellow metal. Marshall picked them up, dropped them into his slouch hat, and showed his find to his workmen as they came out to begin their daily chores.

"Boys, I believe I have found a gold mine!" he said as the men crowded around him. Crude tests convinced Marshall and his associates that they probably *had* found gold, but the full significance of the discovery was not appreciated by anyone. How could it be? There was no precedent for what was about to happen. Marshall himself seems to have been the most excited of the original group. Like many eccentrics, he was quick and volatile in his response to an intriguing new possibility.

When Marshall rode down to New Helvetia a few days later, to show samples of the metal to Sutter, Sutter was also soon persuaded. But the first concern of both men was to have the mill finished before any diversion distracted the hired hands from their job. Therefore Sutter tried to enforce secrecy on all concerned. His own loose tongue and that of the female cook at Sutter's Mill largely frustrated his efforts at concealment; yet only a small number knew of the discovery until March, and in the parochial atmosphere of the little California settlements, a considerable skepticism deadened the effect of the news until May. Even then the military governor was assured by a visitor to Monterey that the reports from the American River were untrue. "A few fools have hurried to the place, but you may be sure there is nothing in it."[3] And the editor of one of the two little newspapers published at San Francisco denounced the whole business as "superlatively silly," "all sham, a supurb [*sic*] takein as was ever got up to guzzle the gullible."[4] But on May 29 the other of the two San Francisco newspapers gave a very different account: "The whole country, from San Francisco to Los Angeles, and from the sea shore to the base of the Sierra Nevadas, resounds with the sordid cry of 'gold,

GOLD, GOLD!' while the field is left half planted, the house half built, and everything neglected but the manufacture of shovels and pickaxes."[5]

San Francisco was stripped of its able-bodied men in May and early June. On June 1 the military governor wrote resignedly from Monterey: "The Golden Yellow Fever has not yet, I believe, assumed here its worst type, tho' the premonitory symptoms are beginning to exhibit themselves, and doubtless the Epidemic will pass over Monterey leaving the marks of its ravages, as it has done at San Francisco, and elsewhere."[6] It soon did, and carried off with it the colonel's troops, who deserted or had to be given leave to keep them from departing illegally. By July and August the whole of California was infected clear down to San Diego, while around San Francisco and Monterey bays the countryside was literally depopulated.

Simultaneously the "Golden Yellow Fever" spread to other Pacific lands. In July and August whole boatloads were leaving the Hawaiian Islands. In early August Oregon and British Columbia had the news, and perhaps half of Oregon's male population hastily started southward. Mexico, Peru, and Chile learned of it by early autumn and sent several thousand men northward before the close of 1848.

*T*HE MAIN PART of the United States received fragmentary reports as early as August and September, but the stories failed to carry conviction until the last week in November. Then the fever caught on with an intense virulence. All over the United States, the New York *Herald* reported in mid-January, men "are rushing head over heels towards the El Dorado on the Pacific—that wonderful California, which sets the public mind almost on the highway to insanity. . . . Every day, men of property and means are advertising their possessions for sale, in order to furnish them with means to reach that golden land."[7]

Country towns and city streets alike resounded to doggerel versions of Stephen Foster's new song, "Oh! Susanna!"

> *Oh! California! That's the land for me!*
> *I'm bound for California with my washbowl on my knee.*

In the seaports every possible ship, whether seaworthy or not, was hastily readied.

> *Then blow, ye breezes, blow!*
> *We're off for Californi-o*
> *There's plenty of gold,*

So I've been told,
On the banks of the Sacramento.

By steamer, sailing ship, and overland wagon tens of thousands of Americans departed in the early months of 1849. In wagons they toiled along the Oregon Trail to the Rockies, thence across the arid lands of Utah and Nevada to the final barrier of the Sierra Nevada. In sailing ships they fought heavy weather off Cape Horn, pumped endless hours to keep their leaky ships from sinking, and lived on poor food and rationed drinking water. The lucky few who found passage on steamers via the Isthmus of Panama traveled more quickly than the rest, but had to endure tropical diseases in Panama and severely overcrowded conditions afloat. All suffered hardship, and some must have wished they had never left home, but most persevered, for truly they were seeking the new Golden Fleece, as enthusiastically as did Jason's men when they set forth in the Argo.

English, Irish, Germans, French, Spanish Americans, Kanakas, Australians, Chinese, Malayans—men from virtually every part of the civilized world—responded with like fervor. One forty-niner said that every nationality save the Russian could be met with in California. Everywhere families were broken up, jobs abandoned, and property liquidated, while outfitters and shipowners rejoiced. Few races, few nations were immune to the unsettling news from Sutter's Mill.

How big was the total influx of population? There are no precise figures as to immigration, and both the federal census of 1850 and the state census of 1852 were incomplete and inaccurate. Stated tersely, there seem to have been about 14,000 persons, other than Indians, in California when the rush began in 1848; by the close of 1849, several thousand less than 100,000; by the latter part of 1852, perhaps 250,000; by 1860, 380,000.[8]

That huge increase demonstrated that gold could attract ten thousand to a frontier where agriculture and commerce would have drawn one thousand. For example, in Utah, where pioneering began in 1847, the highly organized, determinedly led Mormon colonizers built up their numbers to 11,380 persons by 1850; to 40,273 by 1860.[9] Oregon, whose attractions were advertised by nation-wide publicity, had perhaps 10,000–12,000 whites and "half-breeds" in 1848; 13,294 persons in 1850; and 52,465 in 1860.[10] The gains in both Utah and Oregon were impressive, and reflected a more deliberate attempt at recruiting than was common on agricultural frontiers, and yet they were only a fraction of the increase achieved by California in the same years. Overnight growth of great proportions was to be typical of gold and silver rushes. Rapid decline was to be equally characteristic.

In California the gold hunters quickly scattered up and down the foot-hills and lower mountain slopes. Even in 1848, long before they had occupied all the promising spots on the several forks of the American River near Sutter's Mill, men who had suddenly become miners were restlessly trying their luck along the other tributaries of the Sacramento and its southern counterpart, the San Joaquin. By the close of 1848, as one early account describes it, "miners were washing rich auriferous dirt all along the western slope of the Sierra Nevada, from the Feather to the Tuolumne river, a distance of one hundred and fifty miles, and also over a space of about fifteen miles square, near the place now known as the town of Shasta, in the Coast mountains, at the head of the Sacramento valley."[11] When the Argonauts of 1849 began swelling the population of gold seekers, the number of known gold fields increased correspondingly. As some men pushed southward parallel to the axis of the Sierra Nevada, others thrust their way northwestward from Shasta to open diggings in the tangle of mountain ranges that dominate northwestern California and the adjacent corner of Oregon. By the summer of 1849 primitive "camps" and embryonic towns were dotted through canyons and small valleys that could not claim a single settler in January 1848.

This growth of population does not mean that every one who hurried out to this new frontier actually engaged in mining or prospect-ing. Contemporaries, whose estimates were only intelligent guesses, said that at the end of 1848 the number actually at work in the mines may have been only 5000; a year later 40,000; towards the end of 1850, per-haps 50,000; and in 1852, about 100,000, the last figure being approxi-mately maintained during most of the remainder of the 1850s. The census of 1860 reported that 82,573 men described themselves as miners.[12] In other words, even at the peak of the excitement, when few men thought of anything save how to get gold, less than half the population were actually working with their hands at mining.

Of the rest, many were engaged in supplying or serving those at work. A man who spent five years in the mines in the 1850s spoke with astonish-ment of "the crowds of lawyers, small tradesmen, mechanics, and others, who swarm in every little camp, even of the most humble description, soliciting the patronage of the public—of whom they often form at least one half."[13] With equal appropriateness, he might have suggested that in each city, town, or camp were to be found saloons in wondrous numbers, hotels and restaurants, brothels, and "hurdy-gurdy houses." The latter were dance halls in which for a fee and the cost of drinks a miner could dance with a hired partner, who was often an immigrant German girl, and not always especially pretty. "Hurdy-gurdies" were not necessarily prosti-tutes. They, the courtesans, and a few actresses with itinerant troupes were the principal feminine society accessible to most miners.

Hangtown gals are plump and rosy,
Hair in ringlets mighty cosy;
Painted cheeks and gassy bonnets;
Touch them and they'll sting like hornets.

There were always a few wives and children, just as there were always a few ministers and school teachers, and even the roughest gold seeker could usually be counted on to show respect toward such rare and valued creatures. The erratic early censuses suggest that in 1850 somewhat over 90 percent of the California population was male, and that in 1852 the percentage was a little less. In the gold regions the proportion of men must have been even higher, since many of the women who were in California were left behind in the seaboard communities or in the farming and ranching areas when their husbands departed for the noisy, crude, and isolated little camps that existed solely to supply and entertain the miners.

The total number of persons involved in what might be termed the service industries of the mining towns and camps was large; and so was the number of those who were ill, loafing, or simply wandering about from place to place. The last was one of the most popular of all Californian occupations. As one observer remarked, "Thousands are literally homeless. Large bodies of miners keep in perpetual motion from bar to gulch, and gulch to canon, in pursuit of variety, or paying dirt."[14] A song popular among the miners explained why so many saw no reason to remain long in one place:

When I got there, the mining ground
Was staked and claimed for miles around,
And not a bed was to be found,
    When I went off to prospect.
The town was crowded full of folks,
Which made me think 'twas not a hoax;
At my expense they cracked their jokes,
    When I was nearly starving.

In California, even more than in the later excitements, most of the gold seekers were ignorant of everything connected with mining and precious metals. If it had been necessary for the pioneers of 1848 and 1849 to start with the more complex types of mining, the Gold Rush would have been a profitless disaster for nearly every participant. Instead, the geologic history of California had produced physical conditions unusually favorable for the simplest kind of placer mining. Successive geologic cycles had brought to the Sierra Nevada first a subterranean intrusion of molten material out of which countless small gold-bearing

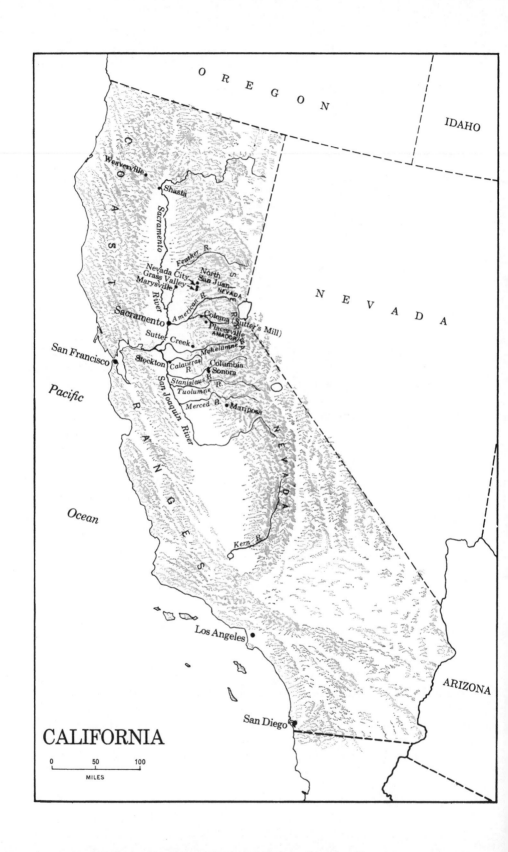

CALIFORNIA

0   50   100
MILES

veins had been formed, then erosion, followed by volcanic eruption, then an abrupt uplifting and tilting of the mountains toward the west, which produced a new erosion because it so greatly increased the cutting power of the westward-flowing streams. Thus one period of vein formation was followed by two periods of erosion and the concomitant deposition of placers, with the result that in 1848 the lower western slopes of the Sierra Nevada were one of the richest gold-placer regions in the world.

So rich were the virgin deposits that the only technique needed was to dig out gold with a knife, horn spoon, or shovel and "wash" it by swirling it around in a pan or bowl to separate the gold from foreign matter. Being heavier, the gold would gradually sink to the bottom, while the lighter sand and gravel was washed over the rim of the pan. Even in 1848, however, men began to seek a faster mechanism than the pan for washing gold. They found it unnecessary to invent anything. For several decades primitive mining for both placer and vein gold had been carried on successfully in Georgia, North Carolina, and other Southern states, while for many generations Mexicans and South Americans had worked in gold, silver, and quicksilver mines. A few "old hands" from these earlier mining regions were in California in 1848, and many more came in 1849, and with them came veterans of the lead mines of the upper Mississippi valley or the coal and iron mines of Pennsylvania, together with men trained in some of the most famous mining centers of Britain and Europe, such as Cornwall, Wales, the German duchy of Saxony, Spain, and Italy.[15]

From these relatively few experienced workers the mass of the latter-day Argonauts learned their new trade. One of their first lessons was that except for its convenience in prospecting, the pan could profitably be replaced by a simple device that had been in use for generations in the thoroughly international world of mining. This was the "rocker" or "cradle," which was essentially a wooden box mounted on rockers and open at its lower end. Cleats or "riffles" were nailed across the bottom to catch the gold. When auriferous gravel was shoveled into the rocker, water was ladled in with it, so as to send the whole mass hurrying along the bottom, with the gold (because of its high specific gravity) tending to drop behind the riffles and be caught, while the rest of the material swept onward. Rocking the contrivance back and forth helped to dissolve the clayey parts of the auriferous "dirt" and wash away the waste materials.

With simple and locally made implements, and with a heavy concentration on placer rather than vein gold, the gold seekers of the early years feverishly exploited the finest opportunity that has ever been offered on any mining frontier. The shallow placers of California were extraordinary not only for their richness but also for their extent, ease of working, and relatively accessible and endurable location. Starting in southern Oregon and the northwest corner of California, they extended inland across the head of the Sacramento Valley and then southward in spotty fashion along the western slope of the Sierra Nevada for a total of several hundred miles, approximately down to Mariposa, below which there was a considerable gap before additional diggings were reached at Kern River. For a distance of 120 miles, beginning north of Sutter's Mill and continuing as far south as Mariposa, the belt or strip of mining country along the slope of the Sierra Nevada came to be known as the "Mother Lode," a term that seems to have been suggested by the usage of Spanish-speaking miners (*veta madre*). The name probably originated in 1850 or early 1851 in the belief that there was a great single source— that is, mother vein—from which all this rich bounty was derived. Actually there was no one continuous vein, but rather an extensive system of "parallel though sometimes interrupted quartz-filled fissures."

Partly because the Mother Lode country was the first area to be exploited, the fame of that region tended for years to obscure the fact that some of the richest districts in California were north of the Mother Lode and at somewhat higher altitudes. Nevada County, whose principal mining center was north of Sutter's Mill by thirty airline miles or fifty miles of winding mountain road, is a good example. In general, the belt of Sierran foothill and mountainside that contained major gold deposits was wider at the northern end of the Mother Lode than toward the southern, and the width increased still further in the latitude of Nevada County and its neighbors. The quite separate diggings that started at Shasta and lay to the west and north of the head of the Sacramento Valley—beyond the northern limit of the Sierra Nevada—never achieved the significance of the Sierran fields.

During 1849 several simple refinements, all of them long known in other parts of the world, were adopted to increase the effectiveness of gold washing. One was the introduction of quicksilver, which had the useful characteristic of amalgamating with gold—that is, of incorporating gold into itself, while excluding foreign matter. The gold could then be separated from the amalgam by vaporizing the mercury in a retort. By a singular coincidence, one of the few quicksilver mines in North America had been discovered in 1845 at New Almaden, south of San Francisco Bay. New Almaden's production presently began to supplement imported supplies in meeting the miners' needs. Another refinement was the building of "long toms," which were similar to cradles except that they were stationary and elongated and were designed to handle a larger volume of auriferous "dirt" with the aid of a continuous stream of water. The long tom, in turn, led in the following year to the sluice, which was simply a line of open troughs with cleats, blocks of wood, or other obstructions placed in the bottom to catch the gold.

Nor were miners content to exploit the deposits left exposed by streams. Even in 1849 groups of men began to form cooperative associations to dam and divert rivers from their courses, so as to expose the beds. At the same time, a few had the courage to venture into the highly technical field of vein or lode mining, often better known in California as "quartz mining." This meant discovering the veins from which gold had been eroded originally and devising means of breaking the auriferous part of the vein away from the solid rock in which it was encased.

Most of the mining of the early years could be done at altitudes of 2500 feet or less, and thanks to the blessing of the famous California climate, this meant a tolerable environment for life and work during all save the period of heaviest winter rains. If there were some who complained about the mid-day heat in summer, there were many more who agreed that the clear, dry air under that superbly blue sky made high temperatures far more endurable than in the humid East, while the sharp coolness that swept down the mountainside at twilight permitted a deep sleep after the day's labor. Some miners grew so to love this new and different land that they became rhapsodic about the wind sighing in the tall pines, the river winding like a silver ribbon far down at the bottom of a green-clad canyon, and the immensity of views out over the distant valleys of the Sacramento and the San Joaquin.

*C*OMMUNICATIONS in the mineral region were never easy, because of the canyons and ravines that cut across the foothills and mountain slopes, and yet difficulties and distances from main bases of supply were moderate when compared to those suffered by later mining frontiers. Almost from the beginning San Francisco became the queen city, the great port where goods from the outside world were landed, bought and sold by merchants, and then loaded onto steamboats or small sailboats for carriage up the Sacramento and San Joaquin rivers to the principal commercial centers of the great interior valley. There were three of these centers: Sacramento (built near the site of Sutter's Fort) on the lower Sacramento, Stockton on the lower San Joaquin, and Marys-ville, which was on the Feather River, the main tributary of the Sacramento. From these interior distributing points supplies were hauled by pack trains and wagons to the larger mining towns, such as Placerville and Sonora, or to the hundreds of picturesquely named, ephemeral "camps": Brandy City, Whiskey Diggings, Red Dog, You Bet, Poverty Bar, and Rough and Ready.

In these camps and interior commercial centers, and in San Francisco itself, life in the early years was a chaos of improvisation. Nearly every one had come for one purpose—to make money—and there was neither the inclination, the time, nor the opportunity to build solidly or permanently in any phase of life, material or spiritual. Most people were in a hurry—but to accomplish what was not always clear. Most were restless and ready to abandon either a mining claim or a business on very short notice. Most expected to be in California for only a few months or a year or two, until they had "made their pile," as they were always saying, and could go back home to "the States," or Europe, or Latin America, or Asia. Most were strangers to one another—some even being cut off from normal communication by language barriers.

Many were inexperienced in the various businesses they entered in California. All labor, capital, materials, and supplies were costly. All things—individual fortunes, prices, or the fate of whole towns and camps—were subject to sharp and quick fluctuations between gaudy prosperity and total ruin.

It is little to be wondered that the early towns and camps were haphazard in their location and appearance. A veteran of five years in the mining regions gave this description, written in the later 1850s:

> What a contrast do these funny little villages present, to the eye of one habituated to the sleepy agricultural towns of other countries; built of all kinds of possible materials, shapes and sizes, and in any spot, no matter how inconvenient, where the first store-keeper choose [sic] to pitch himself. Sometimes they are found on a broad flat with no suburb visible, squeezed together as though the land had originally been purchased by the inch, the little streets so crooked and confined, a wheelbarrow could scarcely be made to go through them; sometimes again, they are made up of detached buildings, forming an extended village two or three miles long. . . . Some, too, are quite invisible until you discover them at your feet buried in a deep chasm. . . .[16]

The buildings were flimsy structures. A common type was one in which rough green timber served as the frame and canvas as the roof and walls. Here and there a log cabin reminded one of the older American pioneer tradition of the wooded East, or an adobe house recalled the Spanish American past. A few wooden frame structures, built in the East in sections and shipped around the Horn, aroused nostalgic memories of New England. Presently, as a precaution against fires, a few stores and financial buildings were constructed out of brick or stone, with iron shutters that could be slammed shut when the all too frequent disaster of a conflagration began to race through a town.

Even more flimsy than the casual physical construction of a Gold Rush community were its governmental arrangements. When the Gold

Rush began, California was getting along with a thinly staffed, badly financed military government that had been superimposed on the very slight existing local government inherited from Mexico. Neither source of law and order could offer much help when thousands of determined strangers suddenly created camps and towns far off in the interior. The old Spanish office of alcalde, which charged its holder with trying civil and criminal cases and supervising what little administrative work there was, did prove useful, however, and it quickly came to be regarded as a California version of the old English and American office of justice of the peace. But what were the laws governing the ownership of the most widely sought type of property, the mining claims? And what was to be done to punish criminals?

Finding themselves left to their own devices, as American pioneers so often had been on earlier frontiers, the new inhabitants worked out their own solutions. On frontiers east of the Missouri, settlers had been compelled to devise their own rules and procedures for protecting individual claimants to land or livestock from being "jumped." The usual solution had been to hold a meeting, elect officers, draft rules, and then use the combined force of the whole group to compel acquiescence. This procedure was precisely what was adopted in California both in regard to ownership of mining claims and in criminal cases.

Of the two, mining claims presented the greater difficulty, most Americans being quite unfamiliar with the special legal problems involved. But lead miners from Wisconsin had had at least a limited experience, while the Spanish Americans had been raised on the mining ordinances of Mexico, which were in turn based on ancient codes devised in Europe. The Cornishmen and Germans were also familiar with well-developed codes grounded on many generations of experience. From these old and tested codes, as explained by those who knew them, the California miners drew their precedents, and for some years the resulting practices were adequate for the relatively simple needs of the day.

Each local area formed itself into a "district" by voting itself that status at a self-initiated meeting. A presiding officer was elected, a code of "laws" was drafted and adopted, and a "recorder" was chosen to keep a list and description of claims. The central principle in determining ownership was that a piece of auriferous ground belonged to the man who discovered it, or bought it from an earlier claimant, provided he did a specified minimum of work to develop it, such as laboring on it "one day out of every three." Maximum permissible dimensions for a claim were stipulated, and, to give every one an equal chance, the early laws ordered "that no man within the bounds of this district shall hold more than one claim." Provision was made for trying the inevitable disputes that were sure to arise. Controversies might be arbitrated by the presiding officer or an elected "judge," argued before a committee, or even heard before the whole community sitting as a mass jury—the "body politic" in fact.

Much the same procedure was used when accusations of robbery or murder were made against individuals. A "miners' jury," which might be either a dozen men or the whole camp, would try the case under the leadership of some kind of presiding officer, with men appointed to serve as prosecuting and defending attorneys. Sometimes such "popular" trials were entirely extemporized; sometimes they were carried out in accordance with criminal-law provisions incorporated into the local mining laws; and in a few major cases the whole procedure was taken over by self-constituted "vigilance committees," which organized themselves on semi-military lines, captured and tried alleged criminals in secrecy, and temporarily superseded all agencies and individuals as enforcers of law and order. The models that all other vigilance committees sought to emulate were those great committees of prominent private citizens who took over the administration of justice in San Francisco in 1851 and again in 1856, when the legally constituted courts and officers were believed to be too far sunk into corruption and weakness to be capable of protecting the citizenry from criminals.

If the jury in a "popular" trial brought in a verdict of "guilty," since there were no jails the convicted man had to be executed, whipped or branded, or banished from the district. In a serious case, therefore, punishment had to be severe. It was intended to be so. A prime purpose of this home-made system of trial and punishment was to frighten other actual or potential lawbreakers into flight or peacefulness by confronting them with the organized force of the entire community.

Much about the psychology of those who took part in the Gold Rush was revealed by their willingness in moments of real crisis to drop their varied individual concerns in order to concentrate briefly on a troublesome dispute over claims or an accusation against an alleged criminal, while their continuing, day-to-day sense of responsibility for good order was regrettably slight. This behavior indicates, perhaps, that except in emergencies there was little feeling of belonging to a community.

Does it mean, however, that the Gold Rush population was completely atomistic—merely an aggregation of solitary individuals? The question is hard to answer. A high percentage of Americans and some foreigners came to California as members of organized "companies," by which is meant formally constituted cooperative associations. Almost invariably these began disintegrating within a few days of reaching California, because some members wanted to rush off to the mines at once without waiting for the rest or for their joint supplies and equipment, or because some became ill and were a drag on the others, or because the members, as they listened to the mutually contradictory rumors and advice as to the most promising "diggings," were unable to agree on where to begin work.

More enduring were the simple partnerships that grew up in the mining regions. Men would join forces because they could work a claim more effectively together than separately—one man to dig, one to operate the rocker or long tom, one to shovel "dirt," perhaps one to keep a supply of water flowing in. A partnership in labor had the further advantage— perhaps equally important—of providing companionship: companionship on the job, around the camp fire or cook stove, and while doing the simple housekeeping chores. Miners spent most of their evenings not in roistering at a saloon, but rather at their own cabins or camp fires, in talk, reading, or cards. Contemporary diaries suggest that the disappointments and discomforts of life in the mines bore more discouragingly on those who worked and lived alone than on those who shared their troubles and anticipations.

Sometimes a partnership would develop because one New Englander, with a somewhat stricter moral code than many of those around him, would find a kindred spirit, perhaps in the person of a man from one of the areas of New England settlement in upper New York State or northern Ohio. Sometimes a group would be formed by like-minded individuals from what was then regarded as the "Southwestern" frontier, Missouri and Arkansas. Still others grew up around a nucleus of Irishmen, or Cornishmen, or Englishmen.

The French, the Spanish Americans, and the Chinese each tended to be separate elements in the population, forced to stick to their own kind. In the beginning the cultural and linguistic differences may have been too great to encourage their mingling with the general population; certainly from an early date the majority displayed toward these nation- alities a persistent antagonism that was easily triggered into bullying persecution and ostracism. This hostility first displayed itself in "the diggings" against Mexican and South American miners, with Frenchmen, Kanakas, and Indians sometimes serving as additional targets for popular irritation. Irish Catholics, who on the Atlantic seaboard in these same years were being attacked by nativist Americans, in California were on the side of the persecutors. When the Chinese began coming to California in large numbers, starting in 1851–1852, they attracted to themselves a fierce enmity that prohibited their mingling with the American and European miners.

Generally, what coherence the population had was the limited one of personal associations, and even these were subject to fluctuation with the changing richness of the particular claim or camp that had inspired the partnership. Ultimately, therefore, the primary element was the individual. Here generalization is made difficult by the extraordinary variety of origins. The majority were Americans—comprising two thirds of the total reported in the incomplete census of 1850. Of these, some were what contemporaries called "Westerners," by which was meant people who, regardless of their ultimate origin, had spent much of their life on those older frontiers of the Missouri and Mississippi valleys or in the lands immediately fronting on the Ohio River. Mingled with the Westerners were New Englanders, in surprising numbers, New Yorkers and Pennsylvanians in abundance, and relatively few Southerners. There were city men and farm boys, sailors and clerks, not to mention those who did not care to discuss their past.

> *Oh, what was your name in the States?*
> *Was it Thompson or Johnson or Bates?*
> *Did you murder your wife*
> *And flee for your life?*
> *Say, what was your name in the States?*

The people who participated in the Gold Rush tended to be below middle age, both because the venture had appealed originally to young men and because the trip to California and the life in the mines were too trying to be endured by those who no longer possessed the recuperative powers of youth. Labor in the diggings was physically hard, most nearly akin to ditch digging, and it often involved uncomfortable exposure, such as working for hours in the falling rain, to take advantage of a temporary water supply, or in the cold waters of a creek during damming operations. Diets were unbalanced, often woefully lacking in fresh fruits and vegetables. Dysentery, diarrhea, land scurvy, typhoid, chills, fever, and ague ranked high among the diseases reported in contemporary diaries. A popular song bemoaned the miners' commonest complaint:

> *I've lived on swine 'till I grunt and squeal,*
> *No one can tell how my bowels feel,*
> *   With slapjacks swimming round in bacon grease.*

In their preoccupation with just existing, and their freedom from the remonstrances of mothers, wives, and sweethearts, these modern Argonauts let their appearance deteriorate into what became the stereotype for all mining frontiers: an unkempt beard and long hair, weatherbeaten face, flannel shirt, shapeless pants, high boots, an old hat, perhaps an old coat that had seen its first service in the army during the recent Mexican War. So accoutered, and equipped with a pair of blankets, a firearm, knife, mining tools, and cooking utensils, the experienced miner or prospector was ready to start off at once if he heard but the whisper of a rumor of rich diggings in some unknown gulch.

"Dame Shirley," an erudite New England lady who lived in the Feather River mines in 1851–1852, remarked: "Our countrymen are the most discontented of mortals. They are always longing for 'big strikes.' If a 'claim' is paying them a steady income, by which, if they pleased, they could lay up more in a month, than they could accumulate in a year at home, still, they are dissatisfied, and, in most cases, will wander off in search of better 'diggings.' "[17]

These were the individuals and this the society that characterized the flush days. And in the life cycle of a typical Western mining community, the flush days were that period of no more than a few years in which a crowd of tenderfeet, led by a few veterans, came pouring into an area to exploit easily worked virgin deposits.

In California this phase continued at least through 1852, and was marked by successive, large annual increases in gold production and a great increase in population. If the somewhat controversial estimates of modern statisticians are to be believed, the output for 1852 reached the astounding total of $81,294,700, a figure scarcely even approached in the palmiest year of any subsequent American mining frontier. The output in the two succeeding years was still extremely large, approximately $68,000,000–$69,000,000 in each, and yet distinctly below the remarkable peak achieved in 1852. More important, after 1852 the trend was steadily downward, until a relatively permanent level was reached in 1865. Starting in 1865, for nearly twenty years California produced between $15,000,000 and $20,000,000 per year, and this annual figure could have been maintained for a much longer time had not legal restrictions been imposed on certain types of placer mining. Even with restrictions, California's output did not fall below $11,200,000 in any year in the remainder of the century.[18]

It would be difficult to say which is the more remarkable feature of this record: the huge total—over $1,300,000,000 by 1900—the fact that it was so well sustained for so long, or the extraordinary richness of the years up through and immediately following 1852. Other new mining states or territories rose only to much lower peaks, suffered a much more severe and sudden decline, and remained in a depressed condition for a long period, if not forever.

Even within the flush period, contemporaries noted significant changes that were adverse to the prospects of the penniless, unskilled majority of the population. For example, in February 1851 the leading San Francisco newspaper, the *Alta California*, warned that the river banks and gulches, which had hitherto furnished "by far the largest part of the gold," could not be expected to continue to "yield as they have yielded. . . . We have now the river bottoms and the quartz veins," both of which would require capital and perhaps hired labor.[19] In July 1851 the same newspaper stated that "now we hear of the complete exhaustion and abandonment of many of the diggings," while everywhere "there was [*sic*] exhibited strong indications of failing resources, in the increasing necessity for systematic labor and the application of science and practical improvements to assist manual labor."[20] By September the *Alta California* was reporting that while "the general profits to all classes have been lessened," nevertheless the total yield of gold had increased greatly, thanks to "the added science and skill" of the operators.[21] Similarly, the leading newspaper of the interior, the Sacramento *Union*, reported in May 1852 that although there were fewer cases of rich individual fortunes than formerly, by the use of more machinery and expert knowledge mining was paying well and was settling down into a more permanent occupation.[22]

*T*HE FREQUENT REFERENCES to a more scientific, more capitalized kind of mining stemmed from three major developments that started during the flush days but reached their culmination at a later date. These were river mining, deep gravels, and quartz.[23] River mining meant damming and diverting a stream so as to be able to dig out the exposed bed. Tried as early as 1849, its great day came in 1855 and 1856 when the winter rains were unusually late and scant. With their primitive engineering and limited building materials, the miners normally had to wait until late June or July before the rivers were low enough to be controllable. Then a summer of hard work, under the pressure of time, would free the bed of water by September, so that for a few weeks the miners could strip it of its gold before the return of the annual rains washed out the temporary dam.

This was a highly speculative type of enterprise that required intelligent planning and the labor of a large number of men. Most commonly such projects were undertaken by cooperative companies that chose their own foreman, pooled their talents and physical strength, and bought their supplies on credit from the local storekeeper. If the rains held off and the river bed paid well, the miners prospered. If not, the companies carried the storekeepers with them into a universal local bankruptcy, in which the distant merchants of Sacramento, Marysville, or Stockton might well share, since they had advanced the initial credit to the storekeepers.

River damming was very profitable in the middle 1850s, but by the close of the decade the river bottoms had been worked out and had been left very largely to the patient Chinese. Having been simple peasants or laborers accustomed to a limited standard of living in their overcrowded native land, the Chinese immigrants were willing to work for much smaller returns than white miners. The significance of river mining is that it helped greatly to cushion the transition from the high prosperity at the opening of the 1850s to the lower plateau that was to characterize the 1860s. It gave temporary employment to large numbers of men who possessed no capital save their own physical strength.

The deep gravels were something else again, for they gave promise of yielding for a considerably longer period. They were placer deposits laid down by prehistoric streams and subsequently buried by layers of dirt, rocks, or lava. The first approach to them was by digging tunnels or shafts, a costly, tedious, and speculative business that often left the miner and his partners heavily in debt to the nearest storekeeper. Despite the difficulties, from a small-scale beginning in 1850 tunnel mining (known also as "drift mining") developed into an important activity during the middle and later 1850s. By that time tunnels 1000 to 2000 feet long were commonplace.

A more effective way to attack deep gravel was by hydraulic mining, a technique that seems to have its origin in 1852 and 1853. The forms of mining hitherto mentioned were in no sense original to California, although some were reinvented there by men ignorant of the achievements of previous centuries and other continents. Mining is a very old art that has often been reported by careful observers, starting with Pliny the Elder in the first century A.D. Had the forty-niners but realized it, most of the basic types of mining used in the early California rush had been described and illustrated in 1556 in a Latin treatise by the German scholar who called himself Agricola.[24] Many a false start in 1848–1849 could have been avoided if the Gold Rush population had been aware of this monument to the technological knowledge of the late Middle Ages and earliest modern times. Hydraulic mining, by contrast, was a California original, and it remains today one of the really notable innovations contributed by the United States and subsequently used in many parts of the world. Credit for discerning its possibilities seems to belong primarily to Edward E. Matteson, the inevitable Connecticut Yankee, although an almost anonymous Frenchman deserves a part of the glory. The locale was Nevada County, California.

Reduced to its fundamentals, hydraulicking meant nothing more complex than bringing in water under high pressure and aiming it, as if through a hose, at a hill that was believed to be underlain by the auriferous channel of an ancient river. The water was conducted through wooden flumes to the top of a hill sufficiently high so that in falling the water would build up a great "head" or pressure. The water was made to fall through iron pipes and at the bottom of the hill was shot out through a nozzle with a force great enough to wash away mountains (or kill miners who had carelessly stepped into its path!). Once washed loose by this violent jet of water, the auriferous "dirt" was run through long lines of sluices to separate and catch the gold.

Hydraulic mining was only adopted slowly until 1856–1857, because it required a heavy initial capital investment to bring in the very large quantities of water demanded. Quite obviously, it was also a highly restricted type of mining. It could be applied successfully only in areas that had extensive deposits of buried gravels, offered access to large quantities of water, and were characterized by a hilly topography capable of giving the water a sufficient "fall." From Sutter's Mill northward California was blessed in abundance with all of these requirements (to the south conditions were much less favorable), and eventually hydraulicking became the most important single source of gold. In this, as in so many things, California was exceptionally lucky. Later mining states and territories were to find that few of their districts could supply all of the requisites.

From the point of view of the individual independent miner, however, hydraulicking had several serious shortcomings. In the first place it was pre-eminently a labor-saving way of operating. The fundamental concept of making water do the work of men hardly helped men who had nothing to contribute but their labor. In the second place, it required a heavy capital investment that would give a return only over a period of years. It also required purchase from the far-off city of patented nozzles, pipes, and other equipment. Hydraulicking was better suited to operations by a hired labor force working under a single direction than to informal cooperative arrangements of the type that sufficed for simple placer mining or even river damming. Finally, hydraulicking was essentially a technique for what might be called mass production. It was premised upon the assumption that the cost per ton of "dirt" handled would go down as the rate of production went up. Therefore, once it became well established after 1856–1857, hydraulic mining showed a pronounced tendency toward large-scale, heavily capitalized operations.

Much the same outcome characterized the third of the important types of mining that developed after the flush days. Quartz or lode mines were first opened during 1849 and 1850 by men whose optimism was the greater because their knowledge was so slight. Californians still chuckle over the legend that when some men whose only experience had been with placers first became aware of veins, they were deeply puzzled to understand how the gold could have escaped from the placers to form these inconvenient solid-rock veins! A speculative excitement over quartz swelled to such proportions during 1850–1852 that it attracted extensive investment from Californians, Europeans, and people in Eastern cities alike. At the opening of 1853 at least twenty Anglo-Californian quartz companies were being "floated" in London alone, with an alleged total capital of $10,000,000.

Since the great majority of the early backers and operators were ill-qualified for this most technical of all kinds of mining, the first enterprises failed in a general wave of bankruptcy in 1852–1853. Most of those who had been interested abandoned the field entirely, and the few survivors spent the next half-dozen years in learning painfully, by trial and error, how to trace a vein, sink a shaft, break loose the ore, hoist it to the surface, crush it, and extract the gold from the resultant mass of ground-up material. Here, more than in the other forms of later mining, Americans borrowed ideas and techniques from the veterans of older mining regions, from Cornishmen, Georgians, Spanish Americans, and Germans.

Since the early shafts were quite shallow and the underground workings small, operators were spared the serious problems that always develop with depth, such as ventilation, hoisting, and timbering (that is, shoring up the underground chambers). Blasting and hewing out gold-bearing rock was a more difficult business in which, presently, help would be sought in the form of improved explosives and better drilling methods. Once the rock was freed from its matrix, it had to be broken up into pieces the size of an egg before it could be given further treatment. This was at first a laborious task, but Californians soon began using mechanical rock breakers similar to those employed by contractors in building highways. Once through this preliminary breaking, the auriferous rock had to be crushed into fine fragments. The grinding machines used for this in 1850–1852 were fancy, imported affairs, and usually worthless. The Californians scrapped them in favor of several ancient, proven devices that had been used in Europe and the Americas for centuries.

One of these was the stamp mill, which pounded the rock into powder in a huge mortar. The "stamps" were heavy iron heads mounted on vertical "stems" that rose and fell in response to the turning of a horizontal shaft to which the stems were geared. The gold contained in the crushed rock was then caught somewhat as in placer mining—that is, partly with mercury that was placed in the "battery" or mortar, and partly by draining it out of the mortar to flow through traps and settling devices somewhat like sluices.

An alternative that was cheaper and simpler, but slower and suited primarily to small-scale operations, was the arrastra. Mexicans and South Americans often used this device. A hard-surfaced circular bed with retaining walls was built and heavy abrasive stones were placed in it and hitched to a horizontal arm that, in turn, projected out from a central pivot. With a mule for motive power, or perhaps a water wheel, the stones were then dragged around in a perpetual circle, over broken-up, gold-bearing rock dumped into the track. A variation on the arrastra, known as the Chili mill, substituted a heavy stone wheel for the abrasive stones.

Americans generally found the arrastra or Chili mill too slow, however, and concentrated on improving the stamp mill. So successful were practical mill men in devising a series of improvements that the resultant machine became known as the "California stamp mill," and under that name passed into use by mining men throughout the world. Like hydraulic mining, this device stands forth as a Californian contribution of international technological importance.

Quartz mining was essentially a long-term kind of mining. Years might be needed to get a vein opened and developed and a mill built and working efficiently. Really successful operations demanded technical skill of a high order, backed by a growing capital investment. Both requirements were met in a few mines, but even in the late 1850s quartz mining and milling was a relatively inefficient, insecurely established business. There was no comparison between the amount of gold returned by it and that supplied by the various forms of placer mining, including the important new technique of hydraulicking. A modern statistician has even claimed that 99 percent of all the gold obtained between 1848 and 1860 came from placer mines.

Progress in improving the various stages of quartz mining and milling was very uneven. Underground operations received much less attention than they deserved because so long as shallow depths and a limited scale prevailed, it was possible to postpone coping with basic problems. Improvement of the stamp mill raced ahead of the other stages. Californians boasted, with reason, that in a half-dozen years they had carried the stamp mill to a higher level of development than had been achieved during several centuries in the earlier history of that ancient device.

Far less was accomplished in improving the final stage, which was separating and saving the gold after the rock had been pulverized. Contemporaries said that in the early years probably two thirds of the gold content was lost—run off into the dump—because of gross imperfections in handling the pulverized material. Californians were fortunate in that most of their gold ores were what is known as "free milling"; that is, after the rock had been crushed, so as to free the gold, the latter would amalgamate readily with quicksilver. There were some exceptions. Mill men discovered that a small percentage of the gold was enclosed within various forms of metallic sulphides, colloquially known as "sulphurets." Mercury could not come into contact with the gold so long as the ore was locked within the sulphides. To the men of that day is seemed that mere mechanical treatment of the ore was not sufficient to release the gold, and that therefore chemistry and metallurgy would have to be used before progress could be achieved. This was too complex a problem for the average California mill operator of the 1850s, and since the loss through sulphurets was relatively small, he was able to thrust it out of his mind for the time being.

But there remained the basic problem of how to handle the pulverized rock. Some stamp-mill men came to feel that their mills did not reduce the rock to a powder fine enough to release the maximum amount of gold. In the later 1850s it became common to subject the pulverized rock to a second grinding, with mercury, but this time in an arrastra. This procedure, in turn, led several different California mechanics, foundrymen, and mill operators, from 1858 through 1860, to design and patent what were really small arrastras in the form of iron pans. The pans, four to five feet in diameter, had a "muller," or stirring device. In the more effective pans the muller became a heavy iron grinding surface as well as a stirrer, and since heat seemed to be helpful, steam was introduced into the pan.

After this fine grinding and amalgamation, it was still necessary to catch the amalgam of gold and mercury while letting the supposedly worthless rock powder run off in a stream of dirty water. For this stamp-mill men invented a variety of devices that operated much as in placer mining. There were sluices, riffle boards, and inclined tables equipped with contrivances to make them shake or jiggle to help settle the amalgam. Most interesting of all, because of its kinship to classical mythology, was the use of coarse blankets, in the interstices of which fine gold was supposed to lodge. In all probability, the similar use of a sheepskin gave rise to the legend of the Golden Fleece sought by the original Argonauts.

The difficulty and intricacy of quartz mining become apparent in the problems encountered in the successive stages of the total process. If measured by the cash returns received by 1859 or 1860, the whole attempt to extract gold from solid rock might well be written off as unjustified. But for two reasons a hasty dismissal is unwarranted. First, the number of men, the amount of technical thinking, the degree of inventive skill, and the capital sunk into this apparently minor branch of gold seeking during the 1850s was out of all proportion to the return in treasure. Second, when the great Comstock Lode of Nevada was opened in 1859 and 1860, it was the California quartz mines that supplied the knowledge, machinery, and experienced hands needed to exploit that rich opportunity. It is true that when the Comstock silver veins were discovered, California gold quartz mining was by no means well established itself, yet it became the inspiration and guide for a vastly greater effort on the far side of the Sierra Nevada.

*M*OST OF THE CAPITAL for the quartz mines of the middle and late 1850s had to come from the mines themselves. Outside capital showed no enthusiasm for returning to the scene of the original failures. Operations necessarily remained small in scale and under the personal direction of the principal owner. As with other types of mining, credit furnished by local storekeepers was of some assistance. At times nearby farmers could be induced to supply produce, and local foundrymen iron work, on credit or in return for shares in the mine. Owners and hired hands alike provided involuntary capital when they were forced to go for considerable periods with little remuneration except the food they ate. When pressed for cash, the owner would forsake orderly development of his mine in order to take out only the richest ore in sight.

In all types of mining after the flush years "city capitalists," as the miners termed San Francisco financiers, seemed not at all anxious to invest in the state's leading industry. The merchants and bankers of Sacramento, Marysville, and Stockton showed similar caution. Indirectly, many of the urban businessmen were involved through their extension of credit to local storekeepers. A letter written from Placerville in 1854 explained: "The Miners are in debt to the Country Merchants, Country Merchants are in debt to the City [San Francisco] Merchants, Our City Merchants are in debt to the Eastern Cities—and as *usual, all* are expecting the money from the *Honest* Miners."[25]

From whatever source financed, the newer types of mining did the state the great service of maintaining the output of gold long after the original primitive technology had been rendered inadequate by the declining wealth of the superficial placers. The increasing sophistication of the late 1850s is the more impressive when one realizes that most of it was the achievement of rule-of-thumb engineers—"practical men," to use a popular contemporary term of praise. While a few men showed an interest in what could be learned from books, for most miners trial and error was the first school and native ingenuity the first source of ideas. University-trained engineers and scientists were few in number and low in popular esteem. Too many of the early men who claimed to be learned and went by the title of "professor" proved to be charlatans or incompetents. As a genuine understanding of mining developed in California, enterprising publishers began to provide a better circulation of information. The first significant attempt at a technical periodical, the *California Mining Journal,* lasted only from 1856–1858. It was an outgrowth of a local newspaper published in the leading quartz-mining town of Grass Valley, with Warren B. Ewer, a New Englander, as its editor. This journal was succeeded in 1860 by the *Mining and Scientific Press,* which presently became a reliable publication that was read by working miners, engineers, and foundrymen throughout the Far West. Ewer moved down from Grass Valley to become its editor. Starting soon after 1860, the services of the *Press* were supplemented by numerous manuals on mining practice, some written by Californians, some republished at San Francisco from European texts.

In analyzing the nature of mining after the passing of the flush years, it becomes evident that aside from river damming, there was little here for the majority of the men attracted to California by the Gold Rush. The growing emphasis put on expert knowledge, long-term development, capital, and hired labor was alien to the habits and talents of the pioneer type of miner, with his characteristic impatience, restlessness, limited technical knowledge, and inability to accumulate capital.

Yet this fundamental shift in the character of mining was simply a reflection of a sharp decline in the amount an ordinary man might win in a day. There are, of course, no precise figures, but estimates suggest that in 1848 a miner's "wage" (meaning the gold he dug for himself) may well have been $20 per day, and in 1849, $16. With a gradual drop in the next three years, talk of a standard $5 daily "wage" (still meaning primarily what a man could earn while self-employed) began to be heard in 1852, and was common for several years thereafter. Starting about 1856 and continuing to the end of the decade, the figure was about $3, and by that time there were many references to hired hands, especially in quartz mines. The reduction was compensated for in part by a decline in the cost of living, as mercantile arrangements improved and locally grown food became available from California farms.

If contemporary estimates were at all correct, the total number of men who called themselves miners did not shrink in proportion to the lessening of opportunity. Some contemporaries claimed that in the late 1850s the total was still not far from 100,000, the figure that had been reached during the days of maximum annual gold output. By that time, however, many of those described as miners were Chinese, who were reworking placer ground sold to them or abandoned to them by discouraged white men. The census of 1860 recorded 34,933 Chinese among the state's 380,000 inhabitants, and of the Chinese, three fourths were residents in counties where mining was the principal occupation. (Most of the remainder were in San Francisco and Sacramento, presumably working as laundrymen, cooks, or servants.) At as early a date as 1855, contemporary newspapers were claiming that there were 20,000 Chinese miners. By the later 1850s this would be, if anything, an underestimation. Since white men rarely allowed Chinese to come into a prosperous district, the ubiquitousness of the Orientals in the later 1850s was in itself clear evidence of the declining appeal of the placers. It is entirely possible that at the close of the decade one quarter of the working miners may have been Chinese.

This still left a very large number of white miners. Some of the latter were relatively recent arrivals from "the States," Ireland, or Britain. Some had been there since the flush days of the early 1850s, or even since 1849. The number of forty-niners was dwindling, to be sure, for among those who stayed in California the death rate was high, while those who could afford it presently went home. At the same time, those who went back to visit the old farm in Missouri or Pennsylvania, or the familiar town in Massachusetts, were apt to find themselves unable to remain there. "It's too slow for me," or too confining as to habits and dress, the complaints ran.

What did the future hold for this restless crowd of "old-timers"? They were like the hard core of virtually unemployable military veterans who have become such a problem a few years after each major war. John S. Hittell, one of the best of contemporary California writers, said of them in 1858:

> The miners were spoiling for an excitement. . . . The country was full of men who could no longer earn the wages to which they had become accustomed. . . . They had become industrially desperate. They were ready to go anywhere if there was a reasonable hope of rich diggings, rather than submit to live without the high pay and excitement which they had enjoyed for years in the Sacramento placers. Many of them had become unfit for the placid and orderly routine of the common laborer in other countries.[26]

These were the men who were to help people the other mining frontiers of the Far West.

◁ **3** ▷

Opening the Far West
1858-1868

*T*o a decisive degree, California dominated the first decade of mining in the Far West. It is true that a scattering of mining camps developed in a few places just beyond California's borders, such as the Rogue River of southwestern Oregon, the Carson River basin of westernmost Nevada, and the lower Colorado and Gila rivers of southwestern Arizona. Isolated gold placers were found also at Fort Colville, far off in the northeastern corner of Washington. None of these was of more than local importance.

Meantime, waiting restlessly in California was a growing army of the "industrially desperate." A convincing indication of what was to come was given by the Kern River hysteria of 1855. Kern River was at the extreme southern end of the Sierra Nevada, well beyond the established auriferous area and 300 miles' journey from most of the mining camps and commercial cities. When a series of dishonest or grossly exaggerated letters suddenly trumpeted "news" of great gold discoveries there, 5000 men departed at once, and many more prepared to follow, before more truthful reports deflated the unwarranted boom.

Three years later, in the spring of 1858, there occurred an even more impressive demonstration. Reports came to San Francisco of fabulous wealth along the heavily forested course of the Fraser River, in British Columbia, sometimes called New Caledonia. The distance from San Francisco was three times that of Kern River, little was known of the natural environment, and the territory was foreign. To get there one had to make a voyage of a thousand miles up the coast or set off on a laborious journey overland through Oregon and Washington. So great was the demand for oceanic passage from San Francisco that nine steamers and twenty sailing vessels set out for what had hitherto been a fur traders' outpost. On the docks and streets of San Francisco could be heard the words of an old song rewritten for the new occasion:

> Oh, I'm going to Caledonia—that's the place for me;
> I'm going to Fraser river, with the washbowl on my knee.

Within the four or five months that the fever lasted, between 25,000 and 30,000 people started for Fraser River. Although Oregon and Washington contributed some of the outflow, most of the adventurers came from California.[1]

Fraser River, unlike Kern River, was a case of inaccurate reporting rather than pure humbug. The gold was there, but there was less of it than expected, and the river could not be worked effectively until September because of the late melting of the mountain snows in British Columbia. In the meantime, life was too expensive and difficult in the overcrowded little settlements. The disappointed began returning in July, and by late October most of those who had rushed there were back in California, Oregon, or Washington. Only a few thousand spent the winter of 1858–1859 in British Columbia—perhaps a fifth to a tenth of those who had gone there during the spring and early summer.[2]

Even though many individuals lost every cent they had accumulated or borrowed, the population as a whole seemed not to be at all discouraged. In 1859 one of the greatest of all mining opportunities opened with the discovery of silver veins near the gold placers in the Carson River basin of Nevada, known thereafter as the Comstock Lode, or Washoe. A year later it was the Humboldt district of Nevada and the Bodie and Esmeralda districts along the California-Nevada border that were beckoning, while from 1860 to 1862 major gold discoveries were being made in the central and southern parts of Idaho and the adjacent districts of southeastern Oregon. Montana boomed into prominence in 1862–1864. British Columbia recaptured its reputation with Cariboo and Kootenay in 1861–1863.

In the huge Southwestern region that now comprises Utah, Arizona, and New Mexico, "rushes" and actual mining were of only limited significance during the decade that opened with Fraser River fever. Utah was not even well prospected until the Civil War years, and its output of treasure remained confined to the product of a few placers until railroad transportation began materially to alter the situation after 1869. Arizona and New Mexico had a more active but exceedingly erratic experience. Indian danger, especially after the regular army was withdrawn to fight in the East during the Civil War, made life unusually hazardous; the climate was severe; and transportation was extremely difficult. Although both Arizona and New Mexico had small booms that attracted bursts of attention, as a whole they, like Utah, tended to be overshadowed for many years by the richer opportunities in Nevada, Idaho, Montana, and British Columbia.

In varying degree, to each of these new mining regions, however distant, difficult, or dangerous, California sent its restless population. From 1858 to the middle 1860s great crowds of itinerant miners seemed always to be in motion in the vast region from the Pacific to the Rockies, from British Columbia clear down into Baja California, Sonora, and even Durango, Mexico. After the mid-point of the 1860s, their pace slackened, but they still hurried to White Pine and Ruby Hill in central Nevada in the late 1860s, to South Pass in Wyoming in 1868, and even as far afield as the Stikine mines of Alaska and British Columbia in 1874, the Black Hills of South Dakota in 1874–1876, and Tombstone, Arizona, in 1878–1879. The mood was well expressed in a song that became popular in the 1860s:

> *Farewell, old California, I'm going far away,*
> *Where gold is found more plenty, in larger lumps, they say.*

Nor were California's adopted sons alone in succumbing to what contemporaries variously called "manias," "fevers," and "hysterias," When the Missouri frontier received reports of gold in Colorado in 1858, hundreds started for the Rockies as quickly as they could equip themselves; and 1859 resounded to the cry of "Pikes Peak or bust!"—a cry that was as inaccurate as to geography as it was correct in the alternative it offered. The tens of thousands who went to Colorado came principally from the Mississippi and Ohio valleys. A few who had once been in California were among them, and the example of California's fabled riches was always in the minds of the "fifty-niners." Yet this was a movement from east and south of the Missouri, not from California. What is more, once exposed to the excitement of mining rushes, the country behind the Missouri frontier was ready and eager to send thousands out to the northern Rockies when Idaho and Montana were opened up in the early 1860s.

What the nation was witnessing was an almost simultaneous advance into the interior of the Far West from the Pacific coast and the Mississippi Valley. Expressed differently, a population highly experienced in mining life was advancing eastward, primarily from California but also with recruits from Oregon and Washington, while a population with little previous knowledge of mining or mining camps was moving westward from that traditional jumping-off place, the Missouri frontier. The two thrusts into the interior hardly met in Colorado because of the vast stretches of desert and mountain that separate the southeastern Rockies from the Sierra Nevada, but in Montana and Idaho they did meet, and the participants specifically recognized their differing origins by their omnipresent distinction between "yon-siders" ("yondersiders") from the Pacific coast, and tenderfeet or greenhorns from the Middle West and South.

In terms of the limited transportation facilities of that day, these were big movements of population. The rush to Colorado was probably the largest of them all, second only to '49. With all due respect for a highly competent modern historian who has asserted that 100,000 set out from the Missouri frontier in the spring of 1859 and that 50,000 actually reached Colorado,[3] it seems safer to accept the estimate of a more nearly contemporary writer who gave a simple figure of "probably over fifty thousand men" for the whole rush of 1859.[4] When the census was taken in 1860, Colorado was credited with only 34,277 residents,[5] which would seem to indicate that contemporaries were justified in believing that thousands either returned to the Missouri soon after reaching the Rockies or else turned back in discouragement before ever seeing their destination.

The problem of those who returned almost immediately makes it even more difficult to assess the rush to the Comstock Lode in 1859–1860. Whereas Colorado was 600 to 700 miles from the Missouri River, the Comstock camps of Virginia City and Gold Hill were only 100 miles from well-established California mining towns. Admittedly, this was a most severe 100 miles, especially when snow was on the trails, but still the journey could be made in a few days and contemporary accounts agree that even at the peak of the excitement the flow of traffic was moving both eastward and westward. Historians have guessed wildly as to how many were involved. The older belief that 20,000 went to Washoe (of whom only half remained) has been reduced by recent estimates by precisely 50 percent.[6] The census of 1860, taken in the latter part of that year, credited the whole of Nevada Territory with only 6,857 residents; one year later a local census reported a total of 16,374.[7]

The influx to Idaho and Montana is also hard to measure, although for a different reason. Their rushes came after the census of 1860; their population rose to a peak during the 1860s and was in a decline by the time of the new census in 1870. In very general terms a nineteenth-century historian spoke of "the 30,000 or 40,000 people who flocked to Montana in the earlier years," and of a total of "about 20,000 inhabitants" who were in Idaho's ten mining towns by the spring of 1863. The census of 1870 recorded a total of 20,595 people in Montana, and 14,999 in Idaho.[8]

*W*HATEVER THE PRECISE figures, it is hardly necessary to suggest how destructive the reality of this two-pronged advance from east and west is to the notion that the frontier moved ever westward from the time it first left the tidewater settlements on the Atlantic coast. Much more important is the question of why thousands of men were ready to join these successive "excitements."

Expressed in the broadest terms, the mining stampedes of 1858–1878 were not without parallels in American history. The Oregon fever of the 1840s and the earlier enthusiasm for Texas in the 1820s and 1830s bore many resemblances, despite their foundation in hunger for agricultural land. The agrarian frontier shared with the mining frontier a persistent American restlessness, an equally pervasive addiction to speculation, and a desire to exploit virgin natural resources under conditions of maximum freedom. Western farmers, like the miners, were all too ready to abandon claims that they had laboriously developed in order to pursue the often chimerical chance of greater success in some still newer region.

Perhaps these characteristics would have been less common if more Americans of the mid-nineteenth century had possessed greater working capital, or had been less optimistically convinced of their own ability to better themselves if they just seized the right opportunity. Always in the minds of those not yet successful was the image of the few well-advertised individuals who had risen from poverty to wealth by well-timed speculations.

Into this general atmosphere of restlessly seeking something better came specific stimuli at strategic moments. Just as the "Oregon fever" of 1843 was inspired in part by hard times in the Mississippi Valley, so the Colorado rush of 1858–1859 drew many recruits from those who were suffering from the effects of the panic of 1857. The Middle West was harder hit than any other section by that financial disaster. A "collapsed real-estate bubble, poor crops, decline in grain prices, a degenerate currency, and a heterogeneous banking structure" all combined to carry the Middle West down to a level of discouragement and hardship that prevailed at least into 1859 and to a considerable degree lasted right into the new dislocations of the opening months of the Civil War.[9]

Goaded by dissatisfaction, Middle Westerners sought relief in the march to Colorado. In its listing of "nativities of population," the census of 1860 showed that of the five states that each contributed more than 2500 people to Colorado, one (New York) was northeastern, while the other four, in numerical order, were Ohio, Illinois, Missouri, and Indiana. The Middle Western predominance that this implies would doubtless increase if one could but know how many of those born in New York, as well as how many of the fairly large groups listed as born in Kentucky, Pennsylvania, and Massachusetts, had in fact spent much of their lives northwest of the Ohio River or on the far shore of the Mississippi. The proportion of foreign-born was surprisingly low for a mining region—only 2,666 out of the 34,277 total.[10]

For immediate inspiration and leadership, the Colorado gold seekers of 1858–1860 turned to men known to contemporaries as "Old Californians." As used in the Colorado rush, this ordinarily meant not men fresh from the Sierra Nevada or San Francisco, but rather men who had been in California in 1849 and the early 1850s, had returned to the Atlantic coast or Mississippi Valley, and now were aroused to fresh adventures by reports from the misnamed "Pikes Peak mines." Many of the early discoveries in Colorado were made by one-time Californians, and in the new diggings "Old Californians" were consulted and copied in matters of mining technique, mining law, and mining-camp life. Veterans of the still older Georgia mines also played a significant part, although they were less numerous.

These few "old hands" were an invaluable element, for there was a distinctly amateurish atmosphere to the Colorado rush as compared to most of the other "excitements" after 1858. Frank Fossett, whose excellent manual on Colorado was published in 1879, said of the fifty-niners: "Probably nineteen-twentieths of these gold-seekers were as ignorant and inexperienced as regards mining as they well could be, and had but a faint idea of the work to be done or the experience to be undergone in this wild rush for wealth."[11]

By the time Colorado was well launched on its course, a new stimulus to emigration had begun to work. Contemporaries often spoke of the large number of families that fled from Missouri to escape the guerilla fighting that characterized the Civil War in that state, and they spoke with equal frequency of the former Confederate and Union soldiers who drifted west from all parts of the Mississippi Valley. By then Idaho and Montana were the new magnets, and something of the deplorable social instability of those two territories can be attributed to the hostility of recent opponents who were unable to forget their antipathies when they met in the Rockies.

If Colorado was pioneered from the Missouri frontier and Idaho and

Montana partly recruited from there, Nevada was opened primarily by an outpouring from California. This was quite a professional operation. Even the "bummers" were highly experienced in their specialty, which was the art of existing on no visible resources. Working miners formed only "a small part of the speculative troop" which crossed the mountains in 1859–1860. "Probably half were a swarm of drones, many of whom were penniless and worthless as laborers in any capacity."[12]

But along with them came able and experienced veterans of the California mines, especially the quartz mines and mills. Some, to be sure, stayed only long enough to buy up good claims before returning to California to sell them at advanced prices. Others remained in Washoe to do the pioneer work of opening silver veins, building stamp mills, starting toll roads, and founding banks and business houses. Saloon keepers, gamblers, hotel men, and teamsters were, as always, among the first to arrive.

In Idaho, Montana, eastern Oregon, and British Columbia there could be no question as to the presence of veteran miners from the old California camps. The pioneer historian of mining in that vast northwestern region has pointed out that "whatever elements of population prevailed in one or the other place, there was one everywhere present, everywhere respected, everywhere vital—the Californian." "Youngest begetter of colonies," he termed California.[13]

Unlike Colorado, in the Northwest the term "Old Californian" usually meant some one who had come directly from the Sierra Nevada or from San Francisco, possibly after a brief inspection of Washoe. There were notable exceptions, especially during the period of initial discoveries. Some of the earliest prospecting in Montana was done by the Stuart brothers, James and Granville, who had worked in the California placer mines from 1852–1857 and had settled in Montana in the latter year. In Idaho the fever started when Elias D. Pierce, a former California prospector who had become an Indian trader among the Nez Percés, was told of placer gold by Indians and discovered deposits on the Clearwater River.

Once a Californian, always a prospector, apparently. But most "Old Californians" came directly from that state when they heard reports of new placer diggings. Why were they so ready and so able to depart on journeys of 500 to 1500 miles through little-known, difficult, and dangerous mountains, forests, and deserts?

Certainly they were subject, to an extreme degree, to the general Western restlessness and speculativeness. The panic of 1857 and the Civil War affected them hardly at all; California was too isolated from the eastern half of America. Most of the answer, of course, lies in the change that came over California mining in the late 1850s. This can be illustrated by a specific example. In trying to explain why so many left so hurriedly on such an ill-starred venture as that of Fraser River, John S. Hittell, whose writings were as thoughtful as they were careful, gave a perceptive analysis in his excellent manual *Mining in the Pacific States of North America* (1861).

There were, Hittell said, at least three classes that were attracted to Fraser River. The first was composed of those who "had become disgusted with California, had nothing to hope for here, and had nothing to lose; and, of course, it was well enough for them to go." A second was in better circumstances. They had savings or capital of $200 to $1000 each, but since most were bachelors, they had "no one to care for (to-day or to-morrow) save themselves . . . and why should they not go? Take it for granted that they should lose all their money; they would see the country, and would run the chance of making a fortune, if the mines should prove as rich as those of California in '48. It was a bet of $1,000 against $20,000. Who can say that the chances were more than twenty to one against the river? And the chance of living through such another excitement as that of California in '49—the fun would be worth a fortune almost." The third group was composed of storekeepers, boardinghouse keepers, and mechanics, who reasoned that even if the mines did not prove rich, they would nevertheless attract a large population that would need accommodations and services.[14] Besides, many of this class had themselves come from interior communities, and after they had seen their customers depart, they decided they might as well follow.

Hittell's tolerant analysis suggests that while some Californians started for Fraser River because they saw no immediate future in California, others went because Fraser River was a gamble that offered a chance for great wealth and a certainty of excitement of a kind familiar and appealing to anyone who had lived in California. Apparently, then, the motives were only in part economic. That was why it was so futile to ask Californians to wait prudently for more definite evidence of the river's richness. "To expect such conduct," Hittell said, "would be to expect Californians to exercise more prudence in regard to Fraser river than they do in regard to other business transactions. They are a fast people; they will attempt to outrun old Time himself, and if they succeed once, it pays them for a dozen failures."[15]

What Hittell said of that first episode in the thrust outward from California applied with minor adjustment to all of the later rushes. Always there was the love of excitement, the willingness to gamble on the long chance, the self-confident conviction that after life in California one could survive on any mining frontier. So many were without family responsibilities and with only such business or professional duties as could be shed fairly easily. Always the yearning was for a return to "regular '49 times," as contemporaries so often expressed it. The cry, with its implied prayer for a new chance at rich superficial placers, was the miners' equivalent of the squatters' craving for well-watered forest lands not yet subject to any man's claim.

*W*HILE IT IS well enough to talk of "Californians," who in fact were these new nomads? Quite obviously, they were people with not more than eight to twelve years' residence in California. Whence had they come originally? From everywhere, contemporaries answered. In what proportions? The question is unanswerable save in generalities. The census data are tantalizingly incomplete and dubious for 1850, and while far better for 1860, that date is so late that it is necessary to use with discrimination the insights it suggests. After comparing the two censuses with the numerous verbal descriptions by contemporaries, the most that can be said is that in two senses the population of California's mining counties during the 1850s was cosmopolitan. First, it contained a far higher percentage of foreign-born than was true of the nation as a whole; second, the native-born were broadly distributed as to origin, with the largest groups coming from the northeastern corner of the United States (meaning from the Mason-Dixon line northward), the Ohio Valley, and Missouri. By contrast with Colorado in 1860, there was not a predominance of Middle Westerners, and the foreign element bulked large.

The makeup of California's population in the 1850s helps to explain why, when the mining frontier expanded during the 1860s, most of the new mining states and territories tended toward cosmopolitanism rather than toward the more narrow selectivity seen in Colorado. In Nevada in 1860 and in Nevada, Montana, and Idaho in 1870, to cite as examples regions devoted almost exclusively to mining, people of foreign birth formed a far larger proportion of the population than was true of the nation as a whole, while the large groups of native-born from the valleys of the Missouri, Ohio, and upper Mississippi rivers were balanced by corresponding groups from New York, Pennsylvania, and New England.[16]

Their ultimate origins were probably less important than the formative experiences to which the Old Californians had been subjected since leaving home. If they came out in 1849 or the years immediately following, the trip westward was in itself a transforming influence. Weeks of struggle on the Great Plains and along the Humboldt River of Nevada, or weeks of cramped confinement on shipboard, perhaps interrupted by a few calls at exotic South American ports, were totally new adventures for farm boys or clerks. Even the much shorter trip via steamship involved dealing with the climate, jungle, diseases, and natives of the Isthmus of

Panama. Once in California the young gold seekers found themselves leading a wholly new life. Theirs was an existence based upon uncertainty, novelty, and freedom from the inhibitions of normal society. Material gain was an omnipresent goal, although as Hittell's analysis suggested, pecuniary advantage carefully calculated was not always as appealing as the long chance. The individual learned to do a lot for himself, in housekeeping, mining, raising money, obtaining transportation, developing his mind. He entered into business relationships upon a brief acquaintanceship that no modern executive would regard as sufficient, yet he was not especially surprised if his new partners proved dishonest or incompetent. This was perhaps inevitable in a society in which background and experience seemed less important than what a person appeared to be.

As the years passed and the Old Californians became older in fact, they felt increasingly separated from their childhood homes. Sentimental appeals to memories of home and mother did indeed appear in every mining-town newspaper, but when the Old Californian actually went back to visit his home, he rarely felt content to stay there. If he remained in the diggings, the intervals between letters grew longer, and the amount of money he was able to remit to his parents or wife grew smaller. As Prentice Mulford remarked when a rainy day provided a good opportunity to write home, "What is there to write? Nothing but the same old story 'Hope soon to do well.' I have written in this strain for the last six years until I am tired and sick of it. It is no use telling any more about the country. All that has been told."[17]

What was it that kept such men from abandoning a way of life that so rarely brought real wealth in return for so much hardship? Why was it that so often thoughts of "home" were displaced by nostalgic memories of early days in the foothills of the Sierra Nevada, and that visits to "the States" were less compelling than pilgrimages back to one's first mining camp? Prentice Mulford, who was a part of mining-camp society from 1857 until the middle 1860s, tried to answer:

> Perhaps [it was] the memory of the new and exciting life they experienced from " '49" say till " '58" or " '60," with its "ups and downs," its glittering surprises in the shape of "strikes," its comradeship so soon developed among men who, meeting as strangers, so soon found out each other's better qualities, its freedom from the restraints of older communities, its honesty and plainness in the expression of opinion.[18]

It is understandable why men so inclined should have preferred to seek a new California in Idaho, Montana, eastern Oregon, or British Columbia, or in Nevada or Arizona, rather than begin a humdrum existence on a farm or in a city. Driven by their restless search for

El Dorado, the Old Californians became a new pioneer type. What the beaver trappers were to the fur-trading frontier of the Far West, the Old Californians were to the mining frontier. By their prospecting expeditions they became the first to push into the remote places of the Rockies, the Great Basin, and the Columbia and Colorado plateaus, until ultimately the whole Far West was explored by them. Whenever good luck rewarded their searches, they excited hundreds or thousands to follow them into the wilderness to exploit its virgin resources.

In January 1863 the principal mining journal of the Far West, the *Mining and Scientific Press,* gave this discerning appraisal:

> The restlessness of the California miner, while, as a general thing it works only disaster to the individual, is exerting a most beneficial effect upon the community at large. It is to this class of our population that the country is mainly indebted for the wonderful development of her mineral resources which has been accomplished within the past three or four years. The Fraser river excitement of 1858 seems to have impressed upon the minds of our mining population the idea that California was not the only portion of our territory, on the Western Slope, which was rich in mineral. Though, to a great extent disappointed in their expectations of the value of the Fraser river mines, the adventurers thither were determined to continue their explorations in other quarters.[19]

Their chief desire, of course, was to discover superficial placers, and whenever a rich new district was found, such as the Boise Basin of Idaho in 1862 or Confederate Gulch in Montana in 1864, then the Old Californians would guide the new diggings through the whole cycle of technological evolution that California had passed through during the 1850s. Prospecting with the pan would soon give way to washing pay dirt with rockers; rockers would soon be displaced by long toms and sluices. Progress from the most primitive to the more advanced stages came much more quickly than it had in California; it was like rereading a novel: one already knew how the story was going to end. Whether the ultimate stage of placer mining, hydraulicking, could be achieved depended on local geographic and geological conditions. Few parts of the Far West had so fortunate a combination of deep gravels, water supply, and elevated topography as that which made possible the large-scale development of hydraulic mining in California.

While placers were the more desirable of the two alternatives, Old Californians were never known to reject a chance to claim a gold-quartz vein, and after the educational experience of Washoe, they learned something about the "indications" that might suggest silver. Gold-bearing quartz required the prospecting miner to develop an amateur competence in analyzing samples, but silver, which usually occurs in far more complex forms, forced him into reliance on professional assayers. The latter were to be found in every mining town, and even in the larger camps. To them the prospectors rather furtively brought their sacks of specimens. The assayer's report was supposed to be secret, so that the prospector could hurry back to his discovery and plaster the area with claims if the assayer's analysis justified it. Sometimes the assayer betrayed his confidence; sometimes the prospector himself "got liquored up" and talked too much; sometimes the watchful men hanging around the saloons and outfitting stores decided to "trail" an obviously excited prospector on his return journey. At any rate, a successful discoverer was rarely alone for long.

Once in a new lode district, the Old Californians were quite competent to build simple arrastras that would serve well enough to test the richness of the rock and return a modest income during the initial stages of opening a claim. The great advantage of the arrastra was that it was essentially a home-made device. Few Americans, however, were content for very long with such a slow process. Soon they wanted a "California stamp mill," the universal instrument for crushing gold quartz. With silver veins, a California mill could sometimes be used effectively; often, however, it could not. Elaborate arrangements for smelting silver ores or "roasting" them in furnaces soon were forced upon the silver men.

*I*N TERMS OF COMMERCE and industry, the discovery of gold or silver veins was a development that had a peculiar significance. Only the crudest and smallest stamp mills could be constructed locally on a home-made basis, and silver was altogether too complex a mineral to be handled in locally-contrived equipment. Thus lode mining forced a dependence on distant urban manufacturers, and this, in turn, presently led to a corresponding resort to urban finance. Where hydraulic mining was possible, the same situation often held true. The patented nozzles, valves, finished iron pipe, and wrought iron to use in fabricating pipes at the mine, all were city-made, and a large hydraulic project was apt to get beyond the resources of local capital.

When the mining frontier began expanding beyond California, the businessmen of San Francisco were alert to the possibilities. San Francisco's predominant position in the Far West was based upon the facts of geography. With the exception of San Diego, which was far to the south, there was no other good natural seaport on the long California seacoast. Nor was there a serious rival north of California. Portland, Oregon, at the juncture of the Columbia and Willamette rivers, developed into a most useful subordinate port or secondary distributing point.

Puget Sound was in the midst of a wilderness that was gradually being cut up by the intrusion of farms and lumber camps.

Of great importance in that prerailroad era was the circumstance that San Francisco's excellent seaport could be linked to so much of the interior of the Far West by water transportation. Regular and frequent steamboat service to the great Central Valley of California ran from San Francisco up the Sacramento, San Joaquin, and lower Feather rivers, while comparable though less regular ocean-going steamers and sailing vessels went up the coast to northernmost California, Oregon, Washington, and British Columbia, and down the coast to San Diego and Mexican ports. At Portland, the coastal steamers connected with river steamers that operated up the Columbia and thence up the Snake River, far into the hinterland of the Northwest. From the mouth of the Fraser River, just north of the international line, other river steamers ran up the Fraser well into the mountainous interior of British Columbia. Still another line of steamers tapped a part of the Southwest by operating on the Colorado River from the Gulf of California, up past Yuma and along Arizona's present western boundary to river ports in southern Nevada, now buried beneath the modern Lake Mead.

In each case, from the head of steamboat navigation, supplies were then hauled the rest of the way by teams of mules or oxen, or by pack trains if the topography was too rough for wagons. Passengers and treasure traveled by stagecoach as soon as roads were built, the treasure being carried by the stagecoaches, although in care of an express company.

Among the items most commonly sent into the interior from San Francisco were food, clothing, hardware, mining supplies, heavy mining equipment, whisky, a surprising number of luxuries to eat and drink, books, and newspapers. While gold was the only product sent out from the mines, along with it came hundreds of miners to spend their earnings in "the city," as Old Californians termed San Francisco. Helping miners to free themselves from the burden of their gold came to be an important part of the San Francisco economy.

Under the stimulus of this trade, San Francisco flourished. Starting with an initial population of less than a thousand in 1848, "the city" had 36,000 residents in 1852 and 56,802 in 1860. Proudly a San Francisco newspaper boasted at the opening of 1854: "San Francisco is the center, the focus, the heart of California. All that the State contains is represented here. The city is the store-house, the trading-post for the State and for all the rest of the North Pacific besides."[20]

Yet after the middle 1850s anxiety was felt as to the future, as men pondered the effect upon the city of the declining yield of the placers. On the eve of the Fraser River rush apprehension as to what lay ahead "caused an almost universal depreciation in the prices of property and a general stagnation of business," while labor seemed "superabundant."[21] When the rush to Fraser River began, it revealed an unexpected but most welcome paradox. With some exaggeration, a contemporary claimed that losses to individual participants in the fiasco totalled nine million dollars. To the mining towns and camps of the interior, the losses were probably greater, because everywhere property values depreciated as the working population liquidated their assets to buy stage and steamer tickets to San Francisco and oceanic passage from San Francisco northward. Much of the money lost by the participants, however, was spent in San Franciso. There the transportation people, hotel men, saloon keepers, and outfitters prospered handsomely; shipping through the port increased sharply; and real estate values, after a temporary decline when the rush began, recovered and went on to new heights. Immigration from the Atlantic coast increased because of the favorable publicity. In other words, San Francisco benefited from precisely the forces that injured the individual gold seekers and the Californian mining districts.[22]

When Washoe boomed into the fascinated attention of the public a year later, it offered even greater possibilities than Fraser River. Again the interior of California suffered as men and capital hurried eastward across the Sierras, and again San Francisco was the beneficiary. This time the latter profited especially because the Comstock Lode opened a huge new market for its iron foundries. Despite the high cost of labor, materials, and capital, iron foundries and machine shops had been established in San Francisco as early as 1849, and at a somewhat later date similar concerns had been opened in some of the chief interior towns. After the initial mistake of trying to manufacture articles that could be produced more cheaply elsewhere in the world, the foundries began to concentrate on a few items in which knowledge of local needs would provide a decisive advantage and in which, because of weight and bulk, transportation costs would discourage competition from Europe and Eastern America.

Mining equipment was the most obvious possibility, and by the latter part of the decade, improved mining machinery had become a California specialty, with the greater part of the industry centered at San Francisco. The California quartz mines had given the San Francisco iron founders good experience in meeting the needs of lode mines, and soon orders from the Comstock Lode were dwarfing those from California itself. Iron working became easily the most important branch of manufacturing, in terms of labor and capital employed. In 1867–1868 there were fifteen iron foundries in San Francisco employing nearly 1200 hands. The value of their castings in 1867 was over two million dollars. At this time about two thirds of all the manufacturing in the state was being done at San Francisco.[23]

The prosperity of the city was plainly visible. By 1868 the population was about 133,000. Over a thousand new buildings had been erected in the previous year, some of them "very costly and elegant structures." Forty-six churches, eight theaters, and an uncounted army of saloons, gambling houses, music halls, beer gardens, brothels, hotels, and restaurants competed for the earnings of the visiting miner in from Washoe.[24] With brutal realism the *Mining and Scientific Press* pointed out that many who had come to California to mine had become penniless, and many once populous mining areas had become virtually deserted, while "on the other hand, nearly all classes in our city are continually gaining in wealth, and capital is becoming extremely abundant."[25]

Trade with Washoe fitted with relative ease into the established pattern of transportation radiating from San Francisco. Supplies and equipment could be sent by river steamer as far as Sacramento, and thence over existing roads to Placerville or Nevada City. Beyond that lay the big barrier of the Sierra Nevada, but with the profit motive functioning nicely, contractors were stimulated to secure franchises for toll roads by two main and several subordinate routes across the mountains. The most important route was that from Placerville to Virginia City, a distance of 101 miles. At a cost of half a million dollars, a well-graded, macadamized road was built between the two points. Over it plodded every day an unbroken line of struggling, sweating mule teams hauling huge covered wagons. Past them would race the rattling, swaying stagecoach, carrying passengers, mail, and express.

When the mining frontier moved past Virginia City into central and eastern Nevada, as it soon did, freighters, stagecoaches, and express companies followed the miners, thus extending to most of Nevada supply and transportation services that were based ultimately upon San Francisco and Sacramento. Austin, which was squarely in the center of Nevada, became an important interior distributing point from which pack trains, wagons, and stagecoaches ran to dozens of isolated camps. On the eastern fringe of Nevada competition was encountered from freighters operating out of Utah and from supplies brought up the Colorado River by steamer.

In 1868, as the Central Pacific Railroad advanced eastward from California across northern Nevada, freighting and stagecoach companies shifted their routes so as to operate northward and southward from the new towns along the rail line. Winnemucca became one of the more important of these. From it wagons could haul their loads not only to many Nevada points, but also up into Idaho and the northwest.

When Idaho, eastern Oregon and Washington, and western Montana began to produce treasure, far more difficult problems of transportation had to be met than were faced in reaching Nevada. Few parts of the United States were more remote from population centers or more cut off by formidable mountains, deep canyons, and barren plateaus. The northern Rockies sprawl diagonally across the western third of Montana, where the gold discoveries were, and stretch northward into southeastern British Columbia, where the Kootenay gold fields developed. Along the western flank of the Rockies the difficult Bitterroot Range forms a further barrier to travel between Montana and its neighbor, Idaho. Idaho itself is a tangled mass of mountains save for the broad crescent of plateau land that follows the Snake River across the southern part of the state. North of the Snake River the Salmon River and Clearwater ranges begin a rugged barrier that for a long time interdicted direct communication except by nimble-footed pack mules.

That was why the principal route across Idaho, the Oregon Trail, carefully followed the Snake River around the southern fringe of the mountains. A branch of the Oregon Trail forked south from southeastern Idaho to Great Salt Lake, and thence to California. Reversing the overland emigrant's direction of travel, traders brought occasional wagon-loads of supplies straight north from Salt Lake City, through Idaho and into western Montana, even before the Northwestern gold discoveries.

When they sought business in the new Northwestern gold fields, Pacific coast merchants were well aware that they must beat overland competition from Salt Lake City. The best approach from the west was the extraordinarily long and circuitous one by water from San Francisco. After sailing up half the coastline of California and all of that of Oregon, supplies from San Francisco were landed at the wharves of Portland, were carried up the Columbia by steamboat and portage to the river ports of Umatilla or Wallula, or were borne still farther by steamboat up the lower Snake River to Lewiston, Idaho. Goods landed at Wallula were hauled inland the short distance to the frontier outfitting town of Walla Walla.

From Walla Walla, or directly from one of the river ports of Umatilla, Wallula, or Lewiston, long trains of pack mules operated to all parts of Idaho, eastern Oregon, northeastern Washington, up into Kootenay, British Columbia, and across the mountains to Montana. In the most rugged and isolated mountains, miners would hear a welcome tinkle as the bell mare approached, with the laden mules skilfully picking their way after her.

"And talk about roads and trails; principally there weren't any; leastwise a tenderfoot would have gotten lost a dozen times a day just trying to follow some of them," one old packer reminisced. "We penetrated into the most remote and inaccessible places; over all kinds of country and in all kinds of weather conditions."[26]

Where toll roads were built, the pack mules were displaced by wagons, but many parts of the Northwest never saw a wheeled vehicle. The most important wagon roads were those completed in 1864 to span the distance of 300 miles between the Columbia River and the Boise Basin of southern Idaho, then the most important mining region of the territory.

Much of the responsibility for the success of this roundabout approach rested upon the merchants of Portland and the Oregon shipping men who monopolized navigation on the Columbia and Snake rivers. Supporting their efforts were the outfitters at Walla Walla and the packers and teamsters who operated between the Columbia and the mines. Through the combined efforts of all, supplies and equipment from San Francisco, together with agricultural produce from Oregon, captured and held the major share of the market in Idaho and eastern Oregon. It was never an unchallenged dominance, for freighters brought up from Salt Lake City goods that had come across the Great Plains, and Mormon teamsters distributed agricultural produce from the settlements in Utah. At times wagon trains hauled loads directly into Idaho from the Missouri frontier, as when Chicago-made quartz millls were transported into southern Idaho.[27]

As an alternative to the over-long approach from California by way of the Columbia River, there was hope that a more direct way could be found by utilizing the existing steamboat service from San Francisco to some northerly point within the great interior valley of California, such as Chico or Red Bluff. From there a road could be built across the arid corners of northeastern California, northwestern Nevada, and southeastern Oregon. Repeated efforts to open a route of this kind produced only spasmodic success. Ultimately the completion of the Central Pacific Railroad to Winnemucca provided direct access to southern Idaho from California, and when the railroad reached northern Utah in 1869, an important wagon trade developed from the Utah railheads to both Idaho and Montana. This trade carried with it a major threat to Californian merchants, for the railroad could bring in supplies and equipment from the Middle West just as readily as it could haul them from across the Sierras.

From the beginning Montana constituted a more intractable problem than Idaho for the Pacific coast merchants. The direct approach from Walla Walla across northern Idaho to Montana was possible for pack trains, and in fact each summer, especially before 1865, pack trains brought in supplies from the Pacific coast. Wagon trains, however, found this route impossible, and had to be sent on a circuitous journey down to the Boise Basin and thence eastward along the Snake River before turning north to Montana.

This routing put the Pacific coast merchants at a heavy disadvantage. They were competing with wagon trains from Salt Lake City, 500 miles from the mines, or those coming in directly from Middle West. It is not surprising that prior to 1865 the larger part of the supplies for Montana came from Salt Lake or from the East via these land routes. Beginning in 1865, shipments by steamboats up the Missouri River began to increase rapidly. During the days of the fur trade, St. Louis captains had pioneered navigation on the Missouri. The route was a highly seasonal one, open only during five or six months of the year, and it was an exceedingly long 2300 miles up that shifting, treacherous river. Yet its rates could and did go below those of all competitors, especially for bulky, heavy items such as mining machinery.

After some initial slowness in recognizing their opportunity, St. Louis merchants began to invest heavily in new steamers. Eight steamboats reached Fort Benton in north central Montana in 1865; thirty-one in 1866; and thirty-nine in 1867. Twenty quartz mills were among the cargoes of 1865. From Fort Benton the distance to the various mining towns was from 100 to 200 miles, over roads passable for wagons.[28]

Montana, then, was well within the reach of St. Louis, and through it of the whole Middle West, including the thriving industrial center of Chicago, but it was at the outer edge of San Francisco's radius of trade. In the southern Rockies the balance was even more decisively against California. For Colorado there could be little question as to source of supplies. The Middle West played the biggest role in founding Colorado, and the Middle West supplied it. Some of the earliest mining equipment was built at Burlington, Iowa, from plans obtained from the experienced San Francisco manufacturers. A government survey in 1870 concluded that Colorado's mining machinery "has been mostly supplied from Chicago."[29] Some agricultural produce came in from Utah, and beef cattle were driven up from Texas and New Mexico.

The exceedingly active life of Colorado, Nevada, and the northern Rockies contrasts with the limited amount of mining in Utah, Arizona, and New Mexico in the decade 1858–1868. During the early and middle 1860s all of the former regions experienced true flush periods that transformed them from desert and wilderness into states and territories that claimed thousands of citizens and hundreds of camps and towns. In the chapters that follow, evidence will be presented to indicate why the rate of development was so uneven between different parts of the Far West. Here it may suffice to suggest that the most important factor was the richness of the precious-metal deposits themselves. It is an old saying that the richest deposits are always worked first. With other and more richly endowed parts of the Far West still at their summit of renown, interest in the Southwest was bound to be only moderate.

The degree of richness, in turn, was modified by the technical difficulties experienced in working each type of ore, by the distance to the nearest major supply base, and by the topographic and climatic problems peculiar to each region. The latter were the chief elements in determining whether transportation facilities could be established on a basis that would reduce the cost of supplies and equipment to a level that made mining economically feasible. It is significant that throughout the Southwest the constant cry during the 1860s was for railroads. Indian danger sometimes greatly accentuated natural obstacles. This was particularly true during the Civil War years, when the withdrawal of the regular army left the Far West badly exposed. Everywhere the Indians showed a tendency to get out of hand. In Arizona and New Mexico, what little civilization there was actually retrogressed during the Civil War. Mines, camps, and towns were abandoned, and the frontier visibly receded before relentless and repeated Indian assaults.

◁ 4 ▷

The Comstock Lode

1859-1880

*W*ith more exuberance than tact, a famous San Francisco newspaper boasted in 1872 that "Nevada is the child of California."[1] The assertion was hardly an exaggeration. Californians had assumed control of Nevada's greatest mining area, the Comstock Lode, as soon as its potentialities became dimly visible in 1859–1860, and thereafter the twin Comstock towns of Virginia City and Gold Hill were operated as an industrial suburb of California, and more particularly of San Francisco. Nevadans have been protesting ever since that in the short space of twenty years California stripped their state of Comstock silver and gold, used it to rebuild San Francisco, and then abandoned the Comstock Lode to the unhappy future that faces all gutted mining properties.

There is considerable justification for the complaint. The profits from the Comstock's huge production certainly did not stay in Virginia City and Gold Hill. Despite the extraordinary record of producing $300,000,000 in the twenty years 1860–1880, after the latter date those two communities and their smaller neighbors gradually sagged down to the status of ghost towns, and there they have remained until the present day.

56

They are America's most dramatic demonstration of the impermanency of a society based solely on gold and silver mining.

San Francisco, by contrast, used the Comstock's wealth not only to finance ornate new buildings, but also to expand and diversify its businesses and consolidate its position as queen city of the Pacific coast and the adjacent hinterland. When the Comstock mines failed, San Francisco profoundly regretted the loss, and yet was not permanently injured by it.

The unquestioned benefit of Comstock silver to San Francisco and central California was the more interesting because so much of the new wealth involved speculation of an extraordinarily widespread and irresponsible kind, and because so much of the net profit was monopolized by a small group. California gold had produced a society that was addicted to taking chances in all kinds of enterprises, and yet until shares in Comstock mines were offered on the San Francisco stock market, there was no single, organized mechanism capable of attracting—and misusing—the hopes, cash, and borrowed funds of all levels of society. Again, the opportunities offered by California gold had brought forth some wealthy individuals, especially among the city business and professional men, but it had not spawned the millionaires and supermillionaires who were so striking a phenomenon of the Comstock era. The chairman of the San Francisco Stock and Exchange Board, who was in a position to know whereof he spoke, remarked that "prior to the Civil War, extremely wealthy men in California were not so numerous . . . , and one could name our millionaires on his finger ends. Men possessing $100,000 were considered well off, while a $500,000 citizen was always addressed with the prefix of 'Mister.' "[2] The distribution of wealth in California was visibly more unequal after the Comstock boom than before it.

Technologically, economically, and sociologically the Comstock Lode represented a big and abrupt stride beyond the farthest limits reached in California during the 1850s. No Californian mining venture of the 1850s had demanded such a huge investment, none had been conducted on such a flamboyantly large scale, none had required such a rapid advance in engineering and technology. Nor had California mining, even in the field of quartz, led to the factorylike industrial relations that so soon characterized Virginia City and Gold Hill.

California's achievements of the 1850s have an enduring significance because they represent the first lessons learned in precious metal mining. The foothills of the Sierra Nevada were in fact a basic school in which the Far West studied the fundamentals of a new profession. Having mastered there the initial exercises, Californians were ready to graduate to the Comstock Lode, which became for them an advanced school in which they discovered how to mine in depth and on a large scale, how to use powerful and intricate machinery and large numbers of employees, and how to cope with metals more complex than free gold.

*T*HE ENORMOUS WEALTH that was to come from the Comstock Lode was by no means a certainty when the rush to Washoe began in 1859. Ever since 1850 a small colony of rather unenterprising placer miners had been making a modest income at what was then an isolated mining outpost in the drainage basin of the Carson River, just east of the Sierra Nevada. The "diggings" were on the slopes of Sun Peak, later rechristened Mt. Davidson, which rose 3600 feet above the valley of the Carson and was the highest point in a local mountain chain, the Virginia Range. The Carson, named for the famous Kit Carson, was one of the few substantial streams that drained the Sierras' eastern slopes. Through its valley, so welcome after arid marches across Nevada, passed many thousands of overland travelers on the last leg of their long journey to California from the Missouri frontier. But of permanent settlers the Carson could claim no more than an occasional farmer, rancher, or trader. Most of those who reached the banks of the stream wished to do no more than rest their draft animals before challenging the barrier of the great Sierra Nevada.

The center of mining effort since 1850 had been Gold Canyon, a sagebrush-covered ravine on the southern flank of Mt. Davidson. There a mining hamlet of perhaps a dozen shanties had come to be known as Johntown. In the winter and spring months of an average year during the 1850s, a hundred or more miners sometimes found temporary employment in the area; in summer, when water became scarce, the number usually shrank to less than half that. [3]

Some picturesque individuals were among the more permanent members of the Johntown community. There were "Old Pancake," who was Henry T. P. Comstock, a gaunt Canadian fraud; "Old Virginia," who was James Fennimore (alias Finney), supposedly a native of the Old Dominion; and Peter O'Riley and Patrick McLaughlin, two Irishmen.

The Gold Canyon people were placer men engaged in mining of the older, simpler type that was already becoming obsolete in California. Their working hours were spent in seeking gold that had been eroded from the numerous little auriferous veins that were concealed in the mountainside. There is evidence to suggest that two brothers, Hosea and Allen Grosh (or Grosch), sons of an Eastern clergyman and better educated than the other Johntowners, correctly guessed that the slopes of Mt. Davidson were richer in silver veins than in gold, but the brothers were killed in 1857 and their secret died with them.

After 1855 the yield of the small Gold Canyon placers was on the decline. The little mining community dwindled correspondingly, and the survivors were forced to shift their operations farther up the side of Mt. Davidson. Early in 1859 "Old Virginia," "Old Pancake," and some others began opening what they took to be promising new placer diggings at the head of Gold Canyon, on a small rise that they named Gold Hill. This was on the southern slope of the mountain. On the northern slope, other Johntowners had for some time been working up a ravine known as Six-Mile Canyon. During the spring months, and without any great expectations, O'Riley and McLaughlin started digging on a new claim at the head of that canyon.

The two Irishmen encountered some curious black dirt that paid surprisingly well when run through their rockers, even though it had the peculiarity of producing a pale gold alloyed with so much silver as to be worth less than the usual amount paid per ounce for gold dust. Just as they were rejoicing at their good luck, "Old Pancake" came riding by, guessed that something good had been found, and by sheer assertion bluffed his way into partnership with the two real discoverers. Their claim was soon called the Ophir mine.

Further digging proved that this was not actually a placer claim, but rather was the decomposed outcropping of a vein. The proprietors found themselves forced first to pound the partly decomposed quartz into fragments, then to contract for two small, simple arrastras. By this time the miners, still with no thought of any mineral save gold, were irritably throwing away quantities of heavy bluish sand and blue-gray quartz—what they peevishly called that "blasted blue stuff." The black sand discovered earlier had been not unfamiliar, for it had been encountered previously in the Gold Canyon diggings, but the "blue stuff" was new and puzzling.

During June it occurred to a settler on the Carson River to gather up a sack of the blue quartz and dispatch it over the mountains to California for assay. The assays were made in Nevada City and Grass Valley. Both were in Nevada County, California, and were two of the most prosperous mining towns in that state, while Nevada County itself was famous for its progress in both quartz and hydraulic mining. Yet the assayers' reports that the "blue stuff" was rich in silver caused an abrupt exodus from the county. The reports were received late one evening, and the recipients of the wonderful news agreed to keep it "a profound secret" so that they could go quietly across the Sierras and have first chance to stake out claims. "But each man had intimate friends in whom he had the utmost confidence. . . . These again had their friends. . . ."[4]

By breakfast time Nevada City and Grass Valley were afire with excitement, and the intensity increased when it was learned that two

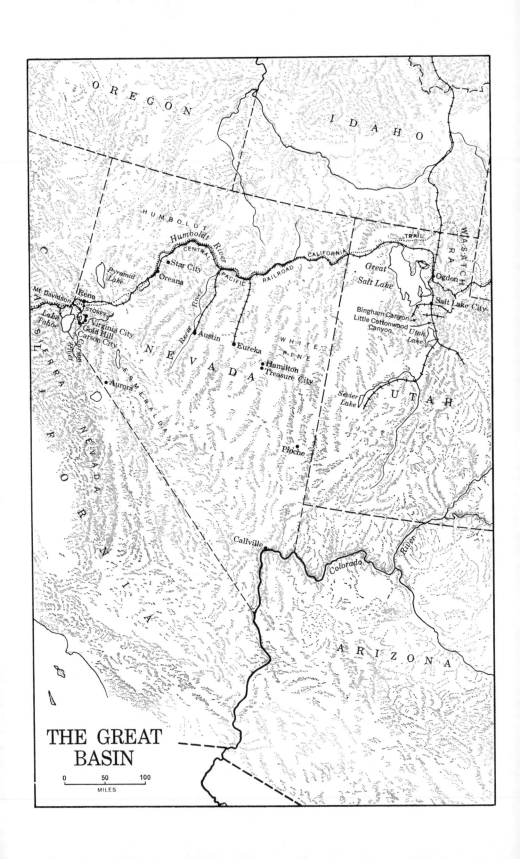

THE GREAT
BASIN

0   50   100
MILES

leading citizens of the latter town had saddled their horses and slipped off before dawn—on what proved to be a highly successful trip to buy claims before the Carson Valley miners knew their true value. Small groups of Nevada County men quickly pursued them eastward over the hundred-mile trail, and as the news spread, men from other mining counties came flooding after them.

Soon the hitherto isolated diggings on Mt. Davidson were inundated by newcomers. A straggling settlement of tents and shanties developed at Gold Hill, and another and larger one sprang up at the site of O'Riley and McLaughlin's discovery. As a tribute to Fennimore, the latter town bore the name of Virginia City, supposedly so christened by "Old Virginia" when he inadvertently dropped his whisky bottle. Perhaps the reflected glory of supplying the town's name was not entirely undeserved; "Old Virginia" seems to have been abler than most of his Johntown friends, even if his mining activities did have to be restricted to his brief periods of sobriety.

Fennimore's sometime partner, "Old Pancake," was even more fortunate in immortalizing himself. By his constant self-advertising and his ill-justified allegations, he caused the great new silver deposit to become known as the Comstock Lode. Under that scarcely deserved name it became famous throughout the world, and as the Comstock Lode it has been studied ever since by generations of mining men and geologists.

Geologically the Comstock Lode had developed when heated fluids bearing mineral constituents had flowed into a massive fissure caused by subterranean faulting. In the fissure and the surrounding walls both silver and gold were deposited. Unfortunately for the stability of Comstock mining efforts, the ores were not distributed evenly during the process of deposition; rather they were bunched into "ore chambers," "shoots," and "branches." Miners lucky enough to strike a concentration of rich ore were said to be in *bonanza* (in Spanish, clear skies); those in the vastly more extensive surrounding rock, relatively barren of minerals, were in *borrasca* (storm). Much of the speculative character of Comstock operations had its origin in this very uneven distribution of ore.

Traceable for two and a half miles, the Comstock Lode ran across the heads of Gold and Six-Mile Canyons—that is, through the eastern face of Mt. Davidson—and underneath the new settlements of Gold Hill and Virginia City. The Ophir mine was close to one end; the alleged Gold Hill placer diggings were actually the decomposed outcroppings of the other end.[5]

Most of the men who came hurrying out to Washoe, as they called the area surrounding the Comstock Lode, were refugees from the decaying placer camps of California, or disappointed men returning from Fraser River, or inexperienced hands from east of the Missouri frontier, or the usual assortment of speculators, saloon keepers, merchants, and drifters who always accompanied any rush. They soon found that a new lode-mining region, and especially one rich in an unfamiliar metal like silver, was ill-suited to their wants and experience. Having neither the capital nor the skill to develop silver veins, and lacking the traditional outlet of most flush periods, superficial placers, they turned to what looked like the easy alternative of speculating in claims and town lots. J. Ross Browne, in his contemporary description of Washoe in March and April 1860, said:

> Nobody seemed to own the lots except by right of possession; yet there was trading in lots to an unlimited extent. Nobody had any money; yet every body was a millionaire in silver claims. Nobody had any credit, yet every body bought thousands of feet of glittering ore. . . . All was silver underground, and deeds and mortgages on top; silver, silver everywhere, but scarce a dollar in coin. The small change had somehow gotten out of the hands of the public into the gambling saloons.[6]

The immediate result of this initial orgy of speculation was to cover the landscape with ill-justified claim notices. Ultimately, nearly 17,000 claims were to be "located." Most were to prove worthless for mining purposes. One half of the total production of the Comstock and four fifths of the dividends were to come from two pairs of adjacent mines: the Crown Point and Belcher, and the Consolidated Virginia and California. So uneven are the rewards in mining.[7]

*W*HILE MOST of those who rushed in were wasting their time on claim speculations, a few veteran quartz men from California were settling down to the difficult task of extracting treasure from Comstock ore. The more typical of these graduates of the California vein mines were men who had achieved only a modest financial success on the western slopes of the Sierra Nevada: some had made and lost sums that were regarded as fair-sized; most were richer in experience than in goods. Having done less well than they hoped, they were ready to leave promising or even profitable small gold quartz mines in California to plunge for bigger stakes in Nevada. In describing the earlier careers of individuals who ultimately became rich through mining on the Comstock Lode, a contemporary biographical dictionary, for all its desire to please potential purchasers, nevertheless dismissed the Californian phase of each man's life by polite euphemisms such as "with indifferent success," "with varied fortunes," or "the fickle goddess withheld her golden favors."[8]

George Hearst, to cite an illustrious example, had been in California since the autumn of 1850. After an unsuccessful year at placer mining and a brief venture in storekeeping, he had decided to concentrate on quartz mines near the twin communities of Nevada City and Grass Valley, which were at that time just starting their development towards pre-eminence in vein mining. Hearst was a hard worker, an intelligent man, and more experienced than most men there, for he had worked in the Missouri lead mines. Yet the first good vein claim he "located" near Nevada City, he had to sell because he lacked the capital to develop it. In association with several other men from Nevada City, he then spent five years prospecting, locating, developing, and selling quartz claims before he found one that looked really promising. He was in the process of developing this one when he heard of the silver strike on the other side of the mountains.

Hearst was one of those who learned "in strictest confidence" of the wonderful assays of "blue stuff" made in Nevada City and Grass Valley in the summer of 1859. He hurried across the mountains, arranged to buy a one-sixth interest in the Ophir mine, then came back to Nevada City to raise the money to complete his purchase. By selling his share in his California mine and borrowing a thousand dollars from a hotel keeper, he secured what he needed. Back he went that same year to Washoe, where he and his associates put two arrastras into operation and, by sheer determination, not only got out thirty-eight tons of selected ore, but packed them across the mountains on muleback through the winter snow. When taken by way of Sacramento to San Francisco, and there smelted, this rich ore paid Hearst and his co-owners $91,000 above the cost of transportation and reduction. It was the sight of the silver bars smelted from this "ore of Ophir" that converted into hysteria California's developing interest in the Comstock Lode.[9]

This was the beginning of the Hearst fortune and the beginning of all sorts of problems for Hearst and his co-owners. In the spring of 1860 they already had ten hired hands working for them on the Ophir. At the fifty-foot level, underground water began flooding the claim, and they found it necessary to install the first steam-pumping and hoisting equipment used on the Comstock. Before the year was out, they had reached a depth of 180 feet on the incline—that is, following the dip of the vein. In other words, they were finding themselves pushed almost at once up to the limits of their California experience.

At a depth of 175 feet they had to face a totally unfamiliar problem. The vein had proved to be extraordinarily broad, when compared to those of Grass Valley and Nevada City. At 175 feet in depth it was 45 to 65 feet in width, and soft and crumbling in composition. Even the strongest timbers, when used as simple pillars, broke under the load, so that cave-ins were frequent and the miners were working under constant threat of being buried alive. It was beginning to look as if the millions of dollars of ore in sight were too dangerous to be touched.

One of the officers of the Ophir company sent for Philip Deidesheimer, an able young German engineer who had been in California since 1851 and was then managing a gold quartz mine in El Dorado County, California. In a month's time Deidesheimer invented the famous "square set" scheme of timbering. This meant that timbers were mortised and tenoned at the ends so that they could be fitted together to form hollow cubes, each cube interlocked with the next in endless series. In large underground chambers some of the hollow cubes could be filled with waste rock, as to make a solid pillar of wood and rock from floor to roof. Deidesheimer's "square sets" became standard throughout the Comstock, and engineers from all over the world came to study and copy this innovation in underground practice. "Square sets" were easily the most important technical development of 1860.[10]

While Deidesheimer was devising a technique that would make underground mining possible, many were struggling with the problem of how to handle the ore once it had been extracted from the mine. Temporarily, the mine owners were picking out their richest ore and shipping it—however incredible it may seem—to England to be smelted. The rest of the ore waited for a satisfactory process that could be used locally.

The principal pioneer in this effort was Hearst's friend, Almarin B. Paul, a veteran California mining man and the owner of a quartz mill at Nevada City, California. Paul was a forty-niner who had tried his hand at merchandising, publishing, and real estate, in addition to mining. He was well-informed concerning California gold-milling practices, and had the good sense to study books on the metallurgy of silver. His long experience included service in the mines of Lake Superior before he came to California. Like Hearst, Paul crossed to Washoe in 1859. He brought back with him sacks of ore on which to experiment during the winter of 1859–1860. By spring he had decided to erect what was for those days a good-sized mill (24 stamps) near Virginia City, at a spot where water was available.

The risk was great, since so little was known in California about silver ores, and since all machinery and supplies would have to be hauled by mules across the Sierra Nevada on the uncertain roads available at that early date. The venture became even more speculative when Paul had the audacity to sign contracts with mill owners by which he promised to start crushing their ore sixty days after signing. He had already ordered machinery from San Francisco. The San Francisco foundrymen responded quickly, while Paul in the meantime was getting his lumber from a forest twenty miles from his millsite. As with his machinery, mules were the motive power for bringing the boards and beams to him, across the rugged and rocky terrain. The transportation costs were extraordinarily high.

With Paul driving the whole enterprise with imaginative energy, the mill was completed precisely on the last day of the contract. Paul was barely in time to win the distinction of putting his mill into operation first. Another California quartz-mill owner had brought over the machinery for an eight-stamp mill. He had his functioning a few hours after Paul's.[11]

As these pioneers realized, crushing the ore was the lesser of their troubles, because it was familiar. The California stamp mill, as it had been developed by 1860, offered a reliable basic model that was capable of enlargement and further improvement to meet Comstock needs. But how should the crushed rock be handled after it came from the mill? An honest man, Paul himself confessed two years later that "in 1860 and 1861 none of us knew anything about milling silver ores."[12] Did it occur to Paul that he was extraordinarily fortunate to be able to think in terms of treating silver in stamp mills and by amalgamation? Most of the world's silver is found in association with base metals (lead, zinc, or copper) and can be separated from them only by the costly and exacting process of smelting.

For reasons that the geologists are as yet unable to explain adequately, the bulk of the silver ores just east of the Sierra Nevada, in western Nevada State, were in association principally with gold, along with only very slight amounts of base metals. Being in that form, they could be treated very much like the California gold ores to which the miners of 1859–1861 were accustomed. In eastern Nevada, as in Colorado, Utah, and Montana, this happy circumstance was not often repeated, and those areas had to struggle to build and operate smelters, instead of being able to employ the much cheaper, quicker, more familiar, and less difficult techniques borrowed from California gold-quartz operations. It was a remarkable coincidence—a case of sheer, unpredictable good fortune—that thrust this basic advantage into the hands of the California quartz men who pioneered the Comstock Lode.[13]

Nor did their good luck stop there. The Comstock ores proved to be almost as rich in gold as in silver. Over the course of twenty years, about 57 percent of the yield was in silver, as compared with 43 percent in gold.[14] In the beginning years, 1859–1861, the gold product was probably distinctly higher than the silver, and it was this factor that saved the earliest operations from being a net loss to their promoters. Without realizing it, Almarin Paul and his fellow pioneers were working under unexpectedly favorable conditions when they began to transfer to the eastern slope of the Sierra Nevada the only techniques they knew.

Paul's first mill was an improved California model equipped with the new iron pans that were just coming into use. Very soon the pans became a most important stage in the whole process, and in an effort to improve them, ideas were constantly being exchanged between the mill operators in Washoe and the foundrymen in San Francisco. The only precedent available for guidance was the primitive practice of the Mexicans, who had been dealing with silver for generations. The Mexicans used two simple processes. One was the *cazo* (kettle). Ore that had been pulverized in an arrastra, with quicksilver, was boiled in a copper-bottomed vat (the *cazo*) with salt and more quicksilver. The same thing on a larger scale could be accomplished by using the *patio* process. With this, pulverized ore from the arrastra was spread out in a paved yard (*patio*) with salt and copper sulphate. Mules or horses were driven through it repeatedly in order to stir the mixture by their trampling (even though this inevitably brought death to the animals within a few months, because of quicksilver poisoning). The only source of heat was the sun, but in a warm, dry climate that proved sufficient provided one were patient.[15]

With relatively easy silver ores, these two simple but slow and labor-exacting processes were adequate. What Almarin Paul and others were seeking to do in 1859–1861 was to reproduce the essentials of the *cazo* and *patio* processes in mechanized form, suited to American ideas of speed, large volume, and minimizing labor. Quite aside from our characteristic national impatience, the universally high cost of labor and capital on all American mining frontiers made the old Mexican techniques inappropriate.

Paul dumped quicksilver, salt, and copper sulphate into his pans. After a trial of hot water, he shifted over to steam as a method of providing heat. He soon adopted heavy iron mullers that would grind as well as mix the pulverized rock. Almost unconsciously, he thus added another chemical. Iron filings worn off the muller and pan by friction proved to be an essential ingredient. By 1862 he and his rivals had evolved these mechanical and simple chemical constituents into what became known throughout the mining world as the "Washoe pan process" or "Washoe pan amalgamation." It was used in association with elaborate settling devices and traps, into which the final product was run after it had passed first through rock breakers, then through the stamp mill, and then through the pans.

The road towards the Washoe pan process was by no means a straight one. For an unhappy period of many months mill superintendents were susceptible to the sales talks of so-called "process-peddlers," who claimed to know secret combinations of chemicals that would surely release the silver. In all seriousness, some superintendents became convinced that tobacco juice and a kind of tea brewed from sagebrush would do the trick. As Mark Twain's friend, the humorous reporter "Dan De Quille," expressed it, "The object with many inventors of 'processes' appeared to be to physic the silver out of the rock, or at least make it so sick that it would be obliged to loose its hold upon its matrix and come out and be caught by the quicksilver lying in wait for it in the bottom of the pans."[16]

The twin victories represented by "square sets" and "pan amalgamation" were by no means the only notable technical accomplishments of the Comstock mines, but they were fundamental, in that without them the mines could not have been developed at all, and the details of their evolution have the special usefulness of showing how intimate and continuing were relations between California and its mining outpost across the Sierras. As the mines went deeper during the next few years, problems inevitably multiplied. The worst difficulties underground were heat and water. Ventilation was never adequate, and there was the constant threat that large bodies of very hot water would burst out suddenly if a miner's pick happened to puncture a hidden underground reservoir. The temperature of the air increased about three degrees with every hundred feet of depth, and when the shafts finally got down to 3000 feet, late in the life of the Comstock, the miners encountered water at 170° Fahrenheit.

In addition to cutting air shafts and installing the biggest and best pumps and blowers obtainable in America, the companies provided unlimited supplies of ice water underground and worked the men in double gangs, so that one crew could rest from the heat and douse themselves with ice water while the other "spelled" them. Rarely could one gang endure working more than every alternate hour; at worst, only fifteen minutes at a time.[17]

Insofar as machines were of assistance in improving work underground, the Comstock companies were ready to borrow from any part of the world that seemed to have promising ideas, but the introduction was usually by way of intermediaries in San Francisco. When the ultimate source was foreign, there was apt to be an American licensee who was located on the Atlantic coast and who did a considerable amount of adapting before the device came west, to be altered still further at San Francisco. Examples were the compressed-air drill and diamond-studded rotary drill, both of which were invented in France, improved by Eastern firms, and finally introduced to the Comstock Lode by way of California. Similarly, following the development of nitroglycerine and dynamite by Alfred Nobel of Sweden, more powerful explosives began to be used in California during the years 1866–1868, and on the Comstock Lode starting in 1868. On the other hand, an original improvement was contributed by A. S. Hallidie of San Francisco, who devised flat, woven-wire cable for use in hoisting from great depths. This wire cable was stronger than hemp and less bulky to wind on a drum than round steel cable. Hallidie was the engineer whom San Franciscans remember fondly as the designer of that city's cable cars.[18]

The Comstock's technical demands, then, were met by a combination of innovation and adaptation from many parts of the world. The process was rapid if compared to the history of traditional European or South American centers of deep mining. A willingness to spend lavishly, and to try and then discard expensive equipment, characterized Comstock operations. Always the emphasis was on quick results and larger gross yields, rather than on steady, efficient work and close attention to the debit side of each mine's ledger. The Comstock Lode became the show place of Western mining. In speaking of it, the newly created United States Geological Survey said in 1881: "It [the Comstock Lode] is the chief focus of mining activity in the region west of the Rocky Mountains, and represents the most highly organized phase of technical mining which has been reached west of the Mississippi River."[19]

By that time the deeper shafts had gone down to 3000 feet, measured vertically (or 4000 feet "on the incline"). The total length of underground shafts and galleries was between 180 and 190 miles, and the subterranean workings reminded visitors of an underground industrial center—an underground "city 3 miles long and a half a mile wide," John S. Hittell called it.[20] Some said that this strange world beneath the streets of Virginia City was suggestive of a series of huge, interconnected tenements, in which everything was at different levels, the whole dimly lit and filled with sweaty, almost naked workmen.

*T*HE NUMBER of men on the payrolls of the mines increased from perhaps 1500 in the 1860s to more than twice that in the 1870s, with possibly two thirds of the men classified as "miners," the rest occupying nearly forty categories of skilled and unskilled labor. One of the bigger mines might have 500 to 700 employees.[21]

A notable characteristic of both the labor force and the Comstock community generally was the high percentage of people who were foreign-born. This was true even in the confused days of 1860. By 1870 the census showed that in the total population of Virginia City and Gold Hill, the foreign-born outnumbered the native Americans. As in the United States as a whole, many of the newcomers were Irish, in flight from the limited opportunities of their homeland. Unlike the rest of America, here Cornishmen were an important element because mining was a traditional occupation for them. Mining in Cornwall, after being notably prosperous in the 1850s and early 1860s, entered upon hard times that became a severe depression in the 1870s. At least a quarter and perhaps a third of the mining population deserted Cornwall between 1871 and 1881. In the Far West, the Cornishmen readily found work in the lode-mining towns, such as Virginia City. Everywhere they were known by the nickname of "Cousin Jack" (and their women folk as "Cousin Jennie"), supposedly because years of intermarriage within their small native land had made every Cornishman the relative of all his fellow countrymen.

On the Comstock Lode, the census of 1880 showed that while native Americans formed more than half of the total population, in the mining labor force they were greatly outnumbered, only 770 of 2770 being American-born. Of the 1966 listed in the special category of "miners," 691 were Irish, 543 English (including Cornishmen, but excluding Welshmen), 394 Americans, 132 Canadians, and the rest scattered among very small national groups. By contrast, Americans had pre-empted jobs that required operating or maintaining machinery.[22]

If this division of labor by nationalities suggests an Eastern industrial city rather than a Western mining camp, the impression is heightened by the success of the miners in organizing themselves and bargaining collectively with their corporate employers. A "Miners' Protective Association" was formed at Virginia City in 1863 and was expanded into a "Miners' League of Storey County" a year later. Its central purpose was to maintain the existing standard wage of $4 per day, in coin, for all work done underground. In 1864 the league demonstrated by parading in front of mines that were talking of reducing pay. Rather than face a work stoppage, the superintendents yielded for the time being. Skilfully they adopted a policy of meeting the principal demand by paying $4, while at the same time quietly finding grounds for substituting nonunion men for league members. Under the twin pressures of blacklisting and of the hard times that so adversely affected employment in 1864–1865, the league disintegrated, and a wage of $3.50 was temporarily established in the spring of 1865. As soon as employment began to revive, the miners moved to regain their losses. They formed a new Miners' Union on the Fourth of July 1867, and this time succeeded. They forced a re-establishment of a standard wage of $4 for all underground work, and when one mine tried to hold out, a "committee" of 300 muscular miners "persuaded" the recalcitrant owners to yield. Having won their point, the union thereafter maintained the $4 rate with remarkable success, even into the years when the Comstock was visibly and permanently declining, and even though less than $4 was being paid in some "outside" districts. An attempt to establish the eight-hour day failed in 1867, but succeeded in 1872.

The miners successfully encouraged other skilled workers on the company payrolls to form comparable unions, until presently all branches of skilled labor, both underground and surface, were enforcing what the employers regarded as arbitrary rates. When the employers tried to avenge themselves by quietly dropping union men and replacing them with outsiders, the unions promptly called a meeting and decided that henceforth no one might work for any mine for more than a month without joining the appropriate union. A potential, if remote, danger of competition from Chinese labor was so vigorously and immediately opposed that there was no further serious consideration of it.

The Miners' Union prospered financially. They had what Dan De Quille described as "handsome and commodious halls" for business and social functions, and they contributed $2000 to establish the only public library in Virginia City. With confidence bred of success, they helped form similar miners' unions in other Nevada towns and in California. In neither place did they win strength comparable to that achieved on the Comstock Lode. The total number of hired hands in Virginia City and Gold Hill was distinctly larger than in any other mining community west of the Rockies, employment was relatively continuous (by the erratic standards of the mining world), and the unions had the good luck to start off at a time when a high basic wage had been for a considerable period not only standard, but also justified because of the high cost of living. When in hard times and amid declining living costs the employers sought to reduce payroll expenses, the unions had the tactical advantage of seeming to fight merely in defense of an established custom.[23]

Most contemporaries agreed that the men employed underground, where the work was unusually demanding and dangerous, were quite proud of their jobs. Above ground, the miners lived a life that was basically simple and yet not without its luxuries and dissipations. Fancy foods, such as oysters, fresh fish and game, and foreign delicacies, were surprisingly common in the Virginia City markets, while the consumption of whisky and beer was impressive. As always in mining towns, the saloons, gambling houses, and billiard rooms were the places to which a man was most likely to go during his idle hours. Hurdy-gurdy dance halls and the bordellos on D Street were conveniently available.

The diary of one working man, James Galloway, happens to have survived.[24] Galloway came to California from Iowa in 1853, at the age of nineteen, and worked as a placer miner until 1861, when he went back to Iowa to marry a home-town girl. Fourteen more years of mining and ranching in California preceded his arrival at Virginia City on February 4, 1875. His diary for February 6 noted: "Went to work in the Con. [solidated] Virginia mine at 3 P.M., wheeled waste [rock], very hot, 8 hours for $4." A later entry reported: "Worked on the south end on 8th floor, was fearfully hot, made me sick." The same theme of excessive heat recurred when he spoke of going to his job on a cold day, working at 110°F. underground, and then catching a bad cold when he returned to the surface.

Some insight into living conditions was given by Galloway's notation that he had purchased a house lot for $225 and had to borrow $800 at 1 percent per month to pay for having his home built. Since the carpenters apparently completed the structure within ten days' time, one can make a good guess as to how substantial and spacious it must have been.

Galloway's diversions included standard American forms of recreation and some peculiar to Washoe. He spoke of taking his wife and children on picnics, of watching Fourth of July fireworks with them, of setting up a Christmas tree, and preparing a New York's Day feast. He made references to attending church, watching a traveling company put on *Hamlet,* and going off on a rabbit hunt. On the other hand, in company with most of those employed in the mines, he speculated frequently in mining stocks, lost badly, swore to abstain henceforth, and soon was back in the market. One of his notations reported: "Lost $300 out of $800 in stocks in 10 days."

Prophetically, he spoke often of accidents in the mines. He himself was killed when his sleeve caught in the blower that he was tending. Forced to choose between having his arm hacked off as he lay there helpless or risking his life in the hope of coming out whole, he gambled on the long chance and lost. With their lives as with their money, the miners were speculators. Galloway left his family little save his insurance policy with the Chosen Friends benevolent fund. A birthday notation for October 7, 1879, is revealing: "43 years of age, after 26 years of struggle on the Pacific Coast I am a poor man, but with a conscience clear that I am an honest man."

Galloway's personal record, which was fairly typical of the lives of his fellow workers, serves as a corrective against two well-established assumptions. The first is that the Comstock Lode continued to be a frontier mining camp because it was located in the Far West during a period when there were indeed many examples of genuine frontier communities. This supposition has received encouragement from the most readable book about Washoe and the mining West, Mark Twain's *Roughing It.* Readers fail to note that the wonderful, bizarre world conjured up by Mark Twain was limited chronologically to what Mark Twain experienced between 1861 and his departure from Nevada in May of 1864.[25] What is more, much of Mark Twain's account was of straggling little places outside Virginia City.

His stories of Virginia City and Gold Hill described a mining town that had already emerged from its initial period of privation and isolation. "Six months after my entry into [Comstock] journalism the grand 'flush times' of Silverland began, and they continued with unabated splendor for three years."[26] Virginia City had become what Mark Twain called the "'livest' town" in the land. Its sidewalks were crowded with people intent on making their fortune. Its streets were jammed with teamsters' wagons bringing in goods or hauling quartz rock from the mines to the mills. Businesses and dissipations flourished. The city was already burdened with a full assortment of municipal officials, policemen, and firemen that would have sufficed for New York City.

Ahead, and starting almost as Mark Twain left for California, lay a depression and consequent reorganization from which Virginia City would emerge with a pattern of life more suggestive of an industrial city than of a frontier mining camp. The unionization of labor and collective bargaining with corporate employers between 1863 and 1867 were one indication of this change, just as the predominance of foreign miners was another.

This is not to say that Virginia City was the sort of industrial city that one would find in Massachusetts or Illinois. But neither was it any longer an ordinary mining camp. There were too many people and too many amenities for that. Virginia City and Gold Hill had a combined population of 11,359 in 1870 and 15,448 in 1880, although the total rose to about 20,000 in the middle of the decade. The community was a remarkable one. A writer who had often visited there said that it had the appearance and location "of a great village perched upon the side of a high mountain," but that it also had the dimensions and character of "a cosmopolitan city, with the diversified interests and varied social features of a large and important centre." There was something of "the features of an old and long settled community mingled with the shifting and strenuous life of a mining camp."[27]

Strangers sometimes felt that the whole settlement was illogical. Certainly there was no reason for its existence except its mineral wealth, and when that dwindled, no substitute justification, such as farming, commerce, or transportation, replaced the mines. The population departed when the underground caverns ceased to send up ore and the great stamp mills stopped their thudding. Elaborate industrial plants and whole streets of substantial brick and wooden buildings were left to dusty silence.

In its heyday it was a breezy, lively place, both literally and figuratively. At any minute, in the spring or fall months, its clear, thin air might become filled with sand, trash, miner's hats, and tin roofs, as the famous "Washoe zephyr" burst furiously upon the city from the west. It was a tribute to the attractive powers of silver that so large a town could be built on such a hostile site. The natural water supply was inadequate in quantity and heavily metalliferous in quality. The miners claimed that it became safe for drinking purposes only when diluted in the proportions of a tablespoonful of water to a tumbler of whisky. The local native timber was equally poor but could not so satisfactorily be improved. Both water and wood were ultimately secured by the notable engineering feat of building flumes down the side of the Sierra Nevada mountains, twenty-five miles away. For household and commercial purposes, the water had to be brought under pressure (in iron pipes) from the base of the Sierra Nevada down into an intervening valley and up a mountain on the other side before being released into the city's water pipes. Lumber was floated down the sides of the Sierra Nevada in V-shaped wooden flumes, and then hauled from the base of the mountains to the city. Food and supplies came mostly from California, although a few farms developed near by along the Truckee River.

If the "Washoe zephyr" kept literally stirring the atmosphere, so did the omnipresent impulse toward speculation make unstable the psychology of the community. Every one speculated in mining stocks, and all were accustomed to sudden changes in their own fortunes or of those of their fellows. Perhaps it was easier to face economic uncertainty because so many led a life underground in which the possibility of fatal or crippling accident was a daily reality. In times of individual adversity, Virginia City was proverbial for its generosity and sentimentality. The climate was masculine and boisterous, and money was spent more easily than in most towns. In 1870, men outnumbered women by more than two to one, and children were not much more than 10 percent of the population. By 1880, both women and children had increased much more rapidly than men, so that together they formed about half the population, and yet it was still a world largely dominated by the values of men who had few family responsibilities. In its masculinity, speculative instincts, free spending, and instability, Virginia City stood apart from normal industrial cities of comparable size.

A SECOND ASSUMPTION that leads to misunderstanding is the idea that the life of a colorful few represented the whole life of Virginia City. The Comstock Lode produced some of the world's great exhibitionists in the "bonanza kings," the men whom silver suddenly made inordinately wealthy. No one could fail to be aware of new-rich millionaires who built houses that looked like grotesque wedding cakes and sent their wives to Europe with unlimited bank accounts to purchase titled sons-in-law. What was the relationship between these indecently happy few and the great majority of the community, including unknown simple folk like James Galloway?

One writer has remarked that the Comstock mines "made enormous fortunes for half a dozen men," while at the same time "creating a score of mere millionaires" and a fairly large number of men with estates of $100,000 or more.[28] In other words, even among those who succeeded there were several sharply different levels of opulence. One might also add that this wealth was achieved at different times. The superfortunes were created in the 1870s, when the biggest bonanzas were found. The earlier bonanzas of the 1860s started some men like George Hearst on their way to vast wealth, but did not immediately dump it into their laps.

Sheer luck alone did not produce great wealth, nor was success solely a matter of individual abilities. Like all mining districts, the Comstock experienced exaggerated fluctuations in economic conditions. The men who finally became richest were those who were, simultaneously, strong enough to survive periods of adversity, wise enough to see that hard times offered a chance to buy up depreciated property, and discerning enough to know which property to buy. Possession of all these exacting requirements still had to be reinforced by persistence and intelligence in developing one's purchases, and by an ability to borrow money at the right time.

The Comstock Lode started off with a preliminary boom of a disorderly kind from 1859 up to 1861. Far too many claims were located and sold, too little underground development work was done, and too many stamp mills were started for the amount of ore in sight. The output of silver increased only slowly. But with a good yield of gold and a rich performance by a very few mines that were in bonanzas near the surface, Washoe as a whole was carried forward into the flush days of 1861–1863, which Mark Twain described so attractively. In the process many individuals suffered disappointments, while a small group made comfortable profits.

Once well launched, the output of bullion seems to have increased by more than doubling itself each year in 1861, 1862, and 1863. In 1864 the rate of increase slowed down sharply, although the total for that year came to the impressive figure of $16,000,000. This output was approximately maintained in 1865, after which a disheartening decline gradually carried the annual yield down to less than $7,000,000 in 1869. In other words, in four years' time the Comstock lost considerably over half its annual product.[29]

For most people hard times began before the bullion yield showed such weakness. The leading mining stocks, as quoted on the San Francisco exchange, tumbled appallingly during 1864. For example, the Gould & Curry mine was selling at $6300 per "foot" on July 1, 1863; at $4550 on April 1, 1864; and at $900 on July 30, 1864. The Ophir mine, in which Hearst was an owner, dropped from $1580 per "foot" on April 1, 1864, to $300 on September 20.[30] (In the early Comstock years shares were in terms of "feet," supposedly in proportion to the number of linear feet owned by the company along the lode.)

Those with "inside" information realized as early as the closing months of 1863 that even the better mines were running out of rich ore (bonanza) and into barren rock (borrasca). Quietly, they begin to liquidate their holdings and withdraw profitably, while the public continued to buy. In the spring of 1864, the general public sensed trouble, and in their scramble to "unload" precipitated a disastrous decline that continued throughout the year and into 1865. A halting recovery in the latter year lacked the strength to conquer a new wave of public doubt, and 1865 closed in an atmosphere of individual bankruptcies and general despair.

Hard times drove hundreds away from Washoe to try their luck elsewhere in Nevada or some more distant part of the mining West. Hard times also greatly reduced the number of active mines and mills— an inevitable happening because so many were unjustified from the beginning. The lessons learned in California during the gold-quartz boom of the early 1850s should have warned the public to scrutinize carefully all incorporated mining companies, but by the latter part of 1860 Nevada mining stocks were being bought and sold daily at the principal business houses of San Francisco. Two years later, the first stock exchange was founded in San Francisco and quickly became the center for speculation and investment by people throughout the Pacific coast. The *Mining and Scientific Press* said at the opening of 1864 that 2933 mining companies had been incorporated during the previous year alone.[31]

The speculative element that is always present in new mining ventures was enormously increased by the resultant divorce between ownership, or risk, and management. The loose ethics of the mine managers and stock market operators coincided with the greedy impatience and ignorance of the public to make possible a thoroughly unsound situation. The hard times of 1864 and 1865 exposed the unreality of many a silver dream.

The years between 1864 and the early 1870s were a difficult period that was at once the Comstock's time of trial and its time of opportunity for those with strength and foresight. Three groups made their start toward superwealth in those years. The first was the "bank crowd." Here the inspiring force was William C. Ralston, the speculative genius who founded the Bank of California in June 1864. Born in Ohio in 1826, Ralston was a clerk on Mississippi River steamboats while still in his teens, and started for California in 1849. He got no farther than Panama, where until 1854 he served successfully as a banker, merchant, and shipping agent. Upon coming to San Francisco, he advanced through a series of banking partnerships until in 1864 he was able to create the biggest and most influential bank California had seen.

For his agent and branch manager in Virginia City Ralston appointed William Sharon, a reserved, shrewd, and cynical man who had at first prospered in real estate speculation in California and then had lost everything in a mining stock venture. Behind Ralston and Sharon stood most of the "big names" of San Francisco finance, including those who had made their money in Nevada and California mines. Among the latter was Alvinza Hayward, an old California quartz man, principal owner of one of the richest mines on the Mother Lode. Although he first profited from his relations with the "bank crowd," Hayward presently broke with them when John P. Jones, then superintendent of the Crown Point mine, gave him private information of a chance to profit richly by buying up the stock of that mine—which the "bank crowd" regarded as one of their properties. When Hayward followed Jones's advice, he and Jones were in the position of setting themselves apart as a force independent of the Bank of California.

The third group, which ultimately climbed to the greatest financial heights of all, was that of the four "bonanza kings," John W. Mackay, James G. Fair, James C. Flood, and William S. O'Brien. All were of Irish stock and penniless backgrounds. All had been in California since the Gold Rush. Of the four, only Fair had been even moderately successful prior to the Comstock era. Fair operated a gold-quartz mine and mill before going to Nevada. Mackay had been a competent and hard-working placer miner, but he was without funds when he crossed the mountains to Washoe in 1860 to learn vein mining for silver. Flood had been a placer miner in 1850–1851. Subsequent to that he and O'Brien had run small businesses in San Francisco until, failing in their respective enterprises, they decided to open a saloon in 1857. From running a saloon they graduated to a partnership as stock brokers and speculators.[32]

The "bank crowd" were first on the scene. A few months after the Bank of California began business in 1864, Ralston sent Sharon to Virginia City. There, although he found a community that was sliding down into severe financial trouble, Sharon began granting loans at a lower rate of interest than that demanded by the local houses. When the notes came up for renewal, Sharon's debtors were not able to pay, and gradually a great deal of property passed into the bank's ownership by foreclosure. Stamp mills seem to have predominated at first. At Sharon's urging, and after a sharp dispute within its board of directors, the bank created a subsidiary, the Union Milling and Mining Company (1867), to which was transferred the foreclosed milling property. Sharon reorganized the mills, moved them to a location on the Carson River where water power would be available, and presented the mines with the uncomfortable fact that henceforth a virtual monopoly of milling facilities would exist. To make sure that the mines would send their ore to the Union Company, the bank acquired an interest in the principal mines. Realizing that a big item in operating cost was the expense of hauling ore in wagons from the mines in Virginia City to the mills on the Carson River, Sharon and Ralston decided to build a short, winding railroad connecting the two points. This they carried out during 1869, when the mines were still in borrasca. While it was true that Sharon raised part of the money for his railroad by inducing the mines and the county governments to make subscriptions, nevertheless it was a gamble to venture upon a railroad at such a moment. As soon as the railroad opened, the cost of transporting ore from the mines to the mills dropped from $3.50 per ton to $2. When, a year later, the railroad was extended to Reno to intersect the new transcontinental line of the Central Pacific–Union Pacific, prices of supplies of all kinds were reduced materially. A fall in operating and living costs in Virginia City greatly improved the prospects of the community.

Not content with having power over mines, mills, and transportation, Sharon caused the "bank crowd" to acquire an interest in the principal water company that served the mills, and in a company that was bringing down lumber from the Sierras in flumes. Irrate Comstockers denounced Sharon's enterprises as a "fortified monopoly," by which they meant that under Sharon's single direction, each stage of the mining business was being made to support and protect the next one. As opportunities dwindled for independent operations, criticism of the "bank crowd" grew into a general dislike that has become an integral part of the Comstock legend. It is easy to forget that the bank's heavy investments began during the disheartening years when the future of the mines seemed questionable. Without the improved facilities financed by the bank, a revival might have been long in coming. Without the lift that its construction program gave Virginia City, the depression would have been longer and more severe, and the loss of population greater.

When a revival did come, it proved, paradoxically, that the "fortified monopoly" was not impregnable. John P. Jones, who was British-born but raised in Ohio, had mined in many parts of California since 1850 and had become a popular and influential figure in Republican politics. He was a handsome, black-bearded individual of commanding personality and alert mind. When he failed to win election as lieutenant governor of California in 1867, he accepted appointment as superintendent of one of the Comstock mines. Apparently he had by this time won the confidence and support of the wealthy Alvinza Hayward, who is said to have obtained the job for him. A year later Jones transferred to the Crown Point mine, where he distinguished himself alike by his energetic search for new bodies of ore and by the sheer courage and physical endurance he showed during a terrible fire in his mine.

In 1870 the Crown Point mine seemed barren of rock worth extracting. Explorations at depths of 1000 and 1100 feet had revealed nothing of significance. Shares of stock were offered at $2 without finding buyers. Then Jones noticed an encouraging change in the character of the rock, a change that suggested the miners were at last approaching rich ore. He seems to have discussed this with the principal owners in San Francisco, where apparently few believed him. Hayward, however, bought heavily in the stock of the mine, and Jones himself purchased all the shares he could finance. By the time that William Sharon realized what was happening, Hayward and Jones had acquired enough shares to control the property. Sharon conceded defeat by negotiating a settlement in which Sharon sold to Hayward for well over a million dollars the 4100 shares that he held on behalf of the "bank crowd," while at the same time buying from Hayward the latter's stock in the Belcher mine, next door to the Crown Point, on what proved to be the correct hunch that if the Crown Point had struck ore rich enough to be a true bonanza, the ore would probably extend over into the contiguous claim.

Both Crown Point and Belcher did indeed go "into bonanza," and by sympathetic reaction the whole mining industry on the Comstock responded with new vitality and hope. Their relations with the "bank crowd" having become embittered, Hayward and Jones refused to deal with the Union Milling and Mining Company. They formed their own Nevada Mill and Mining Company to crush most of the Crown Point ore. Hayward even shifted his banking interests away from the Bank of California and became president of a rival institution.[33]

Apparently, then, the "fortified monopoly" could not defeat an outside challenge by able and determined men who "had a nose for ore." Hayward and Jones started with the advantage of Hayward's wealth and influence. No such favoring circumstance aided the four Irishmen who next defied the Bank of California. They formed their partnership in 1868–1869. Since going to work as a pick-and-shovel man on the Comstock Lode, Mackay had risen to be superintendent of one mine and presently principal owner of another. After his slow start in California, his experience on the Comstock had developed him into a highly competent mining administrator. His quiet, modest, truthful nature, together with a notable generosity, had made him a well-liked figure.

In his own shrewd, grasping, determined way, Fair was as able a mining man as Mackay, and he too had risen to be superintendent, but his nickname of "Slippery Jim" accurately suggested how far apart in personality the two men were. Flood, like Mackay, was a quiet, able businessman. He handled the San Francisco end of the partnership's affair. O'Brien was the least talented of the four.

Like Hayward and Jones, the four caught Sharon unawares. At a time when stock in the Hale & Norcross mine was greatly depreciated, and the mine was regarded as a poor property, the four quietly bought enough shares to control it. With Fair as superintendent, the Hale & Norcross was turned into a highly profitable investment. Again like Hayward and Jones, the new combination promptly used some of their profits to buy milling facilities of their own, rather than use the Union Company's plant. During the next few years they gradually freed themselves from dependence on the "fortified monopoly's" numerous other services.

Following the success of their first joint venture, the four Irishmen tried two other mines. Neither proved profitable. The partners then decided on a venture that was speculative (as are most mines!) but not unreasonable. "The Consolidated Virginia ground, made up of several early claims," to quote the *Mining and Scientific Press*, had been "considered worthless" because although it was adjacent to mines that had paid, it had been a net loss to the companies that had spent many thousands of dollars in prospecting it underground.[34] The four partners acquired the property in 1871, and in the spring of the following year began the expensive business of exploring it by cutting drifts, tunnels, and crosscuts far underground. The principal explorations were made from the bottom of existing shafts, at depths of 500 and 1167 feet. Far from being a case of suddenly "striking" a rich body of ore, the Consolidated Virginia was in fact developed carefully and determinedly throughout 1872, 1873, and 1874. New shafts had to be sunk and costly new surface machinery installed; fierce heat, poor ventilation, and quantities of water had to be fought underground.

Only gradually did it become apparent that all this expenditure and effort were leading to the greatest bonanza of all time. At the opening of March 1873 highly favorable reports came out of the mine, but until the new machinery and new shaft and drifts were ready, operations had to be on a limited scale. By October the press was conceding that "there is no longer a doubt as to the richness and value of the deposit,"[35] yet the first dividend was not declared until May 1874. By the end of 1874 it was clear to observers that in the Consolidated Virginia and its immediate neighbors there was a "body of ore absolutely immense, and beyond all comparison superior in every respect to anything ever before seen on the Comstock lode."[36]

When part of the bonanza proved to be beyond the limits of the Consolidated Virginia ground, the adjacent claims were organized into the California Mining Company. Shares in the Consolidated Virginia could be purchased for $1 in July 1870 or $15 in June 1872; they sold for $700 early in 1875. The California mine's shares were quoted at $37 in September 1874 and at $780 early in 1875.[37]

Dan De Quille, the best mining reporter on the Comstock Lode, said in 1876 that the Consolidated Virginia was extracting 500 tons of ore per day that were yielding an average of $50,000 *a day!*[38] In total the Big Bonanza, as it was always called thereafter, produced $105,168,859 from 1873–1882. This was an almost unbelievable treasure to come from only two mines. What is more, $74,250,000 of the total was paid out in dividends from 1874–1881.[39] And that is why the four Irishmen, once penniless, so suddenly seized rank among the world's richest men. It must have been literally true that for a few years they hardly knew how to use the wealth that came pouring into their vaults. Flood's lavishly ornate houses on Nob Hill and in suburban Menlo Park, Mrs. Mackay's European extravagances, and Fair's purchase of a seat in the United States Senate (by outbidding that other Comstock millionaire, William Sharon) became international symbols of Comstock prodigality.

Yet the Big Bonanza lasted for only a few years. By the opening of 1877 its continuance was in doubt. A new exploratory crosscut at a depth of 1650 feet raised hopes, but the rich ore failed rapidly. The four "bonanza kings" continued the expensive business of underground searching, and took over several other Comstock mines. They sank shafts down to depths below 3000 feet, at a cost of millions of dollars. Meanwhile they lost other millions in unwise attempts to manage their own stocks on the San Francisco exchange.

They could afford to lose; their employees in Virginia City could not. In 1878 the newspapers were speaking of the need to help destitute miners, and that same year the exodus began to other and more promising mining communities. Annual production declined drastically. In 1876 it reached a record figure of slightly over $38,000,000. For the following year it was only a million dollars less. Then in 1878 it was below $20,500,000; in 1879, a little more than $7,500,000; in 1880, $4,300,000; and in 1881, only $1,400,000.[40]

*O*N A LIMITED BASIS, mining on the Comstock Lode continued for many more years, but the great days were past. There remains the need to say something about the several controversies that marred the twenty-year history of the lode. One, which was only indirectly connected with mining, was the failure of the Bank of California. This great institution was primarily Ralston's creation. The daring way in which he allowed its resources to be used to revive Comstock mining in the latter half of the 1860s was typical of Ralston's blend of speculative and constructive instincts. Ralston was a bold, persuasive entrepreneur who was arrogant in his self-confidence and electric in his imagination. His admirers called him San Francisco's Renaissance prince.

A truly passionate desire to build up San Francisco as queen of the Far West, and a willingness to take long chances in doing so, caused Ralston to establish or support local woolen mills, a watch factory, a carriage works, the lavish Palace Hotel, an ornate theater, transportation systems, water works, lumber companies, real estate ventures, and many lesser enterprises. His restlessly active mind seemed always to be sweeping the horizon in search of some new project that could be attracted to San Francisco. To a considerable degree, money from the Comstock Lode made all this possible.

At times Ralston overextended even the resources that California and Nevada made available to him. From 1870 onwards he was under constant pressure from adverse local developments, from the world decline in the price of silver, and from the national financial stringency caused by the general depression that began in 1873. By 1875 the Bank of California was in serious trouble. Most of Ralston's schemes were proving unremunerative, at least temporarily, and yet both the bank's capital and Ralston's own were "frozen" in commitments to them. The bonanza in the Consolidated Virginia was not helping Ralston directly, and the four Irish "bonanza kings" were about to transfer their funds to a bank of their own creating. On August 26 the uneasy depositors started a "run" that the Bank of California could not meet. It closed its doors that afternoon. The following day, after resigning as head of the bank he had created, Ralston was found dead in San Francisco Bay. Had he committed suicide, or was he drowned accidentally?

Dispute has raged ever since over his death and over the subsequent liquidation of the bank's assets and Sharon's handling of Ralston's personal estate. For the general public perhaps that was less important than the bank's ability to reopen within six weeks and pay off its depositors. The crash affected business of all kinds. Mines as far off as southern Idaho were crippled by the suspension, dramatically revealing the extent of San Francisco's influence while under Ralston's imperial leadership.[41]

More directly connected with mining was the long controversy over Adolph Sutro's famous tunnel. From the time when the original Ophir company first struck large quantities of underground water, one of the principal problems had been how to free the mines of increasing floods. Bigger and still bigger pumps were the immediate answer, but were there not limits to how long the mines could stand the expense of pumping an increasing amount from an increasing depth?

Adolph Sutro was a dramatic figure. His personality was a combination of admirable and irritating qualities. In resourceful determination no one was his superior. His innumerable opponents often checked but never wholly defeated him. Yet he was also an egotistical monomaniac whose vanity, boasting, and exaggerated claims alienated precisely the men whose support he needed.[42]

Sutro was born of German Jewish parents in Aix-la-Chapelle (Aachen) in 1830, and, his father having died, he came to America in 1850 as one of seven sons and four daughters who accompanied their widowed mother to Baltimore. He quickly broke loose from his big family to come to California in 1851, where he engaged in small retail trade, chiefly as a dealer in cigars and tobacco. When the Nevada silver discoveries attracted him, he built a stamp mill in the Carson Valley, and even in 1860 began to talk of the possibility of using tunnels to drain water out of the mines. Local newspapers also put forward this idea, and one of them, the Gold Hill *News,* suggested in 1864 the need for a major tunnel capable of draining all the mines.

Adopting the idea, in 1865 Sutro induced the Nevada legislature to grant him a franchise, and a year later he secured a similar authorization from Congress. His notion was that a big tunnel should be driven up from the Carson Valley to the Comstock Lode, a distance of between three and four miles. He believed that the tunnel would simultaneously drain the mines, provide ventilation, and serve as a passageway through which ore could be hauled to mills on the Carson River. He also felt that he might discover paying ore while cutting the tunnel. His plan was to build the tunnel with borrowed funds and subscriptions to stock, and pay for it by charging royalties to all mines using the tunnel.

Initially his proposal was received favorably by the mine officials and the Bank of California, but by the time that Sutro was soliciting funds in New York, the "bank crowd" and the Comstock mine and mill operators had turned against him. Thereafter William Sharon led an unyielding opposition to all of Sutro's plans. Part of the hostility was generated by Sutro's boasting that his tunnel would dominate the Comstock Lode and force the abandonment of Virginia City in favor of the Carson Valley. Sharon had an understandable dislike for people who threatened to grow into a rival power. The mine owners, including Sharon's associates, seem to have regretted their earlier agreement to pay royalties to the tunnel company.

Refusing to be stopped, Sutro sought funds in London and New York. In Washington he lobbied for a loan from the federal government. In Nevada he ran for the United States Senate. Through a series of stirring public meetings in Virginia City, he so aroused the working miners that their Miners' Union subscribed $50,000.

Severe technical problems complicated his financial and political troubles, with the result that the main tunnel was not cut through to the

Comstock Lode until 1878. This meant that it was completed just as the mines were failing. Five to ten years earlier the tunnel would have saved the mines millions of dollars and might have been profitable. Even at its late date of completion it still proved useful for draining the mines, but it was never able to repay the cost of construction, which was said to be $4,500,000 without interest, or $6,500,000 with interest. The tunnel proved of little value for ventilation, no major ore bodies were found along its course, and it was not used for hauling ore to the mills.

Sutro himself quietly "unloaded" his tunnel stock before its value collapsed, retired to San Francisco to speculate brilliantly in city real estate, and finally achieved the paradoxical distinction of being elected the Populist mayor of San Francisco at a time when he was one of the city's richest men—in other words, the millionaire leader of popular protest.

If the merits of Sutro's efforts, like those of Ralston, leave the reader with mixed emotions, what of the biggest question of all, What happened to the money produced by the Comstock? The money for which so many thousands scrambled? Part of the answer is suggested by a tabulation of the finances of the sixty principal mines, some of which represented consolidations of many smaller original holdings. From 1859 to 1882 the total yield was $292,726,310. Of this, $125,335,925 was paid out in dividends, with most of the dividends coming from the four later-day bonanza mines: the Consolidated Virginia, California, Crown Point, and Belcher. Against the dividends should be set $73,929,355 in assessments levied on the stockholders to develop the mines. Virtually all of the mines assessed their stockholders, whereas less than half ever paid any dividends.[43]

These figures do not in themselves tell much about collective fortunes, for they bear only a partial relationship to what happened in the stock market. Playing the market in the hope of a rise or of a fall was probably more common than buying mining stock for income. The chairman of the San Francisco exchange was able to list large numbers of speculators who profited in the market, and a surprisingly large number of brokers who became rich through handling their clients' affairs. But he also stressed the pathetic human wrecks who retired, broken, to a back street in San Francisco known as Paupers' Alley.

Hidden somewhere in the difference between yield and dividends were expenditures that involved the false starts to which mining so often is prone—shafts sunk or drifts cut to barren rock, mills built on the wrong principle or in an inefficient location, equipment bought and quickly discarded as unsatisfactory. Hidden also were many instances of extravagant costs or equally unreasonable salaries to a few favored officials. Of these little is known with any definiteness. Nor can one generalize on any substantial basis about the obvious discrepancy between the small number who profited so richly and the very large number who risked their lives or funds.

It is possible, however, to say something about the efficiency of the ore-extracting process and its relationship to this disparity in profits between the few and the many. When Ralston and Sharon formed the Union Milling and Mining in 1867, they were exploiting an unusually good opportunity. Over much of the West, mines erected their own stamp mills, and in the early days some of the Comstock mines preferred this practice. But as Almarin Paul showed in 1860, there were real advantages to custom mills—that is, to mills that crushed ore for a fee. Resort to custom mills saved a mining company from the necessity of assessing its stockholders for funds to build its own mill, and in the early stages of opening a mine there might not be enough ore to justify a mill for a single mine.

Ralston's and Sharon's scheme, however, involved control of both the mines that supplied the ore and the mills that worked it. Thanks to the legal device of the corporation, the same men who dominated the affairs of a mine could make a contract with themselves, in the guise of the Union Milling and Mining Company, to handle the ore. With Comstock ores the practice was for the mill to guarantee to pay a mine 65 percent of the value of its ore as determined by periodic assays of samples. If less was obtained from working the ore, the mill operator had to make good the deficiency; if more, the excess was supposed to go to the customer, the mine owner.

This sounded fair, and might have been if the mills and mines had been independent of each other, so that the mines would have had an incentive to scrutinize carefully the mills' operating standards and ethics. Lacking this pressure, the mill operators found it to their interest to pay only the 65 percent plus enough more of any excess to make the mill look efficient.[44] A surplus beyond that became a hidden extra margin of profit, which went to the "inside" few. This was not peculiar to the Union Company. When Hayward and Jones, and later the four bonanza kings, broke away from the Union Company's monopoly, they followed the same practice, except that they charged lower rates for their milling service.

Nor was that all. By universal custom, the residue or "tailings" and "slimes" left after working the ore belonged to the mill, even though they still contained a significant amount of additional gold and silver. Thanks to the work of an able and well-trained engineer, Louis Janin, it was shown in the middle 1860s that at least a part of the residue could be saved profitably by a subsequent reworking, and thereafter a further treatment became common. The proceeds did not, however, go to the stockholders of the mines.

Two different federal investigators, Rossiter W. Raymond and James D. Hague, both men of high ability and the products of good training at the famous old mining academy of Freiberg, Saxony, concluded that there was an important gap between what the mills actually obtained from the ore and what they paid over to their customers, the mines. From the limited data available to Raymond and Hague, the gap appears to have been about 8 percent of the total potential value of the ore.[45] Public discussion paid little attention to this until late in the history of the Comstock. From 1876 onward vigorous criticisms asserted that serious abuses and large private profits grew out of the advantageous position of a few well-to-do men who controlled the mines but owned the mills.

The controversy is historically regrettable because it led to concealment of precise statistics and thus increased the difficulty of determining just how efficient Comstock operations were in recovering silver and gold. In the early years the public assumed that the mills were saving only 65 percent of the potential value of the ore, because that was all that the contracts demanded. The work done by Raymond and Hague in 1868–1870 demonstrated that the mines of that day were in fact receiving from the mills close to 70 percent, quite aside from the further amount of treasure that the mills extracted from the ore and from the residue but retained in their own accounts. Another distinguished government investigator, George F. Becker, who did not make his survey until 1880–1881, found that "in late years" the mills had been guaranteeing 72 percent and often returning over 80 percent.[46] Such an increase over the proportion recovered in 1870 reflected in part more efficient handling of the ore, and in part a somewhat improved philosophy as to what constituted a fair sharing of the profits.

But at as late a date as 1882 John S. Hittell, one of the best informed economic writers on the Pacific coast, denounced as a "common abuse" the whole Comstock system by which "the directors of a mining company made contracts with themselves as directors of some other company." He claimed that the abuse was prevalent not only in milling, but also in making contracts for supplies and for work to be done. The result, he concluded, was that a mine could be worked at a loss to the stockholders and yet yield a handsome profit to the "inside" controlling group.[47]

If this sounds singularly like the contemporary scandals associated with the building of the Union Pacific and Central Pacific Railroads, then it suggests that Pacific coast mining, far from being an isolated phenomenon in American life, was in fact a participant in the low national ethical standards that are forever associated with the political era of General Grant and Boss Tweed.

Looking back upon the Comstock Lode, one is impressed alike by its achievements and significance, its controversies and shortcomings. Despite the brevity and the almost unreal glitter of its period of big production, there was so much that proved to be of more than local and temporary importance. Politically, the Comstock's huge output of silver was a major justification for the fierce campaign to establish that metal on a parity with gold as a basis for the nation's currency. Technologically, by 1880 the new understanding of veins and of deep-mining on a large scale had already contributed to the revival of quartz mining in California and to a beginning of vein mining in Utah and in Nevada outside Storey County. It was soon to inspire a boom in vein mines in Montana, Idaho, and the Southwest. The *Mining and Scientific Press* asserted that "The metallurgical experience acquired by explorations on that one vein [the Comstock Lode] has done more to further the mining interests on this coast than any one other thing."[48]

Even before the Comstock mines began to fail, the superintendents, foremen, engine-operators, mechanics, and miners trained on the Comstock Lode were carrying their skills to new jobs at mining centers throughout the Far West. Their presence in the 1870s and 1880s was as important as the Old Californians' had been in the late 1850s and the 1860s. San Francisco manufacturers continued to make and ship not only to the Far West but also to foreign countries equipment whose design was strongly influenced by Comstock experience, just as the enlarged facilities for manufacturing at San Francisco were in great part a response to Comstock demands. From their headquarters in the ornately rebuilt queen city, Comstock millionaires underwrote many a new venture in the American West and abroad.

It was, therefore, only the physical body of the Comstock's own mines and cities that proved evanescent. The iron, bricks, and wood of which the Comstock community was built proved less enduring than the men, ideas, and capital developed there.

◁ 5 ▷

A Study in Contrasts:
California and Nevada
1859-1880

*D*uring the heyday of the Comstock Lode, thoughtful writers kept protesting that Washoe's glitter was causing promising opportunities in both California and Nevada to be badly neglected. Since then, history and biography have perpetuated this imbalance of attention. However natural it may be to focus on what is colorful, it is a pity to overlook entirely what else was happening in California and in Nevada outside of Storey County.

The two states stood in antithesis to one another. Nevada was new country. Throughout the 1860s prospectors were opening new districts as they advanced eastward across the territory. They started by venturing out from Virginia City into the huge empty areas of western Nevada, in particular Humboldt County to the north of Washoe and Esmeralda County to the south of it. A few towns such as Aurora, queen of Esmeralda, temporarily achieved considerable significance. With the discovery of the Reese River mines in 1862 and the founding of their principal town, Austin, precisely in the geographical center of Nevada, the prospectors shifted their base to that booming community and explored first the middle and then the eastern counties.

California, by contrast, was relatively old. With an experience that extended back to 1848, California had had time to sort out the camps and towns that had a future from those that had little chance of survival. Among the former at least two quite different types of society were emerging. One was the retarded mining frontier, found chiefly in the huge northwestern corner of California, west and north of the upper Sacramento Valley. Although its history was almost as long as that of the Mother Lode, it had never reached a high stage of development. Poor communications, a topography of broken, irregular mountains, heavy snows in winter, and more Indian danger than in other parts of California, all these helped to hold it back, although surely—despite the protestations of local journalists—its mineral wealth must also have been less attractive than that of the Sierra Nevada, for miners will overcome huge obstacles if they think that fortunes lie before them.

As a participant in the original placer boom of a decade earlier, the northwest also had by the 1860s its ghost towns and its diggings that had been abandoned to the Chinese. More importantly, the region could still offer opportunities long since exhausted elsewhere. Speaking of river mining in two northwestern counties, the federal mining commissioner remarked in his first report (covering 1866) that "there is a large area of ground that is comparatively undeveloped; and that is the best region in the State for the miner who wants to work on his own account, and on a small scale."[1] Similarly, a compendium published in 1868 said of a north-western county that "the placer mines here not having been worked so extensively as in the counties further east and south, pay better average wages, perhaps, than in any other part of the State."[2]

If this suggested a continuation of chances for simple placer mining, long after such opportunities had been exhausted along the Mother Lode, so did social conditions resemble those of the earlier 1850s. When the California State Geological Survey passed through Weaverville in 1862, one of its members reported that the town reminded him of a Californian camp "in bygone times." Amusedly the geologists counted twenty-eight saloons in the little town and noted that "gambling and fighting are favorite pastimes." After witnessing three street fights, a French geologist attached to the survey wryly remarked that the mining customs were better preserved in Weaverville than in any town he had seen thus far.[3]

There were both quartz and hydraulic mining in the northwest, but both were prosecuted with lethargy. Of a northwestern county that had extensive deposits of deep gravels, Rossiter W. Raymond reported that "it was not until the spring of 1874 that the improved appliances of hydraulic mining, so generally in use" elsewhere were introduced.[4] Of quartz mining in two other northwestern counties, he said, "the quartz interest is but in its infancy."[5] The latter phrase was to recur often. Even after the opening of the present century the State Mining Bureau was saying of one county that "quartz mining is still in its infancy," and of another that "quartz mining was of slow development."[6]

A the end of 1872 a newspaper correspondent described the whole region as being still "remote and hard to approach" and "the least known" part of California. "To anything like an advanced civilization much of the region remains still virgin." Its population, the correspondent discovered, was exceedingly sparse, and was a curious blend of miners, lumbermen, Indians, and men who were half hunters and half stockgrowers. The miners and lumbermen he found to be somewhat ahead of the others in "their progress in enlightenment," while as between "the Indian and the back settler," there was "a moral shade in favor of the aborigine!"[7]

Perhaps the most one can say is that at least this retarded frontier continued to exist in California, on however limited a basis, whereas in Nevada comparable districts soon were being abandoned entirely. Climatic and geologic differences probably do much to explain the difference in survival. Water, wood, placers, and free-milling quartz claims were commonplace in northwestern California; they were scarce in Nevada.

A SECOND TYPE of Western mining society was represented by the Mother Lode country and Nevada County. Along the western slope of the Sierra Nevada, where so many settlements were in decay, there were a few that were growing into maturity. The quartz towns were noticeably larger and more balanced in population than the hydraulic towns, because the one was based on a type of mining that demanded a great deal of labor and the services of extensive repair facilities, while the other was based on a technique designed to save labor and minimize mechanical problems. But both kinds of communities were in pleasant contrast to the dying placer camps. The editors of their little weekly newspapers loved to boast of the number of new brick, supposedly fireproof buildings, of the new churches and schools, and of the growing number of women and children for whose benefit the churches and schools had been called into existence. In some of the towns could be found subscription libraries, literary societies, debating groups, and even temperance associations.

The local editor in the prosperous, comparatively well-settled hydraulic town of North San Juan, Nevada County, provided an excellent insight into the varied life of his particular community when he was inspired to take an informal census in the spring of 1859. He found that among a population of perhaps a thousand, North San Juan had 100 families, some of whom had gone to the trouble of building themselves neat cottages and of planting gardens. There were eight brick buildings on Main Street, and the town had a public school, a church, three hotels, two restaurants, a brewery, four or five sawmills, an iron foundry, about sixty stores and shops of all kinds (at twenty of which liquor was sold), "and more houses of ill fame than we like to mention." North San Juan had a library of 600 volumes, chapters of the Odd Fellows and the Masons, a Mutual Relief Society, "and a Temperance Association consisting entirely of Welshmen." Of the 250 houses in or near the town, about 40 were ramshackle affairs inhabited by Chinese. The number of miners' cabins in the surrounding countryside was unknown.[8]

Despite this complacent census, both hydraulic and quartz mining were to suffer through a difficult experience in the early 1860s. Paying mines and promising claims were abandoned in the diversion of men, capital, and popular attention to the new territories of the Far West, especially to Washoe. After starting to praise the merits of North San Juan, the editor of a Nevada County newspaper despondently interrupted himself: "San Juan, to be matter of fact, is dull, awfully dull. The exodus to the mines of Nevada Territory, which has almost depopulated some of the mining camps of Nevada county, has had its damaging effect upon this town."[9]

Hard times on the Comstock Lode in 1864 and 1865 corrected the situation. Men and money began returning to the western side of the mountains. Those who elected to try hydraulic mining found an industry that was just starting to live up to the high promise it had shown in the late 1850s. A few large companies had remained continuously active throughout the intervening decade, and now their success served as a model for newer concerns entering the field.

The dominant trend, as the federal mining commissioner reported in 1871, was toward "operating with the advantages of large capital, and by concentration of labor and the consolidation of large tracts of mining ground."[10] Hydraulic mining, like the Comstock operations, was becoming large-scale industry. Up in the mountainous county of Butte, for example, the great Spring Valley Canal and Mining Company controlled nearly 11,000 acres, acquired at a cost of $240,527, and had spent over a million dollars on its system of flumes, ditches, and reservoirs. Lines of sluices, each four to six feet wide, totalled ten miles. With 160 men on the payroll, the company took out $476,112 during the fiscal year 1873–1874, spent $125,000, and paid out $150,000 in dividends.

While one of the largest, this concern was not unique. The North Bloomfield Company, in Nevada County, controlling over 1500 acres, spent eight years and over two million dollars developing its investment. Two "enormous" reservoirs were constructed near the summit of the Sierra Nevada, 100 miles of canals and ditches were built or were purchased from smaller concerns, and a tunnel one and a half miles long was cut to provide a drainage outlet. During the greater part of 1874 the company was employing from 500 to 600 men on its construction projects.[11]

Such big companies, based upon a consolidation of many small individual claims and the investment of large capital on a long-term basis, were the important producers. Some were incorporated, owned largely in San Francisco and managed locally by professional superintendents. The "bank crowd" of Nevada fame appeared prominently among the owners of some of them. A few were bought up by British or New York investors. Some, especially the smaller ones, were unincorporated and were owned by a single man or a partnership. As a group, deep-gravel companies were less speculative properties than silver mines. Most were not listed on the stock exchanges and were not available to the general public that "played" the market. Unlike Washoe stocks, their nominal capital was stated in relatively conservative terms. The total amount invested in hydraulic companies, however, must have been very large. Systems of ditches and flumes alone, used principally for hydraulicking, were believed to represent an investment of $30,000,000 by 1882. There were by then 6000 miles of main ditches, plus another 1000 miles of subsidiary lines and an unknown length of small distributors. Land, machinery, shops, and other facilities would add a great deal more to the total.[12]

Hydraulic mining was a relatively efficient process. The California state mineralogist said that "where the requisite conditions exist, an astonishingly small amount of gold to the cubic yard will pay a profit." A gold content of as little as three or four cents per cubic yard of "dirt" might suffice.[13] The loss of gold, which had been high in the 1850s, was reduced greatly by a general improvement in technique, until in 1880 some of the mines were claiming that they saved 90 percent of the gold content. While regarding this as an exaggeration, a government investigation nevertheless agreed that "it cannot well be doubted that the working of an average hydraulic mine gives closer results than does the ordinary mill process" of a vein mine.[14]

To a remarkable degree, the technological improvement of this low-cost, mass-production type of mining continued to center in Nevada County, where it had been invented originally. Successive inventions by different individuals over a period of at least two decades gradually made possible increasingly great water pressures, while at the same time reducing the strain on machinery and operators, and lessening the number of men required.

The more effective it became, the more destructive hydraulic mining was to the Californian landscape. The powerful hydraulic instrument literally washed away whole hills and made huge open cuts in what had once been forested mountainsides. To speed up the disintegrating action, miners learned to undercut a mountain bank with the hydraulic's fiercely powerful jet of water or to help the process along with a charge of explosives. At the strategic moment a little further use of the hydraulic's cutting power sufficed to bring a bank 150 feet high crashing down in a wild avalanche. All of the dirt, gravel, and rocks were then sent thundering down long lines of sluices.

At the end of the sluices the debris was spewed out into a canyon or valley, where it piled up as a huge obstruction until the first heavy winter rains started sweeping the whole mass down into the lower valleys at the foot of the Sierras. There rich farms were being brought into cultivation during the 1860s and 1870s. To any form of agriculture floods of hydraulic debris meant death, for the annual overflow covered and choked the land. Bitterly the farmers sought injunctions to restrain the hydraulic miners from further activity. In a series of suits from 1881 to 1884 they finally succeeded in both state and federal courts, and despite much evasion on the part of the miners, the industry was greatly reduced. A federal statute of 1893 sought, with only moderate success, to encourage a revival under controlled conditions.[15]

Life at a large hydraulic mine was rather like that at a small, isolated factory in a company town. The men lived in barracks or boarding-houses and followed a daily routine that was monotonously unvarying except for the occasions when the water was shut off to permit cleaning out the sluices. An observer remarked with amusement that from the time they went to work at 6:45 A.M. until they quit at 6 P.M., the hired hands labored slowly and unenthusiastically, changing pace only when the lunch gong sounded. Then eagerness suddenly appeared and haste prevailed (as well it might, for the miner was allowed only a half hour in which to load himself with an old-fashioned, heavy noonday "dinner").[16]

Quartz mining followed a course that led to similar industrial-like conditions. As a producer of gold it was still a relatively minor source. Modern use of statistics has indicated that from 1861 through 1870, about 90 percent of California's gold was derived from placers, and from 1871 through 1880, about 70 percent.[17] The chief quartz town was Grass Valley, although its neighbor, Nevada City, was important, and productive individual mines were scattered along the 120 miles of the Mother Lode belt. The richest part of the ·Mother Lode belt was the ten-mile piece in Amador County, where Sutter Creek was the most important center. Grass Valley's pre-eminence was especially significant; just as Nevada County was the leader in developing hydraulic mining, so was that county the pioneer in adapting to California conditions the ancient art of vein mining and milling.

The return to California of men who had been on the Comstock Lode was especially beneficial to the quartz mines because mining on the Comstock had so quickly gone beyond the limits of early California experience. Under the leadership of men who had seen what was being done in Washoe, shafts were sunk to greater depths and equipment was improved. Rock breakers and automatic ore feeders replaced manual labor, with a resultant saving of expense, and the latest improvements in stamp milling were introduced.

In attempts to save some of the gold that was being wasted, new devices were invented in the latter half of the 1860s to "concentrate" the tailings (that is, sort out the still-valuable from the worthless parts of the debris). The Washoe pan amalgamation process was brought back to the land in which it had its earliest beginnings, and after years of neglect, attention began to be paid to the difficult, costly problems involved in treating sulphurets by chemistry. Progress in that field, where a knowledge not only of chemicals but also of metallurgy was essential, was far slower than in the areas of underground mining and mechanical engineering. Potentially its significance was great. A technologically effective process based upon the use of chlorine gas (sometimes called the Plattner process after its German inventor) had gradually been adapted to California needs. Toward the end of the 1860s mining men were claiming that improved California mills could save 75 percent of the gold without chlorination, but 90 percent where the latter was added as a further treatment. The difficulty was that chlorination was expensive, required expert supervision, and was dependent upon there being a larger supply of suitable ores than could be assured in most California localities.[18]

Much of the responsibility for quartz mining was in the hands of a small group of self-trained veterans who had been with that industry since its early days. A modern mining engineer has referred to them as "a few sturdy individuals, hardfighters and not too conscientious with those opposed to them, but generally men of their word."[19] One of the most famous was Alvinza Hayward, who had made his "pile" at Sutter Creek before he began investing in Comstock silver.

The mines that such men owned or operated were, like the hydraulic mines, handled on a much less speculative basis than Comstock silver mines. Few were listed on any stock exchange, and most of them were owned directly by one person or a small group of associated investors. All but a few quartz mines were owned within California; the influence of British or Eastern capital was slight. The smaller mines were sometimes owned in part by the superintendents who actually managed them; the larger ones were the property of men who lived in San Francisco, although they had often had an earlier career in the foothills.

At times professional observers felt that, impressed by the losses of the early 1850s and the continuing mistakes made later in each of the mining counties, the veteran quartz men were excessively conservative toward innovation. There was a tendency for a quartz man of the later nineteenth century to reject further experiments once he had put his mine on a paying basis.

This same conservatism controlled relations with labor. As the quartz mines developed into industrial plants, Americans tended to abandon underground work to foreign-born miners, especially Cornishmen and Irishmen, later Austrians and Italians. In this, California was duplicating the experience of the Comstock Lode. The total number of men employed by any one mine, however, was apt to be smaller than in Washoe. When the North Star mine at Grass Valley had 208 men on its payroll, counting both surface and underground workers, the news was considered worth special comment, even though a Comstock mine might have twice as many employees.

At the instigation of the miners' unions on the Comstock Lode, unions were formed in a few of the chief quartz towns, especially at Grass Valley and Sutter Creek. Bitter strikes broke out at Grass Valley in 1869, at Sutter Creek in 1871, and at Grass Valley again in 1872.

The public seems to have paid little attention to the changing character of its mining labor force until these disputes produced shooting, intimidation, the use of "scabs," and finally, in the Sutter Creek affair, the intervention of the governor and state militia. Only then did the public awake to the realization that Grass Valley had become a Cornish town and that Sutter Creek was a mixture of Irish, Cornish, Austrians, and Italians. At the workers' level, both communities were ruled as much by hereditary European attitudes as by American thinking.

The first strike at Grass Valley, for example, centered in the employers' attempt to introduce dynamite in place of black powder, and the related economy of "single-handed" drilling (one man working alone) instead of "double-handed" (two men working as a team, one to hold and turn the drill and one to strike it). Because of its greater force, dynamite did not require such large holes as had been customary with black powder. Therefore one man with smaller drills could do the work of two.

But back in the "old country" the Cornishmen had for many genera- tions held strong prejudices against single-handed drills. Quite aside from their fear that the innovation would reduce the underground labor force, the Cornishmen, with their strong clannish regard for tradition, objected to it as being contrary to ancient custom. When an angry management tried to reopen one of the struck mines with non-Cornish "scabs," nationalistic prejudice boiled over, and strike-breakers who were so mistaken as to walk without guards, were found beaten into insensibility.

The strike at Sutter Creek, while to some degree based on fear of replacement by Chinese labor, was more directly concerned with wages. Thanks to a lower cost of living, wages in California quartz mines had for many years been less than on the Comstock. First-class miners received $3 per day; second-class, $2.50; and surface laborers, $2. What the unions were really attempting was to duplicate the Comstock unions' feat of elevating pay for the less skilled by establishing a basic minimum wage applicable to all.

Appalled at such interference, the president of the first mine to be approached by the unions came hurrying down from his office in San Francisco, but the unions proved to be as obdurate as he, and presently the governor and militia were involved. At both Sutter Creek and Grass Valley ultimate victory lay with the employers. The unions were not strong enough to enforce their will peacefully, and their resort to violence antagonized the public. The rugged individuals who owned the mines were resolute against what they regarded as dictation by their employees.[20]

Quartz centers, hydraulic towns, and retarded Northwestern camps represented only a few of the many and varied types of mining life that could be found in California in the 1870s. Each of the decaying towns along the Mother Lode had its small operators who still kept their claims active. Off on little dirt roads and mule tracks were many isolated claims. Most of the 9087 Chinese listed as "miners" in 1870 were engaged in simple, old-fashioned placer mining.

What was the daily life and what were the attitudes of these miners of the later era? With such a multiplicity of types generalization is difficult. In his little manual on mining, completed in the spring of 1861, John S. Hittell gave this description:

> Most of the miners live in a rough manner. The proportion of those who work for wages varies from one-third to two-thirds. Not one-half of them lay up any money. Many earn money with ease, and spend it as fast as they make it. Men engaged in mining are not noted, as a class, for sobriety and economy. Their occupation seems to have an influence to make them spendthrifts, and fond of riotous living. Not more than one Californian miner in five has a wife and family with him. Most of them are unmarried, and have no prospect of matrimony. . . . The people as a mass, in the mining districts, are very intelligent. They came from all parts of the world, have seen much of life in multitudinous phases, and have profited by their experience.[21]

*A*LL TOLD, THE CENSUS of 1870 found 36,339 "miners" in California. That was a very large number in relation to output of treasure, and it had increased slightly by 1880. Nevada had only 8241 "miners" in 1870, and still fewer in 1880.[22] Yet by 1870 Nevada's annual output of treasure equalled California's, and from then until 1879 greatly exceeded it. California's numerous and varied enterprises were thus using several times as much manpower to produce an equivalent or less of treasure.

A similar contrast existed between the Comstock Lode and the rest of Nevada. In most years between 1866 and 1880, the Comstock mines supplied at least one half and more often two thirds of Nevada's total yield, while employing less than a third of the miners.[23] Some of the discrepancy was a natural result of the large-scale, heavily capitalized, relatively mechanized type of mining practiced by the Comstock corporations. If it implied also that there was many a dubious, manpower-absorbing venture out in the camps and towns of the Nevada desert, then that, too, was reasonable, for during this time occurred the first extension of the mining frontier into that strange and difficult world of the Great Basin. Here were environmental and geological conditions of an unfamiliar and peculiarly demanding sort, far more difficult to cope with than anything encountered on the western side of the Sierra Nevada.

Physiographically the Great Basin began on California soil, in that thin strip just east of the mountains. It extended across Nevada and into Utah as far as Great Salt Lake. To the first prospectors it must have seemed as unpromising as it did the westward-bound "emigrants" who crossed it on the last, weary stretch of the overland trail from the Missouri frontier to California.

Everywhere in the Great Basin the presence of gray-green sagebrush and scrubby greasewood betrayed the lack of rainfall. When he first saw Nevada in 1861, Mark Twain wrote back to his mother: "No flowers grow here, and no green thing gladdens the eye. The birds that fly over the land carry their provisions with them." Alkali dust, as Twain observed on another occasion, "rose in thick clouds and floated across the plain like smoke from a burning house."[24] Vegetation was sparse even in the mountains. Shortages of lumber, fuel, and water were the chronic basic handicaps against which early mining efforts had to struggle.

Distances were another obstacle. From east to west, it was 300 miles across Nevada by crowflight—if any crow had the bad judgment to attempt such a voyage. From north to south the mileage would be as much or more, depending upon where the measuring was done. Since camps kept popping up unexpectedly in almost every part of the state during the 1860s, it was commonplace to be 100 miles from the nearest Nevada supply center, and such centers, in turn, looked back to the western side of the Sierras for most of their stock. These distances made for a high cost of living, high operating expenses, especially for labor, and delays in obtaining needed items.

The construction of the Central Pacific Railroad was easily the most important boon the region received, although at first its rates were disappointingly high. Reaching the crest of the Sierra Nevada in 1867, the railroad marched eastward across Nevada during 1868, to link up with the Union Pacific near Salt Lake in 1869. "Feeder" lines, which were often narrow gauge, were begun by some of the better capitalized mining interests, with the result that during the 1870s a few favored areas could bring in supplies and ship out ore by rail, while districts remote from both the Central Pacific and the local railroads slumped into neglect.

The mineral wealth, of course, was in the mountainous regions. Long lines of north–south trending mountains are a characteristic of the Great Basin. They stand forth like parallel chains of islands above the elevated plains that have been formed by erosion and outwash. When the earliest miners and prospectors came over from California, they were seeking gold placers similar to those of the western Sierra Nevada. They found a few, and placer mining of modest proportions developed in a scattering of districts. Modern geologists have guessed that perhaps $25,000,000 was produced by Nevada placers between 1849 and 1900. Much of it was the work of Chinese—a sure sign that contemporary white miners considered the diggings second-rate.[25]

Most of the treasure of the Great Basin was silver, and silver is not ordinarily found in placer deposits. Hence there was not much more opportunity here for the old-fashioned miner than there had been on the Comstock Lode. Those who were determined to stick to cradle and sluicebox strayed off disconsolately in search of better fields, while the rest gradually made their individual choices between learning the difficult business of silver mining or else drifting into a lifetime of prospecting.

From the earliest days of the Gold Rush in California there had been a tendency for some men to spend most of their time wandering about in search of gold rather than actually developing such deposits as they might find. These restless souls, even more nomadic than most miners, made what little money they earned by selling to others the "claims" they discovered and "located." As placer mining in California passed out of its richer and simpler days, the number of men who were more pros-pector than miner grew larger. With the advance of the mining frontier into the whole Far West, prospecting increasingly became a separate branch of the mining industry; and here in the Great Basin the adverse natural conditions tended to magnify the distinction between the working miner who would develop a claim and the wandering prospector who sought in order to sell.

The lonely, unkempt professional prospector, with his furtive attempts to conceal his journeyings, became a central figure in Western folklore. Some local merchant, professional man, or mining speculator was always ready to "grub-stake" him in return for a large share of any discoveries made. Native shrewdness, a self-taught knowledge of promising "indications," and a tough, leathery ability to survive anything from desert heat to mountain blizzards were the prospector's chief resources. Packing onto a mule or burro his few tools, a primitive assaying kit, and his bedding, gun, frying pan, coffee pot, and food, the prospector would start off on a solitary quest that might last weeks or months.

With admirable exaggeration Mark Twain tells of prospecting in the western part of Nevada, in Humboldt and Esmeralda counties, during the early 1860s. At that time Carson Valley and the Comstock Lode were still the supply points from which prospectors departed into the desert. Soon thereafter Austin, with its advantageous central position, became what the federal mining commissioner called "the frontier mining town of the State, and the general outfitting point for new explorations." To it came the returning prospectors, "ragged, hungry, and physically worn out, but still jubilant over the brilliant future" that would be theirs if only their load of specimens proved rich when submitted to the professional assayers.[26] Perversely, the assayers insisted upon being far more skeptical than the prospectors.

Enough of the prospectors succeeded to inspire the founding of the many camps that kept booming noisily into notice during the 1860s. Even if judged by California's experience, these camps proved extraordinarily erratic. Some were born, developed, and abandoned within the decade. Others started enthusiastically, then sagged into insignificance for years; while a few began late in the 1860s, surmounted grave difficulties, and flourished for a time during the 1870s, only to decline thereafter. Throughout most of Nevada, the last two decades of the nineteenth century were a discouraging period that saw mining activity at low strength. Without much exaggeration, one could say of the Great Basin that it was a region in which mining made a very large number of false starts for every one real success.

For this situation there were many reasons, some inherent in the environmental limitations already suggested, others attributable to geological and mineralogical causes. Instead of occurring in the familiar form of veins, much of the silver of the Great Basin was in replacement deposits, a type hitherto little known to Western miners. Silver itself is a complex and often treacherous metal. While gold is "a most independent substance" found in commercial quantities in only a few minerals other than native gold, there are fifty-five well-known silver minerals; and while gold is alloyed principally with silver, silver may be found in association with a considerable variety of metals in addition to gold, especially the base metals: lead, zinc, or copper. Complicated difficulties with sulphides are also more common and important with silver than with gold.[27]

The Comstock mines and a few other deposits in western Nevada and eastern California were fortunate in having relatively simple ores that could be treated by stamp milling and "pan amalgamation," although even within that part of the Great Basin exceptions break the rule, as in the case of the Cerro Gordo mines of eastern California, which were in a smelting district. In central and eastern Nevada, on the other hand, smelting was usually essential; the ores were not susceptible to the processes used on the Comstock Lode.

Smelting, which involves converting the ore into a "fluid state by means of heat and chemicals," and then separating "the metallic from the earthy ingredients by means of their specific gravity," is an art that demands both theoretical understanding and knowledge of practical details. Few men of the mining West who had not had formal training in chemistry, metallurgy, and mineralogy were likely to practice it successfully. When Rossiter W. Raymond joined with two colleagues in November 1871 in a review of Greater Basin smelting, the trio concluded that although there were about twenty smelters in Nevada, "very few" had been profitable, even though they had treated only the richer ores of their respective localities.[28]

An inexperienced person was all too prone to select from the contemporary manuals a process that was ill-suited to his particular local ores or to the economic conditions of his district. Even if he chose aright, the local mines did not always produce enough ore to keep a custom smelter in continuous operation.

Many a small mine proved irritatingly unstable in output; a brief period of surface bonanza might be followed by total inactivity, while the owner went off to spend his profits and hunt for some one to buy his mine. In the meantime, the smelter lacked business. Frequently, also, the native ores did not provide what metallurgists call "fluxes"—that is "mineral substances which serve to liquefy others not fusible by themselves." Finally, there were the constant harassments of very high costs for labor, supplies, transportation, and the only fuel available, which was charcoal—obtained by stripping the mountains of their scant stand of nut pine and other local species. Transportation alone could decide a smelter's fate. One of the greatest advantages inherent in smelting, as contrasted with simple milling, was the saving of *all* commercially valuable minerals. Whereas lead was only a nuisance to a man running a stamp mill and amalgamation plant, to the smelter it was a major source of income, *provided* transportation was available for so heavy a product. Even a smelting plant that was technologically successful might fail if a railroad were not within reasonable distance.

It is hardly surprising that many promoters in the new camps, faced by so many difficulties and things unfamiliar, wasted their time and money sometimes on furnaces that neither worked nor paid or, at other times, on stamp mills and amalgamating plants that would have been satisfactory elsewhere but in the Great Basin could not save enough of the silver to be worthwhile. Nor was that all. Silver was not only a complicated metal, it also often occurred in a most deceptive form. One of the commonest disasters in Nevada was to discover deposits that paid richly at shallow depths and yielded what miners called "docile" ore that was so free of sulphides, lead, and antimony as to be suitable for simple treatment. Overconfident at their apparent early success, the owners would draw lavish plans for an elaborate plant, only to have the quality of the ore deteriorate suddenly and permanently at a depth of a few hundred feet.

Modern geologists explain this as having been caused by a process they call supergene, or secondary, enrichment. The ores near the surface have not only been weathered (oxidized), and thus have become free of troublesome sulphides, but they have also been positively enriched, for minerals formerly contained in the eroded upper part of the vein have been oxidized, brought down by leaching, and redeposited into the vein just below the water table, thus adding materially to the original richness of the vein.[29]

A miner whose operations extended downward to a point only a little below the water table might well be working under bonanza conditions—and have considerable justification for visions of a palace on Nob Hill. But farther down he would find himself entering what geologists call the hypogene, or primary, zone, which had not been so enriched. There the quality of his ore would deteriorate to such a disheartening extent that his imaginary palace on Nob Hill might prove to be no more than a shanty at Eureka, Nevada. The erratic history of many a Nevada district is inexplicable without an understanding of this geological phenomenon. To those whose hopes were thereby withered, little consolation could be found in the reflection that at some much later date a combination of lower costs, better metallurgical treatment, and a market for base metals might make it economically feasible to exploit the lower-grade ores of the primary zone.[30]

Under the pressures of so many adverse natural influences, Nevada's camps and towns could hardly help but have an economic development

marked by instability and a high percentage of wasted effort. The incidence of failure could have been reduced if more of the pioneers of the
Great Basin had recognized how much guidance they could obtain by
systematic study of the practices that had evolved in Europe, Mexico,
and South America during many centuries of experience with smelting.
Textbooks were available, but their use was not easy for men with only
the limited, workaday understanding gained from ventures with free-
milling ores. Aware of their own limitations, a discerning minority of
the early Nevada promoters hunted through the varied talents available
in Nevada and California until they found veteran Welsh or Cornish
smelting men or one of the few university-trained engineers. The majority
stumbled forward into adventures that remind one of the disasters
suffered in the Sierra Nevada and on the Comstock Lode during the
early days of milling and amalgamation. There was the same initial
ignorance accompanied by a firm confidence that the business would not
be difficult to learn; the same unwise resort to "improved" processes that
were worthless.

In part, however, the troubles of the smelting promoters were
inherent in the mistake of building many small local smelters, each
entirely dependent for business upon the uncertain supply of ore from
one or two mines and upon charcoal made expensively from the scant
timber. Subsequent experience showed that a few large smelters, centrally located in regard to both ores and fuel, had a far better chance of
surviving. This fact was demonstrated, in precisely the years of unsuccessful pioneering in Nevada, by a smelter established at San Francisco and operated with what appears to have been considerable success
almost from the beginning.

Thomas H. Selby, a New Yorker by birth, was a forty-niner who
came to California because, after building up his own large business in
New York City before he was thirty, he failed and found himself loaded
down with debts. In San Francisco, where he founded the firm of
Thomas H. Selby & Co., importers of metal and merchandise, he became
both rich and prominent, serving as alderman, mayor, president of the
Merchants' Exchange, and the head of philanthropic organizations.
Among his business interests in San Francisco was a shot tower and a
lead-pipe manufactory, for which he had to import pig lead from the
East. With the discovery of silver-lead ores in the interior of the Far
West, Selby was encouraged to build a smelter at North Beach, San
Francisco, in 1867, at a cost reported as $100,000.

Unlike the smelting operators of the Great Basin, Selby had the
capital and could hire the skilled supervisors and large labor force needed,
while his location at the queen city of the Far West also enabled him to
draw raw materials from a wide variety of sources. In 1869–1870 he was

buying ores from about twenty mines in California, Nevada, and Arizona. For most of these mines the Selby works constituted the only market. Although the greater portion of the ores arriving at North Beach were brought from the Great Basin by the new Central Pacific Railroad, a significant percentage came from Arizona and eastern California by older routes. Even before starting construction of his plant, Selby established an ore-buying agency on the Colorado River, from which shipments could be made by water to San Francisco.[31]

*T*HE EARLIEST SUCCESSFUL experiment within the Great Basin preceded the opening of the Selby plant by about a year. The locale was a singularly unpromising one: Humboldt County, in northwestern Nevada, a region that had momentarily attracted attention during a premature boom that started in 1861. Although many claims were filed and several towns founded, little mining work of any substance was carried out during the next few years because the ores proved to be less rich and much more difficult to treat than had been anticipated. By the late 1860s Humboldt was regarded as a largely discredited silver region that was unable to hold its population.

To the Trinity Mountains of Humboldt County came a man of outstanding determination and resourcefulness, A. W. Nason, the superintendent of the Trinity and Sacramento Silver Mining Company of New York City. Nason inherited responsibility for a quite unsuccessful plant for treating silver ores. He moved the works to the appropriately named settlement of Oreana, which was on the Humboldt River and on the line of the prospective Central Pacific Railroad. There, to quote the words of a sympathetic contemporary, he built a smelter "in a region destitute of fuel, and in the absence of all precedent or experience of the kind in Nevada." In the absence also, one might add, of skilled labor.

For guidance Nason turned to smelting techniques that had been used successfully for generations in Europe. To assure a steady supply of suitable ore, he bought a mine, the Montezuma, three miles from Oreana. Intelligent experimentation and careful adaptation to local conditions brought technological success in 1866–1867. Profits proved more elusive. Because of lack of transportation, there was little market for the lead and antimony that Nason produced as by-products of his silver smelting; the latter metal therefore had to pay all expenses. When the railroad arrived, the Oreana smelter temporarily became profitable, because the base metals could be shipped to the Selby company in San Francisco. Highly competent mining engineers praised Nason's efforts as being a model of well-directed Western enterprise. A government engineer who was allowed to examine the account books concluded that the average yield of the ore was "largely in excess" of the expenses for mining and smelting.

But the Trinity and Sacramento concern was hardly in full-scale operation before it was forced to suspend. The company had become deeply involved in litigation—a very common evil in the life of mining corporations—and the financial cost of Nason's vigorous measures had been too high for the resources available. Newspaper reports said that the reduction works had cost close to $60,000. Creditors attached and closed the Oreana plant. Attempts by other parties to reopen it proved unsuccessful, sometimes for technological reasons, sometimes because of insufficient capital.[32]

Despite the brevity of its triumph, the Oreana experiment has usually been regarded as the first instance of successfully working the silver-lead ores that were to be the basis for a major branch of the mineral industry in Western America. Nason's chief rival for the distinction of being the pioneer was W. S. Keyes, a well-trained engineer and metallurgist who had studied at Freiberg. In May 1866 at Argenta, Montana, Keyes carried out what he claimed to be "the first serious attempt" at smelting in the West. When it proved to be economically impractical to operate a smelter in so remote a region as Montana, Keyes came down to Nevada and, after one more false start, found a challenging assignment at Eureka, about sixty miles east of Austin.[33]

Eureka had begun its life in 1864 when prospectors discovered silver-lead ores that were not suitable for milling.[34] Having neither the capital nor the knowledge to develop their claims, the early locators had accomplished little, and excitement over what were called the "lead mines" remained within very modest limits. Attempts to operate small smelters failed in 1866 and again in 1868. Enough rich superficial ore was taken out to give the camp a spasmodic existence, but fundamentally the pioneer miners had little understanding of the problems before them. They were dealing not with veins but rather with the new and puzzling question of silver-lead replacement deposits in limestone. Subsequent geological studies were to show that this was a type of deposit often found in the Great Basin; Eureka differed from the rest primarily in that its resources were unusually valuable. Awaiting the fortunate were some "immense chambers" of ore, more than fifty feet in any given direction, and from the chambers "branches" and "pipes" projected, but the whole seemed arranged in a very irregular fashion. "The ore bodies do not seem to follow any particular direction," the United States Geological Survey concluded.[35]

A local mining man who had more determination than capital or scientific knowledge had the courage to buy control of one of the unsuccessful local smelters. He sought advice at Oreana and was urged to hire two Welshmen who had had practical experience. Together they succeeded in 1869, and several other small plants were erected in 1869–1870 in imitation of this first success. To judge by the events that followed, the real objective of these pioneer attempts was probably not to work the deposits themselves, but rather to make the potentialities of the Eureka claims look sufficiently attractive to catch the attention of well-to-do investors. The stratagem succeeded admirably, for in 1870 the Eureka Consolidated Mining Company was incorporated in San Francisco to take over one group of claims, while a similar amalgamation of claims in 1871 led to the formation of the Richmond Consolidated Mining Company of London. Later San Francisco and London each contributed a second company as well.

Realizing that they were embarking upon an unfamiliar and highly technical business, the San Franciscans hired Keyes to be general manager of the Eureka Consolidated Company, and Keyes in turn employed an experienced metallurgist, Albert Arents, as his principal associate. As Keyes himself described it, the two men "forwith proceeded to erect several large furnaces according to the latest European models." Theirs was not a slavish copying, for Keyes and Arents modified and improved upon the original with such success that they had to spend more than fifteen years fighting off infringements on their patents.[36]

Eureka became a thriving community that was described in the early 1880s as having 6000 inhabitants, two daily newspapers, "an imposing, well built court house, three or four churches, and several blocks of brick stores and warehouses." As in most Nevada mining towns, water was too scarce and costly to be used for anything but housekeeping and industrial purposes. A visitor in 1879 counted only four or five green "front yards" and a few small trees. With vegetation so scant, the town seemed almost as barren as the surrounding desert mountains. Since the beginning of its prosperity in 1870–1871, Eureka had survived two floods, two devastating fires, and one epidemic of smallpox. Such was the resilience of a district whose mines were still paying. San Francisco investors, who included some of the "bank crowd" of Comstock notoriety, were inspired to build a railroad more than eighty miles long to connect Eureka with the Central Pacific.[37]

The town's output of precious metals was impressively large and long-continued when compared with that of most Nevada camps. Nothing approximating precise figures can be cited, because even professional authorities differ greatly in their estimates. A monograph of the United States Geological Survey, published in 1884, asserted that up to the end of 1882 about $60,000,000 in precious metals were produced, of which about a third was gold. This was in addition to 225,000 tons of lead—an amount great enough to influence the world price of that metal, and great enough to establish Eureka as the first important center of silver-lead smelting in the United States. By contrast, a modern recalculation indicates that from very small beginnings Eureka County, which included some districts well outside the town, jumped to an annual production in excess of $2,000,000 in 1871, and remained well above that amount every year through 1882, with 1878 a bonanza year of $5,316,000.[38]

Throughout the 1880s production fell gradually. Before the end of the decade it was under a million dollars. By that time excessive amounts of underground water were becoming a serious problem, and as the bonanza ore bodies were exhausted, the owners of the two principal mines started leasing their property to others. In 1890–1891 the two big smelters were shut down, thereby throwing the whole community into a long period of inactivity that extended into the present century.

Lest Oreana and Eureka suggest that there was only one route to success with Nevada ores, the example of Pioche is worth considering. Pioche, in the southeast corner of Nevada, was prospected in 1863 and organized as Meadow Valley District in the following year, although little happened until 1868, when F. L. A. Pioche, the San Francisco financier after whom the town was to be named, sent in a metallurgist to examine and buy a group of claims. Early experiments with smelters failed because the ores were too poor in lead sulphides to make possible silver-lead smelting. The promoters then turned back to the Washoe pan process and succeeded.

Two large companies developed, one of which sponsored a narrow gauge railroad for local hauling between mines and mills. The distance to the Central Pacific Railroad—273 miles—was too great to justify extending the line to a connection with the outer world. With all supplies coming in by wagon, and ore and bullion going out by the same expensive means, only high grade ores could be worked profitably. The completion of the Utah Southern Railroad to Milford, Utah, 115 miles from Pioche, enabled Utah farm products and Chicago manufactured goods to challenge San Francisco for Pioche's trade.

A brief boom from 1870 to 1873 gave Pioche a population that was said to have reached 6000, as well as the sought-after distinctions of having a post office and becoming the county seat. Bad fires in 1871 and 1872 and a flood in 1873 failed to discourage the town's growth. But production reached a peak in 1872 (with $5,363,997) and declined rapidly down to 1875, thereafter dwindling more slowly until it very nearly reached zero in 1885. By 1875 most of the rich ore in the upper levels of the two principal mines had been exhausted; in both mines water had been encountered in discouraging quantities during the previous year at a depth of 1200 feet. When both companies decided to abandon operations, Pioche's citizens deserted as precipitately as they had come, leaving behind a town that by 1880 had shrunk to very small size and from the middle 1880s until the twentieth century was very nearly dead. Pioche's output of silver was said to have totalled over $12,000,000 during the three big years 1871–1873.[39]

A final illustration of the uncertainties of silver in the Great Basin is the brief story of what was surely the most extraordinary of all the Nevada silver stampedes, the rush to White Pine. The transitory fame of this spot rested upon some remarkably rich claims. James D. Hague termed one of them "probably the most remarkable occurrence of horn-silver on record." Rossiter Raymond went even further when he asserted that White Pine's "ore deposits of Treasure Hill are richer than any that have been discovered during the present century."[40] Horn silver was a soft, "docile" silver chloride mineral that could be worked by stamp mills and the Washoe pan process. It occurs only in arid regions of interior drainage, such as the Great Basin. Twentieth-century geologists say that the remarkable richness of the White Pine deposits was caused by super-gene enrichment, with all that implies in terms of inevitable shallowness.

Although they formed the White Pine Mining District in 1865 and erected a small mill, the pioneer prospectors and miners were not aware of the wealth before them until late in 1867, when an Indian directed a prospecting party to the unpromising summit of Treasure Hill, a mountain 9000 feet high. There they found deposits of dazzling promise. After a brief period of skepticism, the men of the Far Western mining world became convinced that here was one of the great opportunities of their lives.

White Pine was 120 miles from Austin and about 110 miles from the Central Pacific Railroad. The boom began in the spring and summer of 1868, but rose to a peak at a most unfortunate season of the year—autumn of 1868—and continued through the snows and zero temperatures of the winter of 1868–1869. Although smallpox, lack of housing, and limited and costly supplies all worked against a major excitement, nevertheless Raymond termed this "one of the most violent of these extraordinary epidemics ever experienced on the Pacific Coast."[41]

Some Nevada mining communities were almost depopulated by the exodus to White Pine; others sagged into depression. Men came hurrying eastward from California and westward from Salt Lake City. Capital, with almost equal precipitateness, was sent in from San Francisco (especially by the Bank of California), and soon afterwards from Great Britain. The local newspaper claimed that during that first winter 10,000 to 12,000 men crowded into caves and huts on the cold, windswept mountain. Doubtless this was the usual local exaggeration, for when the census was taken in 1870, it recorded 6765 people in the three principal towns that had sprung into existence on Treasure Hill. This was enough to make that bleak mountain the second largest center of population in Nevada, more than half as large as Virginia City and Gold Hill combined. Thirteen thousand claims were filed in two years.

A large percentage of those locating claims were what contemporaries called "old miners." Finding that the chloride ores were rich enough to support small-scale individual mining, these veterans scattered over the mountainside. As Raymond described it, "For months the slope of Chloride Flat looked almost like a placer gold-digging of the early days. Each miner worked with pick, gad, and shovel in his little pit, collecting in a canvas bag the rich ore he obtained." Humorously Raymond described this unusual sight as a fine example of the "retail mining business."[42]

Stamp mills and smelters were hastily and expensively built in numbers far greater than could be justified by even the most optimistic predictions as to how much ore would be produced. They were also erected without scientific guidance as to how much of the ore was "docile" enough for amalgamation and how much was suited to smelting. W. S. Keyes was one of the engineers hired to inaugurate smelting. Finding it impossible to operate his plant at a profit, Keyes resigned and went on to a more promising career at Eureka. By April 1869 170 White Pine mines had been incorporated in California, with the magnificent "paper" capital of $246,884,000—most of which was entirely imaginary.

The end came as suddenly as the beginning. Production had risen to at least a million and a half dollars in 1869 (the local newspaper claimed twice that) and over two million in 1870. Even as the peak was reached in 1870, a local correspondent reported that "the hurry and bustle and excitement of last spring no longer exist in White Pine."[43] In 1871 production was down to a little over a million dollars, and by 1873 to less than half a million. By 1875 real work had ceased except at one notable mine, the Eberhardt and Aurora, which had been bought by a misguided English syndicate and was being developed on a major scale.

When a mining camp failed in the Great Basin, its decline was apt to be more sudden and complete than could have been anticipated from any precedent set in the Sierra Nevada. Lumber was so scarce and costly that the buildings were often torn down so that the boards and beams could be used again in some new venture a hundred miles to the east. Stamp mills, unless they had already been moved too often to be worth redemption, were carted off and erected anew by the first optimist to come along.

Rossiter Raymond, in his report for 1868, was inspired by the brief history of Humboldt County to make some perceptive comments on mining booms in general. As Raymond expressed it, after a crowd of enthusiasts had invaded Humboldt in the early 1860s,

> the difficulty, mechanical, metallurgical, or merely economical, of treating the ores, the lack of ores in many veins in depth, the effect of hasty and ill-considered local regulations, and other agencies, brought about a revulsion akin to a panic. Populous towns were deserted, whole districts abandoned, and mines upon which large sums had been expended were forsaken as worthless. It is usually a long time before one of our mining districts recovers from such a reaction. They are always, so to speak, prematurely settled.[44]

To illustrate his point, Raymond described the fate of Star City in Humboldt County. Star City had been a "flourishing town, with two hotels, post office, and daily United States mail, a Wells-Fargo express office, a telegraph office, connected by a special line with Virginia City, and a population of more than 1,000 souls. So sudden has been its decline that the daily mail, the express office, and the telegraph office are all in operation yet, though the entire population consists of a single family, the head of which is mayor, constable, postmaster, express agent, telegraph operator, and, I believe, sole and unanimous voter!"[45]

Nowhere in the mining West were ghost towns more truly ghostlike than in the Great Basin.

On the way to the mines. Early 1850s. Contemporary drawing by Charles Nahl. The caption reads, in part: "The stranger, as he ascends the mountains towards the mining towns . . notices the contrast in the scenes around him to anything he ever saw before. . . Indians are met in groups, and in every stage of filth. . . . Strings of Chinamen pass, and greet you in broken English with 'how do you do, John?' . . Next comes a Negro, with polite 'good morning, sar'; or Chileno, Mexican, or Kanaka . . . ; then come horse teams, mule teams, ox teams, or mules laden with provisions, tools and clothing for the mines." (THE HUNTINGTON LIBRARY)

"How the California Mines are Worked." From a letter-sheet of the early 1850s. Left to right: operating rocker; washing with a pan; pushing loaded car out of a tunnel; lifting bucket to head of shaft; digging tunnels; using long tom; shoveling "dirt" into line of sluices; flume. (THE HUNTINGTON LIBRARY)

[Published at the WIDE WEST OFFICE, 181 Clay Street, San Francisco.]

[ANTHONY & BAKER 20.]

River Mining. Middle 1850s. A splendidly effective scene that conveys a sense of the physical effort required to turn aside a river and work its exposed bed. (THE HUNTINGTON LIBRARY)

(Opposite) *White miners and Chinese*. From a daguerreotype believed to have been taken in 1852. One of the earliest known photographs of California mining. The miners are standing beside a line of sluices; one is holding a pan. A penciled note identifies this scene as "Head of Auburn Ravine [Placer County] in the early 50's." Especially interesting for its inclusion of Chinese. (Below) *White miners and Indians*. From a daguerreotype. A penciled notation on the reverse side states: "Gold mine of Walter Taylor. Taylorville, California. 1849. Uncle Walter died here in 1850." If this dating is correct, then this must be as old as any surviving photograph of California mining. The machinery seems elaborate for 1849. The inclusion of Indians is a notable feature. (BOTH: THE HUNTINGTON LIBRARY)

Placerville, California. Lithograph of the early 1850s. Note the disorderly clutter of buildings and irregular streets, so characteristic of a mining town. (THE HUNTINGTON LIBRARY)

Grass Valley, California. Lithograph of the 1850s. In foreground, a lumber mill, with Chinese carrying loads on ends of poles. (THE HUNTINGTON LIBRARY)

"Miners Coat of Arms." 1850s. A graphic depiction of the physical objects that filled a miner's daily life: badly worn boots; rocker; fleas; hat and pipe; coffee, whisky, medicine; tools and firearms; playing cards; chewing tobacco and cigar; bully beef, beans, and pork; and an evening scene in a cabin. (THE HUNTINGTON LIBRARY)

An *"Old California" miner at the opening of the 1860s.* From *Hutchings' California Magazine,* V (April 1861), p. 436. The text accompanying the cut remarks: "A Representation of a hardy miner's phiz. Mark the expression of the eye and nostril. A volume of hardy experiences, of sagacity, of early reliant and lion-like prowess reveals itself in his stern glance, and in the deeply graven lines of his face." (THE HUNTINGTON LIBRARY)

Nevada miners. A penciled notation locates this scene at Gold Hill, Nevada, about 1865. Gold Hill was Virginia City's neighbor on the Comstock Lode. Note Chinese cook. (THE HUNTINGTON LIBRARY)

"*Miners refreshing themselves with ice-water in the 1,600-foot level.*" From *Frank Leslie's Illustrated Newspaper,* XLVI (March 30, 1878), p. 61. Underground scene in a Comstock mine in the latter days of the Comstock Lode. (THE HUNTINGTON LIBRARY)

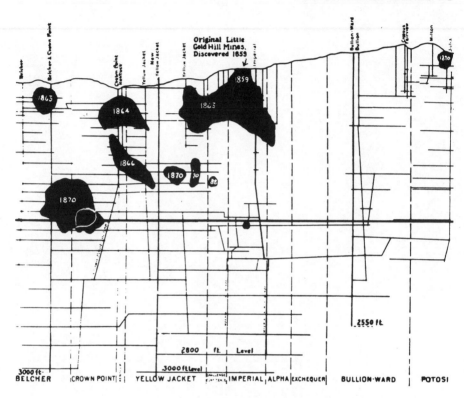

"Vertical Section of the Comstock Lode." Adapted by Grant H. Smith (*The History of the Comstock Lode,* p. 276) from Atlas Sheets X and XI of George F. Becker's contemporary monograph *Geology of the Comstock Lode* (Washington, 1882). Reproduced by permission of the Nevada Bureau of Mines and Mackay School of Mines, publishers of Smith's history, which appeared as University of Nevada "Bulletin," XXXVII, no. 3, Geology and Mining Series No. 37, 1943. (BANCROFT LIBRARY, UNIVERSITY OF CALIFORNIA)

THE COMSTOCK LODE
BODIES WITH DATES OF DISCOVERY

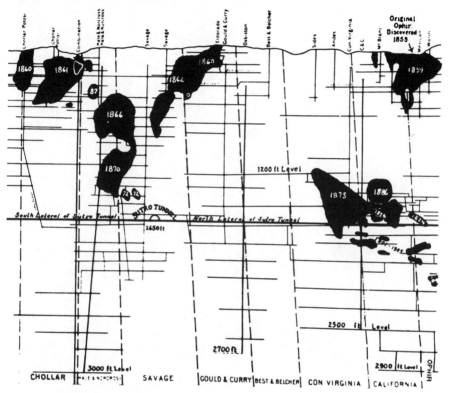

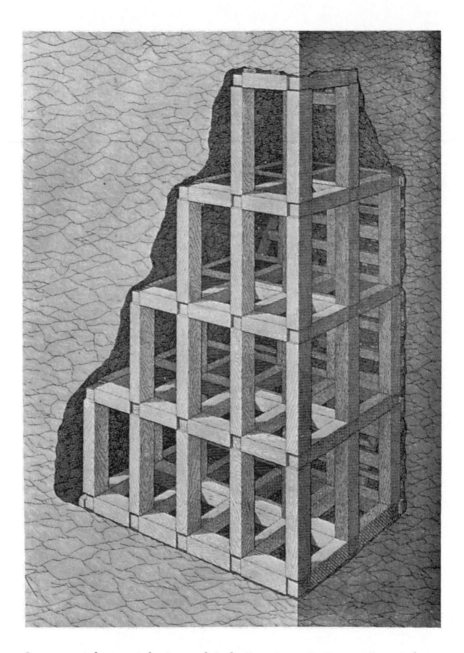

Square set timbering on the Comstock Lode. From James D. Hague, *Mining Industry* (Washington, 1870), plate V, facing p. 114. This book was volume III of Clarence King's *Report of the Geological Exploration of the Fortieth Parallel* (7 vols., Washington, 1870–1880). (THE HUNTINGTON LIBRARY)

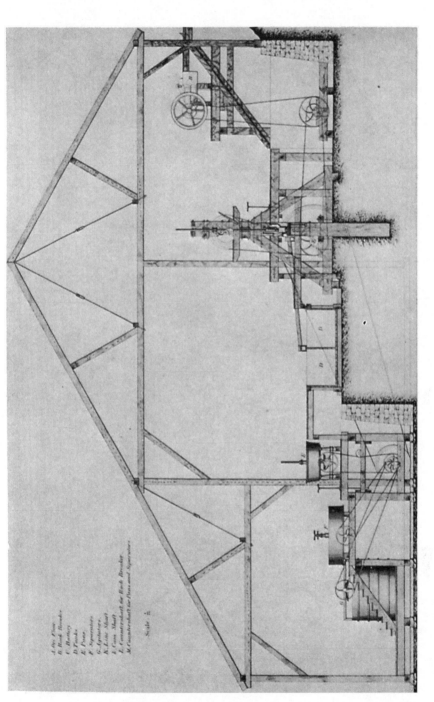

"Sectional view of Mill" on Comstock Lode. From Hague, *Mining Industry*, plate XXIII, between pp. 230 and 231. The machinery that reduced the ore by successive stages, starting with the rock breaker, continuing with the stamp mill, and passing on to the pans and settling devices. (THE HUNTINGTON LIBRARY)

"*Virginia City, Nevada, from the side of Mt. Davidson.*" The mature city, from an undated contemporary photograph. (THE HUNTINGTON LIBRARY)

"*J. C. Flood's Residence, Menlo Park, California.*" A "bonanza king" uses his Comstock wealth to build an ornate mansion in a suburb south of San Francisco. Contemporary photograph. (THE HUNTINGTON LIBRARY)

George Hearst (1820–1891). A major figure in mining throughout the Far West. After experience in both placer and quartz mining in California, he shared in developing the Ophir mine on the Comstock Lode, the Ontario mine in Utah, the Anaconda in Montana, and the Homestake in the Black Hills, in addition to having less important investments at Eureka, Nevada, in Idaho, and elsewhere. United States senator from 1886 until his death, father of the newspaper publisher. (Opposite) *Eureka, Nevada.* A contemporary photograph that shows the town's frame houses, workshops, and smoking smelters, against a background of bare mountains. (BOTH: THE HUNTINGTON LIBRARY)

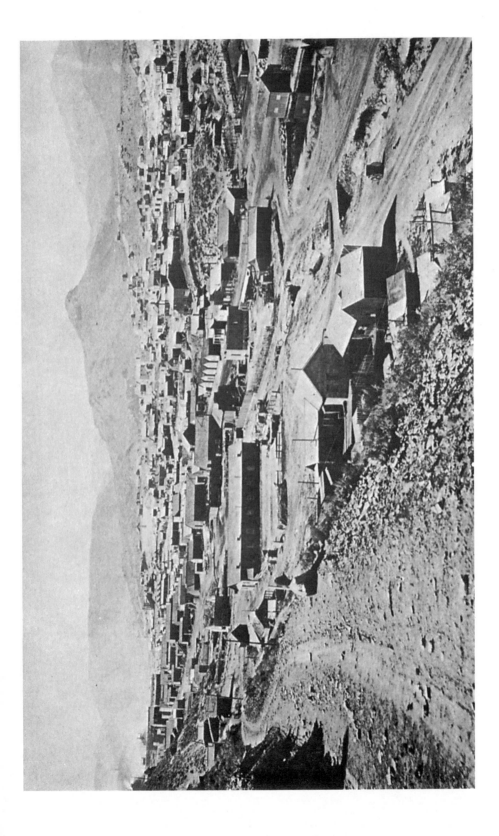

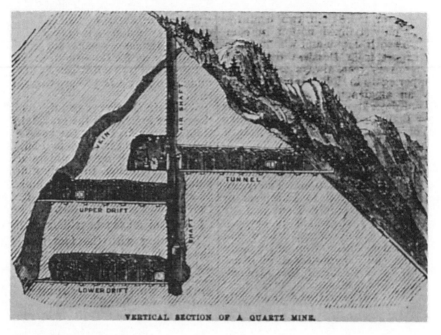

VERTICAL SECTION OF A QUARTZ MINE.

"*Vertical Section of a Quartz Mine.*" From the *Mining and Scientific Press,* January 18, 1873. (THE HUNTINGTON LIBRARY)

(Opposite) "*Hydraulic Mining in 1872.*" From Rossiter W. Raymond, *Mining Industry* (New York, 1874), p. 396a. (THE HUNTINGTON LIBRARY)

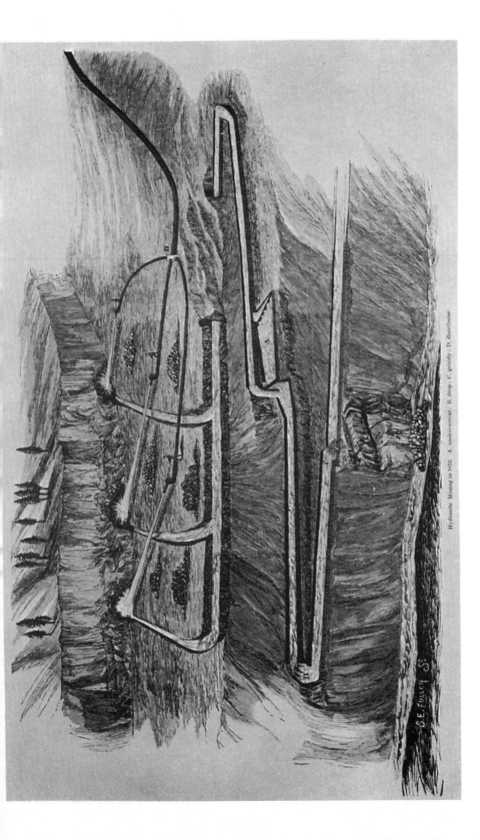

Hydraulic Mining in 1852. A, monitor or *giant*; B, *sluice*; C, *gravity*; D, *distributor*.

S.E. Young Sc.

"Pike's Peak—Our Camp in Auraria, K. T." From *Frank Leslie's Illustrated Newspaper,* VIII (August 20, 1859), p. 182. Gold rush crowd camping on the site of the future city of Denver, then part of Kansas Territory. (THE HUNTINGTON LIBRARY)

Quartz mines of Quartz Hill and Nevadaville, Gilpin County, Colorado. From Frank Fossett, Colorado, its Gold and Silver Mines (New York, 1879), between pp. 324 and 325. (THE HUNTINGTON LIBRARY)

CHESTNUT STREET, LEADVILLE.

(Above) *Chestnut Street, Leadville, Colorado.* From Fossett, *Colorado,* p. 409. Crowded streets in boom time. (Left) *The notorious Emma mine, Little Cottonwood Canyon, Utah.* From Thomas B. H. Stenhouse, *The Rocky Mountain Saints* (New York, 1873), p. 726. (BOTH: THE HUNTINGTON LIBRARY)

Hurdy-gurdy house, Virginia City, Montana. From Albert D. Richardson, Beyond the Mississippi: From the Great River to the Great Ocean (Hartford, Conn., 1867), facing p. 480. (THE HUNTINGTON LIBRARY)

Lynching of Rafael Escobar at Jackson, Amador County, California, August 1855. Engraved from a daguerreotype. Escobar, a Mexican, was accused of participation in a murder and robbery. The caption states that Escobar was captured at Columbia, Tuolumne County, and was brought back to Amador by a police officer. The prisoner was seized by a mob "and in less than one hour's time placed in the position you now see him, making the tenth execution on the same tree." (THE HUNTINGTON LIBRARY)

On the Way to New Diggings—Halt in a Rough Pass of the Rocky Mountains. From *Harper's Weekly,* XIX (May 1, 1875), pp. 360–361. The caption explains that "our artists traveled for several days with such a party." In view of the date, these gold seekers may well have been en route to the Black Hills. (THE HUNTINGTON LIBRARY)

"*The Exodus from the Black Hills.*" From *Harper's Weekly*, XIX (November 6, 1875), p. 904. Disgruntled gold seekers form long, unbroken columns as they abandon the Black Hills and start back across the plains. (THE HUNTINGTON LIBRARY)

Model of timber stope in the Homestake mine. Showing the influence of the Comstock system of square-set timbering. (PUBLIC RELATIONS DEPARTMENT, HOMESTAKE MINING COMPANY)

Stamp mill at a plant of the Homestake mine, Lead, South Dakota. Taken in the 1920s, the photograph shows the continuing indebtedness of the Homestake mine's milling equipment to ideas developed in California in the 1850s and improved to meet the needs of the Comstock Lode in the 1860s and 1870s. Note the massive construction. (PUBLIC RELATIONS DEPARTMENT, HOMESTAKE MINING COMPANY)

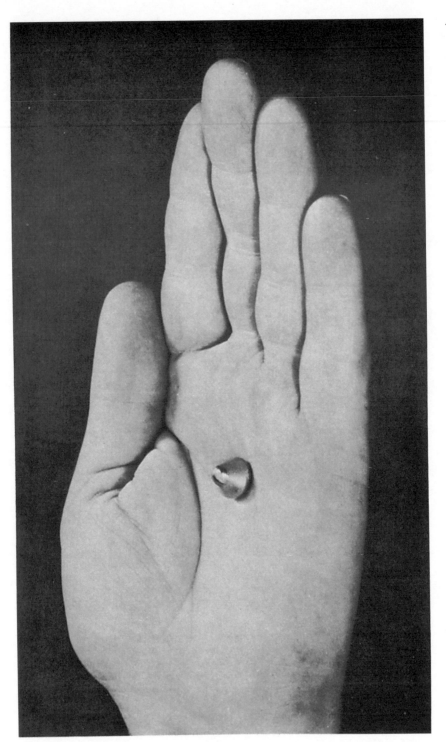

Amount of gold produced from one ton of ore at the Homestake mine. (PUBLIC RELATIONS DEPARTMENT, HOMESTAKE MINING COMPANY)

◁ 6 ▷

Colorado
1859-1880

A few months before California learned of Comstock silver, the Missouri frontier heard rumors of Colorado gold. The resultant rush was the first episode in the mining history of the Rocky Mountains. In Californian thinking this meant that a new mining frontier had been established a thousand miles away, to the east of the great natural barriers of the Rockies and the Great Basin deserts.

Separated by so long a distance and such imposing obstacles, Colorado was almost certain to have a history somewhat apart from that of the mining commonwealths tributary to the Pacific coast. Colorado's natural ties were with the Middle West, or even with the Atlantic seaboard that lay behind the Middle West. Her pioneers, material goods, and capital came to Colorado from the East, and to it she sent her treasure in exchange. At times the relationship seemed a source of strength to Colorado; at other times it seemed to have inherent weaknesses.

Colorado's nineteenth-century history followed the typically episodic pattern so characteristic of mining regions. The opening years from 1859

109

to the early 1860s brought a boom based upon rich, shallow gold deposits. Then came a severe depression that lifted only gradually during the late 1860s and early 1870s. In the middle and late 1870s began a great silver boom based upon new discoveries, new skills and processes, better transportation, and lower costs. By the 1890s this boom was being deflated by the world slump in the price of silver. When gold was discovered in a most unpromising place, Colorado quickly shifted back to the precious metal of her earlier years, and enjoyed a new gold boom that lasted into the present century.

But that was not all. The silver boom received its greatest impetus from the huge silver-lead deposits of Leadville. There, starting in 1877, the silver smelters became also major producers of lead, to a value of several million dollars per year. Copper was a minor by-product for many years before it began to have an annual value of over a million dollars in the late 1890s. Zinc was of little importance until the close of the century. Soon after 1900 it, too, began coming from the smelters in amounts worth several million dollars a year.

In the last two decades of the century, then, Colorado's mines ceased to be dependent solely on the precious metals. The base metals so often associated with silver became a significant, though secondary, source of income. Their large-scale production at an earlier date would hardly have been practicable, because it was so necessary to have railroad transportation, access to large supplies of fuel, and a general lowering of costs. At the same time, their market was much greater at the end of the century because of the general expansion of American industry and the appearance of wholly new demands, such as for copper for electricity. Within the present century, other new industrial and strategic needs have lent importance to Colorado's deposits of molybdenum, vanadium, tungsten, and uranium.

This remarkable diversity of metals has given Colorado an unusually long history of profitable mining, and has credited the state with a record of total mineral production that can stand comparison with any part of the Union.[1] But diversity has not necessarily meant stability. As every tourist knows, Colorado is well filled with ghost towns. Many of the early gold towns had declined before the silver boom started, and only a few of the important silver deposits were close enough to existing gold towns to save the latter. Silver smelters built from 1878 onwards, and located in accordance with transportation routes and fuel supplies, created new population centers outside the mining regions, while the new gold boom of the 1890s drew people away from the silver mining areas. Each change left behind it towns that were stunted or deserted.

Some great fortunes were made for Coloradans by these successive booms, and as the business center for all the Colorado mining areas,

Denver grew to be one of the West's important cities, with its accumulating wealth visibly displayed in new buildings and new enterprises. If Denver did not become as notable a regional capital as San Francisco, neither did it suffer the fate of Virginia City, Nevada. Its continued growth and usefulness were assured not only by the mines tributary to it, but also by its position as a focal point for the railroads, farms, and ranches that became so important in the region after 1870.

Yet much of the capital for Colorado's mines, mills, and smelters came from investors who lived far east of the Rockies. New York contributed part of it, and from an early date. Boston, Philadelphia, and Providence were among the other Eastern seaboard investors. The Middle West had important holdings. The British sent large amounts of capital after 1870. The proportion of absentee ownership was much higher in Colorado than in California—and much lower than in Nevada. This meant, of course, that Colorado was in some degree a colonial province that sent part of its profits eastward.

*C*OLORADO'S LIFE started with a curious contradiction. When the first reports of gold drifted back to the Missouri frontier in late 1858 and early 1859, a gold rush was launched that seems to have been second only to '49 in dimensions; yet there was no substantial basis for the initial excitement. Years of rumors of gold in the Colorado Rockies had finally inspired William Green Russell, a veteran of mining in both Georgia and California, to organize a party in Georgia to prospect the Pikes Peak region in 1858. They journeyed out to what is now north-central Colorado and focused their interest on the area just east of the base of the Rocky Mountains, where many small creeks flow out to the South Platte River.

Russell's party made camp on one of these little streams, Cherry Creek. They found too little gold to stir up real enthusiasm, but by chance a trader who was en route back to the Missouri frontier witnessed their operations and imaginatively conjured up an inflated notion as to the importance of the discovery. He carried back with him a small sample of placer gold, and the Missouri newspapers and frontier outfitting merchants did the rest. All were only too eager to stimulate a boom that would bring business to the little towns that would become the points of departure for Colorado.

A second prospecting party, from Lawrence, Kansas, had started for Colorado before the news was out, and as the early reports of gold spread along the Missouri frontier, several additional parties hastily departed for a destination that was mistakenly identified with Pikes

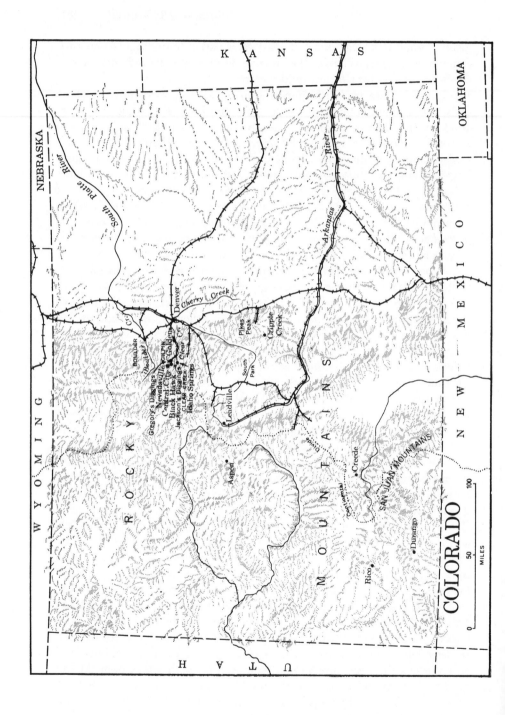

Peak. Before 1858 was over, at least four paper "cities" had been proclaimed near Cherry Creek. The one named Denver survived and became the headquarters for the new gold region.

In 1858 there was little justification for all this speculative activity. Only very limited amounts of placer gold had been discovered. Exaggeration and hysteria had done the rest. When the first "fifty-niners" began to reach Colorado a few weeks later, they found that they had been misled, and discontentedly denounced the whole business as the "humbug of humbugs." By early May, even as the outward-bound fifty-niners were crowding through the Missouri River towns, a reverse current of disillusioned gold seekers was flowing back across the plains, "destitute of provisions or means of conveyance, disappointed and utterly disheartened . . . toil-worn, foot-worn, and heart-weary," as a sympathetic observer reported.[2]

What saved the rush was the presence of a few experienced prospectors. Too much of the prospecting of 1858 had been along the lower course of the creeks tributary to the South Platte, close to the base of the mountains. As 1859 opened, veterans of other mining frontiers followed the canyons up into the rugged mass of the Rockies. In particular, several men retraced a little stream that they called Clear Creek, a tributary of the South Platte that breaks through the mountains directly west of Denver. In January, John S. Gregory ascended North Clear Creek and made a promising discovery in what became known as Gregory Gulch, at the site of the present-day Black Hawk, Gilpin County. Almost simultaneously, George A. Jackson discovered good placer diggings on Chicago Creek, a small tributary of South Clear Creek, where the town of Idaho Springs was soon to be founded. Although both men prospected their discovery areas in January, snow and lack of supplies forced Gregory to postpone further work until spring, while Jackson kept his good fortune secret until the end of April. On May 6, Gregory found a rich outcropping of gold-bearing quartz at the head of Gregory Gulch, and thus gave his name to the famous Gregory Lode. In their personal histories the two men symbolized the twin sources that Colorado drew upon for experience in its earliest days. Gregory had been a miner in Georgia; Jackson in California.

Gregory's and Jackson's "strikes" were separated from one another only by the ridge that divides the north and south branches of Clear Creek. To the north of them, and again in mid-January, a party of prospectors who had gone into the region drained by the branches and tributaries of Boulder Creek found gold at a place that they named Gold Hill, in the center of what is now Boulder County.

The Gold Hill diggings became known very quickly; the other two in the spring. Together the several discoveries, however tardy, justified what had begun to look like another mining fiasco.[3] As always in new mining regions, good luck at a few places inspired prospectors to successful searches in many other directions. Before 1859 was over miners had moved southward into the beautiful region of South Park and westward across the Continental Divide to the Pacific drainage. A year later an expedition even made a thrust clear across Colorado to the southwest, in a premature attempt to open diggings in the remote and difficult San Juan country. By that time it was becoming apparent that Colorado's mineral resources were located in a broad belt that stretched diagonally across the territory from the San Juan country in the southwest to Boulder County in the northeast, a distance of over 200 miles by direct air line.

*B*OTH PLACER AND VEIN mining developed quickly. At first there was not much distinction between the two. Some claims were true placer deposits; others were really the heavily eroded and broken outcroppings of veins. The first miners successfully ran "dirt" from both types of deposits through rockers, long toms, and sluices. Presently, as they went down a little further into more solid rock in their lode claims, they began to build arrastras and crude stamp mills to grind the ores. Former Californians and Georgians were their instructors; from these veterans of earlier mining frontiers the inexperienced multitude learned just enough to get started.

For several years the stress was upon the simpler techniques characteristic of California's own flush days, rather than upon the more sophisticated refinements that were being devised just as the mining frontier started bursting out of its original Californian limits. Perhaps the inexperience of the majority made simplicity essential, while the rich and superficial nature of the first deposits to be worked made it possible to profit from even the crudest operations. Or perhaps, since so many of the "Old Californians" of the Colorado rush had in fact left California several years previously, they were not familiar with the technical progress that had come with the maturing of mining on the Pacific Coast. Whatever the reason, early Colorado tended to repeat the mistakes along with the other experiences of California.

The center of pioneer mining in Colorado was in the mountainous region of gulches and canyons where Gregory and Jackson had made their discoveries. Here, at an altitude of 8000 feet and a distance of thirty-five miles (mainly rough, up-hill mountain roads) from the new supply center of Denver, developed one of the most notable mining counties in America, Gilpin, and its important neighbors, Clear Creek on the south and Boulder on the north. The distinguished mining geologist, Frederick L. Ransome, has remarked that this is the region "where so much in mining and metallurgic technique had its beginnings. . . . In many respects it holds in this country a position analogous to that of Cornwall in Great Britain."[4] Or, one might add, it is even more closely analogous to Nevada County, California, or Storey County, Nevada, since all were centers of practical study and experimentation from which ultimately came major contributions to the art of mining and the several branches of science and engineering essential to it.

That still lay far in the future. In 1859 Gregory Gulch and the Clear Creek country were typical raw frontier districts. A motley throng of the able and the inept, the energetic and the lazy came crowding up the steep, narrow canyons, "claiming" every piece of ground that showed promise or was close enough to some one else's good claim to be hopeful. Of several thousand people, only a dozen were women, and of these five were white wives, the others being described as squaws "living with white men in the capacity of wives."[5] Tents, wagons, shelters made of boughs, or roughly constructed cabins were the only homes. With men doing the housekeeping, disorder and litters of cans and bottles soon marred the landscape. The men themselves were as comfortably unkempt as any forty-niners had been a decade earlier.

Californian notions as to mining codes and mining districts were copied, and the region went about its business, which was mining. Unlike California, lode gold was important from the beginning. Modern estimates for the decade 1858–1867 ascribe two fifths of Colorado's gold product to lodes.[6] No special technical difficulties arose at first, even in vein mining. Yet the total output was small, very small, if compared with the early years of California or Nevada, or the other two principal Rocky Mountain states, Montana and Idaho. Modern geologists estimate it at only $25,000,000 for the decade 1858–1867, and the figures of careful contemporaries confirm this surprisingly closely. One of those contemporaries, Frank Fossett, whose excellent manual was published in 1879, felt that production reached a peak of $3,400,000 in each of the two years 1862 and 1863, fell slightly in the following year, and then began a tumble to a much lower level.[7]

So small a product from so large a rush of gold seekers makes it clear how greatly exaggerated were the early ideas about Colorado gold. Even in 1859 and 1860, when rich new claims were yielding abundantly, there was an exodus of the disillusioned and discontented back to the Middle West, and throughout the 1860s Colorado had a hard time retaining its newly acquired people. Frank Fossett expressed the belief that a hundred thousand people had lived in Colorado for varying periods between 1858 and 1870, even though there had rarely been more than a third of that number in the territory at any one time. The census recorded 34,277 in 1860 and 39,864 in 1870.[8] The latter statistic would have been smaller than that for 1860 if it had been based solely on the mining districts and Denver. It was inflated by Congress's enlargement of Colorado's legal boundaries in 1861 and a subsequent influx of Spanish-speaking farmers and ranchers into the southern counties. If Fossett was right in speaking of a hundred thousand people, then 60 percent of those who came to Colorado in its early years must have abandoned it.

The Civil War, Indian troubles, bad weather, and high prices all helped to discourage population growth in the 1860s. However paradoxical it may seem, it might have been easier for Colorado to hold its pioneer population if the distance from the Missouri frontier had been greater. The journey back to "the States" might well be dangerous in the 1860s, for the Indians did their best to disrupt communications while the regular army was absent on wartime service, but the trip could be made within reasonable time and at corresponding cost by men who were by then old hands and were traveling light. Stagecoach service between Denver and Fort Leavenworth, Kansas, began as early as 1859 and sought, hopefully, to make the trip in a week, although it often took longer. There was a vast difference between going home from California in the 1850s and returning from Colorado in the 1860s. Perhaps this helps to explain why more people left Colorado than stayed.

But the principal reason for Colorado's failure to grow was that the flush days passed all too soon and were succeeded by a difficult era of readjustment and hard times. The placers, while rich in particular localities, were quite limited in total extent when compared with California's in the 1850s or those of Montana and Idaho in the 1860s. They seem to have reached their peak in yield during 1861 and 1862, and to have been visibly on the decline after 1863. Until 1863 it was fairly common to make a "wage" of $3 to $5 dollars per day per man, while using equipment no more complex than sluices, long toms, and rockers. Thereafter the Colorado placers were in a condition similar to that of the California placers in the later 1850s. As a contemporary expressed it, "the ground that had been easiest to get at or handle had been largely worked out."[9]

Some of the best placers had been discovered when prospectors moved westward and southward from Gilpin and Clear Creek counties up toward the summits of the Rocky Mountains. Although even the passes were at altitudes above 11,000 feet, prospectors crossed the Continental Divide as early as 1859, and miners and mule trains followed them. Others pushed southward in 1859 to find gold high on the eastern slopes of the Continental Divide, where thriving diggings were opened in the lovely and lofty South Park and at the head of the Arkansas Valley. When

the census was taken in 1860, there were 10,600 people in South Park—
30 percent of the total population of Colorado.

The upper Arkansas Valley had fewer people, but its chief community, California Gulch, was later described by one pioneer as having
been

> *The Camp* of Colorado. It was strung along through the gulch. . . . There
> were a great many tents in the road and on the side of the ridge, and the
> wagons were backed up, the people living right in the wagons. Some of
> them were used as hotels; they had their grub under the wagons, piled
> the dishes there, and the man of the house and his wife would sleep in
> the wagons nights. They would get some rough boards and make tables
> where the boarders took their meals, and those who did not want to board
> did their own cooking. The gamblers would have tables strung along the
> wayside to take in the cheerful but unwary miner.[10]

For even the most traveled of the "Old Californians" it was a new
experience to be working rich placers at an altitude of 10,000 feet, as they
did at California Gulch. Snow and cold came early and lasted so late
that the season had to be short, but for several years the returns were
easily rich enough to justify it.

After the early 1860s even these high-country diggings were being
abandoned, while the placers of Gilpin and Clear Creek counties had
ceased to be attractive, and the small original placers nearer Denver had
long since lost their appeal. As simple placer mining became less profitable, it was succeeded in only a few places by hydraulicking. Most of
the country either lacked deep gravels or was poorly suited to hydraulic
operations. When the latter were introduced into individual areas, there
was often a gap of years between the end of simple placer mining and
the beginning of significant attempts at hydraulicking. Meantime, the
majority of the gold rush population, who would not have been interested
in hydraulic mining anyway, deserted in crowds for those new magnets,
the placers of Idaho and Montana.

The future of Colorado depended on its lode mines. California had
already shown, and in these same years Nevada was confirming, that
lode mines were inherently slower, more difficult, and more expensive to
develop than any placer workings save perhaps the very biggest hydraulic
projects. Experience in California also suggested that even able and
determined men might have to struggle through years of technological
mistakes and inadequate financing before lode mines could be made to
produce largely and profitably. Contemporary Nevada, building on California's lessons and financial capital, and blessed with real bonanzas very
near the surface, seemed until 1864 to be accelerating the developmental
process. Then it, too, fell into a painful readjustment that was closely
parallel in time to Colorado's troubles.

Colorado, then, was entrusting its fate to a slower and more uncertain enterprise than contemporaries realized. The initial operations went well. The ore at or near the surface was richer than that farther down, and for a short distance beneath the ground it had been so weathered by air and water as to be relatively free from its sulphide matrix. Yields were large and the gold amalgamated with quicksilver without difficulty.

With the undiscriminating enthusiasm so characteristic of mining, many more rushed into the business than was justifiable or desirable. Through defects in the original local mining codes, too many small claims were permitted on each section of the better known lodes, with the result that shafts were being sunk almost side-by-side, while the surface was cluttered with the buildings, shaft-houses, equipment, and waste dumps of neighboring companies. Stamp mills in great numbers were erected before any one had attempted to determine how much ore would be brought to the mills to be crushed.

These were among the troubles of inexperience and poor judgment. When the shafts went deep enough to strike water and need machine-powered hoisting works, inexperience combined with inadequate capital to cause the early promoters to install hoisting and pumping engines that were barely powerful enough for the immediate need, and quite incapable of meeting the increasingly heavy demands that always come with increasing depth. At many of the claims there was the further difficulty that just as income became most necessary, it dwindled sharply, because the vein temporarily "pinched" into a very narrow width. Finally, the practice of piratically stripping the public domain of all the trees that were reasonably close to a camp, was gradually creating a shortage of timber and fuel, with resultant high prices.[11]

Many of these various problems were characteristic of new vein mining regions throughout the West, and by themselves they would probably have forced the early Coloradans into a discouraging period of reduced activity and reorganization before advance could be resumed. But along with them the Coloradans suddenly found that they were delivering to the stamp mills ores whose gold refused to amalgamate with mercury, and hence was lost in the tailings.

At depths that were often no more than 100 feet, the weathered, oxidized, and enriched ores, which had been paying handsomely, gave place to ores in which the gold was not only less rich, but, worse still, was in chemical combination with sulphides, thus constituting the "sulphurets" or pyritic ores already encountered in California and the Comstock Lode. Coloradans irritably labelled them "refractory" or "rebellious." The miners found something highly personal in their gold's uncooperative refusal to combine with mercury in the presence of sulphides.

When faced by this same problem, Californians had been able to dismiss it temporarily, since the percentage of sulphurets in their ores was too small to constitute a major obstacle. By 1867 California mill men were claiming that they could save 75 percent of the gold content by milling and amalgamation without chlorinating the sulphurets. According to one well-informed contemporary, after the Colorado miners got below the weathered zone the mills were saving only one tenth to one half of the potential value. According to another, the proportion saved was between 15 and 40 percent.[12] What had been a minor element in Californian thinking became the central problem for Coloradans.

There were two general ways to go about reducing a heavy wastage of precious metals. In California and on the Comstock Lode, where the ores were very nearly or actually free milling, the response was to make milling processes more efficient by improving the mechanical devices used at successive stages. A few relatively simple chemicals were added at some of the stages, as in the Washoe pan process. To use modern terms, in California and on the Comstock it was possible to evolve a solution by trial and error within the fields of mechanical engineering and very simple chemistry.

The other way was that followed in central and eastern Nevada in the later 1860s, where the precious metals were in association with base metals. There the attempt was to learn smelting, by which all of the commercially valuable metals could be saved. For this a knowledge of chemistry, metallurgy, and mineralogy were essential, and geology desirable. In other words, for successful smelting a training in science was prerequisite.

It would have been asking much to expect an inexperienced mining frontier like Colorado suddenly to produce a corps of real scientists. Nevada and easternmost California, as we have seen, had trouble enough with their attempts at smelting during the 1860s, even though, as colonies of the West's most experienced mining region, they could draw upon a much richer and more numerous body of well-trained metallurgists, together with an increasing amount of competent printed advice put out by the San Francisco publishers.

Nor was the problem simply a matter of science. The economics of smelting were at least as demanding in Colorado as in Nevada, and they were complicated by mineralogical limitations. In Gilpin County, which was the center of lode mining, the ores contained their gold in the form of auriferous iron or copper pyrites. This meant that there was little of commercial value but the gold itself. Iron pyrites, though one of the commonest iron minerals, was rarely used industrially because the sulphur in it "is undesirable in the reduction and treatment of iron."[13] Copper pyrites was potentially industrially useful, but at no time during the 1860s and 1870s did it add more than a very small supplement to

Colorado's mining income. Silver was more immediately important. It was encountered in some of the shafts below the oxidized zone. Even with some silver to supplement the main yield of gold, the precious metals would have to be rich indeed to pay for so much of the cost of so expensive a process as smelting.

The anxious Colorado mining and milling men of the early 1860s understood neither the nature of their difficulties nor the possible solutions to them. Most of the miners were as short on capital as on experience. As their expenses mounted, they had to borrow from the bankers who handled their gold shipments. Continued bad luck brought a transfer of ownership from debtor to creditor. The banks, in turn, exploited their business relationships with Eastern financial interests to secure the incorporation and sale of the foreclosed mines to Eastern speculators.[14]

Thus introduced to Colorado, Easterners proved unexpectedly eager to risk their money, and in 1863 and 1864 capital was raised with comparative ease in New York, Boston, Philadelphia, and other large cities. These were the wartime days when the speculative impulse was strong throughout America. For Coloradans the resort to Eastern capital was caused in part by the justifiable conviction that additional funds were necessary for further development. Presently the further discovery was made that it was easier to work Eastern "suckers" than Colorado ores. As new money came in from the East, it was spent unwisely for elaborate buildings and untried equipment, usually erected before enough ore had been uncovered to justify heavy investment. Expenses of all kinds shot up as soon as mining operators found themselves no longer spending their own money. Worst of all, Colorado became infested with a race of pseudo scientists, charlatans who bestowed upon themselves the title of "professor," and talked learned nonsense about patented processes and ingenious gadgets that they had invented to conquer the "refractory ores." The Comstock Lode, of course, went through a comparable phase of fake science and unsound joint stock ventures.

The inevitable collapse began in 1864–1865. It was hastened by a serious interruption of freighting service across the plains from the Missouri River to Colorado. Severe storms in the winter of 1863–1864 were followed by floods in the spring, and then by Indian attacks when the wagon trains resumed service. Freighting charges mounted as the dangers and obstacles increased, and supplies and services of all kinds were sharply inflated just as the new incorporated companies were trying to develop their properties. At the same time, the companies were ordering their mining machinery from Middle Western cities, where the iron foundries and machine shops proved slow in response because they were busy with war work for the national government. Delays in delivery took valuable months out of the best part of the year, while continuing expenses in Colorado in the meantime ate up the corporate funds.[15]

*T*HE YEARS FROM 1864 to 1868 represent the lowest point in the history of Colorado mining, and they were followed by two or three additional years that brought new disappointments along with more favoring circumstances. By 1868 the placer deposits had dwindled to small-scale operations. Modern estimates credit them with only $320,000 for that year, and these same estimates assign only $1,690,000 to the lode mines in 1868.[16] By way of contrast, California, then in its twentieth year of mining, produced $17,500,000 in 1868; and the Comstock Lode, even though it had not yet struck a new bonanza, nevertheless produced nearly $9,500,000.

In the late 1860s one could reasonably have argued that Colorado had run through its flush period and was gradually dwindling into extinction. The population figures, with their indication of a shrinking mining population, would have seemed to support such pessimism. So would the doleful descriptions of eye-witnesses. The veteran literary traveler Bayard Taylor, writing from Central City on June 26, 1866, said: "The deserted mills, the idle wheels, and the empty shafts and drifts for miles along this and the adjoining ravines—the general decrease of population everywhere in the mountains—indicate a period of doubt and transition."[17]

Mining activity, which had spread over a large part of mountainous Colorado during 1859, 1860, and 1861, contracted back toward Gilpin County, where it had started. For a time it seemed as if Colorado mining were about to become coterminous with Gilpin County mining. But for the persistence of the men who continued stubbornly at work in that notable county, Colorado might well have lost its mining industry for some time.

In Gilpin County activity centered in a series of small towns that straggled up the canyons, sometimes alongside, sometimes actually extended out over a muddy, hurrying stream. Black Hawk, Mountain City, Central City, and Nevada (or Nevadaville) formed a continuous, crowded line of buildings. Many of the structures were cut into the hillslope at one end but rested on stilts out over the stream at the other, like a person standing uncertainly on one leg. Along the "irregular, wandering, uneven" road were "hotels, with pompous names and limited accommodations," saloons, beer halls, bakeries, log and frame houses, and a few cottages "in the calico style, with all sorts of brackets and carved drop-cornices." Everywhere were idle mills and heaps of rusting machinery, while the bare mountainside was pitted with prospect holes, abandoned shafts, and mounds of tailings and refuse.[18]

To the external observer it did not seem a promising setting. Yet it was here, and from this low point in its fortunes, that Colorado was rescued by several simultaneous developments. The first was a slow improvement in the way the existing gold lode mines and mills were handled. Adjacent claims were consolidated into more efficient units. Working miners replaced absentee corporations, by buying or leasing idle properties. At many mines highly professional Cornish or Irish miners took the place of American amateurs. Over Colorado as a whole, the proportion of foreign-born increased moderately after the gold rush years, and the greater part of the gain was experienced by the mining counties and Denver. Unlike the rest of the mining West, few of the foreign-born were Chinese. Most were from Ireland, Great Britain, Germany, and British America. In Gilpin County the Cornishmen became an especially notable part of the life of the community. With their long experience in underground work, they contributed much to the improvement of mining technique.[19]

Out of the tons of abandoned equipment and scrap iron that cluttered the territory after the failures of the middle 1860s, the new operators reconstructed stamp mills on a more sensible basis, free from the fancy Eastern and European notions. In their reconstruction the Coloradans moved decisively away from the California prototype that was so universally in use elsewhere in the mining world. In an attempt to lessen the inhibiting effect of the sulphides, the Coloradans now built mills that would give the refractory ores a longer and finer crushing and a longer period during which the crushed rock would be exposed to the action of mercury. This procedure meant reducing the daily tonnage of the mill by more than one half, and accepting a loss of gold that one government mining expert estimated at 40 to 50 percent, and another at 30 to 70 percent.[20]

Disparaging comments on the efficiency of the Colorado, or Gilpin County, mill, as compared with those of California and Nevada, were expressed by virtually every nonresident mining engineer who studied the Colorado mills during the remainder of the nineteenth century. Always the Colorado millmen replied that their peculiar practices were well suited to their peculiar ores. Rossiter Raymond, in his report for 1869, remarked that "the strong and natural reaction in Colorado against new processes, from which the Territory has suffered so much, has gone so far as to make the mill-men obstinately refuse to adopt even the well-proven apparatus of other regions."[21] Apparently a pattern of thinking that was justified by the local conditions of the 1860s became so well established as to be impervious thereafter to advice from outsiders. Not without reason did mining men nickname this stubbornly independent county "the Little Kingdom of Gilpin."

Although gradually the percentage of loss was reduced, even within the present century the Gilpin County mill rarely saved more than 75 percent of the gold and 40 percent of the silver in its ores, and even this was achieved at a continuing sacrifice in the amount of ore that could be crushed within a given period of time.[22]

In the year 1870, just as this special milling technique was becoming the local standard, the Colorado vein mines were visited by that outspoken veteran of the Comstock, Almarin B. Paul. Paul's comments reflected the point of view of one conditioned by twenty years in California and Nevada. He found the Coloradans to be a slow-moving, secretive lot who were content with what he regarded as small-scale operations and with Eastern-made stamp mills that lost an unreasonable percentage of the precious metal. Acidly he reported: "There is not that 'git up and git' that can be seen in the mining districts of Nevada especially," and "I have yet to see anything that comes within gun-shot of a first-class California or Nevada mill." He admitted that Colorado's ores were more complex and "rebellious," and hence more expensive to treat, than any he had encountered in California or Nevada; yet with all the confidence of a self-taught Westerner, he concluded that Colorado's "whole mill system wants bettering and cheapening, and the way to do it is to introduce Western practice instead of Eastern science."[23]

Coloradans and Easterners investing in Colorado were by no means convinced of the correctness of Paul's prescription. A Colorado mining newspaper pointed out: "In Colorado we are having the privilege of solving some of the most difficult problems of metallurgy."

> We doubt if any other district on the continent can afford a more complete and varied study for the metallurgist. Its gold is found nearly always associated with iron and copper, the latter in quantities varying from three to twenty per cent. Its silver is in a majority of cases carried in zinc or lead ores, and often with an admixture of antimony and arsenic. Were only one or two of these present the difficulties would not be so great. As it is however a very small number of mines yield rock that can be properly handled in any other way than by a long and complicated process.[24]

By testing the potentialties of metallurgy, Colorado achieved the second of the several simultaneous improvements. The Colorado setting was again in Gilpin County. Nathaniel P. Hill, while teaching applied chemistry at Brown University, won the confidence of a group of New England industrialists. With their backing he made trips to Colorado to examine the losses under existing milling practices, and trips to Britain and continental Europe to study well-established techniques for smelting ores. To test the possibilities under working conditions, he had several tons of samples of Gilpin County ores hauled across the plains to Missouri, thence by steamboat down the Missouri and Mississippi rivers to New Orleans, and then across the ocean to the great Welsh smelting center of Swansea.[25]

Hill had good judgment and possessed notable talents as a business administrator. Despite innumerable obstacles, he succeeded in building at Black Hawk, Gilpin County, a smelter that was a modification of those used at Swansea. As his metallurgist he hired Hermann Baeger, a graduate of the German academy of mining and metallurgy at Freiberg, Saxony. From the time it went into operation in 1868, Hill's Boston and Colorado Smelter was technologically successful in reducing Gilpin County ores. Its operating costs, for all Hill's careful management, proved to be so high that only the richest ores could be worked. The rest continued to be treated in the stamp mills, despite the waste.

When he turned for guidance to the famous smelting center at Swansea and the equally famous academy at Freiberg, Hill was tapping the best scientific knowledge in Europe. In 1873 he went further in that direction when he hired Richard Pearce, the son of a superintendent in the ancient tin mines of Cornwall. Pearce brought with him a group of veteran workmen who had served under him in Cornwall and again when he was manager of an ore reduction works at Swansea. Pearce had begun working in the Cornish mines as a boy, had won admittance to the Royal School of Mines in London, and later had gone on to Freiberg, where he specialized in metallurgical processes relating to silver. By instinct and training Pearce was much more of a scientist than Hill, and he continued to be for years a dominant figure in Colorado sciences related to mining. His presence, even more than Hill's and Baeger's, symbolized the beginning of Colorado's long and ultimately successful attempt to bring science as well as engineering to bear upon problems presented by the complex nature of its ores.[26]

Precisely as Hill was putting his smelting plant into operation for the treatment of gold ores, a whole new field opened up with the beginning of silver production in Clear Creek County, adjacent to "the Little Kingdom of Gilpin." Silver had been discovered there at the end of 1864, but until 1869 little silver ore was produced and smelting facilities were minimal. The delay did not check the burgeoning of a vigorous little boom and the discovery of silver lodes at points widely scattered over Colorado. The state's silver production, after a modest beginning at $600,000 a year in 1869 and 1870, rose to more than $1,000,000 in 1871, to over $2,000,000 in 1872, and to over $3,000,000 in 1874. In the last of these years, the value of the silver output exceeded that of gold for the first time.[27]

Fundamental to the success of these promising developments was the advent of the railroads. In the autumn of 1867 the Union Pacific reached Cheyenne, Wyoming, 110 miles due north of Denver. This in itself was a great improvement over the days when the Missouri frontier was 600 miles distant. Better still, it inspired Coloradans to build the Denver Pacific Railroad between Denver and Cheyenne. The Denver Pacific was barely completed in 1870 before it was rivaled by the Kansas Pacific, which started trains running from Kansas City into Denver in August of that year. The first of many local lines also began in that year, when the Colorado Central was constructed from Denver as far as Golden, which was a gateway to the mountains. After an interval, construction continued and the line wound its way up Clear Creek canyon, reaching Black Hawk in 1872 and offering service to the smelter and a whole chain of Gilpin County mines.[28]

Changes for the better followed quickly. Prices for all commodities, including labor, began to decline, and a marked reduction took place in the cost of transporting ores and fuel to the smelters and mills. Mines that had been idle reopened. It has been axiomatic in Colorado that success in mining and treating ore has never been solely dependent on overcoming technological obstacles, nor even on finding rich ores. Rather, it has been a question of what was financially practicable at the prevailing level of costs, and of these costs transportation has been one of the most important, largely because of the rugged terrain for which Colorado is so famous.

Denver was the principal beneficiary from what was in fact a revolution in transportation. As Jerome C. Smiley pointed out sixty years ago, when he was preparing his excellent pioneer history of Denver: "Prior to 1870 Denver was distinctively a little frontier 'city' presenting the aspects apparently inseparable from every community depending wholly on stage-coach communications. The town was crude. . . . The pioneer manners, practices and customs still held sway. . . ."[29] In size the population was virtually the same in 1870 that it had been in 1860.

The little 'city' made varying impressions on visitors. In July 1863 a Congregationalist missionary wrote home to his Eastern sponsors that Denver stood in the midst of plains so hot, dusty, and bare that he was tempted to make his congregation sing Watts' hymn, "Lord, what a wretched land is this!" "Yet," he went on, "some of the Denverites think they have found the best spot on earth. Poor, deluded mortals! The population of the place is now about four thousand. Much of the society is good, business is brisk, and many of the buildings really fine for so young a city."[30]

A French visitor, four years later, gave an endorsement that was less qualified save in that field of such critical importance to one of his race, food and drink. Denver, he wrote in 1867,

> is well built; the houses are attractive, constructed of brick, stone or wood. Denver has numerous buildings, a theatre, a mint, a race track. . . . M. Talleyrand was right when he said that in North America he had found only one dish and thirty-two religions. There are no cooks in this country, but every one is a little religious. . . . Everywhere are stores, banks, hotels, saloons. As in all the Union, one partakes freely, several times a day, of the sacramental glass of whisky, or some of the iced drinks which the 1867 Exposition brought to the Parisians.[31]

After the railroads reached it in 1870, and as farming and stock raising began to supplement mining as sources of revenue, Denver started to grow with remarkable vigor. In 1870 the recorded population was only 4759; in 1880, it was 35,629. By the latter date Frank Fossett was boasting that Denver had "a dash and animation . . . along with a finish and elegance that suggests prosperity, wealth, and Eastern stability, as well as the progressive and aggressive frontier."[32]

Denver's chief importance was as a center for supplies and finance and a crossroads for transportation. Its location was advantageous. Standing on the plains, just east of the Front Range of the Rockies, Denver had ample space for warehouses, stores, industrial plants, hotels, and homes, and yet it was "a mile high," as Denver people still like to point out. The city was thus a convenient point of transshipment between the long routes that crossed the plains from the east and the steep mountain roads that twisted up through the gulches to the mining centers.

An attempt to start the manufacture of mining machinery in Denver in 1860 proved premature. The business was transferred to Black Hawk two years later, presumably to be nearer the customers. A second iron foundry and machine shop also chose Black Hawk in the 1860s, and two more settled at Central City. But in the first decade after the coming of the railroads, at least five mining equipment manufactories were established in Denver, and that city began to take on an importance comparable to San Francisco's as a designer and builder of that type of machinery. This function was in addition to its more familiar role as an importer of equipment from Chicago, St. Louis, and other cities to the east.[33]

Smelting came to Denver in 1878, when the Boston and Colorado Company moved out of their cramped quarters at Black Hawk and built a new smelter outside Denver, where they would be more centrally located in regard to both fuel and ore. By that time Colorado coal and coke were beginning to be important sources of fuel, while ores for smelting were coming into the market from many other areas in addition to Gilpin County. When other concerns followed the example of the

Boston and Colorado Company, Denver became a major smelting center.[34]

*D*ENVER'S RAPID GROWTH after 1870, its creation of manufacturing facilities to serve the mines, and its connection with both the mines and the Middle West, all these favoring developments stood alongside the technological achievements represented by the reorganization of stamp milling and gold mining, the beginning of smelting, and the start of silver production in Clear Creek and elsewhere. Taken together, these related advances suggest that the decade from 1867 to 1876 was a period of gradual recovery from the collapse of the middle 1860s. In the typical life cycle of a mining country, such a period of depression often follows flush times, a depression that lifts as the region responds to new discoveries, greater capital investment, and technological improvements. Thus the Comstock Lode, after its hard times in the latter half of the 1860s, was placed in a better potential position by Sharon's consolidation of properties, the beginning of railroad service, and a lowering of all costs but labor. Jones's bonanza in the Crown Point mine and the Big Bonanza in the Consolidated Virginia then capitalized on these favorable potentialities to sweep the Comstock Lode into high prosperity in the middle 1870s.

By the year 1877 Colorado had experienced all of these stages of recovery except the final one, the discovery of a true bonanza. One of the richest of the old placer diggings had been California Gulch, that camp at the head of the Arkansas Valley, 10,000 feet above sea level. Just as the early placer miners on what became the Comstock Lode were irritated by heavy "blue stuff" in their gold claims, so the placer miners of California Gulch cursed the heavy sands and rocks that interfered with their gold washing. A decade later, in 1874–1875, two miners with a good analytical sense correctly guessed that the decaying gold camp was probably rich in silver. By great good fortune, in 1876 the St. Louis Smelting and Refining Company sent into that area a well-trained metallurgist, August R. Meyer, who had studied at Freiberg. After demonstrating that the ores were lead carbonates, in 1877 Meyer built a smelter for his employers at the little hamlet that became known as Leadville. Several other smelters followed within a year. The most notable was that erected by James B. Grant on behalf of his Iowa uncle. Grant had prepared himself at Iowa Agricultural College and Cornell University before going to Freiberg for two years of study in mining and metallurgy.[35]

Leadville's boom began in the summer and fall of 1877. In the autumn of that year the future Leadville was a hamlet of log huts. Its population may have been as large as 200, and the "business district" consisted of one grocery store and two saloons. Then began the rush. In headlong haste the crowd came throughout both the summers and winters of the next several years. The deep snows and subzero temperatures on the mountain passes in winter sufficed only to cost men their lives and raise prices to unbelievable levels; mere hardship and danger were not enough to block the rush. Three different routes (financed as toll roads) were opened to bring wagons and stagecoaches into this elevated basin where, as one pioneer remarked, a city was being created "on the very crest of the continent."

When this same pioneer first saw Leadville in January 1879, after forty hours of travel from Denver through blizzard and cold, he found the streets "filled to the center with a constantly moving mass of humanity, from every quarter of the globe, and from every walk of life." It made no difference that the hour was well past midnight. Under the light of thousands of flickering "coal oil" lamps, the crowd still surged up and down the icy main street, the saloons were filled to capacity, tired orchestras beat out popular dance music, and games of faro, keno, roulette, and poker ran continuously. At Pap Wyman's combination dance hall, saloon, and gambling place, a large Bible stood incongruously on the counter, while across the face of a huge clock, behind the bar, was painted the little-heeded admonition, "Please Do Not Swear." Appropriately a local couplet ran:

> *It's day all day in the day-time,*
> *And no night in Leadville.*[36]

By 1880 Leadville had 14,820 citizens and was the second city in the state. Like most Western vein-mining centers, it had a substantial percentage of foreign-born, amounting to more than a third of the total. Irishmen, Cornishmen, Canadians, and Germans formed an important part of the labor force.[37] Leadville was as big as the Comstock Lode's Virginia City and Gold Hill combined, and far more lively than that fading mining capital in 1880. By then Leadville had twenty-eight miles of streets, gas lights, a water works, thirteen schools, five churches, three hospitals, fourteen smelters, and about thirty producing mines. Railroad service reached it in the summer of 1880 and enormously simplified the problem of shipping out ore and bullion and bringing in supplies and fuel.[38]

Leadville's annual output of silver soon surpassed that of any foreign nation except Mexico, and its auxiliary production of lead was nearly equal to England's. It never achieved the huge annual figures for silver reached by the Comstock Lode during its bonanza eras, but it was easily the second biggest producer discovered in America up to that time, and its boom years very closely complemented the Comstock Lode's. The Comstock Lode's sudden decline came in 1878–1880. Leadville, after starting up in 1877, had its first big year in 1878, when it surpassed $2,000,000. In 1879 it reached nearly $9,500,000 in value, and in 1880 nearly $11,500,000. This coincided with the peak in silver-lead production at Eureka, Nevada, but Leadville outlasted Eureka by many years and greatly exceeded it in both total quantity and size of output in individual bonanza years. Lead production had its first big year in 1879, when it totalled approximately $1,775,000. Thereafter it was normally above $2,000,000. Copper production began to be recorded in 1884 and zinc in 1885.[39]

This remarkably quick and successful development demands an explanation, and the more so in view of the great difficulties that so frustrated early smelting efforts elsewhere in the West. Part of the answer is technological. One of the early scientific appraisals pointed out that "the ores of Leadville are remarkably pure argentiferous lead ores," and a veteran of the ore business recalled that Leadville's ores "were comparatively easy to reduce."[40] Another part of the answer is economic. Like Eureka, Nevada, but unlike Gilpin County, there was a commercially valuable base metal that was available in quantity as soon as transportation costs were reduced. It was here that the railroad was so important. It made possible the export of lead-silver bullion and ores, and at the same time it also solved what would have been a severe crisis in fuel. Although the spruce forests were being stripped to make charcoal, they produced charcoal of varying quality and high cost. With the advent of railroads, coke made from Colorado coals began coming into Leadville from two different areas. Similarly, limestone for fluxes was hauled into Leadville by rail from points that ranged from 16 to over 100 miles distant.[41]

All the foregoing were favoring factors, and yet perhaps the most important element was not material but intellectual. A governmental report of 1882 concluded that smelting at Leadville, "while not entirely beyond criticism, has been brought to a relatively high degree of perfection, and is extremely creditable to American metallurgists." The lesson taught by Leadville, the report continued, was that the success of each smelter was in direct proportion "to the more thorough training in scientific metallurgy of its managers, the completeness and accuracy with which they have gauged the operations of their furnaces by chemical tests, and the intelligence with which the results of these tests have been applied to the practical conduct of their business."

All of this was in most happy contrast to the widespread conviction that because the American was a jack of all trades, therefore he could "master the science of smelting as readily as he does any branch of trade." Recognition of this fallacy could "prevent an increase of the already very considerable number of abandoned smelters which dot our western hills and valleys."[42]

Smelting, in order words, was a scientific business that needed to be directed by men trained in applied science. It was significant that two of the pioneer smelting men at Leadville, Meyer and Grant, had studied at Freiberg, just as it was significant that success in silver-lead smelting at Oreana and Eureka, Nevada, and pyritic gold smelting at Black Hawk, came after leadership was assumed by men who turned quite frankly to European precedents. The American technical reports and papers of that day were crowded with descriptions of German, British, and French furnaces and techniques. By 1877, after nearly a decade of trial and error in Colorado, Nevada, Montana, and Utah, enough information was in print and enough men with training in metallurgy, mineralogy, and chemistry were available to make unnecessary (although not improbable) a continuance of the wasteful, amateurish false starts against which this government report was protesting.

The principal author of this report on smelting at Leadville was Samuel F. Emmons, a Harvard graduate who had studied at the French *Ecole des Mines* and at Freiberg. When the United States Geological Survey was formed in 1879 by consolidating several existing governmental surveys, Emmons was placed in charge of the Rocky Mountain division, with headquarters at Denver. Unlike some of the early government geologists, he realized the importance of proving that geology was not solely an ivory-tower discipline, just as he was also convinced that the working miner could not afford to neglect geology. "For a time," Emmons said, "the miner may develop his mine successfully by simply following the ore lead, guided by the empirical rules which experience has taught him," disregarding considerations of structural geology, ore deposition, and the like; "but the time is sure to come when without this knowledge he will be liable to make mistakes which may cost him more than he has gained by all his previous labors."[43]

Both the first director of the United States Geological Survey, Clarence King, and his successor, John Wesley Powell, were determined to have their new organization examine "questions of immediate and direct importance to the mining industries."[44] Leadville was one of the three Far Western mining communities for which King initiated research projects intended to produce highly detailed monographs. The other two were the Comstock Lode and Eureka, Nevada—all silver regions, but one of them then beginning its decline.

In August and September, 1879, Emmons put topographers to work in the Leadville region, and in December, 1879, he began studying the Leadville deposits himself. Throughout 1880, despite fifteen to twenty feet of snow in winter, he kept the project going, with a crew of chemists, metallurgists, and petrographers supplementing his own efforts. By the autumn of 1881 his collaborative project was far enough along that a substantial abstract could be published for the immediate guidance of miners. Publication of the full monograph had to wait five years for congressional appropriations.

Emmons' monograph on the *Geology and Mining Industry of Leadville* genuinely deserves that over-used phrase "epoch-making." Even today it is still referred to as "the miners' bible." More than any other event, the publication of this scientific study convinced skeptical mining operators that they could learn something of cash value from university men. The layman's delighted and somewhat naïve amazement was well reflected in a comment by the publisher of Leadville's principal newspaper. Enthusiastically this journalist declared that Emmons and his colleagues had reduced "the pursuit of mining to a fixed science, . . . enabling the miner to sink with intelligence, to drift with knowledge, to cross-cut with certainty, to discover, extract and hoist the ore to the surface with economic appliances, securing the maximum results with the minimum of labor cost."[45]

Central to Emmons' conclusions was the finding that the Leadville ores occurred as replacement deposits in limestone. In his report for 1880–1881, the director of the United States Geological Survey pointed out that the significance of Emmons' research extended far beyond Leadville, because elsewhere in the Rockies there were many other examples "of this hitherto little studied class of deposits—of which Leadville may properly be considered the type region."[46] Powell, the director, might have added that at that same time another team of the Geological Survey was discovering that the replacement deposits of Eureka, Nevada, were very similar to Leadville's. The Eureka studies, published in three installments from 1884–1892, were overshadowed by Emmons' monograph, but together the Leadville and Eureka research projects established the West's new understanding of replacement deposits upon as firm a basis as the long accumulating knowledge of veins.

As an interesting indication of the industry's changing attitude, in 1891 the director of the United States Geological Survey received from Aspen, Colorado, a petition signed by fifty-one local mining men. After appealing for a survey similar to that made at Leadville, the petition concluded: "The undersigned mine managers and owners, impressed with the value of the work being done by your department in Leadville feel that this district offers an opportunity for similarly valuable scientific research."[47]

Nor did Emmons' immediate efforts stop with his notable research at Leadville. At his invitation, on the evening of December 8, 1882, a little group of interested men met in the rooms of the United States Geological Survey, in Denver, to found the Colorado Scientific Society. Emmons was elected president, Richard Pearce vice president, and Whitman Cross, of the United States Geological Survey, secretary. The early members of the society included metallurgists, assayers, chemists, geologists, mining managers, mining engineers, and one minister, all of whom agreed that the time had come to form a society for the exchange of scientific observations and ideas.[48]

To create an organization that brought men of science into contact with those who needed to apply the ideas of science in their daily work was a notable achievement. Colorado, after twenty years of groping, was finding that science was the key to exploiting its complex and varied ores. By using that key, Colorado was at last achieving an annual mineral production that made it rank as very nearly the most important of the western mining States. Yet in as individualistic an industry as mining, all were not converted easily or at once. The history of the Colorado Scientific Society illustrates this. At the New Year's meeting of 1888 the retiring president complained of "the indifference and lack of sympathy of the community" for the society's work.[49] If Denver had not been the regional headquarters of the United States Geological Survey, the society could scarcely have existed. The original inspiration, many of the most active members, and many of the best papers came from men attached to the Denver office of that organization.

The society did not fully come into its own until a half-dozen years later. In the meantime, Colorado was favored with a series of brilliant silver discoveries in all parts of the state, but especially across the Continental Divide, from Aspen in the north to Rico and Creede in the remote and broken San Juan country in the south. Silver and lead production was large throughout the 1880s and was increasing in the early 1890s. With the international price of silver sagging badly, something of the importance of these great districts was taken from them, and mining men began casting about for what a government geologist termed "a more profitable field for their operations than silver mining."[50]

Amazingly enough, nature yielded up this bounty, too, and in a part of Colorado that was easily accessible, one that had been well known for years and had hitherto been prospected unsuccessfully. At Cripple Creek, near Pikes Peak, gold was discovered in 1890–1891. Skepticism as to the genuineness of the alleged discoveries in so well-known a district retarded the usual rush during the first two years, but thereafter Cripple Creek became El Dorado, a miniature California with modern conveniences. A cow ranch in 1891, it had become a town of 10,000 in 1894. At the latter date it had electric lights, telegraph and telephone lines, daily newspapers, and connections with two railroads.[51]

The ores at Cripple Creek occurred in an unusual setting, in the throat of an old volcano, and in an unfamiliar form, as tellurides. Richard Pearce, now a veteran of more than twenty years in Colorado, took the lead in bringing science to the aid of the puzzled mining industry. Pearce presented two papers on Cripple Creek ores to the Colorado Scientific Society at its meetings in the winter and spring of 1894, and a third article a year later. The society arranged a special discussion for its meeting of June 4, 1894. Whitman Cross of the United States Geological Survey, who had been one of the founders of the society and who had worked with Emmons at Leadville, was sent to Cripple Creek in the summer of 1893 to begin a major governmental study that would be comparable to Emmons' research of a dozen years earlier. His associates were Richard A. F. Penrose, Jr., of the University of Chicago, and Edward B. Mathews, of Johns Hopkins University. With the permission of the director of the United States Geological Survey, Cross and Penrose presented preliminary reports to the society on June 4, and these reports were printed at once in pamphlet form for quick distribution.

At the June meeting a lively discussion grew out of the oral presentation by Cross and Penrose. Philip Argall, a young metallurgist who had already seen service in Ireland, Cornwall, Wales, New Zealand, Mexico, and Leadville, and now was beginning at Cripple Creek, commented on the great value of such papers to all engaged in mining work, "giving, as they do, a clear insight into the geology of mining districts, and often indicating with remarkable exactness the probable limits within which active explorations may reasonably be expected to give economic results." The Cornishman T. A. Rickard, then a practicing engineer, but presently to become the most distinguished editor of mining journals of his day, made the further point that Cross's paper was "particularly opportune. Only too often the geological reports of the United States Survey are published so late that, on account of the rapidity of western mine development, they partake very much of the nature of obituary notices. The determination of the different rock species at Cripple Creek, will be of immediate utility."[52]

Here was decisive evidence of the new status science had won for itself in Colorado mining. It would be hard to comprehend the great changes of the late nineteenth century without understanding the new influence of science. But applied science alone could never have made possible the mining that developed in these years. Engineering, also, made notable advances, as a few specific illustrations will suggest. The Burleigh compressed air drill was tried successfully in Colorado in the late 1860s and was being employed in several different tunnels in that state in the early 1870s, before it had won acceptance in either California or Nevada. Electricity as a source of power in mines was introduced as early as 1888 in a tunnel at Aspen, when a street car motor was used for hauling and hoisting. The widespread adoption of electricity by Colorado mines facilitated the working of claims at sites far too precipitous to permit the hauling of fuel for ordinary steam engines. Similarly, Colorado was at least as quick as the Pacific coast to try overhead, suspended tramways as a means of getting ore down from a mountain top and getting supplies up to it.

Such influential technical changes and the vastly increased and varied output of mines, mills, and smelters, as well as the corresponding increase in invested capital that that implies, made Colorado mining in the late nineteenth century a vastly different world from the exaggerated dreams and crude realities of 1859. The fumbling placer miner of 1859 was linked to the Freiberg-trained metallurgist of 1879 only by the continuing faith of the few thousand men of Gilpin County who for a decade refused to admit that as a mining commonwealth Colorado was finished when its initial flush days were over. In their struggle to make mining pay, these stubborn "rock miners" were not always open to even well-tested innovation, but their resolute efforts kept Colorado mining before the public until the day when dramatically new opportunities could once more make Colorado the wonder of the mining West.

◁ 7 ▷

Northwest and Southwest
1860-1880

*I*n January of each year the leading mining journal, the *Mining and Scientific Press,* gave its readers a comprehensive appraisal of Western mining. In the 1860s and 1870s, the *Press's* annual reviews stressed California and Nevada, because those two were the biggest producers of bullion and the leaders in mining technology. As the *Press* pointed out in January of 1882:

> Up to within the past few years the States of California and Nevada have overshadowed all the others in the mining interests. Now these two States are by no means so much ahead of others. Colorado heads the list, California coming second and Nevada third.[1]

Twelve months earlier the *Press's* annual review had used quite similar language but had specified the particular states and territories it had in mind. Where once, the article said, California and Nevada had "far overshadowed Montana, Idaho, Colorado and Utah, . . . now all of them are large bullion producers, and to them are added Arizona and New Mexico," while in the meantime the Comstock Lode had run out of bonanzas and Leadville had rushed into great richness.[2]

Colorado's rise to pre-eminence was thus the foreshadowing of a mining revival that was to affect many parts of both Northwest and Southwest during the 1880s. The decade that opened with the Fraser River rush in 1858 had carried prospectors and miners into the whole vast region from the eastern Rockies to the Pacific. With the brilliant exception of Nevada, more particularly the Comstock Lode, this great mining advance was based primarily upon gold placers. Where rich and extensive placers were discovered, as they were in so much of the Northwest, a quick boom created camps, towns, and transportation facilities within a few weeks or months. Where the placers were limited, as they were in most of such Southwestern territories as Utah, Arizona, and New Mexico, fewer miners and little capital followed after the prospectors; and Indian danger, poor transportation, and natural obstacles became towering discouragements that repulsed all save the unusually determined.

The potentially rich veins that were known to exist in both Northwest and Southwest were an ever promising, usually elusive attraction. Thousands of individuals squandered their health and fortunes, and sometimes their lives, in futile attempts to open a new Comstock Lode in Idaho or Arizona or Utah. Their failures they attributed to lack of railroads and resultant high costs, "refractory ores," and hostile Indians.

Looking back upon this uneven development almost a century later, it is possible to discern certain common features. Throughout both Northwest and Southwest the 1860s were years of intense excitement and eager anticipation. While the anticipation rarely materialized into reality in the Southwest, in many parts of the Northwest thorough-going flush times ruled for a half-dozen years. By the end of the 1860s decline was widespread, except in the special case of Utah presently to be discussed. The 1870s were years of discouragement, as men struggled to put into production the principal remaining resource, veins. In a few favored areas, scattered through both Northwest and Southwest, a new mining boom of major proportions came during the late 1870s and the 1880s. Very commonly, though not invariably, it involved silver more than gold, and it brought into great prominence either lead or copper. Where a base metal was involved, extensive smelting facilities developed, together with the attendant service industries. Always this late boom was closely related to new railroads, new technical knowledge, and a new ability to attract heavy capital investment. The result was that many mining settlements were carried well beyond any stage of society that could reasonably be called the frontier. They became, instead, industrial islands in the midst of forest, desert, or mountain, located in Victorian isolation along a railroad branch line, hours distant from the nearest regional capital, such as Denver, Salt Lake City, or Spokane,

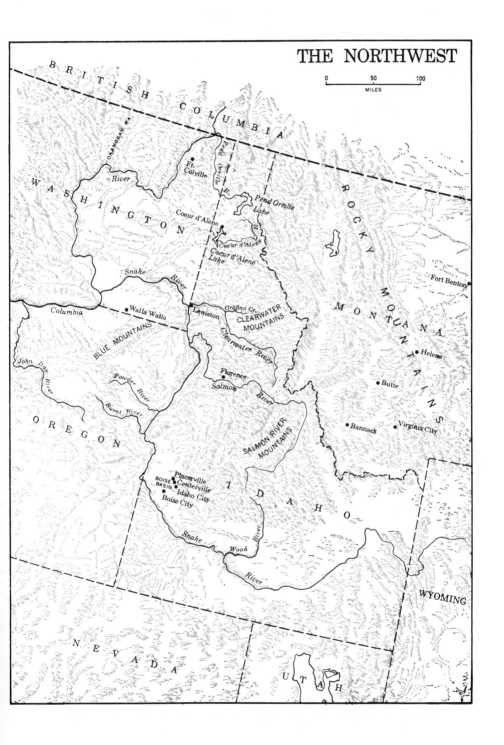

THE NORTHWEST

0   50   100
MILES

BRITISH COLUMBIA

WASHINGTON

ROCKY MOUNTAINS

MONTANA

OREGON

IDAHO

NEVADA

UTAH

WYOMING

Ft. Colville
Pend Oreille Lake
Coeur d'Alene
Coeur d'Alene Lake
Fort Benton
Snake River
Columbia
Walla Walla
Lewiston
Orofino Cr.
CLEARWATER MOUNTAINS
Clearwater River
BLUE MOUNTAINS
John Day River
Powder River
Florence
Salmon
Burnt River
Helena
Butte
Salmon River
Bannack
Virginia City
SALMON RIVER MOUNTAINS
Placerville
BOISE BASIN
Centerville
Idaho City
Boise City
Snake
Wood River
Okanogan R.
Pend Oreille R.

and days removed from the cities that came to control so many of them: New York, San Francisco, Chicago, Boston, or even London.

*O*F ALL THE NEW REGIONS that opened to mining during the 1860s, Idaho and Montana came closest to making a reality of the prospector's dream of finding a new California. Here were rich and extensive placers that could be worked with simple equipment. Here were promising lodes of both gold and silver.

By the thousands men hurried in from the Western lands of California, Oregon, British Columbia, Nevada, and Colorado and from the Eastern lands behind the Missouri River. "Yon-siders," familiar with the ways of the Far West, met Easterners, whom they called "pilgrims" and regarded condescendingly as greenhorns.

Idaho's virgin wilderness was the first to be attacked. Gold was discovered in the summer and autumn of 1860 in northern Idaho, in the region drained by the Clearwater River and its small tributaries, such as Orofino Creek. Although this was Nez Percé Indian country, a few determined prospectors managed to winter along Orofino Creek. A much larger number impatiently assembled during the winter at the frontier outfitting town of Walla Walla, Washington Territory, while others founded Lewiston, Idaho, as an advanced depot on the Snake River, opposite the mouth of the Clearwater.

Before the snow was off the ground, the crowd was hurrying into the wilderness, thrusting aside the Nez Percés wherever they encountered them. Camps like Orofino sprang into existence in 1861, only to be hastily abandoned within the year when news arrived of gold in the Salmon River region, farther to the south. Florence, as the new center of the Salmon River mines, struggled into being during the winter of 1861–1862, despite heavy snows, intense cold, intolerable trails, and a shortage of food so great as to cause scurvy and near-starvation. Then the great placers of the Boise Basin of southwest Idaho were discovered in the summer and autumn of 1862, and Florence, in its turn, was deserted for the new mecca.[3]

Even when judged by Western standards, Idaho's gold rush people were extraordinarily unstable. In a famous and vivid simile, the historian Hubert Howe Bancroft described them: "The miners of Idaho were like quicksilver. A mass of them dropped in any locality, broke up into individual globules, and ran off after any atom of gold in their vicinity. They stayed nowhere longer than the gold attracted them."[4] At each new point of promising discovery, camps of tents and "wikiups" (brush shelters) were quickly replaced by towns of log cabins, frame buildings, and the few brick structures of which each community boasted so inordinately. At first logs and whip-sawed lumber served all purposes, for rockers, sluices, and houses, but soon sawmills were brought in and were run literally day and night. Men waited in line to buy the green lumber as fast as it was cut.

The Boise Basin became easily the most productive and most heavily populated part of Idaho. John Hailey, a pioneer who wrote his account many years later, believed that there were about 16,000 men in the Boise Basin during the warm months of 1864, and a local census taken in that year approximately confirms his figure.[5] A great geologist of a later day made a "rough estimate" that the Basin probably produced three million dollars in 1863, four in 1864, and five in each of 1865 and 1866.[6] This was more than the whole Colorado Territory was producing in these same years.

Since wagon roads into the basin from the Columbia River were not completed until the summer of 1864, all supplies for this very large crowd had to be brought in by pack trains. The distance from the Columbia was about 300 miles; a pack train's normal speed, 10 to 15 miles per day.[7] How this affected prices can easily be imagined.

As Hailey remembered it, perhaps half the people of the basin were engaged in mining; the other half in serving those who mined.[8] This division of labor was not unlike that ascribed to California in its flush days. Merchants, lumbermen, hotel, restaurant, and saloon keepers, gamblers, theatrical people, blacksmiths, lawyers, teamsters, ranchers, even an occasional minister, all these could be seen thrusting their way through the crowded, crooked streets of the basin's towns and camps. Noise and restless activity dominated daily life. As William L. McConnell, later governor and senator, recreated a typical Idaho scene:

> The braying of the pack-mules, and the clatter of the carpenters' and the blacksmiths' hammers gave zest to the hundreds of pedestrians continually moving about the streets from one place to another as fancy or some excitement attracted them. Violin music was heard in most of the saloons, and gambling was an adjunct of them all. New arrivals were almost continuous and departures of prospecting parties were of daily occurrence.[9]

It was a confusing society, lacking in ready coherence. In the early Idaho camps Californians and Oregonians were numerous and prominent, in fact usually the dominant element, although there was also an admixture of dissatisfied refugees from the Colorado placers and wanderers from Nevada to the south and British Columbia to the north. Incongruously, in southern Idaho large wagon trains of settlers bound for the Pacific coast kept passing through over the Oregon Trail. With them came the household belongings typical of farm families, including milch cows, chickens, and sewing machines. At night the flickering fires of their big encampments proved irresistibly attractive to gold seekers, who sought there the privilege of being with white women and children again, and perhaps of getting some "home-cooked" food or buying those great luxuries, fresh eggs, milk, and fowl. A few even worked their way past the suspicions of cautious parents to be allowed to talk with the young girls.[10]

Some of the westward-moving settlers changed their plans and stopped permanently in southern Idaho to start raising food for the market so suddenly opened by the mining camps. As the Civil War dragged out its weary course, many families of Confederate sympathizers fled to Idaho to escape the guerrilla warfare in Missouri. By 1864 they were giving a pro-Southern prejudice to local politics.

The process in Montana started somewhat later; indeed it drew off some of Idaho's volatile pioneers. Key discoveries were made at Bannack in the summer of 1862, at Alder Gulch (where Virginia City was founded) in 1863, Last Chance Gulch (where Helena developed) in 1864, at Butte in the same year, and at Confederate and Emigrant Gulches. Exploitation of them, Rossiter Raymond remarked, seemed to "travel in a circle."[11] One gulch would be abandoned when a better-promising one was discovered elsewhere, but upon subsequent re-examination, the first gulch would again be taken up, presumably by new people.

With its routes of travel favoring the Mississippi and Missouri valleys, Montana had a heavy influx from the center of America. Bishop Daniel S. Tuttle, the universally loved Episcopal missionary bishop, said of Helena in 1868–1869:

> the men were from everywhere. Helena was, indeed, that far cosmopolitan. There were more from Missouri than from any other one state, and the next greatest number I think were from Iowa. Multitudes had come, also, directly from California and Nevada, and there were, besides, a few Englishmen and a good many Canadians. Among the miners were many Cornishmen and Irishmen. To crown all, a considerable squad of negroes, mostly from Missouri, had wandered over from the boats and landing of Fort Benton.

Women, the bishop reported, were still exceedingly few—as was the case in all new mining towns. Bishop Tuttle guessed that the ladies were outnumbered by "seven or ten to one." (The bishop overestimated by a little. When the census was taken about a year later, 81 percent of Montana's population was male.) But if they were lacking in numbers, the ladies were hardly backward in other respects. When Mrs. Tuttle arrived from New York State in 1868 to join her husband, she expected primitive hardship and simplicity. While she unquestionably found the former as soon as she started housekeeping at Helena, she was amazed to have the local ladies come trooping in for social calls "arrayed in silk and adorned with gold and jewels." Mrs. Tuttle, her husband remarked, "had yet to learn that the mountain people would have the best of everything regardless of expense." The display of finery did not necessarily imply luxurious living, for Mrs. Tuttle found that most ladies did their own housework. Among the ladies she was glad to find a few—"comparatively few"—who were people of "refinement, cultivation, and education."[12]

Bishop Tuttle had preceded his wife to Montana by more than a year. The letters he wrote home during 1867 and 1868 vividly described what he saw and heard in Helena and Virginia City, Montana. Like Governor McConnell's recollections of Idaho mining towns, the Bishop was impressed by the amount of noise: the "confused din of auctioneers and teamsters"; a Negro with a handbell crying out a list of goods to be sold that day; dance music and drunken cursing from the "hurdy-gurdy" houses; whisky-stimulated "profanity and blasphemy" from a Democratic meeting.

Helena and Virginia City at that time were large towns filled with log cabins, a few frame houses, and a few stone store buildings. Stores were surprisingly numerous—100 or more in Helena, the bishop thought. Saloons were equally common. Hurdy-gurdy houses were well patronized. On Sunday church services were held, but the stores, auctioneers, saloons, and hurdy-gurdy houses continued in full operation, because that was the day when miners from all the gulches around the town crowded in to buy their supplies and have a carnival good time.

At such times, "jostling men" filled the sidewalks and "be-pistoled and be-knived" men passed on horseback in the street, where they had to thread their way past ox-drawn "huge freight wagons, from which goods were being discharged, that had been dragged five hundred miles from Salt Lake, or two hundred and sixty-five miles from Fort Benton on the Missouri River."[13]

The bishop's reference to the long haul for supplies touched upon a major handicap to the continued prosperity of both Montana and Idaho. Both came into being because of virgin placers that were rich enough to cause all obstacles temporarily to be overcome—to the limited extent necessary for simple placer mining and gold rush people. The realities of physical geography were so forbidding as to make it doubtful whether a more permanent, more exacting society could develop to take the place of the inevitably short-lived placer camps.

Idaho's best diggings were in the Boise Basin, where the topography and climate were not unreasonable and where local traveling distances were moderate; but the other Idaho gold fields were lost in the tangled mass of mountains that dominate the northern two thirds of the state and intrude into parts of the south. J. Ross Browne reported that "the mines of Idaho occur in isolated groups separated by long tracts apparently barren in the precious metals."[14] Some camps were at altitudes quite high enough to produce snow-bound winters. Some could be reached only by pack trails.

Montana's diggings were in the gulches and high mountain valleys of the unevenly furrowed northern Rockies. The camps were difficult of access and difficult to live in. "In ordinary years," a correspondent noted, "the placer miner can count upon eight months, during which the streams are not frozen, and hence he must earn enough during two-thirds of the year to support him during a twelvemonth."[15] It became customary for many Montana placer miners to go south each autumn, either by voyaging down the Missouri River in homemade boats, or by journeying overland to work in the vein mines of Utah, Nevada, and California. Some returned to the Montana placers in the spring; the discouraged failed to come back at all.

Transportation within both territories was difficult and expensive, and transportation to and from the outer world was worse. Contemporaries felt that of the two Idaho was better situated, since it had regular and fairly good service over the roundabout route by water from San Francisco and up the Columbia and thence overland to the mining towns. But this was a long and costly trip, and it is significant that the Idaho merchants protested so often against the high charges levied by the Oregonians for the use of their steamers on the Columbia and Snake rivers and their toll roads from the Columbia to the Boise Basin. Idaho newspapers and merchants eagerly supported each of the attempts to open direct wagon routes from the upper Sacramento Valley of California to southern Idaho. The alternative was to patronize the teamsters who hauled supplies up from Salt Lake City and across the Snake River plains.

Montana's situation was definitely unfavorable. After traveling over Montana in 1871, Rossiter Raymond concluded: "When it is considered with what difficulty and expense communication, travel, and transportation are maintained between the Territory of Montana and the rest of the world, it seems marvelous that any one should come there or stop there at all." Raymond regarded steamboat service to Montana, via the Missouri, as both "tedious and precarious," with low water always interrupting it too soon. Nor did the land route impress him, with its haul of 450 miles northward from Utah, across "the vast basaltic plains of the Snake River" and up through a succession of Montana valleys. "Montana," he felt, "is heavily weighted in the race with other Territories."[16] At as late a date as 1879, a writer of western guidebooks said of Montana that "no other territory has been so isolated."[17]

The obstacles presented by nature were reinforced by Indian troubles of a serious nature. The Northwestern Indians, taken as a whole, were far more competent than their fellows of California and the Great Basin. They had reason to be resentful, for the early gold discoveries cut into reservations that had been guaranteed to them. Periodically the Indians burst out in hostilities that made prospecting and isolated mining very dangerous. Prospectors learned to operate in large, well-armed bands, instead of going off alone or with one or two partners, as was so common in California and the Great Basin.

As between the two territories, Montana's placers were the richer, and they continued to pay well for at least two years after Idaho had begun its decline. More hydraulic mining was introduced there than in Idaho, and with good results, especially after the latest improvements were imported from California. In neither territory was gold found in quantities at all comparable to California's huge yield in the 1850s, nor even equal to California's reduced yield during the 1860s. But both Montana and Idaho during the 1860s had a much larger output than Colorado, and much larger also than that of any of the other Northwestern regions of Oregon, Washington, or British Columbia. The statistics are in too chaotic a condition, however, to justify precise comparison.[18]

As with all new placer regions, flush production developed quickly and fell off with like rapidity. By 1870 both territories were losing population and declining in output of treasure. Idaho was the earlier of the two to suffer and the slower to recover. Its recorded population of 14,999 in 1870 can not have been more than half the number that had come to Idaho for varying periods of time during the decade. Local censuses and estimates by assessors claimed 20,656 residents in September 1863; 24,631 in the summer of 1864, and 21,725 in September 1866. As the pioneer John Hailey remembered it, in the autumn of 1864 many miners left Idaho, some to return temporarily to California, Oregon, or Washington for the winter, others, who had sold out, to leave Idaho forever. Probably the placers of northern Idaho were already declining by then, but with the placers of Boise Basin just rising to their peak in production, the spring of 1865 still saw a large influx of gold seekers into that favored area. A year later the crowd of spring arrivals even into the Boise Basin was thinning, and thereafter Idaho was losing population fairly rapidly. It is quite probable that the decline in gold production was distinctly slower than the loss of people.[19]

Particularly interesting was the transfer of claims from whites to Chinese. Resistance to the Chinese in Idaho was bitter during the early years, and hostile legislation was passed, but as each camp began to decline, the claim holders became eager to sell out to the Chinese, who were willing to work for a more modest return than the whites. In 1870, 4274 of the 14,999 people in Idaho were Chinese. The census's classification by occupation listed a total of 6579 men of all races as "miners." Of these, 3853 were Chinese.[20] In other words, more than half of all the miners the census could find were Chinese. In his report covering 1873, Rossiter Raymond said that in Idaho "for every well-paying claim worked by white men, we find at present probably not less than five or six which return profits only to Chinamen, and a few camps are almost exclusively worked and owned by them."[21] This numerical dominance by Oriental miners continued down to 1880. At that time the ratio of Chinese to whites among the general population was higher in Idaho than in any state or territory in the Union.[22] The origin of this lay in the unwillingness of whites to continue struggling with placers that still contained large amounts of gold, but not in as great an abundance as formerly.

Montana, with a recorded population of 20,595 in 1870, appears to have been somewhat more successful in retaining the people who had come to it. The annual exodus of placer miners at the end of the summer season makes it unusually difficult to guess how many people were in Montana during the 1860s. The assessors and tax collectors said that the size of the population "remained very nearly constant" at a figure of 21,000 to 24,000 between the autumn of 1864 and 1867.[23] If this was true, it still give no guidance as to how great the turnover was, that is, the annual replacement by newcomers of old timers who had decided against returning. The boom years were from 1862 through 1868. Production of gold seems to have fallen sharply during the half-dozen years beginning with 1869.

In contrast to Idaho, in 1870 there were only 1949 Chinese in Montana out of the total of over 20,000 people. Of the 6720 "miners" listed by the census, 1415 were Chinese, a little more than one out of every five. The ratio was approximately the same in 1880.[24]

In both territories the expectation was that vein mines of gold and silver would take the place of the declining placers, and much was said about the greater stability this would bring to Northwestern society. It was hoped that vein mines and their attendant reduction works, since they required considerable investment and might last for years, would attract a steady labor force and a group of service industries that would build up real communities, in place of the evanescent placer camps. Through a most happy paradox, the lode mines of the later 1860s and the 1870s did indeed have much of this desired effect. The pioneer farmers, merchants, bankers, teamsters, and local iron workers and machinists found an important part of their business in supplying the ever hopeful, often unsuccessful vein miners and their associates at the reduction plants.

But the mines themselves, and the reduction plants, fared badly. Most were small, poorly financed, badly equipped, of uncertain value, and managed by men of limited knowledge and experience. Many of the owners and promoters were placer men who underestimated the difficulty and expense of opening veins, overestimated their veins' richness, and expected the quick returns to which they had become accustomed in placer mining. Under such heavy handicaps, cycles of brief prosperity alternated with discouraging periods of inactivity or profitlessness.

*C*OMMON TO ALL in the Northwest was the complaint of isolation. The word runs through the reports on individual mines, mills, and smelters. The mining men themselves used the term to explain why it was so costly to bring in supplies and heavy equipment or to export ore or bullion, why labor was so high and scarce. They also used it to explain why it was so difficult to attract capital from San Francisco, the Atlantic coast, or the Middle West in competition with California, Nevada, or Colorado, all of which had a head start and were then being reached by railroads. Some outside capital was indeed drawn in, but much of it was wasted on ill-managed or dishonest operations that accomplished little except to give the Northwest a bad name among investors.[25]

To external observers it seemed equally clear that intellectual isolation was a significant part of the problem. Rossiter Raymond remarked that "in isolated districts like those of Montana, there is frequently a surprising ignorance of what has been done elsewhere in the way of determining the best machinery and processes; and the miner frequently wastes his time and money in experiments which have long ago been rendered unnecessary."[26] Two years later, in his report for 1873, Raymond reached the unflattering conclusion that Montana "has not been fruitful of inventions and improvements in mining. Its isolated and remote position has caused it rather to lag behind other mining regions of the country, even in the adoption of improvements already known."[27]

This was criticism by an outsider; yet it was admitted and even echoed by discouraged Montanans during the 1870s. Having been one of the West's great placer regions, Montana was now struggling through a difficult transition, one comparable to the experience Colorado passed through after the middle 1860s, an intermediate phase that would lead to a new type of mining based upon successful handling of varied and complex ores. Like Colorado, ultimate victory would be founded upon a combination of silver and base metals, upon an influx of ideas and capital from outside, and upon the opening of railroad service to the main part of the nation. Unlike Colorado, the evolution of a new mining economy was to center in one area, the vicinity of Butte. Butte, by itself, was to Montana what Gilpin County and Leadville jointly were to Colorado.

While not as rich as some areas, Butte had nevertheless been a prosperous placer camp until late in the 1860s. Soon thereafter it began sagging down almost to the level of a ghost town. The census of 1870 credited it with only 241 people, of whom 98 were Chinese. In the middle of the 1870s Butte was rescued by a combination of local and external forces. Local working miners started it. With very little capital but their own labor, miners such as William L. Farlin and William J. Parks stubbornly persisted in trying to develop lode claims. Although the early Butte lode mines had been sought principally for free milling gold quartz, the interest now was in the black, manganese-stained silver ores, which could not be handled by simple stamp mills and amalgamation. An additional treatment was necessary to render the ores "docile."[28]

The discovery of a practicable technique and the opening of veins and processing plants proved too complex and expensive a business for the local miners to master solely through their own efforts. There were in Montana by then merchants and bankers who had profited comfortably from serving the mining camps during the flush days. By the 1870s men such as William Andrews Clark, Samuel T. Hauser, and Andrew J. Davis had money to spare and were investing in local properties and businesses of many kinds. All had had experience with mines in Montana in earlier days, and usually also in California, Colorado, or some other mining region before that. Like most men who had once suffered from the "mining fever," they never overcame the itching desire to speculate in mines. One of them, Clark, was unique in that, recognizing his own deficiencies, he traveled east to Columbia University's new School of Mines to spend the winter of 1872–1873 in studying mineralogy, assaying, and analysis.[29]

When Farlin failed financially, after spending all of 1875 in a promising attempt to open a silver lode and operate a stamp mill and associated furnace, Clark took over, made a success of it, and thus demonstrated that Butte's rather difficult silver ores could be worked profitably. Other men hurried into similar activities, and Butte now began to regain population as word spread that a silver boom was opening.

Through their banking and commercial activities, Clark, Hauser, and Davis were in contact with banks, investment houses, and mining interests in many parts of the United States and even in Europe. As the 1880s opened, "outside" capital began coming into Montana through the agency of these local capitalists, who served as middlemen and often as coinvestors in the purchase of claims and embryonic reduction plants at Butte.

Initially the primary interest was in silver, but discerning local men were aware that Butte had also copper ores of significance. Just how important the copper ores might prove to be was not appreciated by any one. With transportation to the outside world still an obstacle, there was little chance of developing a base metal on a large scale. Small quantities of both silver and copper ores, presumably of very high grade, were exported in ox and mule wagons to the nearest railroad point, which was 400 miles away in Utah. Thence the ores were shipped to smelters in Utah, Colorado, Omaha, Baltimore, Newark, and Germany.

A shipment by Clark to the Boston and Colorado Smelting Company, at Black Hawk, produced such good results that Clark induced the Boston and Colorado Company to join him in creating the Colorado and Montana Smelting Company (1879), which built a successful experimental copper smelter at Butte and thereby established a limited local market for copper ores. When a narrow-gauge railroad from Ogden, Utah, was finally built through to Butte in 1881, after ten years of spasmodic promotion by interests from outside Montana, Butte was ready to add a copper boom to its burgeoning silver output.

In the meantime, back in 1875, a shipment of silver ore from Butte to a Utah smelter had proved so rich that the proprietors of the smelter, the Walker brothers of Salt Lake City, had sent a trusted subordinate, Marcus Daly, to examine and purchase claims. Once a penniless Irish immigrant, Daly had had long experience in California, Nevada, and Utah. He had been a mine foreman on the Comstock Lode. After starting development of a mine and mill at Butte for his Utah employers, Daly secured an option on another Butte silver mine for himself. This was the Anaconda, then a small affair with a shaft only sixty feet deep. The price was $30,000. To finance development of it, Daly drew into his venture George Hearst and Hearst's two associates in mining investments, the San Francisco lawyers and financiers, James B. Haggin and Lloyd Tevis. Hearst, Haggin, and Tevis were all wealthy men by then. They allowed Daly to spend a large amount in 1880–1881 in opening the mine.[30]

Just when Daly came to realize that his silver mine was in fact one of the richest copper mines in the world, is not clear. Early in 1882 he sent for Haggin and Hearst and proposed that they finance the huge investment necessary to mine and smelt copper on a mass-production basis. Daly suggested that they send representatives to Wales to study smelting techniques and that they import Welsh labor to operate the smelter. If Hearst hesitated, as tradition has it, his doubts were understandable. Copper was a new metal for Far Western mining men, and quite aside from the technological problems to be solved, copper production was a field that had been dominated for years by the Lake Superior mines, which marketed their output in a highly monopolistic fashion. Despite all uncertainties, by the end of 1884 Anaconda was producing in such quantities as to influence world prices, and Butte was on its way toward becoming what a twentieth-century geologist has termed "the most important mining center in the United States."[31] Although silver continued to come from Montana in quantity, copper became the chief product.

As a result, when Montana mining finally regained its vigor, it assumed a drastically altered form that soon produced a correspondingly changed society. Butte and its new neighbor, the smelter town of Anaconda, became industrial centers and "company towns." The anarchy for which Butte became notorious at the end of the century was not the turmoil of a mining camp, but rather the lawlessness of labor warfare and bitter feuds between great corporations, or between the millionaires who controlled great corporations.

Idaho's recovery came somewhat more slowly. Even the completion of the Union Pacific–Central Pacific railroads to northern Utah in 1869 did not bring a major improvement in Idaho's prospects. Nor did much progress result from attempts to introduce improved mining methods from California and Nevada. The final humiliation came in 1874–1878 when a railroad finally reached Idaho only to cut through its southeast corner, remote from the mines, because there was no other way to get from Ogden to Butte. Two railroads of greater importance to Idaho were built across the territory in 1882–1883, the one along the route of the Oregon Trail and the other across the narrow "panhandle" just north of Lake Pend Oreille. Both were en route to the Pacific coast rather than intent upon serving Idaho.[32]

New developments, however, were giving the railroads grounds for re-evaluating Idaho. Following discoveries in 1879 and 1880, a rush began in the summer of 1880 to Wood River, which is squarely in the center of southern Idaho. The ores were rich in both lead and silver. Here, within a year's time, smelters began work, and the approaching railroad checked its advance along the Oregon Trail to build a spur line in to the new mines. Railroad service to the Wood River district began in 1883. A telephone system followed in the same year, and electric lights in 1887. Capital came in from San Francisco and London.[33]

Still more significantly, in the Coeur d'Alene region of northern Idaho gold discoveries were made in 1882 and leaked to the public late in the following year. Seizing the chance to build up passenger traffic, the Northern Pacific Railroad, then building toward Lake Pend Oreille, burst into a flurry of publicity that assured the Argonauts of

1884 that they could travel practically all the way by train. How conditions had changed since 1849! Telephones and electric lights on Wood River; Pullman cars almost to Coeur d'Alene! The frontier with modern conveniences.

Advertising the Coeur d'Alene as a gold region proved a mistake, for starting with 1884–1885 it became apparent that lead-silver ores were the real wealth of the region. As capital came in from San Francisco, Portland, and Montana, a series of mines, mills, and smelters began transforming this mountain wilderness into one of the world's great sources of lead, silver, and presently zinc. Unlike Butte, no single industrial center developed; rather, the hitherto beautiful valley of the Coeur d'Alene River was cut up into a succession of drab industrial suburbs. Like Butte, however, the Coeur d'Alene became notorious for the violence of its labor warfare.[34]

*I*DAHO'S IMMEDIATE NEIGHBORS, eastern Oregon and Washington, were not as important as Montana and Idaho, either initially or subsequently. In eastern Oregon mining centered in the extensive Blue Mountain region. A series of districts came into production in 1861–1864. Names like Powder River, John Day, and Burnt River became temporarily famous. Thereafter the placer yield declined and the Chinese, those harbingers of decline, became numerous. Of 3965 "miners" that the census was able to list in the whole of Oregon in 1870, 2428 were Chinese. The ratio was not greatly altered in 1880. A few quartz mines were started on a limited basis in the latter half of the 1860s, but real progress was made only in the 1880s, partly because of inadequate transportation. Eastern Oregon seems, therefore, to have developed in the 1860s as an extension of the much larger placer mines of Idaho, just as southwestern Oregon in the 1850s had been essentially an extension of activities in California. Neither area was of great importance in the 1870s.[35]

In Washington, again, scattered placers and some lode districts were discovered at intervals during the long period between that first rush to Fort Colville in 1855 and a rush to the retarded Okanogan region thirty years later. A modern Washington geologist has remarked of his state: "From the beginning, gold-mining activities were intermittent rather than constant. Periods of activity were followed by periods of stagnation."[36]

Utah was quite a different matter. Geology combined with theology to set its mining development apart from that of its neighbors in the Great Basin and the Rockies. Rich and extensive placers—the usual initial lure of most new Western mining regions—were lacking, and most of the veins, instead of being in the easier form of free-milling gold quartz, were predominantly argentiferous lead ores that required technical knowledge and investment comparable to that utilized at Eureka, Nevada, and Leadville, Colorado.

The mineralogical handicaps could be and presently were overcome when railroad transportation reduced basic costs. In the meantime, Brigham Young and the Mormon Church viewed mining with a cautious reserve unusual in Western history. They were not necessarily opposed to mining as such, for in fact from 1849 onward the Church permitted occasional groups of Mormons to work in Far Western mines and bring home their highly useful profits or pay. But the Mormon authorities were determined to prevent mining from unsettling the ordered society and economy that they were so determinedly nurturing in Utah. What is more, the Mormons were abnormally level-headed in recognizing that many must fail for every one who would find gold or silver.

This qualified attitude was strengthened by the Mormons' first experience with mining in Utah. During the Civil War the army decided to garrison Utah with the Third California Volunteers. As any one could have predicted, the Third Californians proved more interested in prospecting than in soldiering—and more familiar with "indications" than with close-order drill. Their commanding officer, Patrick Connor, was a boastful, aggressive Irishman who appears to have seen in a mining boom not only a chance for personal profit, but also a means of attracting into Utah a "Gentile" population big enough to counter the influence of the predominant Mormons. He succeeded admirably in arousing the Mormons' anxieties as to the possible results of a mining boom.

Connor's soldiers discovered in Bingham Canyon, just below the southern tip of Great Salt Lake, one gold placer area that proved to be of importance. (Contemporaries claimed that it produced a million dollars from 1865 to 1872.) Although they found also some lesser placers, they uncovered, much more significantly, veins of gold, silver, and base metals. Some of these, like the Bingham placers, were in the area directly south of Great Salt Lake; others were in the Wasatch Mountains, east and a little south of Salt Lake City. One of the discoveries in the Wasatch Range, Little Cottonwood Canyon, although too far from transportation for immediate development, was soon to become one of the most widely advertised of Western silver districts. In the meantime, in addition to encouraging his men to prospect, General Connor spent his own and his friends' funds in unskilful attempts to build and operate furnaces for smelting Utah's promising but difficult argentiferous lead ores.

While viewing askance mining within Utah, Brigham Young and the members of his church had no hesitation about profiting from the sudden increase in population in the Far West after 1848. Trade with the mines, like trade with the army posts, proved a most important source of cash income and a means of balancing the economy in what would otherwise have been an agricultural community without a market for its produce or the services of its teamsters. Supplying the forty-niners as they passed through Salt Lake City en route to California was the Mormons' first experience of this kind. A recent historian has suggested that the profits from the Gold Rush were what saved from failure the Mormons' dream of establishing a Great Basin empire.[37]

After gold was discovered in Colorado a decade later, Mormon wagon trains, laden with flour, oats, barley, and onions, were soon making the 500-mile trip across the Continental Divide to Colorado. The opening of mines in Idaho, Montana, and Nevada provided further outlets that were energetically exploited during the 1860s. Flour, dried fruit, butter, and salt were among the local produce sent in wagons each spring and summer, while Eastern merchandise of all kinds was included. The Mormons, in short, benefited greatly from the necessities of their new mining neighbors.

An unexpected result was to create a little group of wealthy merchants and bankers in Salt Lake City, not all of whom were Mormons. With money to invest, these men welcomed the opportunities that opened as railroad service became available after 1869.[38] The Church took the lead in building a branch line to connect Salt Lake City with the transcontinental railroad at Ogden, thirty-seven miles away. The Church took the lead also in initiating a network of small railroads to bring the principal mining districts of Utah into contact with Salt Lake City. Thereby the latter city was able to start developing into the great smelting and ore-processing center that it was presently to become.

In both mining and smelting the response to railroad transportation was remarkably quick. Rossiter Raymond said that in 1868 and 1869 he had found no Utah mines in profitable operation save for the placers in Bingham Canyon; yet in 1870 such a "sudden and rapid" silver fever had broken out that even Mormons were "locating and prospecting ledges with truly Gentile zeal"; or as the *Mining and Scientific Press* reported two years later, "the country is covered with nomadic bands and parties of prospectors."[39] With warnings against speculation and licentious conduct, the Church authorities accepted the inevitable and actually encouraged Mormons to take mining jobs at good wages—partly in order to make it unnecessary for mine owners to import from outside mine laborers who might be of an undesirable kind and certainly would not be Mormons. Utah was unlike most of the Far West in that the farmer, stock raiser, and town builder had preceded the miner. Food, livestock for transportation purposes, simple manufactures, and a considerable labor force were all available locally and at rather lower prices than elsewhere. It was an unusual setting for a mining boom.

A speculative "excitement" over silver-lead developed so quickly that even in 1871 Rossiter Raymond was warning that "the thing is over-done." The only restraining factor, he said, was that "there is little opportunity for persons without capital."[40] Those with capital hesitated not. With the confidence of newly-rich, self-made men, the non-Mormon "merchant princes" of Salt Lake City rushed enthusiastically into this difficult and unfamiliar type of investment. Mines were opened and smelters built. Little heed was paid to the exacting requirements of smelting, which would be the key to success in so much Utah mining. Raymond reported that the furnaces were small, wasteful, and "run very irregularly." "The metallurgical industry here," he concluded, "is conducted in a sadly careless and ignorant manner."[41]

While many of the smelters were built close to the mines in the districts south and southeast of Great Salt Lake, almost from the start of the boom some of the more important ones were erected close to Salt Lake City, the logical central point. The years of the boom brought an extension of mining and smelting southward to the area below Utah Lake, and they led to energetic prospecting in the arid southwestern corner of Utah, where silver deposits of great potential value were to be opened after 1875, when transportation began to reach that unpromising region.

A major force in buoying up everyone's optimism was the dramatic performance of one of the early mines in Little Cottonwood Canyon. The "Emma" was "located" in 1868 and proved to be extraordinarily rich. Rossiter Raymond called it "one of the most remarkable deposits of argentiferous ore ever opened." He explained that although there had been no well-marked outcroppings or other decisive surface indications of hidden treasure, nevertheless excavation disclosed a mass of very rich ore that could be extracted at comparatively low cost. Much of it was so rich that it justified shipment overland by railroad to New York, and thence to Liverpool for treatment.

Lacking funds to develop it, the two prospectors who had discovered the mine sought support from absentee speculators who lived in points as distant as Racine, Wisconsin, San Francisco, Vermont, and New York. These speculators, in turn, decided to incorporate the mine in New York in order to sell it in England! The English brokers who undertook to market the corporation in Great Britain had to seek aid from Albert Grant, a London financier of very dubious repute. Thereafter Grant seems to have been the directing force, although he made every effort to conceal his participation in the scheme. A laudatory scientific report on the mine was obtained by engaging the well-known Professor Benjamin Silliman, Jr., of Yale, for a fee of $25,000. Silliman was the son and namesake of the man who is widely regarded as being one of the "fathers" of American science, but in the words of a recent biographer, he "did not inherit his father's business caution" and was notoriously enthusiastic in his reports on mineral properties. In this particular instance he did not stand alone. By distributing additional largesse, Grant and his associates were able to compile a list of directors and sponsors for the mine that included many names distinguished in British society, among them the United States minister to England.

Rossiter Raymond, a far better mining expert than Silliman, expressed anxious foreboding when he heard that the shares in the mine had been "floated" in London for the huge sum of £1,000,000. The gullible British investors brushed aside the first news of a lawsuit by a rival company and an alarming report that the mine had been gutted, that the wonderful bonanza with which it had opened was exhausted. For the moment, the apparently brilliant success of the Emma mine in international finance enormously stimulated investment in other Utah mines. From small proportions the output of silver and lead jumped to several million dollars a year in the early 1870s, and then rose in the later 1870s to a steady annual yield of four to five million dollars of silver, together with one to two million dollars of lead per year, and a small product of gold and copper.[42] In the Bingham Canyon area, where large quantities of low-grade lead-silver ores were being mined, there was as yet little indication that one of the world's great sources of copper would soon be opened.

Behind the façade of these apparently steady and impressive figures lurked a multitude of general maladjustments and individual failures. The effects of the panic of 1873 in the East forced many of Utah's "merchant princes" into bankruptcy, and at the same time crippled the Eastern and foreign interests that had just begun heavy investments in Utah mines and smelters. Coincidentally, in 1873, the much praised Emma mine was revealed as one of the really notable swindles of Anglo-American history. Its collapse was so universally publicized on both sides of the Atlantic that it scared away prospective investors.[43] As it had helped inflate the boom, so the Emma aided now in puncturing it.

Meanwhile, the mines had gone below the rich oxidized ores near the surface. As happened so often in Western experience, the ores below the water table were more difficult ("rebellious") and required new techniques and expensive new machinery precisely when the investors could least afford it. The smelters likewise continued to give erratic results. A governmental survey in 1880 protested at the typically American tendency to rely "too much on themselves and their own ability," while paying too little attention to "what has been done in other coun-

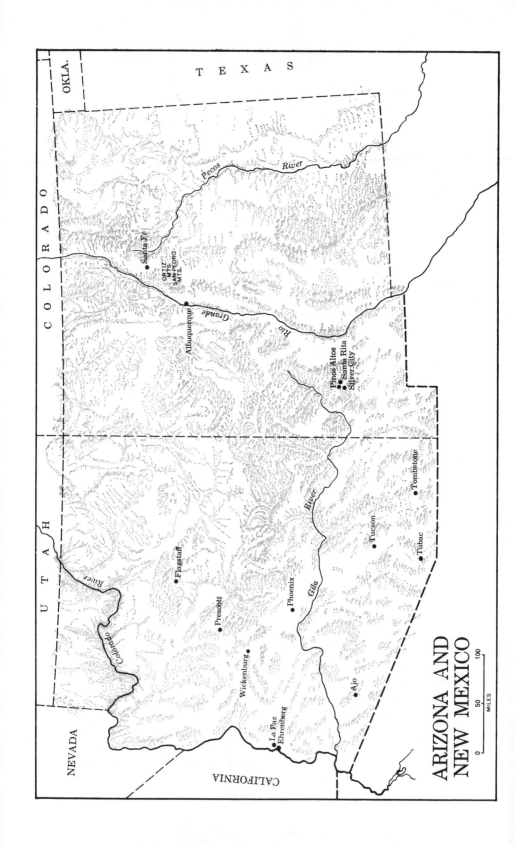

ARIZONA AND
NEW MEXICO

tries" in handling similar ores. "A thorough study of the continental methods would be of great advantage."[44] The contrast between this indictment and the highly favorable verdict upon Leadville's contemporaneous use of European applied science hardly needs to be elaborated.

*N*EW MEXICO AND ARIZONA, the remaining parts of the Southwest, were slower than Utah to begin vigorous development. Both were held back by a highly adverse combination of hostile Indians, poor transportation, a geographic environment made harsh by aridity and topography, and mineral resources in which complex and refractory ores were too prevalent for quick exploitation on an isolated frontier. Contemporaries talked most of the Indians and the difficulty of hauling supplies in and ore out of the area. The complaint was probably right in its emphasis. Some of the fiercest and most militarily competent Indians in North America, the Apaches and Navaho, regarded Arizona and New Mexico as their home and made that vast region one of the most dangerous on the continent.

Western Arizona was by no means cut off from transportation. Today it is not customary to think of the Colorado River as an artery of commerce, but prior to the railroads it was an important entrance into the otherwise landlocked Southwest. In the 1860s sailing vessels made the long voyage of several weeks from San Francisco down the coast of American California and Lower California and up the Gulf of California to the mouth of the Colorado. Subsequently enough business was generated to justify putting steamers on this coastal run. At the mouth of the Colorado, cargo and passengers were transferred to shallow-draft steamers that paddled up the Colorado at least as far as the mining hamlet of La Paz, more than a hundred miles above Yuma, and during favorable seasons they penetrated as far north as Callville, in southern Nevada, now covered by the waters of the modern man-made Lake Mead.[45]

Eastward from the river travel depended entirely upon pack animals and freight wagons, and the further inland one traveled through that hostile region the more hazardous passage became. New Mexico was quite beyond reach of the river's influence. In Spanish and Mexican days its trade had come by overland routes, such as the long road that struck northward from Chihuahua, Mexico, or the Santa Fe trail that came southwestward from the Missouri frontier. After the territory passed under the United States flag, New Mexico still had no alternative to lengthy and exclusively overland approaches, which made for exceedingly expensive transportation whenever a promoter sought to bring in the heavy, bulky equipment and supplies required for any but very simple mining.

Within modest limits, New Mexico was far more experienced than Arizona in mining, for small-scale operations there long antedated the transfer of the region to American sovereignty. Copper mines were discovered near the end of the eighteenth century at Santa Rita, in the southwest corner of New Mexico, just east of present-day Silver City. At intervals throughout the nineteenth century these copper mines were worked by successive American lessees, amongst whose multitudinous harassments the Apache Indians ranked high.

Of greater immediate importance were the "Old Placers" that were discovered in the Ortiz Mountains in 1828 and the "New Placers" that were found at the foot of the San Pedro Mountains in 1839. The two were only a few miles apart, in north central New Mexico, south of Santa Fe. Despite primitive and labor-consuming techniques, a considerable amount of placer gold was dug from them by Spanish-speaking miners long before the dramatic events at distant Sutter's Mill had aroused Americans to an enthusiasm for gold mining. Some lode mining developed in the same area after the discovery of the Ortiz gold quartz vein in 1833. To call this the cradle of Far Western mining, as one New Mexico authority has sought to do,[46] is to overlook the limiting circumstance that the New Mexican gold fields were too isolated to be influential, but in terms of simple priority in time, these fields do indeed rank first.

Activity by English-speaking Americans seems to have started with the finding of placer gold in May of 1860 at Pinos Altos, just north of Santa Rita and Silver City. The discoverers had come over from California, presumably on one of those incredibly long and dangerous prospecting trips to which Old Californians were so prone. In December, quartz claims were added to what were by then flourishing placer diggings. Within a surprisingly short time that remote outpost had attracted to itself people from California, Texas, Missouri, and the Mexican provinces of Sonora and Chihuahua. Unfortunately it also drew the attention of the Apaches, who attacked the miners so relentlessly that by the end of 1861 most had abandoned Pinos Altos. Little in the way of a revival was achieved until near the close of the decade.

When the regular army units were withdrawn during the Civil War for service in the East, the Indians greatly increased their attacks, and to the troubles thus inflicted on the New Mexicans was added a disruptive invasion by Confederate troops in 1861–1862. Mining and prospecting virtually ceased, and were resumed only on a limited basis during the early years after the Civil War.[47]

The war years were equally disastrous to Arizona. Much less mining had been attempted there than in New Mexico prior to the American occupation, and it should be remembered that the southern part of the territory, including some important mining districts, did not come under the United States flag until the Gadsden Purchase was ratified in 1854—half a dozen years after the peace settlement that had transferred the rest of the Southwest to acknowledged United States title. While the area was still under Mexico, a copper mine had been developed at Ajo and some intermittent small-scale mining for gold and silver had been done in the mountains around Tubac, both in the southernmost part of what is now Arizona.

Most of Arizona was Indian country, wild, rough, and little known. The California gold rush brought some forty-niners through southern Arizona, and a little prospecting was done on the Colorado River at that time. Starting in 1854, and at great danger to themselves, the new owners of the territory made spasmodic efforts to reopen copper mines at Ajo, silver mines near Tubac, and a scattering of other isolated claims in the Gadsden Purchase lands. The necessity for smelting their copper and silver ores enormously complicated their already massive problems.

The first real mining boom in Arizona started in 1858 on the Gila River, the southernmost tributary of the Colorado, at a point about twenty miles above Yuma. This was an excessively dry region, ill-suited to placer washing, but the boom lasted into the early 1860s. As it "played out," new placers were opened on the Colorado River, more than a hundred miles above Yuma, where the mining towns of Ehrenberg and La Paz sprang up. Restless Old Californians stampeded to the new diggings.

At almost the same time, both placers and veins of gold and silver were discovered around Prescott and Wickenburg, well to the east of the Colorado and about midway between Arizona's northern and southern borders. One of the mines near Wickenburg, the "Vulture," found in 1863 by Henry Wickenburg himself, produced well for twenty years and was probably the most important single mine in the territory.

These difficult beginnings were adversely affected by the withdrawal of the regular army at the outbreak of the Civil War. In southern Arizona fierce raids by Apaches virtually cleared the country of Americans and established the Indians' power so decisively that the region was not safe for even adventurous settlers until the 1870s. A brief "invasion" of Tucson by a tiny force of Confederates added to the confusion, and gangs of Sonoran bandits seized the opportunity to do any damage that the Indians had failed to accomplish. In northern and western Arizona Indian pressure, while very severe, impeded rather than eliminated the promising developments at Prescott, Wickenburg, and on the Colorado. Ultimately the territory profited from the Civil War, for in Arizona as in Utah the War Department sent in units of the California volunteers to garrison the posts vacated by the regular army. The Californians of course found it impossible to refrain from part-time mining ventures while still in service, and after the war some became permanent and prominent citizens of Arizona.[48]

In general it would be true to say that both Arizona and New Mexico entered the 1870s without having conquered their biggest obstacles— Indians and transportation. The latter need was not met until the Southern Pacific and the Santa Fe finally built parallel lines across Arizona and New Mexico during the years 1878–1883, and at the same time ran a line down the Rio Grande valley to El Paso. Thus connected with both East and West, this vast, neglected region at last began to advance. Its Indian troubles were materially lessened during the first ten years after the Civil War but were not ended. Kit Carson's conquest of the Navaho in 1863–1864 had led to a permanent treaty with that group in 1868. Some of the Apache bands were defeated and forced onto reservations by General George Crook's campaigns during the early 1870s, while others continued to be a terror to isolated southern settlements until the 1880s.

While awaiting transportation and surcease from Indian warfare, miners and promoters in both territories tried repeatedly to bring promising claims into production. In New Mexico they accomplished little until after the middle of the 1870s. In his report covering 1875, Rossiter Raymond commented upon "the small progress of mining" in New Mexico. He blamed it upon poor transportation, "the indolence or indifference" of the Spanish-speaking population, scarcity of water, and the "predominance of base metals" rather than uncomplicated gold and silver ores suited to simple milling and amalgamation.[49]

Arizona fared somewhat better. A few mines of outstanding richness, especially the Vulture, managed to stay in operation with reasonable continuity, and numerous small operators sent occasional shipments of ore to San Francisco by way of the Colorado River steamers. Yet in his report for 1875 Raymond gave this precise and prescient summary of Arizona's condition:

> At present only such gold and silver lodes as would elsewhere be considered surprisingly rich can be worked to advantage, and scores of lodes that would pay handsomely in California or Colorado are utterly neglected, while the great copper interests of the Territory (for copper is nowhere more abundant or of greater purity) are for all practical purposes without value.[50]

If the admittedly faulty federal statistics are at least an indication of comparative standings, then it would appear that for the decade from 1866 through 1875 Arizona and New Mexico ranked very nearly at the bottom of the list of Western states and territories producing gold and silver.[51] In view of the closing of the mines during the Indian and Confederate raids of the early 1860s, the same relative position must have been true during those years also. Of the two territories, Arizona was the more productive.

New Mexico moved gradually into a silver boom during the later 1870s, apparently in anticipation of the railroads and in imitation of the inspiring example of Leadville, Colorado. Towns like Silver City became famous, and mines, mills, and smelters went to work in the hills of southern New Mexico even at a time when the railroad was still fifty miles away, the isolation severe, and the Apache danger very real.[52]

Arizona had a more dramatic experience. Gold had been the mineral principally sought by prospectors in the 1860s; in the 1870s silver was the great enthusiasm. In 1877 one of the most determined of Western prospectors finally struck it so rich in silver that he brought to Arizona one of the last great rushes of the type patterned after '49.

Ed Schieffelen had unsuccessfully followed the crowd to a whole series of mining "excitements"—now to Nevada, now to Utah, or Idaho, or the Oregon in which he had been raised. Like so many prospectors, his appearance had deteriorated along with his fortunes. In 1876 he was described as having a long, unkempt beard, curly black hair that hung below his shoulders, worn-out clothing that had been patched with odd pieces of deerskin, corduroy, and flannel, and a decayed slouch hat mended with rabbit skin. Although actually a young man, hardship had weathered him until he looked middle-aged. He had been born in Pennsylvania in 1848 but had grown up on a farm in Oregon.

After years of failure he returned to his family farm with $2.50 in his pocket. Instead of admitting defeat and taking a steady job, he borrowed $100 from his father and started for Arizona, determined this time to go off by himself into virgin territory, even if a lonely tombstone should be his only reward.

After months of searching in the Apache-infested southeast corner of Arizona, he found what became the rich silver mines of Tombstone. The territorial governor gave Schieffelen and his partners modest financial backing, then drew in "capitalists" from Connecticut and Philadelphia. In the early 1880s Tombstone was a national sensation, noted alike for its silver output and its anarchic society.[53] (Without Tombstone's feud between the Earp brothers and the Clantons the movies and television would have run out of copy years ago.)

Silver soon ceased to be Arizona's principal concern. In the mid 1870s serious if small-scale work began at copper mines in several parts of the territory. As the railroads advanced into Arizona, corporations and individuals in New York and one Scottish firm began buying copper properties. The early 1880s saw the beginning of a well-capitalized development that presently made Arizona a major source of that metal.[54] Montana and Michigan far surpassed Arizona in the production of copper during the last two decades of the nineteenth century, but in the present century Arizona rose to primacy. As one might expect, this industrial type of mining and smelting, under corporate control, produced "company towns" rather than the older type of disorderly mining camp. In this Arizona followed the pattern that was being set in Montana and Idaho in these same years. A late maturing, in an age of railroads and base metals, produced a society very different from that of the original gold and silver rushes.

◁ 8 ▷

First Attempts at Self-Government

*J*ust as the earliest gold mining took place in a part of California that was immune from any effective governmental jurisdiction, so all the subsequent mining booms from the Sierras to the Rockies swept men into wild regions that were almost beyond the reach of established administration. The typical mining area of the 1860s, when the mining frontier was at its widest geographical extent, began its hectic life at the far edge of a huge and thinly administered federal territory. Thus in 1860 Washington Territory, with its seat of government on Puget Sound, extended from the Pacific across the whole of what are now Washington and Idaho, and up to the summit of the Rockies, in what today is western Montana. With the creation of Dakota Territory in 1861, the remainder of Montana was ruled from Yankton, which was only a short distance west of Iowa.

Rarely was there an effective government in such new areas during the early stages of a boom. To supply the lack, Congress had to move with what it regarded as reasonable speed to create new and smaller territories out of the existing vast ones. The act "to provide a temporary

Government for the Territory of Colorado" was approved on February 28, 1861; the gold rush had begun at the end of 1858. Once Congress had acted, the President had to sift through a throng of party stalwarts and "lame duck" Congressmen to find office-holders for the new province. Since the pay even for a governor was a mere pittance, and the tenure uncertain, really able and successful men were unlikely to be among those importuning the President.

Delays inevitably ensued while the fortunate appointees set their affairs in order and traveled to their distant and often isolated domain. There were more delays while the new men tried to learn their jobs, and while a census was taken as the preliminary to holding elections to choose the first territorial legislature. Colorado's first governor did not arrive until May 27, 1861; the first legislature convened September 9. Once the legislature, in all the wisdom it had inherited from older states, had passed statutes, there was still a further period before the text of the latter was printed and distributed. "Township, district, and county" offices could be filled temporarily by the governor, but at the end of the first session of the legislature they had to be replaced by men elected or appointed in accordance with the new laws.[1]

For each new territory the federal government supplied a governor, secretary, three judges, an attorney, and a marshal. The other officials were chosen locally in response to the sovereign will and prejudices of a newly arrived electorate of men who were relative strangers to one another. At best, these national and local arrangements provided a minimum government that came late to its responsibilities; at worst, an inadequate regime that became the butt of constant cynical jokes. In the few instances where statehood replaced territorial rule during the early years (as in California and Nevada), the level of performance was not drastically improved. It was under a state government that local administration in San Francisco was allowed to deteriorate into such weakness and corruption as to require the vigilance committees of 1851 and 1856.

Americans of that day did not expect the kind of strong, paternalistic national government that alone could have moved with a speed and firmness sufficient to keep up with the rapidly advancing frontiers of the mining West. In no small degree the Jeffersonian and Jacksonian "revolutions" had been a rejection of federalist notions that might have made possible a vigorous central administration of the territories. Jacksonian thinking, indeed, had made it a necessity and a positive good to choose officials locally and by popular vote, even though this was asking a great deal of so inchoate a political society as that of a mining frontier. Finally, if the well-established East and Middle West were capable of producing in these same years Boss Tweed, Grant's two administrations, and "shoddy" wartime contracts, then it should hardly be surprising if honesty and ability were not universally present in the public service of the mining West.

Left to work out its own problems, with the aid of the tiny group of officials sent from Washington, the mining West struggled along in uneven fashion. The need for roads, ferries, and bridges was met by voting franchises to ambitious private citizens, who set their tolls at rates calculated to yield a good profit so long as the uncertain flow of travelers and goods continued. Schools and jails were supposed to be the responsibility of the local authorities, although like roads, schools were sometimes started as private commercial ventures. Because children were few, the pressure for educational facilities were small, except in some of the quartz towns and commercial centers. The jails, by contrast, had plenty of potential customers, but they were almost invariably so "leaky" as to make it impossible to hold a prisoner for trial, let alone for serving a sentence. A song of the California gold rush cheerfully described Hangtown jail, as seen by a prisoner who was detained by it for only the briefest moment:

> *Canvas roof and paper walls,*
> *Twenty horse-thieves in the stalls;*
> *I did as I had done before,*
> *Coyoted out from 'neath the floor.*

Twenty years later Deer Lodge, Montana, was complaining bitterly that it was "the site of the most unretentive jail in America—an institution that was never known to hold a prisoner long enough to bring him to justice."[2]

Against this background it becomes understandable why the mining communities often "took the law into their own hands" when dealing with crime. In the early phase there was no alternative. Quite aside from the lack of jails, legally appointed judges and sheriffs were too distant to be realities. Hence the early codes adopted by miners' meetings sometimes included, along with rules for acquiring mining claims, provisions for appointing constables and trying alleged criminals before locally elected "judges" and "miners' courts." Later, when constitutionally established authorities were available, they were not always competent to meet really serious challenges, such as the well-organized gangs of murderers and thieves that made themselves dominant in Idaho and Montana. The real blame in such cases of course rested upon the citizens themselves. What Governor William J. McConnell, a pioneer of 1863, said of Idaho was true of all the mining states and territories:

> If the first settlers in Idaho had intended to remain and become perma-
> nent citizens, as many of them eventually concluded to do, and had
> directed their energies, not only to making money, but also to public

affairs, including the election of good men to fill the offices, life and property might have been as safe from the beginning as in the older and
well-regulated states and territories.[3]

The difficulty was that while he might find momentary excitement
in the hurly-burly of local elections, the average gold seeker was not
eager to sacrifice his time for the public good. A Montana pioneer said
of Bannack in 1863: "Every man had left his home to better his condition. Bannack was not supposed to be a settlement, but simply a mining
camp where every one was trying to get what he could, and then go
home. Consequently the majority were simply trying to attend to their
own business and to let that of others alone."[4]

*N*OR WAS THERE MUCH in the behavior of a camp to
inspire a lofty sense of obligation. Weekday conduct might vary widely,
depending especially upon whether the region was in boom or bust,
but Sundays, incongruously, throughout the mining West were usually
chaotic affairs, because that was when the miners poured into camp to
buy their supplies for the week, get their mail, and celebrate at the bars
and gambling tables. Melodramatically one observer claimed that this
was the Sabbath in an Idaho town in 1863:

> This is Sunday—the solemn echo of the tolling church bell was unheard.
> . . . This is the settling day with merchant and miner; one presents a
> villainous-looking paper, charged with figures; the other, a long, greasy
> bag, charged with gold; Shylock wins; dust loses! Sunday . . . his Satanic
> Majesty the ruling spirit and genius of the hour; thermometer, 92° in
> the shade; rot-gut, twenty-five cents at the bar; myriads of mammoth
> bottle-flies, pregnant with poison, sailing through the air; whisky the
> beverage, and monte the game; . . . a breathless corpse lay weltering in
> his blood; law is violated, and the victim unavenged; the Sabbath closes
> with a clouded moon frowning on the sins of the day! [5]

Heavy drinking and gambling were not universal, but they were
commonplace and quite unashamed. Society was not censorious of either
the occupants or the operators of the saloons and gambling "hells." Sar-
castically, Mark Twain said that "to be a saloon-keeper and kill a man
was to be illustrious."[6] Prostitutes and mistresses, who in other lands
were shunned, were accepted by all but the lonely little group of ladies.
Indeed, "the girls" were more apt than the ladies to be a part of anything
important that was happening.

This was not invariably true. By the time a camp had grown into
a town it usually had a few women who struggled gallantly to establish the social and cultural values they had known in their former homes.

Nor did the ladies' efforts fail to win allies from among the predominantly male members of the community. Merchants were especially apt to contribute money and time to worthy local causes, presumably because they felt an instinctive interest in anything that would help to develop the town. Churches, schools, literary and singing groups, and temperance societies were among the weapons the feminine minority used in attacking what they regarded as the crudities of their new environment. Perhaps equally important was the example they set by creating a few attractive family homes in the midst of so much raw newness, so many saloons and hurdy-gurdy houses.

Sarah Eleanor Royce, whose son Josiah grew up to become the distinguished philosopher and Harvard colleague of William James, reveals in her autobiography an instance of her own influence on her neighbors. In an unnamed California mining village, she found only two or three families nearby. Hearing Mrs. Royce play on her melodeon, these neighbors formed the habit of coming in to "have a sing," as Mrs. Royce expressed it, on certain evenings each week. This, in turn, led to the group's arranging with the only minister in the area to have the latter preach in the Royces' "sitting room" once in every two weeks. Mrs. Royce heard that the miners of the district were making fun of the "psalm singing," as they derisively called it, but she persisted in her purpose as long as her family remained there.

Presently the Royces moved to the much larger and pleasanter quartz town of Grass Valley. There they found "a number of very good Christian people," churches, Sunday schools, a public school, and "one or two social and beneficent societies."[7]

A woman of similar determination was Rachel Haskell of the mining town of Aurora, Nevada. A surviving fragment of her diary shows Mrs. Haskell's leadership in seeing that her family read good literature, played the piano, and had a healthy group existence, even though the head of the family kept inventing transparent excuses for staying out late into the night and feeling mysteriously ill the next morning. With the Haskells as with the Royces, the piano was an attraction that brought in friends for singing.[8]

Women like Mrs. Royce and Mrs. Haskell were decidedly in the minority in the early years of a town, and while their desires were usually treated with at least outward respect, the standards they sought to impose were hardly the ones that in fact controlled the life of the community. Even some of the wives found the uninhibited, masculine atmosphere fatal to their accustomed notions about proper feminine conduct and fatal to stability in marriage. They started by accepting generous presents from their husbands' male acquaintances, and ended by running away or getting well-publicized divorces.[9]

With truthful insight, a contemporary remarked that mining towns "openly wear the worst side out."[10] It seemed to many that flaunting of what elsewhere was custom had much to do with the high incidence of violence and disrespect for law. "Drink, cards, women, and all the baser passions of man, were the primary cause," one man asserted, speaking of Idaho.[11] Men with unstable or weak personalities, who in quieter countries might have led innocuous lives, here became wastrels and lawbreakers, and in so doing they found themselves in congenial company. Each new mining land received among its early citizens a consignment of ready-made thieves and thugs. It started with the riff-raff that came to California in 1849 from the Australian penal colony, the streets of Atlantic seaboard cities, and the frontiers of the Mississippi Valley and northern Mexico. Nevada and Idaho, as children of California, each received a good share of their parent's outcasts, and when the frontier pushed further east to Montana, the bullies and "roughs" went with it. Later still they moved on to the Black Hills, or headed south for Arizona. They were reinforced by an assortment of equally unpleasant individuals who drifted west during the 1860s and 1870s from the notoriously wild river towns and frontier posts to the east of the Great Plains.

Trouble with law-breakers was not a new phenomenon for American border regions, but the temptations were at a maximum in precious metal camps, because the only local product, when it was gold dust, was easy to steal, easy to dispose of, and high in value. In the silver regions robbery was not always so simple. The silver smelters ingeniously reduced temptation by melting their product into bars of several hundred pounds' weight, to the utter frustration of highwaymen mounted on horseback.

With a few professional "roughs" to provide leadership in towns that at best were free and easy, with the saloons and gambling houses turning out recruits, and with most citizens intent on their private concerns, it becomes understandable why so many towns went through a period of something close to anarchy. Old timers who had lived through it insisted that the trouble-causing element was a very small minority. John Hailey, a notable Idaho pioneer, claimed that 95 percent of the people were "good, industrious, honorable and enterprising."[12] Governor McConnell, who had been a vigilante captain in Idaho, indignantly protested that even this left too large a proportion to the undesirables. Real "bad men," he felt, rarely exceeded one half of 1 percent, but through their bluster and recklessness, and their tendency to congregate together, they intimidated the ordinary citizenry and "always succeeded in making their presence felt—whether in saloons, precinct primaries, nominating conventions, or at the polls."[13] Granville Stuart, the famous Montana pioneer, agreed that "the respectable citizens far outnumbered the desperadoes," but the former were strangers to one another and without organization.[14]

The need, therefore, was to arouse the lethargic majority. An isolated case of flagrant murder or robbery could be handled when the miners and townspeople, finally goaded into action, seized the accused, tried him before a hastily chosen "popular jury," and executed, whipped, or banished him if found guilty. When less than death was the punishment, an ear was sometimes cut off so as to mark the man for the rest of his life.

Where the lawless minority was well organized or had obtained the election of friends to key public offices, a more elaborate action was necessary, because the citizenry needed not only to be aroused, but also to be emboldened to risk their lives against desperate men who freely used murder as a means of cowing the majority. At Oro Fino, Idaho, for example, an organized gang shot down in the public street a man who challenged them, then rode up and down the street "defying the inhabitants of the town to come out and take their share of the punishment."[15]

At such a critical moment the majority was helpless without leadership. Sometimes a small group would assume responsibility; sometimes one determined man of commanding personality would risk his life to take charge of the aroused but irresolute crowd. A striking instance was the action of Colonel Wilbur F. Sanders, a Civil War veteran recently arrived in Montana, nephew of the first territorial governor, and noted alike for courage and eloquence. When a notorious criminal had finally been seized for a brutal murder, after months of unpunished gang dominance in Montana, Sanders resolutely led the crowd through the forms of a trial before a "people's jury," despite the presence of armed "roughs" who openly threatened retaliation. Upon the death penalty being voted, Sanders climbed onto the back of a wagon, knowing that hostile firearms were being aimed at him, and persuaded the indecisive crowd to hang the criminal immediately. Out of this episode developed the great Montana vigilance movement which seized and executed, often in secrecy, more than a score of ruthless men who proved to have been led by the sheriff, Henry Plummer, a man with a previous record of crime in both Idaho and California.[16]

"Popular juries" with their hasty trials and lynchings, and vigilance committees with their secret arrests and executions were manifestly undesirable phenomena, but it is not easy to see how else the small lawless minority could have been forced to leave the majority in peace, in regions that either had no law or had been too careless to see that good men got into public office. In retrospect, the probability that mistakes were made in enforcing extralegal "justice" during the gold and silver rushes seems less significant than the continuance of the practice long after legitimate officers and courts were in fact available. It was so easy to argue that the delays and uncertainties of legitimate processes justified resort to the quick, cheap, and frighteningly final action of a crowd of private citizens.

If considered in the abstract, there was no necessity for extralegal maintenance of the peace. The mining rushes were not confined to United States soil. Men from California and the northwest crossed the international line into British Columbia; some crossed the Pacific to Australia and New Zealand. In the regions that flew the British flag they introduced American mining methods and machinery, and operated transportation and supply services. Their views on matters of mining and economics were listened to with respect.

At that point acceptance of American influence stopped. Law and order were maintained in British, not American fashion. To be sure, there was a necessary concession of tolerating petty uproar, gambling, and drunkenness, but crime was quickly repressed by the legitimate authorities, and self-constituted vigilante movements were neither necessary nor permitted. In each British colony, Gold Commissioners were appointed by the provincial authorities and sent out to the diggings as resident representatives of the central government. A few police, similarly appointed, backed them up, and a still smaller number of judges, appointed by and usually sent out from Great Britain, tried disputes. At the head of the hierarchy stood the governor of the colony, who was not infrequently some one with a background of service in authoritarian organizations like the Hudson's Bay Company or the Royal Navy. On the very rare occasions of real threats to legitimate rule, troops were used.

There seems to be no question but that crime and violence were less and security of life and property greater under the British colonial system than under the United States flag. The Americans who found themselves temporarily subject to this relatively firm regime accepted it—as they never would have at home. This was a question of national attitudes, not of something made inevitable by the unquestioned confusion that always attends gold and silver rushes.[17]

*T*RYING ALLEGED CRIMINALS was the most dramatic work of the miners functioning as a self-constituted "body politic"; it was not necessarily either the most frequent or most important task assumed by them. With only a very few exceptions, the early mineral discoveries were on land that was part of the national public domain; yet neither in 1848 nor at any time up to 1866 were there federal laws to authorize exploitation of mineral lands or to provide a means of acquiring a title. Technically speaking, the miners were trespassers on the public domain, and as such stood outside federal law for those eighteen years.

Man may or may not be a social animal, but he is certainly a creature that finds it difficult to live and work alongside other humans without rules for handling disputes and determining title to property. In default of other regulation, the miners therefore adopted their own local rules governing ownership and tenure of mining claims, and extended their rules to the related field of diverting water from streams for mining purposes. Recognizing that presently disputes would reach legally constituted courts, a young assemblyman, Stephen J. Field, the future justice of the United States Supreme Court, induced the new State of California to pass a statute (1851) which declared that "in actions respecting 'Mining Claims,' proof shall be admitted of the customs, usages, or regulations established and in force at the bar, or diggings, embracing such claim; and such customs, usages, or regulations, when not in conflict with the Constitution and Laws of this State, shall govern the decision of the action."[18]

This acceptance of the miners' codes by the legislature was confirmed by successive court decisions in California. The local rules of the various districts thereby became a kind of common law, based upon universal use and consent. They gave the miners what were essentially possessory rights, held subject to the will of the paramount owner, which was the government of the United States. California lawyers rationalized this by arguing that through its silence the federal government "tacitly consented" to the proceedings.

When California's adopted sons began migrating to all parts of Western America after 1858, they carried with them this "customary law" of mining property on the public domain, and the legislatures and courts of the new territories accepted it, as California herself had done earlier. When the Public Lands Commission examined the situation in 1880, it concluded irritably that "California common law," to quote the Commission's phrase, had become in fact the American law of mines for the whole vast area west of the Missouri, regardless of the English common-law precedents and federal land policies that prevailed east of that river.[19]

Whether in California or the newer territories, this body of law was not an ideal way to settle disputes. The local rules were sometimes loose in phraseology, the local records were often kept in a most careless and impermanent fashion, and local districts did not always trouble themselves to reassemble and revise their codes when mining conditions changed—it was easier to fall into a universal disregard of outmoded clauses. With records of this kind and men's fallible memories as the only evidence, litigation between rival claimants became an expensive and prolonged disaster when possession of very rich claims was at stake, as notably on the Comstock Lode. The lawyers rather than the owners profited from such controveries, and in their eagerness to win, litigants were not above mutilating the local records or using perjured witnesses to testify that such and such was done on the famous day when the claim was "located."

"Claim jumping," under cover of some alleged prior right, became a regular kind of legal blackmail, in which the hope of the "jumpers" was not that they might win, but rather that they would be "bought off." Part of the trouble here was inadequate enforcement of the rule that a man must continue actively to develop his claim in order to retain title to it. Carelessness in describing and marking boundaries increased the chances for chicanery. Then again, there was danger that the discoverers of a district would try to "rig" the rules in such a way as to monopolize the promising ground.

Especially critical was the practice in regard to lode claims. In many of the other details the Western mining codes followed the simple and well-tested provisions of the old Spanish and English ordinances, but in their local rules for ownership of veins, the Californians made an important innovation at an early date, before they could have had much technical information about the nature of veins. With some exceptions, the Spanish and English precedents specified that the underground boundaries of a quartz claim were simply the downward extension of the surface boundaries.

But suppose an inexpert claimant, forced to guess the behavior of his vein after it disappeared beneath the surface, erroneously fixed his surface markers in such a position as to miss most of the vein? The Californians tried to avoid this by asserting that the vein itself, rather than the surface boundaries, was the criterion. Ownership of the upper part of the vein gave the claimant the right to follow the vein, including all its "dips, spurs, angles, and variations," wherever it might lead underground, even though this might mean penetrating under a neighbor's claim.[20]

The superficially logical nature of this provision won for it widespread acceptance within California, and later throughout the West. Had geologists been consulted, they could perhaps have warned that many a vein "pinches out" or becomes discontinuous, and at a distance beyond that terminus there is a vein which may or may not be a resumption of the original vein—depending upon which side of the litigation you are supporting. Costly cases have centered upon this question.

As originally conceived, some variation in the content of different codes was inevitable, since a code covered only the district which drafted it. During the 1850s a perceptible trend toward standardization of codes developed in California, especially in regard to lode claims. At times the county was substituted for the much smaller district as the geographical unit covered. When mining expanded into the rest of the West, there was an attempt in several of the legislatures to adopt standard codes for the whole territory. Nevada tried and failed, and went back to reliance on local regulations. Arizona passed a code that was regarded as being "far preferable to the multifarious and generally ill-digested local laws which have hitherto prevailed in California and Nevada." Montana adopted a standard lode law whose provisions seemed to one observer to involve an unwise thrusting aside of California precedents in favor of Eastern notions that had come westward by way of Colorado. In statesmanlike fashion Colorado passed a lode statute that required the records, laws, and proceedings of each district to be filed in the office of the county clerk, so as to insure reasonable custodianship. Idaho, too, tried legislating for lode claims.[21]

As recognized and molded by the Western legislatures, and as interpreted by their courts, particularly the California supreme court, the codes became gradually a fairly definite body of customary law. In the words of Chief Justice Silas W. Sanderson of the California supreme court, in a classic decision in 1864: "Having received the sanction of the legislature, they have become as much a part of the law of the land as the common law itself, which was not adopted in a more solemn form. . . . These customs and usages have, in progress of time, become more general and uniform, and in their leading features are now the same throughout the mining regions of the State."[22]

Better still, in December 1865 Chief Justice Salmon P. Chase of the United States Supreme Court, in deciding a Nevada case, conceded: "And we cannot shut our eyes to the public history, which informs us that under this [local] legislation, and not only without interference by the national government, but under its implied sanction, vast mining interests have grown up, employing many millions of capital, and contributing largely to the prosperity and improvement of the whole country."[23]

*W*ITH SO SWEEPING an endorsement by the highest courts, the Western mining interests were content to continue with their customary law, even though English and Eastern investors sometimes balked when urged to put money into mines held only under a possessory right. But a great war had just ended. For some time the secretaries of the Treasury and the Interior, and the Commissioner of the General Land

Office, had been urging that the mineral lands be sold, partly as a means of paying off the war debt. The influential John Sherman of Ohio, brother of the general, introduced a bill into the Senate, while Congressman George Washington Julian of Indiana, chairman of the House Committee on Public Lands, began a personal crusade to sell the lands.

Of the small representation the Far West then had in the Senate, one member, William M. Stewart of Nevada, was a true product of the mining frontier. He was loudly assertive, resourceful, and able. His shrewd brashness was so great that it was hard to distinguish between his bluffs and his real intentions. Stewart had abandoned his studies at Yale to go to California in 1850. There he energetically made a career for himself in the three fields that were to occupy him for the rest of his life: mining, mining law, and politics. Like many another Western politician, the money he made from the latter two was largely lost in unsuccessful ventures in the first.[24]

He "read law" and was admitted to the bar in 1852 at Nevada City, Nevada County, that county which was to be so prominent and progressive in the development of California mining. He was elected district attorney in the following year and was acting attorney general of California by 1854. If his autobiography is to be believed, he served also as chairman of a committee which carried out the pioneering task of writing a quartz-mining code to cover all of Nevada County. This code was widely copied in other counties and became something of a model for the Far West.

In 1856, Stewart transferred his law practice to Downieville, Sierra County, and from there went to Nevada in 1860, after the Comstock Lode had opened. Four years of handling some of the most important litigation on the Comstock Lode made Stewart a practiced specialist in mining cases and temporarily a rich man. Having served in the Nevada territorial legislature and constitutional convention, he became one of Nevada's first United States senators, and with a hiatus of a dozen years, he remained in the Senate for the rest of the century.

The threat to his constituents' mining interests in 1866 caused the new senator to start a determined battle to persuade Congress that it could not in justice take any action that would upset the existing legal status of the industry that had in fact developed, without authorization, on the public domain. The statute that he maneuvered through Congress in 1866 applied only to lode claims.[25] A parallel act for placer claims was not passed until 1870.

Stewart's statute of 1866 made three major points. First, it gave both retroactive and future sanction to the miners' action in going onto the public domain and exploiting minerals. Second, it established a procedure for obtaining United States patents to mining claims. Third, it specified throughout that the existing local arrangements were to be respected and continued. Thus the preamble prescribed that the lands were to be open "subject to such regulations as may be prescribed by law, and subject also to the local customs or rules of miners in the several mining districts." Again, within general limits "the local laws, customs, and rules of miners" were to be controlling when the federal government undertook to accept and survey claims.[26] In the words of a great student of mining law, Stewart's lode statute "was but a crystallization of the local rules."[27] The *Mining and Scientific Press*, the unofficial spokesman of the industry, complacently agreed.[28]

The acceptance of the miners' "customary law" in the lode statute of 1866 and the similar placer statute of 1870 was not changed in fundamentals in the several amendments passed by Congress during the 1870s. In the important revision of 1872 Congress very wisely made a beginning at specifying what information the local records should contain, how claims should be marked, and how much work had to be done annually to avoid forfeiture.[29] This was advance in the right direction, although hardly far enough. For example, the local records would never be safe from loss or tampering until they were placed in the safekeeping of a recorder who was selected and bonded like any other public trustee charged with custody of valuable property. Nor would new congressional stipulations be of major service until some means was provided for enforcing them continuously and honestly.

In that same revision of 1872 Congress made a change that seemed almost an encouragement of expensive litigation. Responding to recent court decisions hostile to the unlimited license of the California doctrine in regard to veins, Congress now ruled that henceforth a claimant must fix his surface boundaries in such a way as to embrace the apex (that is, the top) of the vein. If he succeeded in so doing, he might follow the vein through the side limits of his rectangular claim but not through the end limits, as extended downward from the surface. A failure to include the apex vitiated one's right to pursue the vein on its downward course. In practice, this meant that millions of dollars would depend henceforth on the geologically uncertain question of whether the apex of a vein was within a claim.[30]

When replacement deposits became economically important at Eureka and Leadville, the words of the statute had to be bent by judicial interpretation to include a type of solid-rock deposit not foreseen by Congress. A costly suit between the Eureka Consolidated and Richmond Consolidated companies at Eureka, marked by the mutually contradictory testimony of a procession of mining experts, established the legal precedent that "a single deposit" of silver-bearing ore in limestone could be regarded as constituting a "lode," "within the meaning of the mining acts of Congress."[31] At Leadville, "much expensive and savage litigation resulted" from attempts to apply the statutes to replacement deposits. Local lawyers who had some understanding of economic geology, such as Charles S. Thomas, were able to demand fees that were "huge for those days."[32]

At the end of the 1870s, more than a dozen years after the first statute, Congress created a commission to investigate the public lands and land laws in the Western part of the United States. This action led the *Mining and Scientific Press* to remark that the old customary mining law had been good enough in its day, when mining conditions were simple and decisions as to title were settled by direct local action, with the implied threat of armed retaliation against recalcitrant losers. "That style of enforcing laws has, however, become nearly obsolete, and as it faded out sharp practices grew," partly because "dishonest shysters" no longer feared "the quick decisive arbitration of the revolver." At the same time the development of mining into a great industry demanded a corresponding alteration in the laws. These two considerations, the *Press* argued, were the real justification for congressional intrusion into the field of mining law. Yet even after amendments to the original statutes, congressional intervention had been moderate so far. "Except, as to those sections relating to patents to mineral lands, the idea seemed to be merely to establish a few general rules for future guidance in locating and holding claims, while details were left to district laws to provide for."[33]

The Public Lands Commission itself was more harsh than the *Mining and Scientific Press*. It agreed that the local laws had been sufficient in their day, when the mineral lands were not unduly crowded and when there was no alternative to self-constituted local regulation. But, the commission reported, most of the mining men who had testified had asserted that the local laws were no longer of use and should be abolished by Congress. The commission so recommended. The evidence gathered by the commission had revealed "an extraordinary and characteristic difference" in the frequency and costliness of litigation over titles in the area west of the Missouri, as compared to that east of it. In the latter there were almost no lawsuits; in the former "the most frequent, vexatious, costly, and damaging litigation." For this deleterious condition they blamed two features of the federal statutes: the recognition of the local regulations and records, with all their increasingly dangerous imperfections, and the doctrine that the vein rather than the surface boundaries was the basis of rights to a lode, especially as revised in the apex provision.[34]

Congress did not see fit to enact the major changes proposed by the commission. The "apex law" in regard to veins thus continued. But the district rules, even though sanctioned by statute, were in fact falling into disuse even at the time that the Public Lands Commission was making its report. The obsolete nature of so many of the provisions of the local codes and the decay of so many of the districts that had drafted them left mining men no alternative but to turn elsewhere. The way was thereby opened for a gradual displacement of the codes by a growing body of state and territorial legislation that supplemented the basic stipulations established by Congress in the act of 1872.

Disputes over old titles that ran back to the early days of the mining booms of course continued to involve the local codes, with all their failings. This situation led R. S. Morrison, a Colorado attorney and the author of a mining-law manual that ran through sixteen editions between 1875 and 1936, to observe caustically in his 1880 edition:

> Frequent eulogies have been made upon these District Rules in forensic efforts and even in solemn opinions, but such compliments seem to come more frequently from courts the furthest removed from a knowledge of their practical operations. They answered a good purpose where there was no Statute Law, but the remnants left of them are only used to cloud and blight titles otherwise honest and fair.[35]

Morrison's condemnation was virtually identical with the Public Lands Commission's conclusions and those of the *Mining and Scientific Press's* editorial, and occurred almost simultaneously with them. Taken together, the three criticisms form a disheartening commentary on the suitability of the "California common law" for a later day. The parallel to the continued handling of crime by lynching, "popular juries," and vigilantes is obvious. In both fields of law an informal local action had sufficed for the era in which it was first used. While a few men undoubtedly suffered unfair treatment, for most miners rough and ready "justice" made life and work possible in the face of challenges by a small minority of law breakers who did not respect other men's lives or property, and law evaders to whom sharp practices were commonplace. As mining society and the mining economy changed, the legal system changed with it, but at a slower pace and with serious lags and occasional blacksliding. Practices that may have been justifiable on a frontier were no longer appropriate two or three decades later.

Culmination in the Black Hills

*N*early all the mining rushes were confined to that geographical third of America that extends from the Rockies to the Pacific. Because of the configuration of the Rockies, the miners' world reached as far east as the 105th meridian in Colorado, and almost as far in New Mexico. In Wyoming the Rockies start a sharp slant toward the northwest. Wyoming itself was not important in mining. A considerable "excitement" over gold near South Pass, the historic route through the Rockies, burgeoned briefly in 1867–1868, just as the Union Pacific Railroad was being built; but it soon collapsed, leaving behind it empty "cities" and little groups of miners working their isolated claims. North of Wyoming the area of active mining shifted westward with the slope of the Rockies, to approximately the 112th meridian, which passes through Helena, Montana.

Well to the east of the Montana and Wyoming Rockies, and almost due north of Denver, was a group of mountains whose forests of dark-colored evergreen trees caused them to be called the Black Hills. Located in the southwest corner of South Dakota, this isolated range lay well outside the known mining regions. The Oregon and California Trail passed to the south, the Missouri River route to Montana to the east and north. The big rushes swirled by without breaking the peace of its precipitous peaks, dense forests, and lovely "parks." This "magnificent mass of mountains," in the words of a contemporary army officer, rising above "a desert of dreary alkaline plains,"[1] was part of a huge reservation guaranteed to the Sioux Indians by treaty in 1868. The fierceness of the Sioux and the vigilance of the army kept prospectors out of the Black Hills until the middle of the 1870s.

Repeated rumors of gold were confirmed in the summer of 1874 by a military reconnaissance under the command of the ill-fated George A. Custer. Reports by Custer himself and by members of his expedition, when publicized not only in local but also in national journals such as *Harper's Weekly* and the Chicago *Inter Ocean*, stirred up a frenzy of excitement across the country.[2] In San Francisco the *Mining and Scientific Press* editorialized on September 19, 1874, that "the glowing reports from Custer's expedition to the Black Hills have had the effect of exciting a lot of prospectors who want some new country to work in." By the autumn of 1874 expeditions for the Black Hills were being organized throughout the mining West by men who saw in this late discovery of virgin mining territory an opportunity of a kind once common but becoming increasingly rare. Elsewhere in the nation men who had suffered in the severe depression of 1873 saw in the new gold region the possibility of re-establishing themselves financially.

The army's policy of ejecting miners as trespassers on treaty lands proved increasingly futile during the latter part of 1875. Local pressure proved irresistible and the civil authorities were in sympathy with the trespassers. New treaties with the Indians were negotiated in 1876, and the Black Hills were legally opened early in the spring of the following year. But by that time the "excitement" had in fact carried thousands into the forbidden mines, from Dakota, Iowa, Kansas, Nebraska, Montana, Colorado, California, Nevada, "and other border States and Territories," as a contemporary observer summarized it.[3] Crowded diggings and "wide open" boom towns demonstrated, as they had on so many earlier frontiers, that gold seekers were far too impatient to wait for permission from their distant government in Washington.

Local enthusiasts have been claiming ever since that the Black Hills were the "last frontier" of Western mining. Tombstone has been a rival claimant, and there are other areas that could make a good case for the title. Taking the Black Hills at their word, they represent the culmination and a kind of summation of the successive mining frontiers. The rush to them opened with gold placer diggings that aroused nostalgic memories of the vanished frontiers of '49 in California, '59 in Colorado, and the '60s in the Northwest. Extreme Indian danger and a good supply of highwaymen gave it the isolation of those much more remote earlier regions, even though the railroad was only 260 miles distant. The chance to exploit rich virgin deposits seemed to be there, and in part actually was, although events soon showed that the future lay in the "rich man's quartz mines" rather than the "poor man's placer diggings." Of white men there were none before 1874. No permanent settlers preceded the miners there, as they did in Utah. Few even of trappers or explorers had ever invaded that mysterious and lovely mass of dark mountains that towered so dominantly above the surrounding flatness of the plains.

*W*HAT KINDS of people crossed the plains to found Deadwood, Lead, Central City, Custer, Rapid City, and the other Black Hills towns that grew up suddenly in 1875–1876—those boisterous camps that boomed so noisily while quieter folk elsewhere in America were celebrating the centennial of the nation's birth?

Like all previous mining frontiers, the Black Hills attracted a mixture of the restless, the ambitious, the curious, and the outlaws from all parts of the country. In Deadwood on a Sunday, when the prospectors and miners crowded in to get their mail and supplies, and to drink and gamble away their earnings,

> could be found representatives of every prominent mining district of the west, as well as 'tenderfeet' from every state of the Union. In the throng the buckskin clad hunter jostled the dandified gambler and the pilgrim from New England. On every side was heard the sound of the hammer and saw, in the construction of new buildings. . . . On one hand could be heard the impassioned call of an itinerant minister of the Gospel. . . . In close proximity would be a loud-voiced gambler crying his game.[4]

How much like Idaho or Montana of a dozen years earlier! The resemblance was understandable enough because so many of the people who were now in the Black Hills had once been in the Boise Basin or Helena, and were leading essentially the same life that they had known in the Northwest. A few were bona fide survivors of California. All, whether veterans of the mining West or new arrivals from Illinois, were sharply conscious that they were reliving an old pattern. At Deadwood in 1876 a favorite song to demand of itinerant entertainers like "Banjo Dick" Brown was *The Days of Forty-Nine:*[5]

> *You're looking now on old Tom Moore, a relic of by-gone days;*
> *A Bummer, too, they call me now,*
> *But what care I for praise?*

For my heart is filled with grief and woe,
And oft I do repine
For the days of old,
The days of gold,
The days of Forty-Nine.

It is suggestive to find a Deadwood audience demanding *The Days of Forty-Nine*. Throughout the nation, at just this time, mining-camp life was coming into vogue as a subject for literature. Bret Harte's phenomenally successful stories and poems of California mining camps had begun appearing in the summer of 1868. Mark Twain's *Roughing It* had been published in 1872. Dan De Quille's *History of the Big Bonanza* was issued in 1876, the year of the big rush to Deadwood. Westerners were already protesting that Harte's stories were romanticized unrealities; yet here was a real gold rush crowd in a real boom town listening enthusiastically to a nostalgic song that linked the Black Hills to golden memories of California in '49.

In the Black Hills the prospectors' early discoveries had drawn in placer miners, and now, as in former regions, gold dust was the medium of exchange when purchases were made or drinks ordered. Merchants, teamsters, assayers, blacksmiths, and bankers had started flourishing businesses. Lawyers found few clients at first, because there were no legally constituted courts and because, as one lawyer said, people tended to settle disputes with a six-shooter. The attorneys soon had plenty of cases, and in the Black Hills as elsewhere in America, they always had the arena of acrimonious local politics in which to spend much of their time. Journalists, despite the high freights, brought in type, presses, and paper so that they could keep the isolated "Hillers" informed as to news and inflamed as to politics.[6]

Less reputable professions were well represented. The promoter and speculator, whose activities wavered between outright fraud and a courageous pursuit of the long chance, were to be seen daily, sometimes seeking money for a mining claim, sometimes organizing a new town or water company, sometimes trying to "corner" the limited supply of some necessity. Gamblers, saloon keepers, hurdy-gurdy–house proprietors, and "madams" were as numerous as in most mining camps.

For those who wanted theater, there were soon offerings of drama, comedy, and variety shows. Jack Langrishe, a favorite of the mining West, began performances as soon as a wood-and-canvas theater was ready at Deadwood in July 1876. Langrishe was famous as a comedian and theatrical manager, and has been called the "father of the Colorado theater." His little troupe had made its headquarters at Denver during most of the 1860s and had toured through mining towns, railroad camps, and army posts all the way from the Missouri frontier to Nevada.[7]

Through the perseverance of an interested few, religion and education received a modest start almost as soon as the theater. A brief preaching mission in the summer of 1876 by a Methodist ended in the latter's mysterious death, presumably at the hands of Indians. A Congregationalist missionary sent out by the American Home Missionary Society arrived in Deadwood in November 1876, and after holding services in whatever buildings were made available to him, he "organized" a permanent congregation early in the next year and erected the first church building in the Black Hills. The Catholics, similarly, dispatched a priest to Deadwood, where the first mass was celebrated in a carpenter shop in May 1877. A church was built that same year.

Tiny little private schools, taught in log cabins, advertised for pupils in Deadwood in the autumn of 1876 and in Lead (with a spinster school ma'rm!) the following year. Small public schools were inaugurated in 1877–1878. Lead's first public school attracted thirty-two pupils (by way of comparison, Lead had a population of 1441 in 1880).[8]

These were the pioneers. Their widely varied occupations suggest that the Black Hills resembled the earlier frontiers in that only a part, and probably not the greater part, of the total population engaged in mining. The rest served the miners, or victimized them, struggled with ill-health, loafed about the towns, or caused the crime and violence for which Deadwood became famous.

Actual mining started with simple placer operations based upon the use of equipment no more novel or complex than the pan, rocker, sluice, and pick and shovel—as if this were 1849 all over again. Even in late 1875, however, lode claims were being "located," and in the spring of 1876 increasing attention was being given to them. A year later, in June of 1877, the San Francisco triumvirate of George Hearst, James Haggin, and Lloyd Tevis had an advance agent at Lead. At his urging, Hearst, Haggin, and Tevis purchased a claim known as the Homestake mine and began the development of what was to become one of the greatest gold quartz mines in the world.

Others with capital to invest in quartz appeared in town at the same time. Following their purchases came experienced mining engineers, and soon thereafter great wagonloads of heavy equipment began arriving for the stamp mills and amalgamating plants. Capitalized quartz mines brought also an influx of the varied personnel always associated with vein mining: professional underground miners, who were often of Irish or Cornish stock; mechanics; bookkeepers; and equipment operators, together with an increasing number of families.

When a well-known mining engineer, Louis Janin, submitted a report on the Black Hills in July of 1878, he said that "all the conveniences, and even the luxuries of life can be obtained in this section of the Black Hills [that is, Deadwood, Lead, and Central City]. It is by no means the rough mining camp that exists in the imagination of many. On the contrary, it is one of the pleasantest of all mining localities I have visited; and in no other district is justice more ably administered, or greater security afforded to life and to property."[9]

This suggests that social and economic development had been rapid, even though the region was still dependent on stagecoaches and freight wagons for its connections with the outer world. Railroads did not reach Rapid City until 1886, nor Deadwood and Lead until several years later. In the meantime, the closest stations on the Union Pacific and Northern Pacific railroads were well over 200 miles distant. But mining booms were an old story to the West by now. If there were many tenderfeet who responded to the "excitement" of 1874–1876, so were there veterans of every economic level and the most diverse ambitions who know how to seize the opportunity. That is why experienced leadership, men with special talents, and capital for investment appeared so readily once indications of real richness were advertised. In the case of quartz mining, Louis Janin pointed out in 1879 that in the vicinity of Deadwood, Lead, and Central City, "the first attempt at vein mining was in 1877, and now, in the short space of two years, there are numerous mills engaged in crushing the quartz and among them are several as fine and as large as any in the world."[10]

In their basic design the stamp mills reflected in a most interesting way the different sources of leadership and investment in the Black Hills. The California companies, including the great Homestake syndicate, firmly insisted on mills designed and built in San Francisco according to the well-proven California model. Some of their neighbors in the Black Hills turned to the Colorado version, as designed and built in Chicago. Watching the rival models in operation, Louis Janin noted that the Colorado pattern was lighter, cheaper, and required less horsepower, quite aside from the basic advantage that freight from Chicago was about two cents per pound less than from San Francisco. The California mill, by contrast, would "crush more ore than the lighter and slower stamp of a Colorado mill," and thanks to its heavier construction would last longer. "In outward appearance and in their general arrangement, the Colorado mills of the Black Hills cannot compare with the California mills."[11]

In underground operations a similar competition between rival ideas prevailed. Some mines were content to excavate ore through open cuts in the hillsides; the managers of the Homestake mine turned quickly to the shafts and square set timbering that they had learned on the Comstock Lode. With a supply of timber much closer at hand than in Nevada, the "square sets" devised so long ago by Philip Deidesheimer served well for years before being displaced by more economical methods.

The ores extracted from the group of claims that were ultimately absorbed by the Homestake company were free-milling gold quartz—whence the successful resort to stamp milling and amalgamation—but they came not from veins, as in the original California gold lode mines, but rather from replacement deposits, as in the silver mines of Leadville and Eureka. Thus the new understanding that was being gained in Colorado and Nevada in 1879 and the early 1880s by Emmons and his colleagues of the United States Geological Survey was applicable also to this newest of gold mines.

Because of the quartz mines, towns like Lead ultimately had a working population of quite mixed nationality, but initially this was not true. The census of 1880 listed 3570 "miners" in Dakota Territory. Of these 2134 were native-born Americans, and nearly a thousand more came from English-speaking countries—Great Britain, Ireland, and British America, in that order.[12] Soon after quartz mining began, a "Miners' Union" was formed at Lead, with the familiar objectives of "just wages" and mutual protection in dealing with employers. The union prospered and was able to build its union hall in the following year. By mid-1878 wages for skilled mining labor were $3.50 per day; surface labor and mill hands less. This means that the pay scale was intermediate between Comstock levels and the rates prevailing in California. Yet by Western standards, according to Louis Janin, the cost of living was "not high."[13]

The Chinese, who often formed a part of a mining region in the West, were not numerous in the early years. There were only 238 of them in the whole of Dakota Territory in 1880. They were a picturesque if small element in Deadwood, performing such services as doing laundry, running restaurants, and growing vegetables.[14]

The presence of this varied crowd, so hastily assembled, proved decisively that even after thirty years of "excitements" the West was still volatile, still ready to respond to the magic of that word "gold." It was all very well for Lieutenant Colonel Richard I. Dodge of the army to predict that "of each twenty men who will rush to the Black Hills as miners, nineteen would have been better off if they had remained at home." The colonel may have been right, but the crowd went anyway. As the colonel resignedly explained, "the American people are so constituted that each man expects himself to be the twentieth."[15]

*W*HO WERE SOME of the individuals that pushed their way through the Sunday crowd on the main street of Deadwood, or of Lead, four miles away? The stories of the lives of a representative group of them are a recounting in miniature of the history of the mining West, and each individual experience fits into some phase of the life cycle of the Black Hills as a mining region.

Since so many who took part in each gold rush were the veriest transients, perhaps it would be fitting to start with two partners whose whole adventure, from the time they left home in Cordova, Illinois, until they returned to it again, covered only the five months from March 13, 1876, until August 20. Of the two, Jerry Bryan was the more experienced. He had been in California, and his diary speaks of having been on the overland trail, south of the Black Hills, seventeen years earlier. His companion, Charles Hallenbeck, seems to have been a tenderfoot. He was "thinking of Home" before they had been gone three days, and was feeling "a little Blue" by the time they had been on the road two weeks.[16]

The two men traveled on crowded trains to Cheyenne, then hired a wagon and struggled north through driving snow and with a cautious lookout for those "Red Devils," the Indians. When they reached Custer on April 7 they found there "A Ruff crowd" and decided that they didn't "like the looks of" either the country or its new occupants. As redeeming features, at Custer they were able to get "a good Square meal of Slap-jacks and Bacon" and have the privilege of doing their own laundry. They inspected a "Hurdy gurdy Saloon" without being impressed by its shopworn entertainers.

Like most new arrivals, they prospected fruitlessly at first. In mid-May Bryan wrote wearily in his diary that he would have done as well had he remained in Cordova. On May 19, near Deadwood, the mood changed abruptly: "Whoop Hurrah We have struck it at last." For the next two months they did fairly well, first working their placer claim with sluices, later by ground sluicing. They were interrupted at one point by a scarcity of water, at another by a flood that followed after snow and rain. Bryan suffered a back injury and a return of a stomach trouble he had experienced in California. In mid-July the two were selling their tools and sluice boxes in preparation for returning to Illinois. On July 21 Bryan noted in his diary that he was "a few hundred Dollars" richer than when he left home, but somewhat "reduced in flesh" and still a long way from Illinois.

A far more successful pair were the Manuel brothers, who "located" what became the greatest gold mine in the region. By birth French Canadians, Fred and Moses Manuel had grown up on the edge of Sioux

Indian country in Minnesota.[17] Hunting, trapping, and Indian fights had taught them how to survive hardship and danger. In 1867 Moses Manuel started for Montana, whither Fred had gone a year earlier, after finishing his wartime service in the army. Moses was not yet twenty years old. The two brothers tried the full range of possibilities in Montana: they placer mined, prospected endlessly, opened quartz mines, and built an arrastra. Like many other miners, they found that Montana's distance from the nearest railroad was so great it took the profit out of the small veins in their quartz claims. When Montana brought them only modest rewards, they turned south to Utah. At Salt Lake City, Moses was persuaded by a prospector friend to start for Arizona, but another prospector, apparently more convincing than the first, induced them to change course and go instead to Idaho, to seek a "lost" mine.

Finding more Indians than gold in Idaho, Moses joined a new partner to prospect in Utah and Nevada. Once more the small silver veins they found were too far from railroads to be worth development. Returning to his earlier desire to try Arizona, Moses Manuel got up a party to prospect in that Indian-infested territory. When a new Indian scare drove the others back, Moses stubbornly continued alone—and narrowly escaped being killed in a night battle.

Some unprofitable and nearly fatal adventures followed in the arid region that stretches from the Mojave Desert of California across southern Nevada to the Colorado Plateau of Arizona. Apparently undismayed and still ready for anything, Moses departed by steamer in 1874 for southern Alaska and northern British Columbia, when that region was "boomed" as a new gold country.[18] He found gold near Great Slave Lake, but disliked the climate so much that he resolved to go to Africa. Returning with his gold dust to Portland, Oregon, he was waiting there for passage to Africa when he read in a newspaper Custer's report on the Black Hills.

"I had always wanted to go into that country and when I saw that report I saw my opportunity," Moses Manuel later claimed. Instead of sailing for Africa, he bought two horses and rode across the mountains of northern Idaho to Helena, Montana, where he rejoined his brother Fred. While waiting to start for the Black Hills, the two brothers worked a quartz mine and arrastra. Then they headed south to Idaho and eastward across Wyoming, despite a heavy snow that literally buried them. When Indian danger made other gold seekers hesitate to start for the Black Hills, the Manuel brothers organized a small party and went through to their destination without trouble.

By purchase and "location" they finally acquired three good quartz claims, the Homestake, Old Abe, and Golden Terra, but only after prospecting unsuccessfully for some time in the early months of 1876. With a small arrastra and later a ten-stamp mill, they made a little money and proved the potentialities of their claims. A California company proposed to buy the Homestake for $40,000, and posted bond to that effect. By good fortune the Californians failed to complete the purchase before the bond expired. That opened the mine to L. D. Kellogg, who was acting as agent for George Hearst. He raised the offer to $70,000. The Golden Terra was sold for $35,000 to a man from Denver and his partners from Cheyenne; the Old Abe was sold for $45,000.[19]

It was a long-delayed reward for ten years of hardship, danger, and self-instruction in the arts of prospecting, mining, and milling. Even then it was not the end of the trail for the Manuel brothers. They went back to Minnesota to find themselves wives, and thereafter their adventures were more circumscribed, although they continued prospecting and operating mines for years. Moses made Helena, Montana, his permanent headquarters. Fred, some years later, had trouble with his health and decided to sell his claims and move to Los Angeles. Moses lived long enough to fall a victim to one of the new engines that were revolutionizing mining in the present century. His daughter states that he "was killed on July 5, 1905, by an explosion of gasoline fumes in the shaft of his Minnesota Mine near Helena, Montana."[20]

By their standards the two brothers had done well at Lead, yet the big profits went to Hearst, Haggin, Tevis, and those who later bought stock in the great Homestake corporation. The total received by Moses and Fred Manuel, the pioneers, was exceedingly small when compared to the returns that went to the urban investors who could raise the capital and hire the talent to exploit the property extensively and efficiently.

This is not to criticize the corporate owners. They risked their capital not only to buy the original Homestake mine, but also to acquire adjacent claims, purchase water rights, and erect expensive machinery for reducing ore and supplying lumber and cordwood. As an index to the scope of their initial operations, before the mine had proved its profitableness, their first mill had eighty stamps, which meant that it was of Comstock proportions. Their mines and mills became famous throughout the mining world for highly efficient reduction of low-grade ores on a mass-production basis. While to be sure the ores were free-milling and unusually easy to work in stamp mills, nevertheless the notable success of this famous mine would have been impossible without the well-capitalized, highly experienced handling that it began to receive a year after its original "location" by Fred and Moses Manuel and their partners.

"Major" Andrew Jackson Simmons was another example of the veterans who came to the Black Hills from earlier mining regions. Born in 1834 and raised in Indiana, he made the long journey across the plains to California in 1851.[21] When the Comstock Lode became the new sensation, he crossed the Sierras to Nevada. There he joined in the rush to Humboldt County, and from that temporarily promising county was elected and re-elected to Nevada's territorial legislature.[22] Perhaps in Humboldt County or perhaps at Carson City, he knew Mark Twain and later claimed that he was once the roommate of that writer.

Simmons took his Nevada earnings back to California and sought to "play" the San Francisco mining stock market. Like so many others, he was ruined by the manipulations of persons and forces bigger than himself. Having failed in San Francisco, he sought a fresh start in Idaho, but then moved on to Montana, where he served as agent on an Indian reservation from 1871–1873.[23] Resigning in the latter year, he returned to mining in Montana until news of the discoveries in the Black Hills sent him off once more.

"Always an optimist," as a contemporary described him, he entered enthusiastically and confidently into both mining ventures and community affairs in the Black Hills. With a genial, attractive personality, and a quarter century of experience with life in the Far West, he won many friends and made himself a force for good in the community. He served as a councilman and mayor of Rapid City. When, just after the turn of the century, the local mining men formed the Black Hills Mining Men's Association to cultivate "a better feeling among the mining men of the district," as well as to share technical information among themselves and with the world—instead of being secretive as mining men were apt to be—Simmons was one of the committee of six that sponsored publication of a thick pamphlet of the association's technical papers; and with his son Jesse, he was coauthor of the introductory article in the pamphlet. The committee reported that requests for these articles had come in from mining centers in all parts of the world—even from places as distant as South Africa.[24]

The fate of Simmons' mining ventures was suggested by the euphemism used by the journalist who wrote his obituary: "During all these years [in the Black Hills] he was active in promoting and endeavoring to promote and establish upon a profitable basis one mining enterprise after another." The notice concluded: "A complete story of Major Simmons would necessarily include a large part of the history of the development of the western part of the United States, in the making of which development he played an important part."

*W*HEN SIMMONS was serving as one of Humboldt County's two representatives in the Nevada territorial legislature, his fellow member from Humboldt was William Horace Clagett.[25] Clagett was born in 1838 into an old and distinguished Maryland family. His father moved to Keokuk, Iowa, in 1850, where he became well known as a lawyer and judge, and as a newspaper editor of allegedly Southern sympathies. The younger Clagett "read law" in Keokuk and was admitted to the bar before he was twenty, at a time when his father was judge of the local district court. He had the good sense to go east to study law for a year at a school in Albany, New York, before beginning practice.

. After practicing briefly in Keokuk and campaigning for Stephen Douglas for president in 1860, young Clagett decided to go west to Nevada. He married, and on the day of the ceremony departed with his brother on the long overland trip to Carson City. His bride of a few hours was to follow by sea to San Francisco eighteen months later. Clagett practiced law in Carson City until the beginning of the "excitement" over Humboldt County. He then joined another young lawyer named Oliphant, an elderly blacksmith known only as Mr. Ballou, and a young Missourian, Samuel L. Clemens, on the most amusingly recorded of all prospecting expeditions.[26] (Anyone who has not read Mark Twain's account of this financially profitless adventure has missed a real experience.)

"Young Clagett," as Mark Twain referred to him, was elected to the lower house of the territorial legislature from Humboldt County in 1862 and 1863, but his real distinction came in the confusing year of 1864. In January of 1864 he was elected senator from Humboldt, and in November was chosen senator from Storey County (the Comstock Lode) when the first state legislature was selected. After a long struggle at the Republican state convention in 1865, he failed by five votes to win his party's nomination for Congress.[27] In the meantime his law practice at Humboldt and later at Virginia City was proving none too remunerative in those discouraging days when Humboldt County was being deserted and the Comstock Lode was in depression.

He decided to try his luck in Montana, and in 1866 moved his family first to Helena and then to Deer Lodge, which remained his home for a decade. In Montana as in Nevada he entered energetically into law practice, politics, and mining. Despite his Republican allegiance in a territory where Democrats were strong, he was elected territorial delegate to the national Congress in 1871. His two years in Washington were very active. The bill to establish Yellowstone National Park was passed in large part through his efforts.[28] In promoting the great mining statute of 1872, he joined his friend of Nevada days, Senator William M. Stewart, in earnest advocacy. He urged legislation against polygamy and Mormon control of Utah. He obtained additional national banks, post offices, and an assay office for Montana, and intervened in Indian affairs.

Bancroft, the historian of the West, said of him that he did more for Montana in the first eight months of his term than his predecessors had done in seven years.[29]

When even this notable record failed to win him re-election, he went back to law practice in Deer Lodge, but Montana in the 1870s, like Nevada in 1866, was in a depression because of the transition in mining then taking place. To quote one who knew him for fifty years, "Clagett became restless and impatient, as he generally did when not actively employed." A brief test of the possibilities in Colorado in 1877 proved unencouraging. Meantime the newspapers were full of news from the Black Hills.

Clagett hurried off to Deadwood, where soon he was listed as one of the half-dozen attorneys with offices in "lawyer's row." There he found himself in stiff competition, for the boom had brought to Deadwood "the best legal talent from the mining states and territories of the west."[30] But Clagett was by then famous as an able and hard-working trial lawyer in mining and criminal cases. As an orator he was noted for "his clear, ringing, well-modulated voice; his well-chosen words and graceful gestures." He was handsome, courteous, and generous, with manners "somewhat of the old southern style." Surprisingly for one who had lived so long amidst earthy comrades, he did not drink. For all his polished manners, he was careless in dress and appearance.[31]

Raw mining towns were Clagett's proper stage, and he soon established himself as a major figure in the new Dakota courts. He either did not seek or did not find in the Black Hills an outlet for his aggressive, uncompromising political stands and his Republican affiliation. Unlike Simmons, he became dissatisfied, and after making his contribution to the life of the new community, he left Deadwood in 1882 to return to Montana. There he tried briefly to work a quartz claim at Butte, but soon restlessly drifted west to open a law office at Portland, Oregon. He was hardly established there when news of the mining rush to the Coeur d'Alene took him off again. Years later a pioneer who had been a fledgling attorney in 1883 could still remember the electric effect upon a crowd of hitherto disorganized miners in snowbound Idaho, when Clagett came into camp and "stood before us like a prophet," bringing "the message of law and order," and instinctively assuming leadership. Clagett was only forty-five by then, but with Nevada, Montana, and the Black Hills behind him, he was already known as "the 'Gray Eagle' of the mining frontier."[32]

Idaho offered Clagett a greater opportunity than the Black Hills had given him. He handled major law suits over mining claims, "engaged actively but not very successfully in mining," and became a leading figure in the politics of northern Idaho. When Idaho held its convention in 1889 to draft a state constitution, Clagett served as president.[33] Twice he was a candidate for the United States Senate from Idaho, once as a Republican and once as a Populist and free-silver advocate. Ultimately he became a campaigner for William Jennings Bryan and was certainly closely allied with the Democratic party if not actually a member of it, thus very nearly completing his circuit back to the party of his prewar youth.

He died poor, soon after starting still another new law practice, this time in Spokane, Washington. He left an enviable reputation that lingered for years in the mining West. A lifelong friend said of him: "Old miners all over the West will tell you they heard 'Billy Clagett' make a speech at such a time and place, and what a wonderful talker he was."

If Clagett seems a perpetual wanderer of the mining frontier, consider an even more peripatetic figure, a veritable Baron Munchausen of the West. "Jim" Wardner, who boasted that towns were named after him in Idaho and British Columbia, was a well-known promoter who was part P. T. Barnum and part Colonel Sellers, the figure made famous in Mark Twain's *The Gilded Age*. He took the trouble to write up his own life story, and a wonderful tale it is, especially in the parts that are so palpably untrue.[34]

Wardner came late to the mining West. Born in 1846 of a quiet Milwaukee family, he had served in the army and had lived by his wits for years before he reached California in 1871. He tried mining in Arizona, but sold out because of the Apaches. At San Francisco he tried "plunging" in Comstock mining shares. In the Black Hills, if one can believe him, he tried absolutely everything: storekeeping, saloon keeping, freighting, running an oyster bar, mining, farming, and trying to "corner" the market in feed and eggs. He claims he even sought to organize a walking contest.

News of the Coeur d'Alene boom of course drew him away once more. His Idaho adventures started in familiar fashion with a speculation in synthetic butter when the real article was in short supply. It is a maxim among men of Wardner's type that every promoter strikes it rich at least once. Wardner's chance came unexpectedly, when he stumbled into partnership with the prospectors who were "locating" what became one of the great mines of America, the Bunker Hill and Sullivan. Wardner forced his way into a part interest in the claim, and presently induced Samuel T. Hauser of Montana to invest. Wardner's share of the venture was $100,000 and the honor of christening the Coeur d'Alene mining town that still bears his name.[35]

The $100,000 was all lost. How? With good-humored self-depreciation Wardner admitted that a "man with good sound judgment and a reasonable-sized head" would not have lost it. "But the shoddy man, the lucky shoddy man, the man who never before had a hundred dollars, a man who begins to feel poor when he gets the first $50,000, a man who constantly and wilfully and determinedly persists in getting over his head in the confusing waters of speculation," such a man is sure to lose his hundred thousand, and not one in a thousand ever wins it back.

It was a revealing confession. It helps to explain why the mining West was so cluttered with unsuccessful hopeful men—why so many mining ventures were launched against unlikely odds.

Wardner tried to regain his losses in South Africa, Nevada, British Columbia, and the Klondike. His autobiography ends as he readies himself to sail for the new gold fields at Cape Nome, Alaska, "with all the glowing aspirations and ambitions of twenty-five years ago." Modestly he signed himself "Jim Wardner, of Far Western mining fame— one of those mortals of such intense activity of mind and body that the best conditions of the present are naught by comparison with the possibilities of the future, and who are, therefore, in mining parlance, 'up to-day and down to-morrow.'"

*J*IM WARDNER was a promoter, not a business man in the ordinary sense of that term. His outlook was quite different from that of a local merchant such as P. A. Gushurst of Lead, who had an inherent interest in the continuity and prosperity of his community. Gushurst was the nephew by marriage of Fred Manuel and the man who took down Moses Manuel's autobiography when the latter dictated it. A native of Rochester, New York, Gushurst left home at sixteen and went to Omaha, then important as a main point on the recently completed Union Pacific Railroad. Most of the half-dozen years he spent at Omaha were passed in the shops of the Union Pacific Company, though he worked for one year in a grocery store.[36]

He reached the Black Hills in May of 1876 and was in Deadwood on June 1. En route, he and his partner had bought a considerable supply of goods from disgusted men who had given up and turned back. Upon reaching Deadwood, Gushurst began selling this stock while his partner did the firm's prospecting for gold. Gushurst spent the early summer building and operating a store at Deadwood, then yielded to the urging of miners who wanted him to move his stock to Lead to establish the first grocery store in that camp. His store at Lead was built out of lumber that he himself cut during the winter of 1876–1877.

Gushurst's marriage in May 1878 to the niece of Fred Manuel was the first wedding ceremony performed in Lead. The couple began married life in a two-room house that, with many subsequent additions and improvements, was to be their home for fifty-five years.

For many years Gushurst simultaneously managed his "extensive" mercantile business, was owner or partner in a series of mining ventures, and carried a succession of public responsibilities that reflected the changing nature of Lead's economy and society. At first he was elected recorder of the local mining district (Gold Run Gulch). When a citizens' meeting was held in 1877 to devise a somewhat more formal organization for the growing camp, then beginning its quartz boom, Gushurst was chosen one of three "trustees." He served as school treasurer and for six years as a member of the Board of Education.

When the whole future of Lead was threatened by litigation with the monopolistic Homestake Mining Company over the validity of the town's title to the ground on which it stood, Gushurst was chairman of the group that dealt with the mining company, and was one of the three trustees who subsequently handled the complex business of obtaining valid individual deeds for the citizens who were in actual occupancy. Similarly, when Lead felt sufficiently mature to transform itself into a municipality in 1890, Gushurst was one of the members of the first Municipal Council. Before the end of the century he was elected mayor, was a director of the local national bank, and was president of the Society of Black Hills Pioneers. When the Black Hills Mining Men's Association was formed, Gushurst served with Major Simmons on the committee that edited and published the association's very useful technical papers. All told, he carried as balanced a set of responsibilities as one could ask.

In their old age Gushurst and his wife moved to Denver. There this fine old couple celebrated their seventy-seventh wedding anniversary. Gushurst died in 1955 at the age of 102, his wife in 1961 at 101. Their lives thus extended from those exciting days of 1876 down virtually to the present moment.

The life stories of these Black Hills pioneers, each with his particular role, sometimes in local affairs, sometimes in the larger history of the mining West, tie together and give reality to the first three decades of gold and silver mining. The insights offered by these biographical sketches suggest that while many who took part in a mining rush were not working miners, nearly everyone speculated in mines at least part of the time. The sketches also reveal the distinction between the many who were birds of passage and the few who stayed on to build something permanent out of such communities as had a future.

The occasional presence of men like Gushurst who showed a real concern for the town's welfare and continuity does not mean that Deadwood and Lead had none of the gunmen and gamblers so dear to fiction.

On the contrary, the Black Hills had their full share of colorful personalities who would have been rejected in a more conventional society. There were "Wild Bill" Hickok, the dead-shot killer and gambler; "Calamity Jane," the prostitute who dressed like a man; "Poker Alice" Tubbs, the female faro dealer; and all those stage robbers that the volunteer posses finally caught and hanged.

Conversely, ministers of several different sects labored devotedly against the heaviest odds. In their own often solitary struggle to establish religion, they would have understood immediately the saddened comment of Bishop Daniel Tuttle, one of the most loved and most universally remembered of all the mining-camp missionaries. Of his first winter in Montana in 1867–1868, Bishop Tuttle wrote:

> Next to the sense of loneliness, I was most oppressed with the sad conviction of the prayerlessness and godlessness of the people among whom I found myself. Of them, women, especially good women, were a very small minority. Men were kind personally, generous in giving money, respectful and courteous; but I was appalled to discover day by day how almost universally given up they were to vicious practices.[37]

A pioneer California clergyman, as he looked back on thirty years' labor remarked: "One of the lessons my California life has most thoroughly taught me is, that transplanted people do not begin life on new ground on as high a plane as they occupied before removal."[38]

Perhaps that unflattering conclusion helps to explain why mining camps and towns so often seemed one-sided in character—one-sided in that the emphasis of daily life was primarily on individual gain and community impermanency. Most people had come to the mining West to seek wealth and to enjoy excitement and change. How fortunate it was that a few had from the beginning a sense of public responsibility, and that as the frontier era passed, an increasing number came to value and even to love the strange, demanding, and sometimes beautiful country to which they found themselves devoting their lives. By 1880 there were in the surviving camps men who not only had lived through most of the stages in the life cycle of their own area, but also, like Clagett, Simmons, and the Manuels, had witnessed much of the history of the whole mining West.

*T*HAT HISTORY falls into several principal eras. The first, from 1848 to 1858, belonged almost exclusively to California and to gold. For most of those who took part in it, this first period was a time of apprenticeship and learning by the expensive method of trial and error. The percentage of wasted effort and squandered capital was correspondingly high. The loss of the former must have far exceeded the latter, for although more sophisticated techniques began to be developed during the decade, the principal stress was still upon simple placer mining, where labor was the chief investment. What little mining there was elsewhere in the Far West during the decade was essentially a spilling over of Californian effort.

The second era, from 1858 to 1868, brought three simultaneous phenomena. Of these the most important was the expansion of the mining frontier into the whole Far West, primarily through simple placer mining for gold. In large part this meant a re-enactment in thousands of new camps of California's experience in the previous decade. Almost equally significant was the beginning of large-scale vein mining for silver on the Comstock Lode, which led very quickly to a revolution in finance and form of ownership, as the stock of big incorporated companies was placed on sale on newly established stock exchanges. In scale of underground operations and size and costliness of mechanical equipment, the Comstock Lode produced as significant an innovation as it did by its resort to incorporation and popular marketing of stock. In the meantime, in California both hydraulic and quartz mining matured into comparatively stable industries, while in the Great Basin of Nevada camps rose and fell as inexperienced men struggled to master a hostile environment that presented such unfamiliar problems as silver-lead smelting and deposits that were deceptively richer near the surface than further down.

The third era, 1869 to 1879, belonged to Nevada, and primarily to the Comstock Lode, which was then in its great bonanzas. Splendid technical accomplishments and the achievement of a highly professional standard of workmanship stood in contrast to speculation, stock-market jobbery, and a sometimes extravagantly wasteful expenditure of resources. Except for California and Utah, the rest of the Far West either slid down toward decay—wherever dependence still rested on superficial placers—or stood waiting, with hopes centered on an underground mining that was dependent on better transportation, complex ores, and more abundant capital. But this was also a period that saw an increasing investment from outside the Far West, reflecting an interest that was sure to grow as railroads reached additional mining areas. California maintained its relatively stable development, while Utah, under the stimulus of its new transportation facilities, entered upon a remarkably quick although often unsound growth as a silver-lead producer.

The fourth and final era opened with 1879, as the Comstock Lode's prosperity came to an end and Colorado rose to pre-eminence, thanks to its silver-lead and its intelligent adaptation of European smelting practices. Colorado's importance included the first large production of a base metal, with all that that implied economically and sociologically. A few years later Montana, Idaho, Arizona, Utah, and New Mexico, in varying degree, were to follow Colorado's example. All began producing silver in quantity and, increasingly, one of the two base metals, lead or copper, in addition. By that time investment was flowing into Western mines from many Eastern-seaboard cities and England, and San Francisco could no longer confidently assume that it would provide the financial leadership. Colorado, much of Montana, and parts of Idaho and Utah had long stood outside California's sphere of influence. Now, in 1881, the *Mining and Scientific Press* revealed that within the "past two years" the center of mining stock transactions had shifted from San Francisco to New York. The financial columns of that same newspaper showed that Far Western mines were paying out dividends through offices in New York, Boston, Philadelphia, and London.

This is not to say that the center of investment had moved eastward, for throughout the first thirty years of gold and silver many more mines were operated with locally contributed funds, on an unincorporated basis, or as "closely held" incorporations not subject to public sale of stock, than as joint-stock companies whose shares were dealt in by the public daily. The shift to New York, however, does suggest the same conclusion toward which the development of the new railroads and the base metals pointed: namely, that mining was being integrated into the national economy rather than continuing to be largely an isolated Western effort. The changing social character of the mining towns was a further revelation that the frontier phase had already passed in most parts of the West, and was being greatly altered in all.

Within each of the four generalized eras of Western mining, individual camps, districts, or even whole states were passing through varying stages of the life cycle typical of mining regions. To illustrate, many of the boom camps founded in California in 1849 passed through all of the stages of that life cycle within the 1850s, so that by the time the second era began, such towns were already dead or dying. Their fate was in contrast to the fortunate few that during the 1860s were struggling through a difficult transition into maturity. The same phenomenon was even better illustrated by the fate of so many of the camps that sprang up in the Rocky Mountains during the second era. Many of these camps were born, rushed through their flush days, decayed, and died, all within one decade. Indeed, the whole state of Idaho came dangerously close to suffering that fate.

Where the rate of mortality was so high, the early mining civilization bequeathed to the succeeding generations an inheritance that seems relatively slight when compared with the labor and capital that had been invested or the gold and silver that had been taken out and sent eastward or to Europe. That is why Idaho and Montana had such a difficult time when their mines seemed to have failed by 1870, and why Nevada suffered when the Comstock Lode and many a Great Basin outpost underwent a similar decline by 1880. California was not injured so severely because the initial impetus of the Gold Rush was never entirely dissipated. Productive mines of a capitalized kind, a prosperous San Francisco, and a growing agriculture and livestock industry replaced the dwindling energies of the old placer miners. To a lesser degree the evolution of Denver and beginning of farming and ranching gave similar help to Colorado when its declining mines temporarily threatened disaster. Oregon and Washington, similarly, benefited richly from the nonmineral industries to which the gold and silver booms gave rise, even though these areas themselves played only a lesser role in actual mining.

Ultimately Colorado, Idaho, and Montana were carried into a new prosperity by a wholly new kind of mining that brought its own problems along with its rewards. No comparable mercy blessed Nevada; once gutted, it remained depressed for twenty years, and has never found a real substitute for the silver of its vanished greatness. Utah, like Oregon, profited handsomely from the needs of the mining camps for supplies before it became in its own right an important mining region. Arizona and New Mexico might long have been left to the Apaches and Navaho had not miners and prospectors dramatized the need for effective military campaigns and better transportation.

The heritage of early mining was thus a varied one not easily reduced to a single generalization. The most significant gain brought by the miners was the sudden introduction of people, capital, transportation, and commerce where none had been before. Whether this advantage could be retained permanently was always a matter of uncertainty. So much depended on the physical resources and commercial geography of each region, although part of the outcome was determined by the ingenuity and perseverance of those pioneers who decided to see their new home through its period of trial.

Manifestly, a much larger proportion of the Far West was in a frontier condition during the first and second of the four principal mining eras than in the latter two. It follows also that there was never a single mining frontier, nor a frontier line. Mining development was not that orderly. Rather, there were many mining frontiers, not necessarily contiguous in place or time. No two were precisely the same. Geographic setting, distance, geology, and the special attitudes and knowledge of the early population all gave local variety within the general pattern of uniformities. If any one characteristic stood out in common to the mining West, it was instability. Even within their lifetimes, the camps and towns fluctuated sharply in size and prosperity. Today most of them can be seen only as ghost towns, as silent, dusty monuments that recall a colorful if transitory society to which a large part of the Far West owes its beginning.

The Mining Frontier
Another Viewpoint

*I*n the preceding chapters Rodman W. Paul traced the evolution of the
mining frontier across the Mountain West, the technological and scientific
innovations that made it possible, and the establishment of its economic
and political institutions. In the three chapters that follow, Elliott West asks
questions that Paul could not consider or, had he thought about them,
would have been hard pressed to address because many subjects had not
yet been adequately researched. Moreover, in the years since Paul's book
was published, the study of the American Frontier has broadened as well
as deepened in its level of analysis. Today scholars look beyond the creation of institutions to the lives of people influenced by them. Today scholars look as keenly at folklore, songs, and humor as a way to understand a
society as they once did by studying its economy. Little wonder then that
race, ethnicity, gender, social hierarchies, and the environment are the subjects that West's chapters discuss in detail.

These are significant subjects, but Elliott West has an ear for a good
story, and eye for an interesting character, and an ability to write a narrative that brings history to life. Like all good storytellers, West is always

informative and insightful. If, as many historians believe, we as a people are what our history tells, West tells us much about our nation's past, both good and bad; and he does so with wit and shrewdness. His narrative is judgmental, and he is aware that the frontier story, more than any other part of American history, is marked by irony and the unanticipated consequences of what appear to be small individual acts.

Elliott West focuses attention on Native Americans, the original inhabitants of the mining regions, to see how widespread was the impact of the mass migration of alien people on the Indian way of life. Indians who lived in immediate proximity to mining areas were hit the hardest. Many were ruthlessly exploited, brutalized, and killed. Their life-giving resources were plundered. Even the tribes that lived along the overland trail, miles from any mining camp, suddenly found their lives drastically disrupted as thousands upon thousands of gold seekers crossed the Great Plains, first to California and later to the mountain West's gold fields. The Argonauts' livestock consumed precious grass and polluted the streams. They carelessly exploited the limited amount of wood in the arid plains and mountain areas. Deadly diseases too followed in the wake of the great migration of gold seekers. West recounts the events that brought the displacement, degradation, and near extinction of many western Indian communities. The western mining frontier proved to be a vast source of national wealth but it virtually destroyed the Indian way of life on the northern plains and mountain West. Indigenous peoples, West argues, paid the high social cost for the nation's quest for gold.

West also demythologizes the life of the average miner, both as prospector and industrial worker. He gives many examples of the romance of life in the mining camps that make for lively reading, but he also indicates that they are at best distortions and at worst bad history. Living conditions were extremely harsh in most camps because they were often situated in inhospitable places. Women were in short supply, and although working women, whether prostitutes, miners, cooks, or laundresses, were well rewarded, their lives were hard. Men longed for female company but the sex ratios were so out of balance that men were often compelled to find recreation in gambling, drinking, and whoring. Social institutions were rudimentary. Work, either as a placer miner or underground laborer, was neither very financially rewarding nor easy. West offers a new hypothesis when he argues that workers in mining camps craved order, and they struggled to create a sense of community even though they were transients. The quest for wealth usually created an environment hostile to community formation, but West points out that men found their sense of community in the act of work itself. His evidence for this idea warrants serious thought. Because men and women are social beings, West insists, the mining frontier should also be seen as a constant struggle to fulfill this natural urge for community.

The mining frontier was always more ethnically and racially diverse than even the immigrant-filled cities in the eastern United States. Native Americans themselves represented scores of different linguistic and cultural groups. Miners from Chile and from Mexican Sonora were often mestizos. European miners came from virtually every national entity; they rubbed shoulders with Pacific Islanders and Chinese, who early on found transit to the Gold Mountain, as the Chinese called California. Americans from the North and South, black and white, joined in the competitive search for gold and silver. Their raucous voices reflected racial and ethnic social tensions, and the mining frontier, as West points out, exposes the seamier aspects of prejudice. It was not a peaceable kingdom. Racial and ethnic conflict was present almost from the beginning. The mining frontier extended into the West the ongoing national debate over the nature of whiteness and what it meant and was to mean in America. West highlights the irony of ethnic hostility by explaining that the Chinese were criticized not for having bad habits, but for demonstrating the same character traits that whites claimed for themselves.

Elliott West brings his story through the passing of the frontier era. The railroad was part and parcel of what brought the major changes in western style. The transition from gold hunting and simple placer mines to lode and hydraulic mining brought with it environmental damage that was left for a later generation to repair. The prospector's get-rich dream faded within two generations. Mining by the end of the nineteenth century was as representative of a capitalist society as any eastern steel or manufacturing city. Its population was as varied, its labor force as much exploited, its women's roles parallel, and its financial management centered in eastern capital markets. Mining towns were islands of industry supplied by the same agricultural small-scale market economy that sustained eastern industrial communities.

The story of how all of this occurred is in the chapters that follow. It is a bright and refreshingly new narrative. Just as Rodman Paul has explained the origins and expansion of the mining frontier, Elliott West illustrates in surprising ways the unanticipated consequences of the discovery of a few gold nuggets in the gravel at the bottom of Sutter's mill.

◁ 10 ▷

Breaking and Building
Communities

*G*iacomo Puccini's operatic melodrama, *La Fanciulla del West,* opens in a California mining camp saloon, the Polka. Roughhewn customers in wide hats and gum boots at first carouse with songs of "Doo Da Day!" and set-em-up good fellowship (*"Whisky per tutti!"*). Then the guitarist begins a plaintive tune:

> My mother, what will she do if I do not return?
> How much she will cry!
> My old people, what will they do?
> They will think I will not come home!
> My dog! Will he recognize me?

Suddenly one of the men, Jim Larkin, breaks into sobs:

> I can't stand it anymore! Send me away!
> I am sick, and I don't know what is making me sick!
> I am ruined! I am tired of being a miner!
> I want a plow! I want my mother!

200

Moved by this litany, the men pass the hat and send their friend home with strengthening words (*"Corragio!"*), then return to their revels in a slightly more somber mood.[1]

For all its sentimentality, the scene has a lot of truth. Gold and silver camps, like Puccini's stage, did hold mostly men. Miners swilled plenty of whiskey in lots of barrooms like the Polka, and they were fond of stomping dances that often reverberated into the early mornings. As implied by the tattered dress of the operatic performers, life outside the saloons was consumed by backbreaking drudge labor.

Jim Larkin's tearful confession touches on another fact of frontier life. Many who were drawn to a gold or silver rush found themselves pulled powerfully by what they had left behind. They may not have sobbed publicly for a plow, but the memories and comforting sureties of a familiar past always tugged against the excitement and hopes of their unsettled present. A man caught in these emotional cross-currents could end up literally sick for home.

Beneath this tension was the question of community. As far back as we can see in the historical record, communities have been central to staying alive and to being human. People fit their different tasks into a mutual reliance—farmers and millers, freighters and blacksmiths, hunters and hide-scrapers. They find a common identity by recalling the same memories, praying to the same gods, laughing at the same old jokes. Structures vary, and the particulars are a dazzling diversity, but all betray the need to join into a functional and emotional whole. "What life have you if you have not life together?" T. S. Eliot wrote, "There is no life that is not in community."[2]

Mining frontiers seemed to violate this historical universal. They rolled into Indian communities, broke them up and scattered their parts. The motley of strangers who crowded the natives off their land showed little obvious interest in building ones of their own. The one thing they had in common, a fierce competitive drive to profit themselves, drove them apart. Many, like Jim Larkin, asked something like T. S. Eliot's question and wondered whether life in its fuller meanings was possible in the disorienting gatherings where they found themselves.

Exactly because mining frontiers seemed such a killing ground for communities, they are especially worth studying. For communities prevailed. With adaptive imagination Native Americans kept their cultures alive. The throngs of wealth-seekers found some common ground, if only out of a need to work and feed themselves. As social animals they reached around for human connections, using the oddest tools and most eccentric maneuvers. In the end a mining frontier revealed the power of these ancient collective urges.

*T*HE *WEST OF* 1848 was a mosaic of scores of Native American communities. Each had a long history of adapting to changing circumstances, including the disruptions and opportunities brought by Euro-Americans. But gold and silver rushes brought changes on a scale and of a speed no one could have imagined. Every aspect of life was touched. Within twenty years of the first great gold discovery at Sutter's Mill, no western native community was unaffected. Some teetered on the edge of annihilation.

A Native American community was more than individuals and village boundaries. People, landmarks, spirits, physical forces, animals, and plants were bound up in a network of kinship and common memory, influence and obligation. The Pimas of southern Arizona considered the fruit of the mescal cactus to be descendants of a pair of Pima brothers who had been transformed while returning from their father and uncle, Clouds and Wind. The Crow people told erotic tales about beautiful women cuckolding the sun, men fathering children by bison-women, and the courageous wife who dealt with her cruel husband, Worms-in-the-Face, with the help of her friends, the badgers, porcupines and ants.[3] The Miwoks of California said that good people became great horned owls after death; the bad became meadowlarks. The dead among the Nisenan loped about as coyotes and spun over the land as whirlwinds. Everyday life was crowded with spirits. The benevolent Gahe watched over the western Apaches. Once they opened a cave in a mountain, drove some Mexican soldiers inside and sealed them up forever. The soldiers' boots are said to still sit outside.[4]

This does not mean that Indians and their surroundings were necessarily in harmony. Spirits could be threatening and relations touchy among the many members of these communities. Native peoples did, however, see their physical settings as alive in ways that whites did not. Human community was indistinguishable from its particular place and the dense associations among that place's many parts—landforms, four-legged and two-legged and no-legged creatures, weather, unseen presences. There were clear rules of behavior for everyone and everything. Respect for those rules was at the foundation of social order and of what security could be expected from life.

Such a community will always be disrupted by outsiders, simply because the newcomers will not recognize its members, much less how they fit together. Back home mining frontiersmen had their own attachments of memory and belief—affection for some founder's oak on a town square, faith symbolized in steeple and cross, social distinctions among people and neighborhoods. But they were wholly ignorant of the corresponding connections of the Indian communities they entered. Because nothing they saw resonated with larger implications, everything reverted to simple, pragmatic meanings. A creek was a creek, distinguished only by whether it had gold in it, while to a Yurok one stream offered spots where he or she could speak to salmon and another was due special respect because it separated them from a panther-woman who collected men's heads. A prospector looked at a tree, not as a local character, but as something either useful or in the way. The Sioux considered magpies allies who had saved human beings in the Great Race around the Black Hills; miners shot them as pests that stole their biscuits.

Without laying hands on a single Indian, white intruders assaulted native communities merely by acting, by their own standards, normally. We shake down acorns and pine nuts and use only dead wood, an elderly Wintu (California) woman commented, while whites attacked trees indiscriminately:

> The tree says, Don't. I am sore. Don't hurt me. But they chop it down and cut it up. The spirit of the land hates them. . . . They blast rocks and scatter them on the earth. The rock says, Don't. You are hurting me. . . . [But] the water, it can't be hurt. . . . The white people use the water of sacred springs in their houses. The water says, That's all right. You can use me but you can't overcome me . . . I am awfully smart . . . I came from the ocean and I shall go back into the ocean. . . . When I am out of sight I am on my way home.[5]

By this view of things a few shrewd participants, like water, might survive, but as freighters and meat-sellers, dam-builders and gardeners violated well worn rules of proper action at every moment of every workday, they put terrible pressure on the intricate arrangements among people, acorns, rocks, badgers, and sagebrush. Sooner than later, those communities would shudder and crack.

A gold or silver rush also decimated Indian communities by introducing devastating diseases. This danger was not new. Three centuries earlier Europeans had brought the first epidemics, diseases previously unknown in North America. With little acquired resistance, Indians suffered horrific losses. Now men and women converged from across the world, pooling their illnesses and passing them on to whoever was nearby and susceptible. California's Maidu Indians first were struck by cholera in 1849, then smallpox, malaria, typhoid, influenza, and pneumonia over the next several years. Others were hit by all these, plus measles, diphtheria, whooping cough, and tuberculosis.

The calamity was not confined to the camps. If anything diseases were spread more easily along the trails to the gold and silver fields. Overland emigrants lived in conditions often as crowded and filthy as in any mid-nineteenth-century urban slum. They camped in one another's garbage and drank from the same fouled water sources. They left their own dead scarcely buried and their dead stock lying by the road to rot. Along the Humboldt River an overlander visited some desperately ill Paiutes dying at a rate of several each day. On the short ride to their camp he saw six emigrant graves as well as carcasses of thirty-seven horses, forty-two oxen and five mules. During the next night's march he noted that "from *Nasal* evidence we were continually passing dead stock."[6] Inevitably, contagion was passed from overlanders to the Pawnees, Cheyennes, Kiowas, Lakotas, Shoshones and others who visited and traded in their camps.

White Americans would recall 1849 as a symbol of adventure and opportunity, but the Southern Cheyennes still call it The Year the Cramps Came. They lost up to a third of their population that year from cholera contracted from forty-niners, as did the Kiowas, who depict the year in their calendar as a man howling in agony.[7] On Independence Day in that year a government engineer visited some Lakota lodges along the Platte River. Inside he found several decomposing cholera victims lying beside weapons and saddles meant to carry them to a better life.[8] Assaults of small-pox corresponded suspiciously with some of the heaviest traffic to the mines—1850–51 among the western Sioux and 1860–61 among the Kiowas, Cheyennes and Arapahoes.[9] Soon endemic diseases settled to stay along commercial routes to the mining centers. In 1863 a special medical agent along a road to Colorado reported influenza, pneumonia, bronchitis, catarrhal fever, dysentery, gonorrhea and syphilis as well as an unidentified disease that brought high fever and grotesque swelling and often killed its victims within days.[10]

The secondary effects of diseases were almost as bad. When every fourth or fifth person died from cholera or smallpox, an economy unraveled. Animals were not hunted, food went ungathered, infants unsuckled. Survivors, weakened by hunger and stress, were more susceptible to other diseases and less able to cope with the other challenges that seem to come from all directions. A general malaise set in, a listlessness of despair. As in epidemics everywhere, the toll was highest among a tribe's basic human resource, its infants and young. "We found some Indian graves in the trees and on platforms of poles," an army officer wrote of an abandoned camp near the overland road during the cholera epidemic of 1867. "The dead were mostly children—very little fellows most of them!"[11] A Californian diarist in 1855 estimated half of a nearby tribe had died within three years: "There is not a child under nine years of age."[12] But because women and men of prime child-producing years had little resistance to the new diseases, they also died in great numbers, and among surviving potential parents smallpox, tuberculosis, malaria, syphilis and gonorrhea impaired conception and made miscarriages more likely. Communities, that is, were whittled from both ends. As disease was thinning the number of the living, it was disabling the survivors' ability to refill their ranks.

This reproductive crippling suggests a broader, especially devastating assault. The basic cells of communities are its families. Without them

physical and cultural life cannot continue. Mining frontiersmen dismantled Indian families much more intentionally than by bringing diseases.
One of the most appalling practices in California was the systematic theft
of Indian children. An army officer in 1850 wrote contemptuously of a
militia column returning with a crowd of mothers and children, the latter
"mostly yet drawing their sustenance from the maternal fount. . . . Oh what
a world for humbug."[13] Child theft was so extensive in some regions that
a vigorous market for kidnapped boys and girls developed. Two brothers
left their farm in Sacramento Valley for the easier work of raiding Indian
villages and auctioning children from a wagon. A Humboldt newspaper in
1855 reported large numbers sold in rural areas at prices ranging from
$50 to $250, and two years later the *Sacramento Union* noted several "bright
little specimens" available from a raid near Yreka. Some children were
bought as sources of amusement. The officer who scoffed at the "humbug"
campaign acquired a boy, dressed him in a tailored uniform, and called
him one of his two "pets"—the other being a wounded eagle.[14] Most were
sold into domestic labor. So many were purchased in Ukiah, according to
one account, that a typical family kept at least one and often two or three,
like caged birds, working around the house.[15]

Indian women also were common targets of young men who were
often frustrated and always freed from most social restraints. Brutal assaults
took place in all mining regions, but once again California saw the worst.
From the first weeks there were reports of rapes and raids on rancherías to
kidnap women for extended sexual abuse. Families that were captured or
persuaded to move to reservations were even more vulnerable. Employees
of a reservation reportedly were daily and nightly engaged in kidnapping
the younger females, and three men in charge of prisoners from one campaign were confronted by a mob of local miners demanding the women.

Understandably, Indians struck back. A young boy taken from his
family set fire to his master's home, then was lynched by a mob. When a
miner refused to return a woman he had stolen, he and his companions
were all killed and his body butchered. A rancher, furious at his servant
boy for running back to see his family, killed the boy and five of his relatives and floated their bodies downriver to taunt white neighbors who had
criticized similar acts in the past. Indians then killed and feasted on the
man's cattle. Such exchanges escalated to a pattern of indiscriminate mur-
ders of native children and their mothers, widespread killing of livestock
by enraged relatives, then further reprisals against the Indians.[16] All sides
suffered, but the cost was far greater for the Indians, who were much more
likely to be killed, whose numbers now were considerably smaller, and
who were already reeling under other pressures.

Families were being pried apart in other ways. When recruited into
labor, men and women typically were separated. Women were put into

household service, men sent to work in fields, mines, or as servants in other homes. Because women were at much greater risk of violence, many fled the new settlements or were hidden far away. Soon the native census profile was bizarrely out of whack. In 1860 Indian men outnumbered women, usually substantially, in every California mining county. Ordinary Indian households were an endangered species; in a sampling of two counties not a single Indian conjugal couple was found. The effect was predictable. In Butte County, where men predominated and where 84 percent of Indians lived outside any sort of family household, native or white, the birth rate dropped virtually to zero.[17]

Here was a grotesque mimicry of the mining frontier. A gold or silver camp was also made up mostly of men living apart from their families. But its imbalance was an expression of sass and optimism. Men left their families behind in the confident hope of bettering their lives. The Indians' community profile—fractured families, absent women, missing children— by contrast was a measure of disaster and desperation. Diseases gnawed at their numbers and blighted their future. In the most populous mining region child-stealers and rapists pulled apart their families. Massive disruptions shattered their connections to the world as they knew it and shocked their understanding of basic realities.

The wonder is that any Indian communities survived. Some did in fact vanish. Many more, however, held onto enough physical, cultural, and spiritual basics to maintain an irreducible core of collective integrity. That persistence would be one of the more remarkable stories of frontier history.

*T*HE MINING FRONTIERSMEN who flooded over Indian communities at first seemed incapable of making ones of their own. There were many impediments, starting with the environment itself. Some areas, notably the California hills, were pleasant enough for much of the year, but a lot of the mining West had some of the most extreme conditions on the continent. Desert camps like Tombstone were blistered by heat, swept by desiccating winds, and starved of life's most basic need, water. What was available was often close to undrinkable. A New Englander dismissed the stagnant pond water near his camp, adding a sectional touch: "[It] is not fit for humans, though Missourians wouldn't mind it."[18] Many towns sat seven to ten thousand feet up in the Sierra Nevada and Rocky Mountains. Winters were bitterly cold (the lowest recorded temperature in the contiguous United States, minus 69.7 degrees Fahrenheit, was in the Montana Rockies) and the weather turbulent. Near the continental divide winds have been measured at three times the minimal velocity of a hurricane. Some of the richest mining sites received more than twenty feet of snow annually. Towns like Silverton, Colorado had houses with doors on the first and second floors, one for summer and the other used when winter snows turned the first floor into the basement. Storms arrived early and left late. Silver Lake, Colorado once got six feet four inches of snow in twenty-four hours—still a world record. This blizzard hit in mid-April.

Famous horror tales, such as Alferd Packer killing and eating several companions when snowbound near Lake City, Colorado, were only exaggerated cases among hundreds of persons swallowed by the mountains during the cold time. Life in town wasn't always safe, either. Camps usually were built in valleys, where they had best access to streams and least exposure to winter winds. But that made them vulnerable to snowslides. The silver mining camp of Alta, Utah lost more than one hundred fifty persons in seven major avalanches during the 1870s and 1880s. One in 1885 killed sixteen residents and carried off twenty-seven of the town's thirty-nine buildings. In 1902 three avalanches in one day killed eighteen men in Telluride, Colorado. In spring and summer the snowmelt and rains sent devastating floods off the steep watersheds into the valley towns.[19]

To put it mildly, these conditions did not encourage much local loyalty. Some tried to cope through humor. The snow never melted in the northern Rockies, some claimed; it just blew around until it wore out. How dry was it in the central Nevada hills? When a man fainted from the heat, his friends revived him by throwing a bucket of sand in his face. The shock of water would have killed him. Laughing or not, sensible men and women fled whenever they could. Most camps emptied during winters when work was slowest, and whether they stayed year-round or not, few of the first arrivals had the slightest notion of remaining for the long term.

Natural discomforts were made even worse by the frantic pace of settlement. Almost overnight a small gulch like Colorado's Gregory Diggings was overrun with "thousands of cattle, hundreds of wagons, and tents and people innumerable" as well as lean-tos, crude cabins, the first stores and saloons, and around them prospect holes and primitive mining equipment.[20] If rumors proved true, the population continued its steep rise. Leadville, Colorado exploded from two hundred persons to more than fifteen thousand in the three years after 1877. When silver was found around Gold Hill and Virginia City, Nevada, the county population, already considerable, spurted by 275 percent in the 1860s, then another 72 percent by 1875.

The surrounding country was quickly plundered to build the mushrooming camps. With the hillsides stripped for lumber, erosion brought down mud and debris in a slow-motion reprise of winter avalanches. Creeks ran chocolate brown. Swollen by increased runoff, they roared through the towns, chewing their beds wider and deeper, carrying away precious human living space. A new employee in a Montana dance hall stepped out the rear door for some fresh air—and fell twenty feet into a rushing stream that had eaten its way to the building's foundation. High winds filled the air with eroded dirt, small stones, and miners' trash, inspiring more folklore. A Montana editor reported cook stoves and crowbars flying down the street. When he asked about a coat lodged against a lamp-post he was told that its owner was last seen blowing over the hotel.[21] During wet times storekeepers were constantly shoveling and sweeping mud back from their doors; women customers wore knee-high rubber boots beneath their long skirts. In a Colorado town a mule stumbled while laboring down the main street and the pack on its back shifted, pressing its head forward into the muck. It drowned before its owner could pull it to safety.

The overcrowding, the unruly weather, and the primitive facilities made a wonderful home for diseases. "Death is busy among the Californians," one man told his journal, and another agreed: "This is one of the *unhelthyist* places in the known world."[22] Illnesses contracted by personal contact and polluted water were most familiar, and for many dysentery was a constant fact of life. Diseases and infections from insects also were common, and even when these buzzing, biting, stinging companions brought no sickness they could make life miserable. "The air was black with the fleas," Dame Shirley wrote of Bidwell Bar, California. "Confound these big ants," a miner wrote his wife, "they are crawling over my paper so thick that I can't get them out of the way of my pen." In his next letter it was "the fleas [that] are biting me so that I can't write straight. I first scratch one place and then another, so that I have to stop and scratch every few words." Two peeping Toms, after creeping to a window to watch a Frenchwoman undress, enjoyed the sight until, partly disrobed, she stopped to pick various vermin off her body.[23]

All told, western mining camps were arguably the most wretched living spaces in America. The world traveler J. Ross Browne went farther than that. "In all my travels on the four continents, I have never before visited such a desolate, comfortless, miserable region, and never experienced such a series of mental and physical privations," he wrote of Nevada's Washoe district in 1860:

> It is absolutely frightful to think of it. At Virginia City, where people are huddled together thirty or forty in every little hut and tent, sleeping (when they can sleep) two or three together, some on the bare ground and some piled up in tiers, the wind blows a perfect hurricane all the time, and is piercing cold. The air is filled with gravel, and the barren rocks are covered with snowdrifts. . . . [There are] several hundred tents, holes in the ground with men living in them like coyotes, frame shanties and mud hovels. . . . [T]he water is so bad that hundreds are sick from drinking it. Alkali and arsenic are among the mildest ingredients found in it.[24]

Collective commitment for the long haul would not come easily in such places. The frontier's human makeup added to the difficulty. Mining camps were the most sexually imbalanced, diverse, and transient gatherings recorded in American history. Males typically comprised 80 percent or more of an early camp's population; cases of 90 to 95 percent were not unusual. This peculiar condition was doubly unsettling. Not only were towns sadly lacking in families, the basic cells of any community; the rarity of women, as much as blizzards and floods and flying crowbars, also sent many men packing as soon as they could manage it. Camps were also the most ethnically jumbled gatherings in the nation. From throughout America and much of the world they came—New England merchants, deep southern cotton farmers, cedar choppers from the Missouri valley, immigrants from Ireland, Italy, Germany, Australia, China, Hawaii, France and a dozen other countries. Simply finding a mutual vocabulary was difficult. Widely accepted principles and cultural norms seemed hopelessly out-of-reach.

This human mix was turning over at an astonishing pace, a stew at full boil. Demographers use the term "persistence rate" to measure the percentage of persons who remain in place over a given period, usually a decade documented by the census. The lower the rate, the more transient and unsettled a town or city. Persistence rates were low everywhere in urban America, but those in the mining country sank well below the rest. Picture a typical camp during its first months. Of every hundred persons you see hacking at the earth or slogging among the tents, five or fewer will be there ten years later. Most will be gone within the year.

Their attitudes drove the emigrants even farther apart. "The thirst for gold . . . overruled all else, and totally absorbed every faculty, . . ." wrote a visitor to California. Several men panning by a creek summed up for him the new El Dorado: "They addressed not a word to each other. . . . All the sympathies of our common humanity, all the finer and nobler attributes of our nature seemed lost, buried beneath the soil they were eagerly delving. . . ."[25] Search, work, spend, eat, drink, sleep, and search again: the frenetic clip of life became its own justification. A newcomer in the diggings approached a friend for job-hunting advice, but the man had no time to chat: "If you want a hundred dollars, you can have it, but I must not waste a moment. Keep moving, do anything, no matter what. Everybody else does."[26]

Not surprisingly, there was not much hint of even rudimentary order. Governments were limited and extraordinarily unstable. Shoshone County, Idaho had a board of commissioners and four other officials. In one year there were five resignations among the three commissioners; every other office—treasurer, coroner, auditor, and justice of the peace—changed hands at least once.[27] Minimal law enforcement and fire control usually were established within several months, protection for an emigrant's main concerns, his property and life. Everything else was left to individuals, which left a lot of fundamentals ignored. Often there were few or no outhouses, for instance. Men retired when necessary to nearby spots just out of sight—but close enough to be noted in other ways. Horse and cattle manure, garbage, and offal were tossed aside. Even in the relatively well developed city of San Francisco slaughterhouse workers threw unusable heads and hides, twenty or so a day, just outside their yard to rot or be eaten by crows and dogs. All this fouled the water, fed diseases, and made life generally unpleasant. Disagreeable deposits might freeze in winter, but a February chinook or the spring thaw brought first a thin stench and then waves of odor that left hardened residents wet-eyed. By some accounts migrating geese passing overhead fell senseless from the sky.

If a town survived its first months, its crudest conditions began to soften. The chaotic jumble gave way to a basic grid of streets, more substantial buildings, and some public services. Yet the same destructive dynamic was still at work. Mining is rough on land and people. More advanced methods only added to the miners' ability to tear apart the places where they lived. An astonished visitor described a hydraulic at work: "With the turning of a handle came a savage hiss—a smothered crash, as the fierce stream smote its mark, then a rumble and rattle, as great clots and crusts from the cliff hurled themselves into the whirl of water beneath, to be swallowed by the greedy sluice-way." The costs were appalling:

> It was difficult to believe that human force, unaided by earthquake or volcano, could have produced such hideous desolations. . . . [T]he spot might have been ravaged by some of the fantastic fiends of Cornish legend and German 'folk-lore.' On the soil, seamed, torn, scarified, and bestrewn with boulders, the foot finds no level resting-place; the cliff-face displays no sloping shelves, nor smooth sheer descents, but only yawning rifts and chasms, and gibbous crags nodding to their fall; and, here and there, tower uncouth islets of gravel—their dusky sides streaked with dull red and blue—marking the level where was opened the first parallel in this cruel war against the Great Mother.[28]

Smelters brought their own corruptions. A Comstock booster, complaining of Nevada's dreary public image, still agreed that furnaces gave out "dense . . . black smoke, redolent with the fumes of lead, arsenic, and other volatile elements." Boiling from the stacks, they spread outward and coated everything deep in soot. Life there, he admitted, had "a somewhat somber aspect."[29]

By then dreadful living conditions were a tradition. In a camp's first months the stern climate, primitive facilities, shattered landscape, and lack of families and social amenities kept people on the move. That instability, plus the promiscuous human mix, diluted any sense of common purpose, so residents were slow to join in changing what made their lives miserable. Besides, a mining camp was there in the first place because it offered a chance to make money, and that money was made in a business that took a heavy toll on everything around it. The basics of the frontier—its impulse, its setting, its people, its attitudes, and its physical workings—constantly challenged the old urge to form communities.

Occasionally the point was driven home dramatically. At first camps were built at the edge of the mines, but as miners followed the veins of ore they sometimes found themselves digging beneath the same houses and stores where they slept and shopped. While taking tea with a friend, a woman in Virginia City, Nevada could hardly visit because of the loud voices and hammering in a tunnel directly under her feet. "You could hear them as plainly as if they were in the yard," she remembered. Soon she saw the streets wizened by cracks as the honeycomb spread under the town. Buildings tilted and sagged. A year earlier, she recalled, a major tunnel had imploded and a large two-story house with a grocery and dry goods store had collapsed into the yawning pit and caught fire: "It was completely swallowed up, not even the chimney being visible."[30]

A TOWN EATING ITSELF: conditions continually undermined these frontier communities—sometimes literally. Never had Americans faced greater obstacles in the ancient drive to find some common meaning and identity and to meet mutual goals. Nonetheless, miners searched and found what they needed to create some collective order and bonds of identity. They started with the oddest materials and unlikeliest impulses.

The same passion for profit that set men against each other, for instance, could bring them together. Except in its simplest and least lucrative forms, such as squatting with a pan beside a creek, mining was rarely done alone. In the placer diggings a few men would build long toms and the sluices to bring them water. A few more would break up and haul gravel, passing it to others who shoveled it into the long tom's head while still others regulated the flow and watched for problems—five to ten workers all together. At least that many were needed to build a diversion dam to expose an especially promising creek bed. The Englishman Joseph Milner and several companions took four months to construct a dam and a five-hundred-foot race. Another option was for colleagues to pool their funds and issue shares, divide responsibilities, then hire out much of the labor.[31] Whatever the method, cooperative groups were essential, and as miners moved on to more complex operations, they joined in ever larger combinations. Hydraulic mining demanded companies of workers to install water systems, build settling ponds, and accomplish the final gathering. Even in its simplest forms, lode mining almost always required cooperative labor to construct and maintain tunnels and extract and process the ore.

The result was workingmen's clusters, a community's first elemental blocks. Often they grew from their members' common backgrounds. Many emigrants had come with men from their neighborhood or region in companies with names like the Buckeye Rangers or Illinois Hearties. On arrival some groups stayed together. Soon other miners with the same roots were drawn by familiar customs and accents, like the New Yorker who settled with some fellows from back home, "all tough and smart as crickets." Quickly a system of bunking-by-origin appeared. Of every fifty cabins in Nevada City, California in 1850, thirty-seven housed two or more persons from the same state. This pattern built outward into neighborhoods given names like French Camp, Virginia Gulch, and Ohio Bar.[32] The pattern replicated itself in later booms. In the turn-of-the-century camp of Goldfield, Nevada veterans of the Colorado and Alaska rushes formed societies like the Sons of Colorado and Arctic Brotherhood.[33]

This cultural snuggling, rooted in work, gave a mining town its first social shape. The bunkmates in these workingmen's clusters looked to each other for nursing in sickness and protection in a new and chancy setting. Out of this mutual reliance, plus the common trials of grueling work, often grew an ease and affection that bound the men still closer. Frederick Gerstacker wrote that he and his friends at Rich Gulch, California were "a little world of ourselves, in closest neighborhood and amity, eating, working, and sleeping together, and not caring more for the world around us, than if it did not exist."[34] Homosexual intimacies are, as usual, kept in the shadows of the record. Miners were clear, however, that at least in one sense, as unions of trust and loyalty, these all-male households grew into something like surrogate marriages. Hubert Howe Bancroft wrote of the California camps:

> Sacred like the marriage bonds, as illustrated by the softening of partner into the familiar "pard," were ties which oft united men vastly different in physique and temperament, the weak and the strong, the lively and the sedate, thus yoking themselves together. It presented an affinity of opposites, with the heroic possibilities of a Damon or Patroclus.[35]

Every working mess in turn was linked with others as men switched from one company to another, borrowed each other's tools and expertise and worked together when floodwaters or some other crisis threatened their common enterprise.[36] Individual friendships and socializing extended these connections. An Irish miner from Dublin Gulch might drink regularly with the German proprietor of a dry goods tent, who introduced him to the Carolinians next door, who suggested they all drift down to the gaming tables at Ohio Bar, where New Yorkers, Pennsylvanians, and more Irish joined them to pass an evening with mutual gab while tossing a drop down their necks. Exchanges of all sorts, story-swapping, and mutual sweat began to knit together the body of strangers.

America was full of men's subcultures—railroad workers, cowboys, telegraphers, steel mill laborers and others—but only here, on the mining frontier, did the *sub* fall away and male-to-male converse dominate whole towns and sometimes large portions of the country.

Community-making was nudged further along by the appearance of public gathering places that seemed specially designed to bring strangers together. All shared three traits. They satisfied basic urges among people with little else in common. Each had a particular look and feel instantly recognizable by anyone who had patronized similar places elsewhere. And once inside these establishments, patrons behaved in highly distinctive ways. They slipped into mannered actions and language that would be strange or laughable in the building next door but, like the place's layout and appearance, would be immediately familiar in another such establishment far away.

Together these three elements—the patron's need, the physical setting, and the unique customs and motions—created what might be called a moveable institution. If such a place were picked up in Pittsburgh and plopped down in Santa Fe, the New Mexican locals would instantly see it for what it was; they would know exactly how to act when they walked through the door. Conversely, if fifty strangers from as many towns throughout the nation all traveled hundreds of miles and suddenly found themselves tossed together in one of these institutions, each would immediately know where he was and how to behave toward the others. It was a paradox: a piece of home that could be anywhere.

Three moveable institutions were universal on the mining frontier—saloons, churches, and fraternal lodges. Saloons appeared immediately, as if materializing from the ozone. Church services usually were not far behind. Fraternal societies appeared in modestly successful camps, and in a place like Virginia City, Nevada, one woman wrote, "Every society has a lodge, and some of them . . . branches of different degrees."[37] All three institutions fed basic human hungers—physical, social, cultural, spiritual. Each had its universally recognized arrangement. In a church were two sets of pews and a central aisle leading to pulpit and altar; the fraternal lodge had a large open space and a seat of authority; the saloon featured a bar, back bar, and tables for drinking and gaming. All had their own icons and decorations—a cross, the Masonic or other fraternal symbols and seals, and the barroom's nudes and sporting prints—as well as specialized language, stories, and inside humor. Each had well worn rules and decorum enforced by a commanding figure in distinctive clothing—priest or minister in collar or robe, lodge master in his vestment, and barkeeper with a starched white shirt and arm garter. These men oversaw binding rituals: the order of worship and communion, fraternal pledges and songs, the treating and choreographed motions acted out with elbows on the bar and boots on the rail.

None of these institutions helped miners do what they had come for. All, in fact, took money away. Yet they flourished. Miners handed over their dust and money because these places gave them something vital in return: social bearings. A barroom, chapel, or Odd Fellows hall was an island of the familiar. Everything outside might be alien and uncertain, but when a man pushed through the batwing doors or knelt in prayer, he suddenly was more in place and closer to home. As others came in, called by God or a glass of beer, everyone joined in the same motions toward a common purpose. That acquaintance, repeated hundreds of times, grew outward into a social netting that gave some coherence to a camp's human confusion.

Miners found other kinds of spontaneous community. Dances were a favorite. Tunes sawed on fiddles and plunked on banjos were broadly known, as were the steps meant to go with them. A schottische, quadrille, or reel was a variety of ritual that brought strangers together even more inclusively than communion or the Masonic oath. The first dances were held almost immediately. "Think of the idea of a ball way out among the Shoshone indians in a town hardly a day old," a man wrote his fiancée from Austin, Nevada. When no women were around men took both roles, as at Angel's Camp, California, where every dancer "who had a patch on a certain part of his inexpressibles" played the woman for the evening.[38] With or without women, decorum at first suffered. An Ohioan in Boone's Bar, California attended "a ball to dance, and a bawl, to cry aloud . . . it was a perfect rookery." At another a woman thought the crowd might have been swept away by spat tobacco juice, but luckily the brown flood collected in puddles on the uneven floor.[39] As towns took form residents poured energy and resources into balls and masquerades. Guests found elaborate decorations, the best musicians available, and vast spreads of food. Dances became unifying revels, with class and group tolerances stretched as wide as they ever would be. And there were plenty of them. A North Carolinian apologized for being slow to write from his Colorado camp. After four dances in six nights, he was exhausted.[40]

Besides these slightly formalized frolics, mining frontiersmen met in other indulgences. As they pursued these common urges they created communities of appetite and style. Especially when those passions reflected the camp's mood and human makeup, what were essentially selfish pursuits became powerfully cohesive.

Gambling was an obvious example. Where every man expected to beat the odds in prospecting, leisure-time wagering became a passion. Barrooms and gambling halls were stuffed with customers who tossed away their money at faro, roulette, monte, twenty-one, poker, rouge-et-noir, and "every game that was ever played on earth."[41] But that was only the start. Children boxed in the streets for a cut of the dust changing hands in the crowd. There were dog fights, bear fights, and dog-and-bear fights. An Idaho bartender put up his "killer duck" in battle against any local hound. Miners staged races of body lice, bet on the date of the first snowstorm, on the timing of the next crack of thunder, and on which of several rain-drops would roll first down a window pane. By the turn of the century there were auto and motorcycle races.[42]

Gambling was a prime example of the creativity behind frontier com-munity-making, at once perverse and conservative. On the one hand it summed up every enemy of a collective sensibility—self-indulgence, greed, and the relentless drive to grab wealth and deny it to anybody else. But it also brought men together, often in continuing relationships. After all, play-ing faro and betting on body lice were collective acts. They bound com-petitors to each other, if nothing else through a need to win money back. And gambling was an active metaphor of the frontier itself. Lay down your dust and turn the cards: It was an affirmation of what brought these men there in the first place.

Eating, the most basic consumption of all, worked in similar ways. Sharing food is both a symbol and means of community-making in virtu-ally every culture. In the camps it was quickly put to work. Men called their working clusters "messes;" their hours spent together cooking and dining sometimes drove them apart but typically sealed their friendships. Breaking common bread became a central ritual in a camp's moveable institutions—dinners and picnics of fraternal orders, the saloon's free lunch, and the com-munion rail at church.

The style of eating was as important as the act itself. Observers were stunned by the range and amounts of food consumed. The people of Virginia City, Nevada "are not only epicures but gormandizers," a woman wrote: "[They] live very high, eating the best food in the market, at all hours of both day and night, both in season and out of season."[43] The bill of fare at Denver's first Christmas dinner included trout in oyster sauce, elk tongue, roast beef, grizzly bear, mountain rats, swans, pumpkins, Brazil nuts and almonds, pudding, six kinds of pies, and thirteen types of intoxicants.[44] Fremont, California was "literally stuffed, crammed with eatables of every description," Israel Lord wrote, "[E]very thing . . . may be had by present-ing the great 'open sessame' [*sic*] here—gold." Prices were exorbitant, but still customers crowded restaurants to order from long menus, some printed on silk. Like "wolves or anacondas" men bolted down beef, oysters, salads, fish, cakes, peppered pickles, and heady sauces. Just before bed, Lord noted, "[they] must have sardines at 3 to 5 $ a box or a pie at 1 dollar."[45] Hard-worked men needed plenty of calories, of course, but the flamboyant choice of foods and the immoderate belly-stuffing were one more expression of the frontier's blustering optimism. Splurging a last few pinches of dust on a three-course dinner was another act of faith in tomorrow, and gobbling steaks and sardines an outward sign of an inner extravagance.

By every familiar standard, societies emerging from the initial rush shocked the morally orthodox. "Saw Leadville by gaslight," wrote the New Englander Charles Francis Adams, "An awful spectacle of low vice."[46] Selfish impulses were openly, even boastfully indulged. A young Californian explained to his sister:

> You ask me what temptations I had. I did not have any. If I wanted anything, I had it. If I wanted to do anything, I did it. . . . If we are very anxious to do anything that is wrong and find it very difficult to restrain ourselves from doing it, that is temptation, but when we do it, that is wicked[ness], not temptation. . . . Now do not try to refute my arguments with a long sermon.[47]

Traits usually expected of mature men—restraint, discipline and self-denial—receded, and public conduct became a flaunting of fast living and chest-puffing virility. Many miners seemed to deny growing up at all. Men of thirty and forty had the scruffy look of summer schoolboys and took rootless nicknames like "Long Sam" and "Pepper Ed."

The resulting human excess impressed the most toughened observers. The rate of drinking was astounding. An early Comstock historian calculated that county residents consumed 75,000 gallons of hard liquor and 225,000 gallons of beer in 1880, or about five and fifteen gallons per person. So great was the guzzling in Idaho that an editor called for a new definition of sobriety: No man should be called drunk as long as he could make a noise.[48] Other drug use was also widespread. An official in Goldfield, Nevada estimated nearly four hundred residents were opium addicts and thousands of others patronized the town's dens. Miners fought fatigue with shots of bourbon laced with cocaine, a blend sometimes marketed in stores with names like "Bright Eye."[49] Given the turbulent circumstances, killings and serious non-lethal violence were less common than might be thought (with the crucial exception of that toward Indians).[50] But some conditions, especially hard times and a rise in ethnic tension, could turn towns into some of the bloodiest in American history. In the ethnically mixed Sonora, California during the economic downturn of 1850–51, the homicide rate (the number of killings annually per 100,000 persons) has been estimated at 506, fifty times the national average in the late twentieth century. Leadville, Colorado's rate the year after the peak of its boom was 105 and Bodie, California's was 116; the corresponding numbers for Boston and Philadelphia were 5.8 and 3.2.[51]

The human costs were high, but outrageous conduct and wrecked lives could be misleading. Shocked outsiders were looking at a variation of American communities, albeit one never seen before. Men found connection in work that was intended, not to build a collective future, but to help each other abandon this place as soon as they could. They knotted together a social mesh with the unlikeliest materials, such as liquored romps and card game acquaintances. Communities emerged, tentative and shifting but there nonetheless, taking their shape from a collective spirit that was turbulent, hyper-competitive, homosocial, highly masculinized, and dedicated to the impulse of plunge and grab.

*M*ANY MINING CAMPS were deserted within months or even weeks. Buildings were dismantled and the lumber and fixtures taken to some new strike to be hammered again into slapdash stores and saloons. Brush and trees began a slow revival over the abandoned foundations. Communities dissolved without growing beyond their early fantastic shapes.

In towns that survived, society soon moved in a new direction. The strange communities of the early days persisted, but other forms arose as well. A town's appearance changed. So did its human composition and its people's behavior. The blending of older and newer patterns gave the evolving camps a distinctive feel. Even as it moved toward a more familiar appearance, the mining frontier remained a place apart.

Maturing towns took on a more traditional look. Along a crosshatching of streets merchants sold a widening array of goods out of sturdier stores featuring a common western architectural feature—the false front, a facade that gave an improved building a still grander disguise. Citizens built sidewalks and made a feeble try at coping with the dust beds and mud wallows pretending to be streets. Disasters hastened these improvements. A shamble of tents and crude shacks made perfect tinder for a fire begun by some poorly vented stove or overturned lamp. In less than an hour a town could be devoured. The site might then be abandoned, especially if its diggings had started to go dry; however, if mines were still paying, an improved town quickly rose from the ashes. Canvas gave way to wood; seasoned lumber replaced sappy rough sawn planks. The true badges of permanence were imposing business blocks of fireproof brick and locally quarried granite, with substantial churches and civic buildings close by. Thirsty customers now could find spacious saloons with fabulous bars, diamond dust mirrors, and billiard tables with beds of slate. They surrendered their dollars and dust to the finest gambling equipment.

Entertainments grew more refined. The earliest public performances were at best crude melodramas and, at worst, freak shows. The highpoint of one came when a man hammered out a horseshoe on the chest of a four-hundred-pound woman. Soon, however, troupes arrived with a mix of classics—any Shakespearean tragedy was a sure draw—and current favorites like "Love's Fetters" and "The Female Bandit." Deadwood residents attended 130 performances of Gilbert and Sullivan's *The Mikado*. There were dramatic and comic readings, gymnastic exhibitions (with trapeze and rings), and a range of burlesque. Prosperous towns drew some of the best artists available, Edwin Booth performing *Hamlet,* Eddie Foy in comic skits, and even Oscar Wilde, who lectured and read from his works to wildly enthusiastic audiences in Leadville. The first crude facilities were replaced by increasingly elaborate theaters with orchestra pits and private boxes. A town's crowning boast was an opera house. Verdi and Bellini were occasionally performed, but mostly it hosted the commoner theatrics.

New social allegiances spread over the changing town, supplementing the first lodges. By 1870 Virginia City, Nevada had the Band of Hope, Sons and Daughters of Temperance, Good Templars, the Order of the Red Men, Fenian Brotherhood, the Anti-Chinamen, Grand Army of the Republic, the Turnverein, the Hebrew Benevolent Society, and German Benevolent Society, as well as several military organizations. A resident looked back and did "not think it . . . possible for any other city to have more different societies."[52]

Among the most active groups were "hose companies," volunteer fire units found in virtually every town of significant size. They met and trained regularly to protect what was now a community worth saving. Georgetown, Colorado had four, each in an impressive fire house with its own name and symbol. It was an honor to win a place among athletic firemen who ran through the streets pulling big-wheeled carts with large spools of hoses and battled the flames to the cheers of the crowd. A high point of holiday celebrations was a race among companies pulling hose carts down a main thoroughfare. Like a camp's first working messes, a fire company was a cluster of close-knit men celebrating a macho comradery. This one, however, was rooted in faith in a community's future, and it spent its competitive energy protecting a place that a year earlier men were trying to loot and leave.

A newspaper gave a maturing town a voice and personality. Its mere appearance was a vote for the future, since the original investment was at least three thousand dollars and the wages five hundred dollars a month. On a paper's masthead might be the usual *Press* or *Herald* or perhaps a regional wrinkle, like Tombstone's *Epitaph,* Ruby City, Idaho's *Owyhee Avalanche,* and Ouray, Colorado's *Solid Muldoon.* Nationally, journalism was in transition, and frontier editors became pioneers balancing a newspaper's older and emerging roles. As in traditional small-town weeklies, they provided changing particulars of familiar life, from notices of meetings to lists of letters and prices of goods. As with new urban dailies, they also reached over the globe through telegraphic connections and boosted sales with flamboyance, syrupy sentimentality, and unblushing scandals and controversies. To the world outside an editor was a community's advocate, now combative, now sweetly persuasive. Judging strictly from his columns, his town had a grand future undeniable to anyone but a dolt or pettifogger. Whatever its realities, on newsprint a camp was crystallizing into a respectable community.

By then other services were in place: law enforcement, water deliveries, disposal of animal carcasses and the most offensive garbage, burial of the destitute human dead, and even minimal care of the alarming numbers of insane. A cemetery, typically planted high above town, was a poignant contradiction. It was a sign of irreversible departure that implied a collective permanence, sanctified ground for accumulating memories as the years unrolled and a town recalled its losses. Communities felt the first twitching of reform. Pulpits were pounded in attacks on bordellos, gambling holes, and the most outrageous swilling spots. Women's groups appeared and organized benefits for the first clinics and improvements of churches. The Sons of Temperance held their first meetings, often with impressive turnouts.

Appearances could be deceptive. The turnover of officials was still high, especially among poorly paid lawmen who faced occasional dangers but were saddled mostly with shoveling offal, shooting stray dogs, and other degrading chores. New facilities had their problems. When firemen in one town inaugurated a water system that drew from a nearby lake, several small trout flew from their hose and flopped among the crowd. Elsewhere a graveyard dissolved in heavy rains and sent caskets and corpses sliding and tumbling into the camp. After a Leadville prohibition rally, saloons were jammed with temperance converts toasting their cause with whiskey and beer.

Still, unmistakable changes came at a quick clip. One of the most fundamental was a dramatic shift in the towns' human makeup. Families arrived in substantial numbers, and neighborhoods full of crying babies and ball-playing boys and girls appeared next to the sprawl of bachelor cabins. The implausible social contours of the early days began to bend toward the normal. By 1870, more than twenty years after the first gold was panned in Nevada City, California, men still outnumbered women two-to-one. In 1850, however, the ratio had been nearly forty-five-to-one. Single miners were drawn to these new family households as places to board and as semblances of homes they had left. Once again strangers were bound through rituals of eating, now with solitaires pulled out of all-male messes into traditional homes. Gradually this intimate familial landscape spread, especially in the market and governmental centers not so dominated by a workingman's economy. Fifteen years after the boom of Silver City, Idaho, half its dwellings held nuclear families, and another quarter had families with boarders.

*F*AMILIES SIGNALED ANOTHER transformation. As a town matured physically, a different structure of values was taking hold. It directed people's actions, much as the new grid of streets channeled their movement. Like stone cornices and brick facades, these public values were long-distant transplants into new cultural terrain.

This was not, however, simply a case of one social and moral order, secure and distinct to the East, being carried in to replace another set of values, also discrete and unique to the frontier. Something more complicated was going on. Society in the East was undergoing its own changes. New attitudes and values were challenging ones that had been widely respected for generations. A mining town, whatever else it was, can also be seen as an extravagant projection of this contest over America's moral posture.

Mining frontiers coincided with a rapid expansion of American industry and an explosive growth of eastern and midwestern cities. Factories and urban neighborhoods were crowded by a great surge of foreign immigration and by rural Americans leaving farms and villages. This great unsettling produced broad opportunities. It also brought unimagined problems and, for many, a deep uncertainty. Concern was especially sharp among "old stock" Americans, mostly English in blood and tradition. Their values had dominated the republic since its first days, but now, as the nation moved into a new era, the old stock traditions seemed to be challenged at every hand. The old order stressed self-discipline, sacrifice, frugality, honor and civic responsibility; the newer mood favored individual achievement and gaudy consumption. The old stock tradition respected success through steady effort and modest, gradual accumulation; the Gilded Age admired great wealth gotten by heroic risk-taking and the big payoff. The moral center of the first was the family home and the small town; the focus of the second was the city, the factory, and the marketplace. This clash of values made many people uneasy. To some it was nothing less than spiritual Armageddon, a battle for the American soul.

When this contest is kept in mind, mining frontiers take on another dimension. In the most obvious ways they were places apart; geographically they were on the far fringe of America; the form of their first communities was like nothing the country had ever seen. But as moral theaters they were squarely centered in national life. Nowhere could the pull and shove of older and newer values be seen more vividly.

To critics worried about the moral direction of America at large, mining camps seemed to have taken all the wrong turns. Here, they said, was the national character at its worst. Drunkenness stood for a general irresponsibility and a loss of self-control. Swearing was an erosion of class and character. "You know that at home it is considered *vulgar* for a gentleman to swear," Dame Shirley wrote her sister, "but I am told that here it is absolutely the fashion."[53] Were Americans more and more obsessed with material gain? Well here everything seemed for sale. "What shall a man give in exchange for his soul?" an editor heard a street preacher shout one Sunday morning. A nearby auctioneer answered: "I am offered forty-five dollars! Do I hear any more?"[54] Instead of putting their faith in frugal persistence, men trusted to luck. "Gambling seems to be the business, and not the pleasure of this place," wrote Israel Lord. He saw the same deplorable bet-it-all behavior in the diggings, the crowded restaurants, and the smoky gambling hells.[55] With so many interlocking corruptions, men who arrived as respectable citizens might slide quickly into the frontier's behavioral sink, becoming "gamblers, then black-legs and soon ruffians and murderers."[56] Over it all was the disturbing fact that, just at the moment when so many troubling trends were taking hold nationally, these communities were making those trends the very basis of their being.

In towns like these the job of promoting traditional proprieties was such a march against the odds, such fly-swatting in an abattoir that the smallest victory carried quite a weight. The first Sabbath schools and Christian education were hailed as milestones. Most books in the early diggings were trash that had been "written by depraved minds," an Ohio forty-niner wrote, and he thought he knew why. Overlanders had started out with excellent literary works, but along the way the classics "were discarded on account of weight." When heavier works finally arrived and libraries were founded, the numbers of books, like Sabbath school enrollments, became barometers of moral progress.[57] Lyceums and more serious lectures marked a turn toward higher yearnings. An organized effort against prostitution, gambling houses, or selling whiskey on Sunday at first might bring laughs and jeers, but it signaled at least that forces of change were out in the open.

Families and respectable women took on enormous importance in this context. The idealized family summed up the best virtues of the Victorian moral order, and the woman who stood at its center defined the cultural high ground. There were plenty of other reasons, of course, for men to welcome women. Lonely husbands wrote letters home pouring out their emotional and, sometimes explicitly, their physical longing; some single men dreamed of female companions resembling the ones back home; all welcomed women's hands at cooking and other domestic work.[58] But the social value of women—what they accomplished simply by being female and on site—was always a priority. A miner explained California's "tainted moral atmosphere" by the "want of respectable female society" (as well as the lack of books and "rational amusements"). And nothing would improve, Hinton Rowan Helper wrote, until these towns could attract "an influx of the chaste wives and tender mothers that bless our other seaboard."[59]

When eastern women of passable reputation did appear, they caused quite a stir. Denver residents, hearing rumors of a bonnet on the streets, rushed out to "gaze upon its wearer as at any other natural curiosity." Stories circulated of miners paying a dollar apiece merely to look at a matronly dress on a millinery form. Delegations sometimes greeted the first wives with cheers and gifts of gold nuggets and even town lots.

The high social value of women placed restraints on what they might do. Briefly in the early camps, the fluid conditions and crazy imbalance of male and female meant opportunities unthinkable back home. Women prospected, opened saloons and stores, and occasionally took a hand in heavier work like freighting. Some dressed as shabbily and bathed as seldom as the roughest gutter tough. Then the drive for respectability set in, with female propriety at its center. Because women carried such symbolic weight, they often felt more pressure, not less, to toe the Victorian mark in their work, dress, speech, and general behavior. Expectations stiffened, although they were not applied the same to everyone. Women of Irish, German, and other European extractions had a slipperier status; Hispanics were lower still; Indians were beyond the moral pale. But middle class women closest to old stock origins found the new standards at least as rigid as what their eastern cousins knew.

By then communities were sorting themselves into new social arrangements. Earlier, camps had divided into working precincts of men with similar origins, Hoosier Gulches and French Flats. Now they were compartmentalized by social class, money, public decorum, and permissible conduct, all with an ethnic overlay. Well tended homes of the social elite often stood symbolically on rising ground above town. The author and artist Mary Hallock Foote lived in Leadville with her engineer husband up Capitol Hill, from which she descended only rarely into what she called "the mob."[60] Down there, in "that life that twilight covered," was the main business center of banks, law offices, larger mercantile operations, better restaurants and the finer drinking and gambling houses, like Pap Wyman's on Harrison Avenue, with its plush back rooms open only to the highest rollers. Spreading away from this center were working class neighborhoods that were reasonably secure financially but by Foote's standards looser and more suspect in behavior. Family homes mingled with liveries, smaller shops, modest eateries, and middling bars and hurdy-gurdy houses. Farther to the fringe were the cheapest quarters occupied by the randomly employed, the floaters, and the down-and-out. In a reversal of Leadville's pattern, Virginia City, Nevada's hillsides were a sprawl of crude cabins where the city's poor paid a pittance of rent or squatted for nothing. Every larger town had its zone of cheap rooms squeezed among the squalid grogshops and the cribs where street whores did their business with the sexually desperate.

Newer and older moralities were jumbled together when the first families arrived. A twelve-year-old girl described a Sunday in Helena, Montana in 1865:

> At two o'clock in the morning a highway Robber was hung on a large pine tree. After breakfast we went to see him. At ten o'clock preaching, at one o'clock a large auction sale of horses and cattle. At two o'clock Sunday school. At three o'clock a foot race. At seven o'clock preaching. The remainder of time spent by hundreds of miners in gambling and drinking.[61]

Gradually but steadily, the modes of living then pulled apart. A snobbish emigrant found "the most unthinking savage is neighbor to the well-read scholar" during the first rush, but soon residents with literary tastes could withdraw into the expanding respectable neighborhoods and meet in groups like the Sauhara [*sic*] Club of Florence, Arizona to discuss Hawthorne, Irving, and Goldsmith. A reformist editor in Silverton, Colorado complained that the nightly uproar from the twenty-seven saloons "is hideous. A loud piano in one den runs through three charming chords, drowning a vilely squeaking fiddle from seven in the evening until sleep has mercifully closed one's ears." But in time those with other tastes, like a musically inclined wife in a Sierra town, found new friends with similar interests. When they gathered at her cottage, the clamor from the bars was offset by "voices cultivated in the Handel and Hayden Society of Boston."[62] Churches, one of those moveable institutions that appeared almost immediately, at first were tossed together with all the rest. Tombstone's first services were held in part of a thin-walled theater with a torn canvas roof. An attendee thought it "hard work . . . to preach on account of dance hall racket in the rear," with calls of "Hug gals in the corner" drowning out the sermon: "The place is rather a poor one for divine service—but best at present I suppose." By 1882, however, St. John's Episcopal church had been built on the relatively sedate west side of town, about as far as possible (five blocks) from the freestyle nightlife of the Bird Cage Theater and the nearby bordellos.[63]

This social sorting was a sure sign that a town was nearly beyond its frontier stage. Not only had it acquired most institutions found in eastern communities. It had also arranged its public space as in any town or city in Massachusetts or Indiana. Sleazier amusements were kept behind a "dead line," as in any eastern city. Beyond this line, established by law or custom, brothels, grogshops, opium dens, and other base entertainments could operate at full tilt. On the near side were the more refined diversions—theaters, a few gilded saloons, and perhaps a discreet and expensive bordello, and farther away neighborhoods of middle class and elite respectability. Across the dead line anything short of clearly dangerous behavior was condoned. On the near side the utmost decorum was expected in every public act, including language and dress.

Outwardly hostile, the community's two sides actually supported each other. Gamblers, prostitutes, and bartenders lived by a steady clientele from respectable neighborhoods. Moral leaders reasoned that red light districts absorbed the depraved impulses of workingmen, especially immigrant groups considered lustier than usual. Honorable womanhood was segregated, and thus safe. The stark neighborhood division between the righteous and the fallen visually reinforced the Victorian view of humanity as neatly separated into good and evil. Scenes from across the line were constant reminders of what was heard in Sunday sermons and read in school primers.[64]

One man's remarkable diary shows how residents shifted among these zones of respectability. Alfred Doten was a prominent editor, fire company member, and handsome bachelor-about-town in Virginia City, Nevada. He was also an enthusiastic rounder. He spent chaste evenings with daughters of the social elite: "after supper were in parlor awhile, chatting with Miss Kelsey & Miss Pollard—sang them a song or two—Miss Kelsey leaves for Excelsior again early in the morning—we passed an agreeable evening . . . " Other nights, and sometimes in the small hours after leaving some sitting room, he crossed the line to revel in the saloons and brothels. Those in Chinatown were a favorite. Here, where sinning was expected, his descriptions are detailed and candid. With a friend he visited "Mary's house":

> we were in her room with her—she gave us each a cake left from the holi-
> day of yesterday—filled with nuts and sweetmeats—we laid on the bed with
> her & smoked opium with her. . . . long & interesting chat with her . . . On
> my way home I stopped in at the Great Republic saloon—big whore ball going
> on—bed at 2—[65]

Doten also carried on a vigorous affair with his landlady, Mrs. Eunice Morton. Apparently he did so with the tacit consent of her husband, Doten's friend and former schoolmate, and probably with the knowledge of mutual friends. Still, he was violating two boundaries of the new moral order—invading another's marital bed, and doing it on the respectable side of the dead line. That double trespass possibly explains a curious duality in these entries. Doten wrote as explicitly about the affair as he did of his parlor flirtations and Chinatown prowls. He describes the lovers' positions, notes their successes and failures at orgasm, and keeps a careful tally of their couplings—526 over a little less than two years, each signified by the notation "OK." But because his OK's with Mrs. Morton, unlike his other shenanigans, disobeyed public rules about what to do where, he hides them doubly away. Keeping them between the covers of his secret diary, he buries them even deeper by writing about these adventures, and only these, in code.[66]

Alf Doten's diary is a handy map of moral geography. Men and women still broke the rules in this new Virginia City of firm Victorian standards.

The point is not that standards were obeyed or not—after all, Boston and Charleston had plenty of middle class rakes like Doten—but rather that they were recognized and imposed, as a kind of block-by-block overlay, on a town where, not long before, individual desire had strutted around wherever it wished. Doten indulged every impulse, but even as he counted his adulteries and wrote secrets to himself, he bowed at the waist to propriety and churchly virtues:

> 1 PM OK 33—Evening Mrs. Morton & I attended Rev A B Earl's meeting at Presbyterian Church . . . good many converts—Prayer, sermon on "Prepare to die, be ready. . . ."[67]

By no means, however, had the frontier community entirely passed away. The conditions that inspired it were mostly still there. Men often outnumbered women, sometimes substantially. Society stabilized, but the turnover rate remained higher than almost anywhere else in the country. Streets and mines were still a Babel of tongues and a confusion of customs. The coming of families did nothing to improve the climate, and the business of mining still chewed at the environment and poisoned the air. A workingmen's culture, with its virulent masculinity and extravagant, hard-living mode of life, persisted alongside the new codes of restraint and familial values.

It was exactly this stark abutting of older and newer communities that gave surviving mining towns their distinctive feel. The frontier West and the Victorian West were both there. Both were seen in exaggerated forms, often compressed into some narrow valley, chafing against one another in towns of a square mile or less. The juxtapositions were jarring. Georgetown, Colorado had two opera houses, a town park, Episcopal and Roman Catholic churches, the Hotel de Paris with its fine library and excellent wines, and several magnificent homes, one with a solarium and a nine-seater outhouse with a servants' entrance. The dead line was along Clear Creek. Just over it was a full-blown romping ground of whiskey dens and gambling hells. On the far side of the line silver miners drank and whored virtually uncurbed. On the respectable side of the creek a woman once was arrested for refusing to ride sidesaddle.

The paradox of these towns, and of mining frontiers generally, was that they could be so outlandish, so full from the start of such aberrant sights, yet every oddness, from another angle, turns out to be some familiar part of eastern America projected and amplified into the West—in this case with the plunging spirit of the Gilded Age bumping hard against the moral order of an earlier America desperately trying to hold its own. Perhaps that is what the British engineer Daniel Pidgeon understood on his western tour when he wrote of "that most strange and characteristic sight, a rough American mining camp."[68]

◁ 11 ▷

The World's Convention

*D*ame Shirley was in love with her camp at California's Indian Bar. She praised the "primeval splendor" of its fir-fringed stream, the flocks of doves scattering in the bright sunlight, and the distant peaks and dazzling snow-fields. The soundscape, however, spoke of profound changes in paradise. Every day she heard picks and shovels biting into the earth, the carpenters' hammering, and the voices of those who had come to "gather to the golden harvest":

> You will hear in the same day, almost at the same time, the lofty melody of the Spanish language, the piquant polish of the French . . . , the silver, changing clearness of the Italian, the harsh gangle of the German, the hissing precision of the English, the liquid sweetness of the Kanaka [Hawaiian], and the sleep-inspiring languor of the East Indian. To complete the catalogue, there is the *native* Indian, with his gutteral vocabulary of twenty words! . . . I fancy them a living polyglot of the languages, and a perambulating picture gallery, illustrative of national variety in form and feature.[1]

The mining West was "a boiling mass of people from all nations," one miner wrote, and an Idaho editor marveled that he shared his streets with "Saxon, Celt, Teuton, Gaul, Greaser, Celestial and Indian." As much as the rowdiness and the splurge of wealth, observers were impressed by this jumbling of humanity. Here, one declared, was "emphatically the world's convention."[2]

Like the brawls, gambling, street preaching, and fire cart races, the ethnic mixing revealed plenty about the nature of mining frontier society, its psychological contours, and its place in the larger American story, including that story's most tormented and disquieting chapters.

*T*HE WEST HAD been a cultural jumble when first Europeans showed up, and so it remained at the time of the mining frontiers. California held more distinct cultures than any comparable area on the continent, perhaps in the world. About eighty languages were spoken there, forty in the mining regions alone. Near the Montana and Idaho placer beds were Bannocks and Shoshones, with Crows, Cheyennes, and Lakotas on the approaches. Utes lived around the strikes of the southern Rockies and descended onto the plains to fight with Cheyennes, Arapahoes and Lakotas, who made their own forays into the mountains from their homes close to where gold would be found along the Front Range. Washoes and Paiutes inhabited a broad region around the Comstock lode and the eastern watershed of the Sierra Nevada. The southwestern desert mountains, rich in gold and silver, were home to the Chiricahua, Mescalero, and Western Apaches, with Yumas and Yavapais on the fringes.

They lived finely patterned lives adapted to mountains, plains, deserts and forests. They regarded the cosmos through dozens of religions, expressed themselves by an array of artistic traditions, and fed their families with everything from grubs and acorns to salmon and seals. They differed in customs as much as Japanese fishermen and Kurdish herdsmen. Gold and silver rushes, however, gave them one thing in common. Quickly, they all found themselves in deep trouble.

Nowhere did that crisis come faster or with such brutality as in California. Although Native American population is extremely difficult to calculate, a conservative estimate would set it at a hundred fifty thousand in the 1840s. Conditions were in flux in those years. Spanish priests and lords of the ranchos had kept a fairly tight grip on Indians close to the missions, but Mexican independence in 1821 brought a new instability. Aggressive hill tribes stole horses and mules from the Californios to swap for goods carried overland by New Mexican traders. Once the missions were secularized in 1834 many Indian neophytes joined the increasingly assertive raiders. By the early 1840s some landowners considered abandoning their more exposed positions because their overseers and workers "no longer have security of life."[3] The Indians' cockiness shocked the first American arrivals. John Charles Frémont's party of 1844 once found itself briefly besieged by Southern Paiutes who massed "in every direction over the hills," taunted the expedition and scoffed at its weapons and pitiful numbers. In 1850 miners near Sonora pursued a band of Miwoks who had stolen some mules. The Indians withdrew to a hilltop and "used the most insulting gestures and language, slapping their arses and daring the Yankees to come up there."[4]

The everyday life of these peoples is mostly out of sight, but occasional glimpses suggest they lived rather tight in their world, with reasonable assurance and some touches of grace. Isidora Filomena de Solano, born in northern California in 1784, was kidnapped as a child by the native leader Solano. Later he married her. Isidora recalled her pride in Solano's command over ranks of warriors who fought nude except for feather crests in their hair. Her people ate much fish, she remembered, polished their teeth with animal hair, and buried their dead with ear ornaments of finely shaved duck bones. She and Solano, secure in their standing and advised by the best astrologers, looked confidently toward the future.[5]

The discovery of gold, however, turned that future onto a disastrous new course. Besides the unraveling of Indian communities—the disruption of connections within their immediate world, the infusion of diseases, the dismantling of families—every mining frontier posed the more obvious threat of direct assaults. A strike drew crowds of young men, a few of them genuine sociopaths. They arrived with great ambitions but many quickly found themselves living lonely and dream-dashed lives in some of the most uncomfortable settings on the continent. Violence was only an impulse away, and Indians were some of the handiest targets.

California's story was the bloodiest. Three differences help explain this grim distinction. A relatively dense Native American population lived in vulnerable villages, called *rancherías,* close at hand to the diggings. Indians, that is, were more accessible and more obviously in the way. Second, the civil authority that might have provided some protection was slow to come, and, once established, was divided, often ineffective and always subject to local pressures. Finally, in contrast to almost all other mining frontiers, California Indians were a significant labor force in mining and attendant enterprises, including domestic service. This left them vulnerable both to those who forced them into drudge work and to others resentful because they could not afford to hire them.

Almost immediately there were appalling episodes of the kind that tore apart Indian families and communities, followed by Indian reprisals, all of it escalating quickly to what one New Yorker called "the most brutal acts. . . . Such incidents have fallen under my notice that would make humanity weep and men disown their race."[6] In the 1850s the state launched a dozen expeditions of volunteers and militia, funded by bonds later paid by the federal government, but the deadliest attacks were by smaller independent bands of whites who killed some Indians, sold others, and took the rest to military confinement. A participant described such a raid:

> the party would start out [in] the afternoon, and by dark they would [approach] the locality whare they expected to [find] an Indian camp. . . . When they found one, [they] got as [near to] it as possible, and in the morning as soon as it become light enough to see to shoot they made the attack by running into the camp. That many were killed in these conflicts goes without saying, but it was something of which the men engaged did not care to talk; and unless one was present, he never knew much about it.[7]

An army investigator reported whites around Weaverville had massacred scores of Indians, forty or fifty alone during a recent "New Year's Day frolic." He wrote that the Indians, not the whites, needed protection.[8]

Yet California's rapid rise to statehood left Indians almost entirely without even the federal government's limited protection. When California senators blocked a package of eighteen treaties that would have created reservations away from the mining regions, Indians were left with no legal claim to land and no promise of support. The small military reservations had no official standing and offered no real protection. Continued white attacks, plus epidemics and the disruption of their economies, left tribal populations folding in on themselves. The Yana and Yahi, two tribes near the northern mines, numbered about eighteen hundred in 1852, already down considerably from a few years earlier. Starved out and hounded, they lost many more before whites killed scores, perhaps hundreds, during a five-month frenzy in 1864. In 1872 there were twenty survivors. Most were hunted down over the next several years.[9]

Other mining frontiers rarely approached the grotesque excesses of California but all fell into a similar pattern. Each ended with native peoples holding only shreds of independence. Serious conflict usually came several beats later in the frontier's development as isolated assaults set off an escalating tit-for-tat of mutual violations and as Indians saw more clearly the unraveling of their social and material life. By then many whites were feeling frustrated themselves. Latecomers found the best claims taken, while even in the richest regions output and income invariably slumped within a few years.

Paradoxically, Indians and whites both felt that time was running out— the first for their way of life, the second for finding personal bonanzas. It was a perfect formula for trouble. When serious conflict came the last two pieces of the pattern showed themselves. In what Richard White has called the language of "inverted conquest," whites cranked up the rhetoric.[10] Acts of native resistance and retaliations were called vile outrages that demanded harsh and final punishment. And once the fight was underway the over-whelming advantages of the whites became clear. They had a population many thousands of times that of Indians, resources unimaginably greater, and a technology and delivery system to focus that strength with terrible effect. In the field numbers and clout sometimes favored the Indians, and the military could be laughably clumsy in pressing their advantage, but the white apparatus of power was like a clodhopping farmer stomping at a few wasps. When it finally connected, there was no doubt about the outcome.

Nearly every major far western Indian war was provoked by a gold or silver discovery and the changes it brought. Apaches in New Mexico and Arizona had raided and fought mostly with Mexicans on both sides of the border before the rushes of the 1860s. Soon a few nasty assaults by Anglos began a quarter century of southwestern war, grinding and increasingly bitter. Gold strikes along the Front Range of the Rocky Mountains in 1858–59 were followed by rising tension, clashes, intermit-tent war and by 1869 the defeat of the Southern Cheyennes and Arapahoes on the central plains. Red Cloud's War of 1868 was a determined effort by the Sioux and Northern Cheyennes to close the Bozeman Trail opened to the new diggings around Virginia City, Montana in 1863. They won a temporary victory, but eight years later another discovery brought a rush into the Black Hills, holy land to the Sioux. In the war that followed, the crushing victory by the Sioux and Northern Cheyennes on the Little Big Horn spawned a relentless pursuit that ran them to ground or drove them into Canada. The next year accumulated pressures from strikes in Idaho flashed into open war between whites and several bands of the Nez Perces, which quickly became a dramatic running fight as the Nez Perces tried to flee over the Rockies to the plains and then to Canada.

Native leaders who tried to accommodate to the new order did not fare much better. The infamous Sand Creek massacre in 1864 was an attack by Colorado volunteers on the camp of the Southern Cheyenne's most prominent peace advocate, Black Kettle. Others who tried to negotiate them-selves out of harm's way were either pushed onto the worst land or thrown against their enemies. A gold strike in 1870 spawned the towns of South Pass City and Miner's Delight on lands in southwest Wyoming promised to the Shoshones. The next year an agent offered to exchange that area for another to the north. "You know that you cannot eat the rocks or the gold," the agent pointed out. The Shoshone leader Washakie, one of the shrewdest diplomats of that era, answered that, besides rocks, their home had "plenty of grass, berries, prairie squirrel, and fish—plenty of everything of good land." What was offered, on the other hand, was not only poor; it was also being bitterly contested by the Crows and Sioux: "If we went there, then the Sioux might come in and scalp us."[11] Washakie won a few concessions, but finally surrendered the area.

Washakie's bargain was part of one of the biggest stories of the nineteenth-century West—the passing of ethnic control from Native Americans to European Americans. Gold and silver strikes were the great precipitators of that change, just as every rush set loose the transforming energy of a new urban industrial America into the country around it. A mining camp was like an artillery shell lobbed into the outback. Its concussion spread outward and rolled over native peoples who would never see a sluice or a mine, and as the expanding waves rippled into one another every part of the interior West felt the force of change, including regions so remote and so lacking in the usual attractions that they surely would not have drawn much interest for decades. The expansion and metamorphoses of white society were probably inexorable, but nothing accelerated this ethnic conquest of the West more effectively than its mining frontiers.

The final step was to rewrite the story. A local California historian called it "a conquest without resistance, followed by dependency without servitude." Indians, she added, "welcomed the whites as a superior race, and legitimate owners of the soil." Other accounts, however, persist beneath the rhetorical surface. Isidora de Solano, at ninety, looked back and dictated the miseries that began with the arrival of the "blondes" and the rush for gold. After her husband's death she married a white man but despised him as a weakling. Now she lived as well as she could, she said, and took brandy as her communion.

The men and women who flooded to those frontiers, like the Indians whose lives they disrupted, were an extraordinarily varied bunch. Mining camps were far and away the most ethnically mixed gatherings in American history— arguably, in fact, the most cosmopolitan places on earth at the time. Nothing showed more vividly the mesmerizing power of gold and silver. Into the frigid, windswept reaches of the Sierra and Rockies and the blistering southwestern deserts came Irishmen, Frenchmen, Mexicans, Hawaiians, Germans, Finns, Swedes, Chinese, Chileans, Portuguese, Australians, East Indians, Italians, and more. "Here they come in every steamboat, hundreds from every place," wrote a Kansas City journalist: "Hoosiers, Suckers, Corn crackers, Buckeyes, Redhorses, Arabs and Egyptians. . . . [They] blindly rush headlong into the wild delusion of glittering sands full of golden eggs."[12]

Nine-tenths of the first two thousand persons to the California diggings, according to an official dispatch from Thomas O. Larkin, were "foreigners."[13] His use of that term was interesting, given the unsettled diplomacy of the time, but by any standard California was a human scrambling. First to come were Spanish-speaking Californios from the nearby villages and larger towns like Monterey, and with them San Francisco's

Anglo workers and deserting sailors. Hispanics and Anglos at first were outnumbered by local Indians hired or coerced into the heaviest labor. Difficulties of travel kept the news from northern Mexico until October, 1848, but by the end of the year Sonorans, who had mined their own region for generations, were moving northward in considerable numbers. For the first couple of years a steady stream moved along the old routes between Sonora and California. Many shuttled back and forth, placering in the warmer months and going home for the winter.

Because news traveled much faster by water than land, an early surge came from a radius of several thousand sea miles around the Pacific. In Honolulu more than a dozen ships set off for California soon after word arrived in mid-June, 1848. Throughout the summer and fall the exodus continued, with the decks crammed with Sandwich Islanders, called "Kanakas" by Californians, and the holds stuffed with mining tools and with onions, pineapples, potatoes and chickens to feed the multitudes. By summer's end Chile and Peru were abuzz after a ship docked at Valparaiso with twenty pounds of gold. Response from this part of South America was particularly vigorous, given its long and persistent legacy of mining; the German traveler Frederick Gerstaecker had seen commonfolk panning streams in Valparaiso after floods.[14] By 1849 more than a thousand persons had sailed northward from South American ports. Five thousand more followed during the next few years.

Just before Christmas, 1848, a ship from the Sandwich Islands docked in Sydney, Australia, and within days locals were reading of California gold being scooped up by the shovelful. Excitement in Van Dieman's Land (named Tasmania four years later) was especially keen among the many graduates of the island's penal colony. They gathered in pubs like the Generous Whale and the Bird-in-Hand to talk up the increasingly outrageous reports, including news of California Gold Grease, smeared over the bodies of men who merely rolled around to pick up the precious dust that covered everything in the new El Dorado. With a severe depression sharpening the incentive to take the long voyage to San Francisco, the first vessels set off in late January. A berth went for thirty pounds, cabin class, or ten pounds in steerage. In the holds were rum, wines, dried meat, clothes, guns, tobacco, bundles of picks and placering paraphernalia, prefabricated houses and blankets of kangaroo hide.

Meanwhile Europe was being swept by revolutionary upheavals. Governments fell in France and Austria and a Roman revolt drove the Pope from the city. Twelve thousand persons died during a Parisian workers' uprising. Ireland felt the tremors; several revolutionary leaders, first sentenced to death, were exiled to Tasmania. Just as the shocks of 1848 were subsiding, and thousands were licking their wounds and looking gloomily into the immediate future, word arrived that gold had been found an ocean and continent away. Enthusiasm soon was fanned by translations of President Polk's confirmation of the discoveries and Colonel Mason's feverish descriptions of fabulous wealth.

The response was especially strong in France. Early in the rush California's French consul wrote home that, although the wine in the diggings was "ordinary," the region's riches had been "scarcely touched [and] will neither be exhausted in a few years nor even in centuries."[15] Soon investors were buying millions of shares in more than eighty emigration societies with names like *La Californienne* and *L'Eldorado*. Income was used to pay the way for gold seekers who promised to split their fortunes with shareholders. Another three thousand men were sent to California with proceeds from a gigantic government lottery for 224 gold bars. Thousands more took ship at their own expense. A new bi-monthly paper, *La Californie,* urged emigration and the cultivation of Pacific markets for French products: "Let us then not lose this chance to increase our riches and to efface from our memory the suffering of the past year."[16] Into 1850 the interest grew more fervent and the claims more preposterous. A popular illustration suggested that a miner's main trouble in California was carrying the golden boulders to the bank; an inventive fellow had harnessed a gigantic crocodile to haul his.[17] Later that year the bubble burst and most investors lost every *sou*. The emigration slowed, but by 1852 more than twenty-five thousand had made the trip.

No other Europeans were as caught up as the French, although a few thousand Germans, Italians, and Spanish took ship to the goldfields in 1849. Nevertheless, between the Europeans, Kanakans, Chileans, Peruvians, and Australians, it was a mixed crowd that awaited the first Argonauts arriving from the eastern United States.

Several cultural steps away from these were the Chinese. Although a few thousand came to California before 1852, the great wave began that year. The vast majority were from the southern province of Kwangtung and its main city of Canton. Beset by inflation, social disorder and an exploding population—their numbers had grown by 75 percent in a little more than sixty years—they set off on rafts, junks and lorchas for nearby Hong Kong to find passage across the Pacific. Many paid their way with savings or with loans, sometimes using their families as collateral. Many more contracted their labor with Chinese and foreign shippers, who paid for the trip, helped the immigrants find work and loaned them initial living expenses at a robust rate of interest. Debtors turned over a share of their wages until obligations were paid. After enduring shipboard conditions that sometimes resembled the "middle passage" of African slaves, Chinese were met at the wharves in San Francisco by agents who steered them toward temporary housing and employment. Many would stay in the city; many more would fan out into the hills on the scent of gold. About thirty-five thousand were in California by 1860.

Adding to this ethnic variety were African Americans, native-born but distinct among forty-niners from the states because of their imposed social and legal status. By 1852 about two thousand were in California and about twice that number ten years later. Most were free blacks, although a considerable minority were brought as slaves by white southerners.[18] The latter apparently found it relatively easy to break with their owners, like the two slaves reported by W. T. Parker who left their dissipated master and returned to check on him after considerable success, only to find that he had been murdered.[19] The mix of emigrants gave them choices never before encountered. They settled among themselves (as shown in place names like Negro Bar, Negro Flat, and Arroyo de los Negros) and with the least discriminatory groups, such as Chinese, Latin Americans, and New Englanders, and engaged in cooperative enterprises like dam-building with friendly whites.[20] At least during the first few years blacks reported the diggings were promising both financially and socially, "the best place in the world to make money," one wrote home, and "the best place for black folks on the globe."[21]

Those uninclined toward mining found other opportunities. Some worked at tasks traditionally given to blacks in the East. A diarist wrote of hearing "a band of darky musicians" in a gambling hall playing music "as only darky bands can git up." Others found jobs as waiters, porters, barbers for other blacks, laborers in hotels and liveries, and at other menial occupations. Inflated prices offered generous incomes even in these jobs, although the frontier's uncertainties left them vulnerable. A bootblack charging a quarter per shine had saved four thousand dollars when the slump of 1855 drove his bank under. He lost it all, and wailed "Sixteen thousand pairs of boots all gone to smash!"[22] The frontier's fluid conditions opened other avenues. Israel Lord stayed at a roadhouse, "neat . . . and scrupulously clean," run by two African Americans, one of whom had come around the horn as a ship's steward.[23] Mary Ellen Pleasant was probably the best known of many blacks who entered the ranks of San Francisco's property owners and speculators. Most presumably came west with the optimism common to the day. "Gold is plenty in California & some are making fortunes while others are not more than paying expenses," a slave wrote home to family, "I have strong faith to believe that we are going to be lucky."[24]

California's pattern was repeated on later mining frontiers. Until late in the century, in fact, the far West had by far the nation's highest percentage of foreign-born population, largely because of the mining rushes. The percentage on the Comstock rose from 35 percent in 1860 to just over half in 1870. In 1880 half of the Tombstone vicinity (Pima County, Arizona) had been born outside the country, and 30 percent of the Leadville area (Lake County, Colorado). Seven out of ten persons in the Boise River basin in 1870 had been born abroad—the Chinese alone outnumbered the native-born by 1.4-to-one—and for every native-born person in Idaho's Shoshone County, nine had come from elsewhere.

Ethnic patterns differed from place to place, like varieties of plaid. The French never showed much enthusiasm for rushes outside California; they made up only about 1 percent of residents in Virginia City, Tombstone, Leadville, and the Idaho camps, for instance. A few made a special mark. Louis Dupuy, apparently a U.S. Army deserter when he was badly injured as a laborer in a Georgetown, Colorado silver mine, opened the Hotel de Paris, which became famous for its fine fittings, its superb cuisine, and its host's crankiness. Dupuy's outspokenness and contradictions—he was an anarchist who helped conceive home economics education for young women—qualified him as a genuine western eccentric. But apart from such occasional touches, the French presence was not as noticeable as others in the interior mining West.

Chinese moved in swelling numbers through Pacific ports and across the Sierra Nevada, although California remained home to the largest number. Some mined from the start, while many were recruited for railroad construction in the late 1860s and remained in mining towns once the job was finished. Alone among the many groups, the Chinese faced organized efforts in some areas to keep them out or expel them, resulting in a mottled pattern of distribution. Leadville, Colorado never permitted them to settle in, and in Idaho's Owyhee district, Comstock, Tombstone, and other silver towns the relatively small populations were battered by riots.

Other groups, rarely seen during the first years of the California rush, were commonplace later, particularly two from the British Isles. As the development of lode mining created a demand for skilled labor, workers were recruited from the declining tin mines of Cornwall. The first arrivals in turn sent back word through the "Cornish grapevine" about high wages and strong demand, meanwhile asking bosses to hold jobs open for "cousins" on the way—thus gaining the nickname for Cornishmen of "Cousin Jacks." So many were in Grass Valley by 1861 that a local editor dubbed the town "the Cornwall of California."[25] Thousands were working the Comstock as well as Central City, Leadville, and other Rocky Mountain towns by 1870. The second group, the Irish, were present from the start, but their great immigration also came with large scale industrial mining. Most had settled first in the northeast or midwest, then gravitated to the mining frontier with special enthusiasm during and after the Civil War. Like the Cornish, their numbers grew by the siphon principle: a community in place drew more of its own. The cumulative effect was impressive. One out of five foreigners in Montana was Irish in 1870 and 1880. On the Comstock it was nearly four of ten.

Germans, too, were coming far more often by the 1860s. From Prussia,

Hesse, Wurtemburg, Hanover, and other states they formed distinctive neighborhoods in every interior mining town of more than a few hundred. Out of Canada came thousands of British citizens, especially to the northernmost rushes in Montana and Idaho. By the 1880s a new immigrant wave arrived when some of the Czechs, Poles, and Italians crowding into Atlantic coastal cities kept going, often stopping awhile in Chicago before pushing farther west to the Rockies. Leadville, Butte, and most other lode mining centers had their "Bohunk" districts.

As with the mining frontier's odd social behavior, its soaring optimism, and its nagging problems, its ethnic variety was a compressed version of the nation at large. A visitor to northern Idaho's Bunker Hill and Sullivan mine would have found in that one hole in the ground a living exhibit of Victorian America's spread of cultures. Besides the 84 native-born workers, there were 76 Irish, 27 Germans, 24 Italians, 23 Swedes, 19 English, 14 Scots, 14 Welsh, 12 Finns, 11 Austrians, 8 Norwegians, 7 French, 5 Danes, and a couple of Swiss, as well as a Spaniard, a Portugee, and an Icelander.[26]

Mining camps consequently were often as colorful and cosmopolitan as they were crude and uncomfortable. Early Sonora, California was like "the brilliant Bazaars of oriental countries," with flags and banners of brightly colored Mexican cotton draping the tents and huts that sat in shady bowers of tall trees. The Mexican majority wore *serapes* and leather trousers; Chileans sported black ponchos and wide belts for money and tobacco; Sandwich Islanders had colorful shirts with silk sashes; the first "Saxons" from the states wore heavy pants, flannel shirts, scarves and every imaginable headgear except "chimney pot" top hats. Indians wandered the camp, some with military jackets but no pants. A few peddled iced liquor from pails on their heads. Mexican women sold tortillas rolled around meat and peppers while their husbands ran games of chance on tables and on blankets on the ground.

Those gamblers' favorite, monte, "the great national game of Mexico," would spread across the West. It was one of many customs communicated to the nation at large through the mining frontier. South Americans and Mexicans brought a song, "Donde Vas, Bueno Caballero." Anglos liked the catchy melody, so they devised their own verses to fit the circumstances ("'Twas a miner, Forty-niner").[27] The result, "My Darling Clementine," became the mining frontier's anthem and one of the most familiar songs in English. (When Winston Churchill was awarded the Nobel Prize for literature in 1953, celebrants at the ceremonial ball serenaded his American-born wife, the former Clementine Hozier, with this song.) Cuisine from a dozen countries mingled on restaurant tables: in the early days tongue salad in Mexican chili sauce, then German sausages and Chinese noodles, and later Italian breads, Croatian sweets, and Cornish saffron cakes and pasties. According to some traditions, the two most common Chinese-American dishes, egg foo yung and chop suey, were invented in mining town kitchens.[28] Outlanders were intrigued by the new foods, and sometimes surprised. An eastern visitor, familiar with green peppers back home, bought a Mexican red pepper "about the size of a minnow," chopped it onto her salad, took a bite, and

> Shades of Vulcan!... I gave it a pass or two with my family grinders and swallowed it. Tears would not have flowed more freely if I had taken a coal of fire into my mouth. I manipulated my parching tongue with the soft parts of a slice of bread, dried my tear with a napkin. . . . The principal sources of heat are said to be the sun, the fixed stars, chemical action and electricity . . . [but] I am the first person who has ever discovered a latent hell in a red pepper. . . . I would warn all persons to beware of the pepper family entire.[29]

The men and women who sat down to this mix of dishes once again were forging bonds by eating together, although now with a frontier twist—by finding common ground in what was new to most of them. Communities of habit and style were further built by mingling other customs. Indiana miners sported sombreros and smoked strong Mexican cigarillos. Irishmen tried ponchos. Chinese quickly replaced their flimsy cane headgear and slipper-like footwear with felt hats and rubber boots, and over time many switched to flannel shirts and overalls. An archeological dig found the ruins of a Chinese camp littered with suspender buckles and buttons from pants flies.[30] Those trousers were themselves a cross of influences. The Bavarian immigrant Levi Strauss, seeing the raveled clothes worn by shoveling, rock-hauling prospectors, used a durable blue French sailcloth, *serge de Nimes,* to make work pants styled like those of Genoese sailors, with brass rivets from horse harnesses to strengthen seams and pockets. The result was denim (shortened from *de Nimes*) blue jeans (from *Genes,* French for both Genoa and the sailors' trousers). In this classic cultural shuffling a German shaped French material to an Italian cut and created America's most successful contribution to global fashion.

Daily life became an ethnic mix-and-match. The common term for Irish toughs, "highbinders," was transferred to rough Chinese characters who collected bad debts and pursued escaping prostitutes.[31] On household walls of Cornishmen and Chinese were sporting prints and nudes from bankrupt Irish saloons; Italians and Finns stored food in Cantonese ginger jars, served it in rice bowls, and ate it with green-on-white Chinese porcelain spoons. When Georgetown, Colorado hosted a special fat men's race between two German brewers, with a keg of beer as the prize, the pair waddled rapidly by the Englishman William Hammill's magnificent home, with its African camel's hair wallpaper and its fireplace of Italian marble, then puffed past Louis Dupuy's famous Hotel de Paris. There was plenty of vice-swapping. New Yorkers lay stuporous in Chinese opium dens; whorehouse patrons chose among women with names like French Kate and the Irish Pig. "High-grading," the theft of nuggets and ore by wage miners, combined the Cornish tradition of secret chambers in lunchpails, the American use of false-crowned hats and cloth socks within trouser legs, and the Mexican innovation of clay tubes concealed where not even a close search of naked bodies would reveal them.[32]

Workplaces, in fact, seemed a blend of custom at every turn. Placermen trapped fine dust by straining water from tailings through Brussels carpet. In a simple Mexican recovery technique they roasted placer sands in a pan with a thin mercury film; to separate the gold they then baked the amalgamate inside a large scooped-out Irish potato. Ore was crushed early on by the Mexican *arrastra,* a simple mule-powered device that powdered rock by dragging stone over stone. It was one of dozens of workaday tools and methods with Spanish and Mexican roots. The word *placer* itself was a Spanish double entendre; it meant both a sandbar, where gold dust often was found in a stream, and pleasure, suggesting methods that were easier than lode mining (*a placer* translates as "at one's convenience"). From Cornishmen came stories of Tommyknockers, tiny miners both friendly and malevolent, who lived in the shafts. Children were told to listen closely while falling asleep for the hammering of their little single jacks deep underground.[33]

From the start some pride was taken in this human diversity. The sheet music for "California; or the Feast of Gold" had on its cover caricatures of Scots, Chinese, Africans, Indians, French, and Irish all digging riches from a Pacific seashore, and inside:

> Oh! list to the Yankee proclamation!
> "The smartest nation in all creation,"
> Has issued a gen'ral invitation
> To folks of ev'ry denomination,
> To cross the main,
> And drain, and strain,
> And share in the feast,
> The wondrous feast of gold!

The verses went on to say that the precious dust had first been found by "the Mexican crews," and now "The Yankees are getting rich as Jews/And all are at liberty, who choose,/To cross the main, etc."[34] Independence Day bombast included toasts like this one:

> Ye are welcome, merry miners! in your blue and red shirts, all!
> Ye are welcome, mid these golden hills, to your Nation's Festival. . . .

Ho! children of imperial France; Ho! Erin's brave and true;
Ho! England's golden bearded race—we fain would welcome you;
And dark-eye'd friends from those glad climes, where Spain's proud blood
   is seen—
To join in Freedom's holy psalm, ye'll not refuse, I ween.[35]

Beneath the surface of this theme of come-one-come-all is another message, however. The song's opening lines make clear that the "gen'ral invitation" is issued by a particular nation ("the smartest . . . in all creation"), and the poem's salute to ethnic variety was read pointedly on that "Nation's Festival." We've got a lot of different peoples working here, these refrains said, but never forget who is in charge and on top. This point might seem benign—evidence, in fact, of the republic's open arms and wide toleration. But the words take on a sharper edge when read against the events and conditions around them.

*F*RONTIERS WERE ABOVE all fluid. The same dynamic mixing that made mining towns such a colorful cross-fertilization left unsettled basic questions of power—political, social, economic, ethnic. Resolving those questions could be a tense business indeed. That tension sometimes flared up into some of the ugliest moments in the region's history.

Conditions in California in 1849 were especially primed for conflict. The reasons lay in the peculiar timing of the discovery of gold and what followed over the next several months. It began with the most stunning coincidence in American history. James Marshall found those famous glittering flecks in the American River barely one week—just about two hundred hours—before Mexican authorities initialed the treaty that gave California to the United States. American possession, at this point, was a paper fiction. The United States might have owned California, but it definitely did not control it. The seat of national authority was twenty-two hundred crow-flying miles from Sutter's mill; the nearest concentration of military power, besides the skeleton crew at San Francisco, was fourteen hundred miles away in the Missouri valley.

Because of the way the gold rush story is usually told, it is easy to miss the implications of this coincidence. The story typically opens with Marshall's discovery, but shifts almost immediately to the eastern side of the continent. There farmers and haberdashers hear the news and prepare to set out the following spring to walk to the Pacific or to sail around the horn. After their arduous journeys they set up camps and begin the work of prospecting. Told this way, the mining frontier doesn't really crank up until that point, deep into the summer of 1849.

This distorts the picture badly. A more telling view would keep us on the Pacific through the summer of 1848, not fly us back to the Atlantic. We would first watch Californios hurry off to mine their native hills. Then would come Kanakas, Sonorans, Australians, Chileans, and Peruvians during the summer and fall, alongside a smattering of American citizens from Oregon. Finally, nearly a year after those groups were well entrenched, we would see Anglo-Americans arrive from the eastern states—alongside English, Belgians, Germans, and French.

Forty-niners, that is, were preceded by a lot of forty-eighters. The great majority of those early arrivals had no allegiance to the United States, and they felt no special deference toward American citizens who showed up well after they had started their own work. As for the forty-niners, they headed west thinking of themselves as the masters of this, the site of the most spectacular opportunity on earth. They arrived to find the gold fields crowded with just about everybody *but* people like themselves.

So discovering gold at exactly the moment when California was being signed over from Mexico might have been a fine stroke of luck in the long run, but at first this posed an unprecedented problem. Rarely in modern history has an event of such promise as the gold rush occurred so far beyond the practical reach of the people who supposedly owned the place where it happened. No wonder that some of those who came out from Massachusetts or Kentucky felt like a dinner host entering his house to find his rowdy guests starting the third course while slipping silverware into their pockets.

There was never a threat of losing California outright, although at least one French editor proposed sending an international force to keep the diggings open to all comers.[36] Cultural dominance, however, was another matter. Establishing national institutions and lifeways was an uphill effort in a camp like the one described as "a 'Germano' 'Chineso' 'Americano' settlement—three-fifths German, one-fifth Chinese, and one-fifth American, Scotch, Irish, French and Chileno."[37] And beneath any cultural concerns—literally just under the surface—was the real issue: gold, and who would get it. Abstractions of citizenship aside, would the wealth be controlled by the tardy immigrants from the states, or by serape-draped Sonorans, silk-sashed Kanakans, and French veterans of the revolutionary barricades? As the competition for prime sites intensified, such questions became more and more pressing.

By 1850 the great glut of miners (more than forty thousand) had severely limited the opportunities for newcomers, while the rising number of Anglos gave them the confidence to act. California's legislature levied a tax on all foreign miners, an exorbitant twenty dollars a month, more than enough to drive marginal prospectors off the field. Protests followed quickly in camps of the San Joaquin watershed, where the ethnic mix was especially rich. Three to five thousand French, Chileans, Mexicans, and

Germans organized loosely, sent delegates to Sonora to plead their case, and either peacefully showed their strength or blustered with threats of mayhem, depending on which accounts are read. Soon hundreds of armed Anglo miners flocked to the area in support of the new tax. Rumors flew over the next days—the French had raised the banner of revolution and were singing the *Marseillaise*, a lawman had decapitated a Mexican with a Bowie knife—but serious violence was avoided and the immediate crisis receded. The next year the tax was repealed, partly under pressure from merchants anxious to please their customers, Anglo or not. The sentiment behind the law, however, remained.

Anglo miners rankled especially at the French, who kept to themselves, bridled easily at affronts, and seemed to look down their Gallic noses at everyone. With the arrival of a few hundred of the Garde Mobile, a unit that had suppressed the Parisian uprising, Americans were increasingly suspicious. Early in 1850 a large group of "pretty saucy" Frenchmen were given five minutes to strike their tents and leave Mormon Gulch when confronted by a force of a hundred armed Anglos.[38] The next year, when locals claimed some of the Garde tried to control all the rich diggings at Mokelumne Hill, a serious confrontation followed between the French and more than three hundred Americans and Indian recruits. The Garde backed off and were ordered out of the region; their tents were burned and in a humiliating flourish their stylish shirts were given to the Indians.[39]

The most violent clashes were with Spanish-speaking miners—the Californios, Sonorans, Chileans, and Peruvians who were initially a strong majority in many areas. In an ugly outbreak fueled by liquor and patriotic gas, Chileans and Mexicans were booted out of several northern diggings on July 4, 1849. More violence soon followed in San Francisco when mobs sacked Chilean businesses and threatened refugees from the mines.[40] As the first great wave of forty-niners arrived in the fall Anglos first flexed their growing power by harassing and arbitrarily fining Mexicans. Then two weeks before Christmas came the so-called Chilean War in Calaveras County. Anglos had begun mining some dry diggings that Chileans had worked earlier, and when the latter returned for the winter the two groups soon were at odds. In a called meeting the Anglos formed a mining district and drafted regulations, beginning with "No foreigners shall be permitted to work at these mines." When evictions began, Chileans acquired warrants of arrest from a judge in nearby Stockton and raided a few Anglo camps, killing two men and seizing several more. There followed a confusion both of action and authority that ended with no Anglos prosecuted, three Chileans lynched, several whipped and, by one report, two with their ears cropped off.

Trouble continued in this region for nearly two more years. The rhetoric, like that against Indians, pictured foreigners as the aggressors and the Anglos, now the majority, as pressed reluctantly into defensive action. The summer following the Chilean War saw a mass gathering in Sonora that a critic derided as "the great Greaser Extermination meeting." The Anglo crowd resolved that "the lives and property of the American citizens are now in danger, from the hands of lawless marauders of every clime, class and creed under the canopy of heaven." With dark warnings about Mexican renegades and Australian convicts they concluded that all foreigners in the country, "except persons engaging in permanent business [that is, non-mining] and of respectable character," had to leave within fifteen days.[41] Many Mexicans, Chileans, Peruvians, and French did vacate the mines. Others remained but accepted subservient roles or withdrew to towns that were more tolerant or were dominated by their kinsmen. Collectively, California's settlements were sorting themselves in terms of ethnic power and standing, in a fashion similar to how each community, within itself, was sorting and separating its classes, public purposes, and zones of behavior. It was part of the mining frontier's integration into a new American empire and its ruling values.

The period of 1849 to 1852 might be called the second conquest of California. The first had come with the Mexican War and had ended with the Treaty of Guadalupe Hidalgo in 1848. In the second the Anglo latecomers secured economic and cultural control of their new, suddenly rich possession. They relied on their growing numbers and their obvious institutional advantage, from the military to the state legislature to county governments and impromptu gatherings that carried the force of law. Their actions had the sheen of high purpose—the coming of government and civil order—but mixed in was the drive to wrest control away from those who had beaten them to the bonanza. Forty-niners, arriving with manifest destiny at its fullest strut, were especially galled by any dark-skinned Spanish-speaking sorts. These were the same people they had condemned in the recent war as sleepy incompetents who could never make the land pay. But here they were, flush and cocky. The response was summed up by the chair of the public meeting that precipitated the Chilean War: "the d——d copper hides, every s-n of a b--h of 'em, should be driven from our diggings. They've got no business here in the first place, gentlemen, . . ."[42]

By 1852 the second conquest was finished. California remained a stew of cultures and traditions, but there was no doubt who was atop the ethnic order. Poetizers were secure in welcoming the "children of imperial France" and "Erin's brave and true." Three years to the day after Chileans and Mexicans were driven from the region where this orator held forth, the "dark-eye'd friends" of "Spain's proud blood" could safely be invited to join in singing "Freedom's psalm," since everyone understood who was now leading the choir.

Outside California serious ethnic conflict between native-born Americans and immigrants was unusual—with one great exception, considered below, of an ethnic group met with hostility from just about everybody. Because economic and cultural dominance by Anglo-Americans was never in doubt in the interior mining West, tension was greatest among immigrant groups competing for the best position lower in the pecking order. Trouble usually arose from economics. When a Cornish boss of a Nevada mine was fired and replaced by an Irish one, workers from the two groups went at each other. Five were killed, "most of them Irish who got their brains beat out . . ."[43] In Gilpin County, Colorado Italian newcomers in 1888 were suspected of working for less than the scale of $2.25 to $3.00 a day. In mass meetings Irish and Cornish workers passed resolutions against "the Dago, who does not speak our language, does not respect our laws, does not understand our institutions" and was "treacherous" to boot. When an investigation showed that Italians insisted on standard wages, the movement fizzled quickly.[44] A leading authority concludes that for three reasons western mining towns were much less riven by ethnic conflict than eastern industrial centers. So many Europeans of so many origins worked in the mines that there was rarely a concentration of any one group large enough to line up against any others. Rumors aside, most foreigners were unwilling to work for cheaper wages—the most common source of antagonism from other laborers. And because most unions were formed by the workers themselves, not imported from elsewhere, they tended to be inclusive, unlike movements in the East that often kept some nationalities out of their ranks. Union membership brought ethnic solidarity more often than division.

This is not to say that the mining frontier was a peaceful garden of ethnic lions and lambs. Where numbers and space allowed it, groups tended to pull apart into neighborhoods of their own kind, and there was plenty of the prejudice and pettiness common to any human mix. Fiorello LaGuardia, who went on to become New York City's most famous reformist mayor after growing up in the mining town of Prescott, Arizona, received his first ethnic jibes from friends taunting an Italian organ grinder: "Hey, Fiorello, you're a dago, too. Where's your monkey?"[45] The Irish, butts of jokes and insults in eastern cities, caught the same in the West, where some Anglos set them on the social border with the Indians. After watching the burning of an Indian corpse, a forty-niner thought the performance little different from an Irish wake, and another miner made the same point about a returning war party: "They bewailed their dead with dismal howlings, like the wild Irish."[46]

Nonetheless, relations outside early California were remarkably free of ethnically directed violence, given the mining frontier's extraordinary range of peoples, the stresses of the time and place, and the relative lack of social control. As mentioned above, however, there was one great exception to the security of immigrant miners—the Chinese.

Persecution of Chinese immigrants has to be kept in context. As the historian Liping Zhu points out, in areas like Idaho's Boise basin relations were mostly amicable, and although often described as compliant to the point of toadiness, Chinese often defended themselves quite effectively. Because of their superior diet and excellent medical skills, their mortality rates were well below those of non-Asians.[47] Ultimately they integrated nicely into mainstream society. Seen from this angle, theirs is one of the West's better success stories.

But seen comparatively, in a ranking of maltreatment among immigrant groups, the Chinese are in a grim league of their own. The range and level of abuses were surpassed only by those suffered by Indian peoples. There were mass expulsions from the Comstock region (1869), the Owyhee district of Idaho (1873), Leadville, Colorado (late 1870s), Tombstone (1887), and Idaho's Coeur d'Alene country (1891). On a two-day murderous rampage in May, 1887 thirty-one Chinese miners were shot or beaten to death in Hell's Canyon on Idaho's Snake River by whites intent on robbing them. There were lesser atrocities. Near Chico, California in 1877 five Chinese woodchoppers were killed when whites fired a fusillade into their cabin without warning, then set fire to it.[48]

Day-to-day abuse was documented in mining town newspapers like the *Territorial Enterprise* of Virginia City, Nevada. Its editor wrote of young boys commonly pelting Chinese men with rocks and broken bottles while local whites stood by laughing and applauding. "Recently a thirteen-year-old had pulled his revolver and shot in the neck a Chinese man who had not moved quickly enough out of the path of his sled." Another story described police placing a rope around the neck of a Chinese robbery suspect and conducting a public interrogation by dropping him several times from a rail yard derrick. In what was meant as an amusing human interest story, a journalist told of men soaking the coal in a cookstove with kerosene, so when the Chinese cook bent to light it the fuel exploded in his face, burning him badly. The writer chuckled, but then urged caution and common sense: "a little heavier charge of coal oil might have set the building . . . on fire." Virginia City was not much worse than other towns. The midwestern journalist Samuel Bowles wrote that "To abuse and cheat a Chinaman; to rob him; to kick him and cuff him; even to kill him have been things done not only with impunity by mean and wicked men" but by high and solid citizens as well.[49]

The California legislature and courts classed Chinese with Indians and denied them the right to testify in court, effectively taking away any legal protection from assaults. In 1852 the state also revived the foreign miners' tax and focussed it almost wholly at the Asians who began arriving in large numbers that year. Tax collectors had the power to confiscate and auction within an hour the property of anyone accused of tax evasion—an especially pernicious touch that made the system heaven for bullies and thieves with badges. The diary of Charles De Long, a twenty-three-year-old tax collector in 1855, offers a glimpse of how the law worked. "Had a China fight," he wrote one evening: "knocked down some and drawed our tools [pistols] on the rest and they put out." And later: "Sold out a Company of Chinamen [that is, auctioned their property] to Jack [a friend]. They followed him and bought the claim back. He made fifteen dollars." And: "Chased a train up a ridge, collected of them, found two [more] Johns, made them come down the hill with me, liked to have scared them out of their senses." And: "Loafing around doing nothing but picking up a few Chinamen . . . had a great time. Chinamen tails [queues] cut off." And: "Went down to the little Yuba . . . shot a Chinaman. Had a hell of a time." De Long might be dismissed as some lout out-of-step with the times, except that he was later elected to both houses of the state legislature and then appointed by President Ulysses Grant as U.S. minister to Japan.[50]

Ordinary converse among Chinese and their neighbors is much harder to recreate, but hints can be found in a pair of language phrase books published in California in the 1870s.[51] One was meant for English-speaking persons looking for useful expressions in daily contact with Chinese; the other offered Chinese the same sort of guide for communicating in the opposite direction. Here are a few phrases white housewives used to hire a Chinese domestic:

> Can you get me a good boy?
> I think he is very stupid.
> I want to cut his wages.
> Sweep the stairs.
> Wash the windows.
> Brush my hat.
> Take care of the baby.
> Light the fire.
> Wash the clothes.
> Wash the floor.
> Trim the lamps.
> Make some tea.
> Go to bed just now.

The phrase book is nearly two hundred pages long, but it does not include either of these two expressions: "How are you?" or "Thank you."

As for the other side of the conversation, here are some expressions that Chinese apparently found useful in speaking to and about whites:

You have made an agreement to hire me, but if you find that I am not suitable, you can discharge me, only you must not strike me.

He took it from me by violence.

I have made an apology but still he wants to strike me.

He assaulted me without provocation.

He claimed my mine.

He tries to extort money from me.

He cheated me out of my wages.

He pushed me against you.

I only mind my own business.

And for speaking to whites about other Chinese:

He was choked to death with a lasso.

He was frozen to death in the snow.

He was smothered in his room.

He was shot dead by his enemy.

He was flogged publickly twice in the streets.

He was imprisoned, with hard labor on the road.

He was starved to death in prison.

He committed suicide.

Mistreatment of emigrant Chinese is partly explained by what was missing. They had no well established population of Chinese-Americans to speak for them. Diplomatic contact was so recent that the Chinese government had no real leverage to press for protecting its people here. Most importantly, the Chinese were alone in having virtually no common cultural heritage with any other groups. They were the ultimate outsiders, and so the least likely to be given any protective empathy.

Lack of protection, however, cannot explain why so many people attacked them so viciously in the first place. That hostility is best understood through two sets of reasons, the first more obvious than the second, but both telling us plenty about mining frontiers and their economic and psychological dynamics.

The most obvious explanations were timing and money. The first Chinese in 1849 and 1850—merchants and artisans and a few hundred miners who posed no serious competition—were "welcomed, praised and considered almost indispensable," according to one authority. An early governor went so far as to propose land grants to lure more across the Pacific.[52] But between 1850 and 1852 the number landing at San Francisco grew from 450 a year to more than 20,000. Five years later there were more than forty thousand on the Pacific coast, and more than fifty thousand three years later. The timing of the great wave of 1852 was terrible. It washed into California in the final moments of the second conquest, just as Anglos were establishing their dominance over Hispanics and other perceived challengers. Primed to see any mass arrival of foreigners as a threat, the Anglo majority easily shifted its aroused emotions and overheated rhetoric from the freshly cowed Mexicans, Chileans, and French to the Asians suddenly there in the thousands. Unlike the others, furthermore, the Chinese kept coming, especially after the late 1860s when railroad recruiters brought them in to punch their enterprise through the Sierra Nevada.[53]

Making matters worse, the influx of 1852 coincided with California's first serious economic slump. Gold output sagged badly that year, and with the best claims already taken up, many whites found they could barely eke out a living. Now came the Chinese. Not only did they mean more miners scrambling for what little was left. They also showed a remarkable (and humiliating) talent for squeezing a respectable income from marginal claims through persistence, hard work, and a highly effective cooperation—by mastering, that is, traditional American virtues. As a Nevada editor later admitted: "Because of their patience, industry, and thrift the Chinese are enemies more terrible to us as a nation than . . . all the armies of the Czar . . . [They have a] peculiar intelligence and dreadful vitality, . . . and we are willing to admit that our people cannot, on even terms, compete with them."[54]

Responses came quickly. In May, 1852, shortly after Governor John Bigler warned that an Asian tide was threatening to engulf the mines, expulsions began in several mining regions, with rabid resolutions reminiscent of French and Chilean hysteria. This, coupled with the new foreign miners' tax, drove thousands of Chinese into other sorts of labor and service.[55]

A new economic threat arose as independent placer operations gave way to lode mining. Now, with large-scale companies hiring wage labor, it was feared that the Chinese, with their reputation for diligence and docility, would replace white workers, or at the least would depress the general wage. Chinese laying the Central Pacific railbeds looked especially menacing. Gangs of workers, bending and heaving in lockstep as they pushed the rail lines forward, seemed an above-ground vision of a laboring machine that might replace white workers below the surface, pushing tunnels deeper and pulling out the ore, relentless and pliable and cheap. The catalyst for one of the state's first unions was the sight of hundreds of cane-hatted railroad workers: "The talk among the miners was about as follows: Look at those pigtails! When they get that road finished, see how easy it will be to change white miners at four dollars a day for John at [a dollar and a half]."[56]

It was no coincidence that several moves to expel Chinese from Nevada's silver towns came as the Asians' work at railroad construction was ending. "Our town is under control of a mob," a mine manager wired his boss early in 1869, a few months before the golden spike was driven to complete the first transcontinental line. In company of an American flag, fife, and drum, fifty members of the Miner's League were roaming the streets of Unionville with rifles, shotguns, and axes, pulling Chinese from their houses and hauling them twenty miles away by wagon. Dreadful predictions were made for eastern workers who would face the "long-tailed rascals [who] will soon stand squinting their pig eyes across the Mississippi River."[57] The height of this economic reaction came with the rise of California's Workingmen's Party in 1877. With the slogan "The Chinese Must Go!" they called for the harshest restrictions. In the constitutional convention of 1879 party delegates pushed through provisions that declared Chinese dangerous to the state, prohibited their employment by any corporation or by a public agency, gave towns the power to remove them, and classed them with idiots and the insane as persons denied the franchise.[58]

These explanations remind us that understanding mining frontiers begins with money, the competition for it, and the frustrations over not getting it. But as usual there is more behind the obvious. The depth of resentment as well as specific accusations against the Chinese suggest other, subtler reasons. Just as other social tensions reflected the nation's doubts about itself, so too we can hear in the railing against the Chinese an uneasiness and anger felt by many Americans toward the transformations of their own society during the Gilded Age.

A couple of revealing themes run through anti-Chinese rhetoric. First, Chinese were described as so different and so alien that they were off the cultural spectrum. The French might be called irritating and Latin Americans debauched, but these Asians were beyond normal measurements—a "parody on humanity," as one writer put it. "Their costume is absurdity itself . . . , too ridiculous to be singular, or picturesque," another wrote. Yet another found their language scarcely human, more like "the Barking of Dogs and the squealing of Hogs." With such primal aversion some of the most vivid expressions naturally drew on the bodily sense humans have used for millions of years to distinguish others from "our kind"—the sense of smell. When Chinese were nearby, many whites seemed always to have their noses to the breeze, nostrils at full flare. One writer detected "old fish, a suspicion of sandalwood, and an unpleasant remainder that no man can analyze." Another combined the ancient instinct to sniff out aliens with the modern passion for quantification; a Chinese laundry, he claimed, emitted "over 150 distinct and separate villainous smells."

As Chinese were pushed further and further from the normal, their very humanity began to blur away until observers, like one touring journalist, finally felt a disconnection, a sense that what was in front of his eyes somehow was not of his world at all. In San Francisco's Chinatown he was repulsed by the alien architecture and teeming streets, the alley merchants selling everything from charms to cups of curdling blood. His nervous metaphors edged toward the animal; a streetside dentist, standing by strings of hundreds of pulled teeth, wore huge eyeglasses that "make his head look like a cobra's." By the end of the day he was questioning all he had seen: "In so strange a place, with such strange and stolid beings, it seemed as though it must be all a dream, that nothing could be real." The obvious consequence of such distancing is moral disengagement. If people are shoved far enough to the fringe of reality, all sorts of otherwise unthinkable acts can be justified or tolerated. Native Americans and African Americans had learned this lesson already.

The second theme seems puzzling in light of the first. When critics went beyond gut impressions to specific customs and behavior, they again said that those traits were so alien, so different from their own that they were almost beyond recognition. But on a closer look what they called bizarre and sinister suddenly is familiar. Virtually every social criticism of the Chinese had its counterpart in some popular anxiety about white society in the camps—and beyond that, in the new America of the late nineteenth century.

Chinese were condemned, for instance, for having no intention of staying. "These people are not immigrants; they are only visitors," one critic fumed. They would head home as soon as they had made some money, as implied by the vast predominance of males and the tiny minority of women brought for sexual services. Yet precisely the same could be said of those get-it-and-get-out camps of white miners, with their male domination, hardworked whores, and record rates of transience.

Mining camps, in fact were exaggerations of what many critics found deeply disturbing in the new America—crowds of young displaced men ready to go wherever opportunity called, caught up in dizzying movement and driven by manic materialism. Cities, it was said, would swallow the best of our youth. With identical imagery San Francisco's Chinatown was a grim vision of individuals "disappear[ing] like sugar in water" as they crowded "into a nest that would have been restricted for a chicken-yard." Especially worrisome was the effect on politics. City bosses, it was charged, would grab and control transient farmboys looking for work. They would have an even easier time manipulating immigrants in cities like New York and Chicago because those newcomers had no grasp of our political traditions. This fear, too, was projected onto the Chinese. Because they had "a bad handle of . . . English" and because "scarce a Chinaman in ten thousand can understand an abstract idea in our language," one writer warned, elections would become auctions, with a vast Asian franchise sold to the highest bidders.[59]

Authorities also warned that slums of the urban East—as well as gold and silver camps—were cesspools that threatened to set loose waves of disease. So too the city-prone Chinese were condemned for loathsome habits and accused (with no evidence) of importing leprosy. Nativists claimed that this illness, which in western culture had traditionally summed up all others, "would sweep through the entire length and breadth of our glorious America" unless Asians were deported. Medical fears generally were merging with new notions of racial pollution; warnings about Chinese were amplifications of the same. A prominent California doctor wrote that Asian immigrants were nests of hereditary diseases, including "mental alienation," that would threaten the "Divine excellence" of Anglo Saxon America and eat like a cancer at its "biological, social, religious and political systems."[60]

One institution in particular—the opium den—was held up as conclusive proof that the Chinese were both dangerous and hopelessly foreign. Nativists said it was a vile snare for America's best, who reportedly became listless, pale, and yellow-streaked after smoking the dreaded drug. (Some British medical authorities added that opium produced in the smoker Chinese customs and attitudes as well as appearance, which in turn became a transmittable disease, "Orientalness." Being Chinese, it seems, was a contagion.[61]) With its silk-robed proprietor and dim interior painted with flying dragons, an opium den was called too exotic and strange to ever be absorbed. And yet cities and mining camps supported tens of thousands of businesses that were, except in details, identical. Saloons, like the dens, had their distinctive decor and notable presiders, and they flourished by offering whites what the dens gave to Chinese: instantly recognizable surroundings, ritual exchanges, and an overpriced chemical that temporarily deadened loneliness and disappointment. Prohibitionists leveled many of the same charges at home-grown saloons that nativists leveled at the dens, and nativists in turn used rhetoric from the prohibitionist arsenal, including the famous warning of the fatal glass of beer, the first drink that supposedly would send ruddy farmboys into an unstoppable slide to hell. "It is utter ruin to smoke the first pipe," according to one writer, "for there is but one way to keep them from it afterwards, and that way is the walls of an asylum."

Over and over, the same pattern: Chinese were lambasted for things virtually identical to what was worrisome and all-too-familiar in a changing America, but in the same breath they were condemned as hopelessly, poisonously alien. A final example concerned, not habits and institutions, but what critics said was the innate character of Chinese men. One of the most important and contentious changes in the new America was unfolding inside middle class homes. The line between the worlds of men and women was being drawn more and more sharply, and although the spheres of male and female always overlapped, the sexes were called irredeemably different as social creatures. Men were suited for the corrupt and competitive struggles of public life, women for the sheltered moral haven of the home. Drawing and maintaining this keen division naturally added to the strain of American life during these years.

Once again the Chinese were set in the midst of this tension. While women were being maneuvered away from power and position, in the name of their basic being, nativists defined Chinese men as inherently feminine. They were called "half-made men" who were "destitute of . . . the wants" that drove lusty European-American males. Much was made of their slender frames, delicate hands, and their relative beardlessness. Noted, too, was their reluctance to confront, their impulse to smile and concur. This was called a mask that hid a "sullen implacability" and a guileful, merciless character, "but then," a critic added, "the same . . . might apply to divers classes of females all the world over."[62]

Feminizing Chinese men had the double advantage for white males of stressing their strange and alien natures while also excluding them from men's work. Outside their own neighborhoods Chinese found employment mostly as laundrymen, cooks and domestics, all part of what now was called the female sphere. And how natural, one man wrote, "that they should be so apt at washing, cooking, and other household drudgery that in most countries falls to the women's share."[63] But as womanized men, set on that line between male and female, Chinese were easily caught in any crossfire of the sexes. Working class women resented the competition for jobs as housekeepers and laundresses; some Irish women, offered work as domestics, "replied that they were not going to do a Chinaman's work." Middle class women might enjoy the help of Chinese servants, but it is worth asking whether they resented them as well. The female arena of power was limited and crowded already. A woman who hired a man into her home, even a "half-made man," was inviting a male into the only social space that was honorable and hers alone. Perhaps this dilemma helps explain the favored phrases in those books, with their imperious tone that left no doubt about who was on top and who on bottom: "Wash the windows," "Brush my hat," "Sweep the stairs," "I think he is very stupid," "Go to bed just *now*."

Whatever the roots, some of the most rabid diatribes came from middle class women, especially if they had other reasons to attack. Mrs. M. M. Mathews of Nevada, an ardent defender of unions and white labor, warned that the Chinese were "a miserable, thieving, murderous, licentious, filthy, pestilential race of heathens." They were Darwin's missing links, cunning as monkeys but without human graces. They broke the families of honest labor. When hired as servants they defiled our homes, she added, "our little daughters are not safe under the same roof with them." Banish them and save yourselves, she warned Americans elsewhere, "or in five years more you will see these Celestials come pouring down over the eastern side of the [Sierra] Divide like a herd of buffaloes."[64]

Hate that deep usually has a lot of sources, a useful reminder of the many crosscurrents in the mining frontier's ethnic relations. Feelings were by no means all hostile. Especially before 1852 California's white miners often approached their Asian neighbors with open and friendly curiosity. They wondered at their dress and tonsure, commented on their elaborate funerals, and questioned them on their homelands. "Of their morrals, they are very exemplary," one wrote, "Christians might do well to coppy after them."[65] In the years ahead others admired these immigrants' hard work and sympathized with their trials.[66]

Still, the depth of malice suggested a larger, peculiar dynamic at work. Chinese were portrayed as so different that they seemed pressed to the edge of the human condition. They were made the ultimate Others. Yet most of what was called so alien was in striking parallel to trends and habits carrying the American people toward a new—and to many a frightening— way of life. Those who lashed at the Chinese seemed to take their fears about a changing America, hand them to these vulnerable newcomers, exile those aliens to the fringe of reality, then to dismiss them as everything we were not and demand that they be packed up and sent away forever.

Once again the mining frontier was taking its curious part in the nation's search for itself. Visitors thought mining towns were far from the American center, both in behavior and in miles on the map. And so they were, although their oddness lay mostly in their fabulous overstatements of national character. The same was true of frontier ethnic life. Even in an age when immigrants crowded into eastern and midwestern cities, these far western towns were a startling scramble of customs and accents. Their confrontations, from split lips to lynchings, were a condensed, intensified version of the effort to sort and align our new mix of peoples. Chinese served double duty. Out there, on the national fringe, they were called the epitome of unmixable peculiarity. Yet their habits and traits, paradoxically, were pictured as a distant and broad enactment of much that was frightening in our own uncertain future. "Strange and characteristic," Daniel Pigeon called a typical mining camp. It held true as well for the darker performances of this flamboyant American theater.

◁ **12** ▷

Worlds of Work

Indians and whites on mining frontiers had at least a couple of things in common. They worked, and how they worked largely determined how they lived with the people around them and with the places they inhabited.

The earliest mining camp communities were built from men clustering together to share their labor. Simply by doing their work they pried apart Indian societies, starting by cracking the connections native peoples had devised in working the land in their own manner. Labor was a rare common denominator among what was otherwise one of the most diverse human swarmings in modern history; the hostility that did develop among ethnic groups was primed by jealousy over labor and its profits. Work was the clearest mirror of its society's transformation. Each step of change in every job said something about a town's transition beyond its frontier beginnings. While not the alpha and omega of mining frontiers, working life expressed the spirit that set them loose and the force that sustained them. A prospector kept this poem in his journal:

253

But Hope, the stay of honest hearts,
Yet bids me not despair
And tells me I shall make my "pile,"
Yet does not tell me where;
Hence, I will work with energy,
Through seasons dry and wet;
I'll work 'till I shall make my "pile,"
For I will make it yet.[1]

The site of every gold or silver strike had been a working world of other peoples for thousands of years. Each was supporting Native Americans when miners suddenly rushed in. What native residents thought at first can only be speculated. Luther Schaeffer wrote of Maidu women gathering roots and wild onions beside him as he panned for color in a creek near Grass Valley, California. Suddenly he and the women were laughing, great bellydeep guffaws, moved by each other's silliness in working so hard for what each considered worthless.[2] Others probably watched with bewilderment. A Californian wrote home in 1850 that "the 'redskin' who four months ago roamed in his nakedness, the undisputed lord of these mountains and valleys, may now be seen in the hilltops gazing with surprise upon the scenes below—the habitations, the deep-dug channels and the dams built."[3]

Any surprise or amusement, however, soon turned to alarm. The cabins and tents, sluices, long toms, diversion dams and the other mining paraphernalia were outward signs of a far wider transformation. One system of work was quickly choking out all others. Indian peoples, unable, unwilling or forbidden to play meaningful roles in the new order, soon faced a full-blown disaster.

Almost all Indians in mining regions lived by some variation of hunting and gathering. Whites typically thought such an economy inferior to farming, but by one definition it was actually more efficient. Especially where game and plants were abundant and diverse, as in California and some parts of the interior West, hunters and foragers could bring in more calories in less time than laborers in many agricultural societies. This was possible, however, only by reaching widely and with an exceptionally intricate knowledge into the surrounding country. Hunters and gatherers did manipulate their surroundings in limited ways—protecting especially valuable wild plants, for instance, or using controlled fires to move animal herds here and there—but success depended most of all on accepting and understanding a place on its own terms. The trick was to see the land's innate possibilities and to link its many parts into dynamic combinations.

The Yana of California were an example of what might be done. They hunted deer, antelopes, rabbits, mink, wood rats, and other small game;

they strung their bows with deer sinew and glued them with residue from fish heads. They took mussels and salmon from the streams, gathered and leached acorns and buckeyes and ground them into flour, ate yellow jacket grubs and drank soup made from powdered bones. For food storage they wove baskets out of willow bark, rushes, and cordage of milkweed. In pipes whittled from cane they smoked tobacco (their one cultivated crop) and other herbs that brought physical and emotional relief. One prevented dreams of the dead. They greased their hair with deer marrow and combed it with anise root. Animal hides, tanned with animal brains, gave them most of their clothes. They cinched their long shirts with belts made from the topknots of woodpeckers.[4]

Particulars and nuances varied but all Indian peoples of the mining regions supported themselves through an intimate engagement with their surroundings. No clear line existed between working and social communities. Indians saw all things—bears, bison and wild turnips, oaks and trout, gooseberries and cattails—as social beings who pursued their own needs. Directly or indirectly all fed each other, and all were joined through mutual obligations. Things might go awry. This was no idyllic order. Just keeping these communities reasonably untroubled could generate enormous anxiety. It was, however, a view of reality that had worked reasonably well for a long time.

This way of life did have two significant drawbacks, however. Hunters and foragers had to have access—relatively undisturbed access—to the particular region they knew the best, country where they could apply this elaborate understanding. That territory had to be quite large if they were to find all the resources they needed. Each band needed a lot of acreage per person. Thus the second drawback: hunting and gathering communities usually remained relatively small, a couple of hundred persons at most.

Those two requirements made hunting and foraging societies doubly vulnerable. Their smallish communities were more easily attacked, harassed, and generally dominated. California rancherías often seemed little more than holding pens of outnumbered Indians assaulted at will by hostile miners. Plains bands, no matter how skilled their warriors, rarely could muster the numbers to hold up under a sharp military strike. George Armstrong Custer's disaster in June of 1876 is explained not so much by his overconfidence as by his reasonable (but wrong) assumption that he was attacking a village of the usual modest size. As he quickly discovered, Lakota and Cheyenne bands, frustrated by encroachments from mining rushes in Montana and the Black Hills, had gathered in numbers seldom seen before. The battle, in fact, emphasized just how rare such a gathering was. When Custer had the poor luck to stumble onto it, the great village, after rapidly consuming game within a huge radius, had eaten its way into a crisis and was about to disperse. Never again would the western military face a concentration close to the size Custer found along the Little Big Horn.

A second threat, however, took a far greater toll than any direct attack. A mining rush instantly began to shatter the intricate connections that bound Indian communities to those of plants and animals. To live successfully in the eastern Sierra Nevada, for instance, the Paiutes had to be able to gather bulbs from spike brush in the spring, pine nuts in the summer, and the seeds of giant rye grass and love grass in winter; they dammed streams and pulled from pools the fish they stupefied with natural poisons made from plants and animals taken elsewhere; where rabbits and deer were especially numerous they conducted collective hunts in summer and fall; they gathered salt, shaped it into balls and cakes, and carried it great distances to trade for cloth, blankets, and a few other manufactured goods.[5] Such an economy relied on its people being able to follow a carefully choreographic pattern of movement. Those closely timed steps of survival were quickly disrupted by newcomers simply setting up their first crude camps.

Soon the damage was far greater. Miners and professional hunters depleted populations of deer, elk, bison, bear, and other game animals. The massive cutting of trees deprived Indians of fuel, acorns, and pine nuts; erosion fouled the streams and suffocated fish; the furious runoff swept away mussels and other riverine resources. The area immediately around the mining towns soon was unlivable to Indians, at least on the previous terms.

Next, in the mining frontier's distinctive pattern of development, supporting enterprises took root where a non-Indian presence had been felt faintly or not at all. The cultivators who cleared and broke land and the cattlemen who set their herds on the mountain pastures were destroying trees and other plants that had fed, clothed, and housed native peoples. In the Sierra and Great Basin the rich seed-bearing grasses were mostly devoured and replaced by courser, inedible varieties. Bans on burning interrupted old methods of renewing wild plants, and fencing further disrupted the cycles of shifting among resources. Grazing and farming drove out rabbits, many bird species, and other small game crucial to Indian economies. White settlers preempted the most protected wintering grounds, leaving Indians in more exposed sites that often lacked the basics of living.

Consequences soon were felt much farther away. New market towns and distribution centers required roads and established lines of transport and travel. Along these routes, the veins and arteries of the mining economy, flowed everything from flour and bullion to whiskey and corsets. Tens of thousands of wagons, horsemen, and people afoot, as well as herds of cattle, sheep and other animals, passed up and down these commercial corridors that reached out thousands of miles into the far Southwest, across the plains and Great Basin, into the mountain recesses of Idaho and Montana.

This bustling business became a force of change as great as mining itself. Indian peoples along these routes felt the full effects.

On the central Great Plains, for instance, several famous tribes of semi-nomadic horseback Indians—Cheyennes, Arapahoes, Lakotas, Comanches, Kiowas and Kiowa-Apaches—lived by the usual patterns of hunters and foragers. They subsisted on bison and other large game and a variety of plants; they raided against tribes to the east and traded bison robes for vital goods. During the ten years after 1849 more than a quarter of a million persons (and two to three million oxen and other animals) crossed the plains via the great overland trail along the Platte River. Travelers and their stock overgrazed the forage, cut the cottonwood groves, and generally fouled the sites that Indians and their horse herds required to shelter them during the vicious winters. Then word of Colorado gold brought a new rush of a hundred thousand persons across the worn terrain. In the South Platte valley, spared until now, Cheyennes and Arapahoes were "uneasy and restless," wrote agent William Bent, because whites were "laying off and building Towns all over the best part of [the] country" used for winter refuge.[6] A year later the valley had slipped entirely beyond their control, and soon mercantile outposts were set on the best spots along the routes between the Rockies and the Missouri valley. Surviving forage was rapidly depleted, and herds of bison and other game, already feeling the effects of Indian overhunting, shrank dramatically. The Indians' sustaining system of trade began to unravel.

Details varied, but the lesson was the same. The western country could be the working world for gold seekers like Luther Schaeffer or for Indians like the women who gathered plants at his elbow. But it could not be both. As the transforming power of each mining frontier spread steadily outward, native peoples within its widening circumference soon faced economic catastrophe.

Indians had few options to meet this crisis, none of them good. They might fight back. But the same disruptive forces that triggered the Indians' resistance crippled their ability to keep it up, and on the way to defeat they lay open to appalling atrocities. Idaho's Bear River massacre of Shoshones in 1863 and that of Cheyennes a year later at Sand Creek in Colorado both grew from struggles over resources along trails to the mining camps. Armed resistance by Indians in California and Arizona invariably brought the harshest reprisals from locals and the military.

An obvious alternative was to shift into the new economy. The modern mining era, in fact, opened with Indians as prominent workers. Before the rush John Sutter had relied heavily on Indian labor at his settlement at New Helvetia, paying local head men to supply gangs of workers who slept locked in crude huts and ate meals of porridge out of troughs of hollowed logs.[7] Once gold was discovered—by one account it was a local Indian who found the first nugget and showed it to Marshall—it was an easy step simply to redirect native labor into placering. Colonel Mason's report of 1848 estimated half the workers in the diggings were Indians; the former mountain man James Clyman thought the portion was two-thirds. The French consul found most of the workers along the Feather River were local Indians pressed onto the job by American settlers.[8]

Economic arrangements were flexible at first. Some Indians probably were forced to work, much as they had been under Sutter's reign. Others apparently were freer agents. Aylett Cotton bought plenty of "hickory shirts and pants" to hire native workers, and Colonel Mason wrote wonderingly of Indians suddenly able to buy "the most gaudy dresses" and "the luxuries of life" with what they had earned. More independent peoples like the Miwoks of the San Joaquin valley operated diggings of their own, sometimes as neighbors of the first white miners. These natives seem to have considered placering women's work, a variant of gathering. By still another arrangement Indians apparently worked more or less on their own but dealt with the new commercial system through a trusted white agent. James Savage of Mariposa County was one example of a middleman who dealt, not in animal hides as elsewhere in the West, but in gold dust.[9]

Indians, however, were muscled to the edges even more quickly than other ethnic groups. The growing white majority preempted independent native operations, and Indians were relegated to huge labor gangs. Charles M. Weber reportedly had a thousand working for him in exchange for "the necessaries of life and of little trinkets that so win an Indian's heart." With his partner he cleared fifty thousand dollars. Bayard Taylor wrote that Indian labor was paid a dollar a day, but by most accounts they received trade items, and not much of those. The major general of the state's militia condemned as "highly disgraceful" employers who paid workers with a little calico and food "when they would be content with the pay of one-fourth of the wages of a white man." Otherwise native families lived as best they could in the cracks of the new society. Timothy Osborn wrote that as winter approached Indians moved onto nearby deserted claims of whites to wash a little dirt, to gather acorns and to fish.[10] A resident of Truckee complained that local natives would slip into the neighborhood and "resort to any unlawful means to catch trout" and a diarist wrote of Indians visiting his camp frequently to "beg for something to eat . . . or for old clothes."[11]

Their options narrowing, Indians preyed on both the working stock around the towns and the cattle raised to feed the miners. The Paiute Sam Newland remembered harvesting cattle found mired in mud and stealing horses to eat.[12] Faced with this new—and deteriorating—situation, his people were applying traditional practices of raiding and hunting. "The Indians seemed to think they had the Same wright to the white man's stock, that they did to the deer that ware runing wild every whare," as one man recalled.[13] Those deer, he might have added, were rapidly disappearing, but when Indians turned to the livestock to replace wild game they soon faced reprisals. In a valley where he found "no wild animals except Indians, lizards, and black-tailed hares," W. T. Parker reported some Missourians had killed eighteen Indians for taking some horses.[14] This cycle of theft, killings and counter-killings was a prime precipitant of pitched conflicts that invariably cost Indians far more than the whites.[15]

It was out of those clashes that white Californians began taking and selling children and women for their labor and sexual services, a practice given some legal standing in state laws in 1850 and 1860. In the first statute whites could obtain young Indian "apprentices" by pledging to feed and clothe them. The second provided that children could be acquired with consent of parents or of third parties currently "having the care or charge" of them; adults and children could be taken outright if they had no apparent livelihood or were prisoners of war. Men could be kept until the age of thirty, women until twenty-five. From the perspective of the new white majority, these extraordinary measures, establishing de facto slavery on the eve of the Civil War, would ease a labor shortage while controlling Indians by fitting them firmly at the bottom of the ethnic order. "Call them slaves, coolies or apprentices—it is all the same," an editor wrote of what he considered a "most humane disposition." Some suggested taking the system farther. "What a pity the provisions of the law are not extended to greasers, Kanakas, and Asiatics," a journalist wrote with only slight irony: "It would be so convenient to carry on a farm or mine, when all the hard and dirty work is performed by apprentices!"[16]

California's case as usual was extreme, but essentially the same process unfolded wherever gold and silver were found. Mining and its supporting economy rapidly changed the physical setting of the Indians' working world. A journalist summed up what followed: "The complaint on the part of the Indians is that the white men have driven the game from their accustomed haunts; that the rivers which aforetime so abundantly supplied them with fish, cease to afford them food; and that the Americans kill their young men."[17] Apart from brief possibilities in the new world of work, native peoples were pressed toward drudge labor or they found no place at all. When they entered the white world of commerce, it was hardly on equal terms. A correspondent in the California placers told of a supplier who brought in "five hundred steers that he sold to the whites for twenty-five dollars and to the Indians for one or two hundred."[18]

Most whites were oblivious to the calamity they brought. Beyond the simplest observations (natives "are wild, live in small huts made of brush and go naked as when they are born . . . Their character is timid and imbecile"), they had no clue of the intricate adaptations sustaining Indian economies, and thus no sense of how it was all coming apart. If they found any meaning in the unfolding catastrophe, it was a natural replacement of a backward people by superior civilization.

The hungry, ragged, increasingly dissipated Indians who gravitated to the towns and campsites were called proof that, however degenerate the mining camps might be, the new society was far ahead of what it replaced. "Playing cards seems to be about their only lesson in Christianity," a visitor wrote of Nevada's Indians. Others dismissed notions that Indians had ever lived well in their world. "Could those blear-eyed bedlams, . . . stretching forth skinny claws for alms, be the sisters of 'Little Fawn' or 'Laughing Water'?" a traveler wondered: "Could those shambling, knock-kneed loungers, sodden with the fire-water for which they still craved, ever have backed a wild *mustang*, or met a foe fairly with bow and spear?"[19] In the working world of sluices, farms, and groceries, native peoples now were annoyances and, in brushing them out of the way, occasional sources of amusement. John Eagle wrote his wife of three women and their infants approaching him and his friends during dinner to beg for bread. First the men pretended to offer to buy the babies for a quarter, but this failed to frighten the mothers, so they tried another ploy. "We insisted them to come in and go to *bed*, and jumped up from the table to catch them," he wrote, "and then they vamoused with a forced march."[20]

*N*ATIVE AMERICAN ECONOMIES were not overwhelmed by any one or a few changes. They were displaced because the miner's world of work, like their own, was so utterly encompassing. The first labors of prospecting quickly diversified and new enterprises sprang up in their support. The site of a rush was suddenly within the orbit of the national economy. When strings were pulled in distant cities, mining towns twitched. Frontier society's conquering values—acquisitive, supremely confident, transformative—were in a seamless weave with its people's labor.

It started with the search. A prospector entering a new area first hunted for "sign," some indication that he might find gold or silver in amounts worth pursuing. He kept an eye out for likely geological forms, then tested the gravel and sand in streambeds or dug a prospect hold to gauge the dirt at bedrock, the foundation at the bottom of soil laid down over the millennia. His first goal was to find small amounts of silver and gold eroded from their original home in the surrounding terrain. He tossed a bit of dirt or gravel into the broad, shallow pan made famous in illustrations of the mining frontier. He poured in some water, then gently swirled the mixture so that lighter material rose and washed over the side while the heavier sank and remained. Black granules in the residue might be silver chlorides. Silver combines eagerly with much that it meets; the result is compounds, such as chlorides, worth nothing in themselves but indicating purer deposits nearby. If on-the-spot smelting or acid testing showed promise, the prospector began his search for the original source, hopefully close by. It took a good eye and experience to recognize silver sign. Gold seekers in Nevada in the late 1850s cursed the "black sand" and "blasted blue stuff" that clogged the riffles and cleats along the bottoms of troughs meant to catch gold. They tossed it aside, blind to evidence that they stood atop one of the world's richest silver lodes: the Comstock.

Gold, by contrast, was easily recognized. Because it is heavy and combines with almost nothing else, it remains pure and settles quickly when carried by erosion from its mother deposit. And of course it is shiny. When a prospector saw glittering grains and flecks in his pan, he knew instantly, in what would become slang for all good fortune, that he had "hit pay dirt." But except for finding an occasional pea-sized nugget, panning for gold was no way to make money. Like silver chlorides, a sifting of dust suggested that something richer was nearby. Unlike silver, however, eroded gold was still worth mining for its own sake. Its stubborn refusal to join with other elements meant that this "free gold" lay scattered in a more or less pure form downhill and downstream from its origin. Time and chance had left it sprinkled thinly in some places and more thickly in others. Occasionally its concentration was extraordinarily rich. Especially in California's mother lode, it was sometimes packed into ledges, cracks and pockets along present or ancient streambeds where lucky prospectors simply scraped it out with a knife or spoon. One two-foot fissure yielded two hundred dollars. Even more valuable deposits might be found in the potholes of streams.

Typically, however, the wealth was infused in gravel and dirt in varying concentrations. The challenge was to find a claim worth the effort, then to extract the precious dust as efficiently as possible. Gathering eroded gold was called placer mining, a term taken from the Spanish. Placering took several forms. At its simplest, one or two men shoveled dirt and gravel from a promising spot into a rocker, also called a cradle, moving it back and forth as water was poured through it. Gold particles would settle to the bottom and catch behind pieces of wood, called cleats or riffles, nailed crosswise to the flow. A "long tom" was an exaggeration of the rocker. Its head was a broad surface where gravel was shoveled and washed down to a "riddle," a sieve-like metal sheet that allowed only finer material to pass into a long "riffle box" where the lighter, worthless dirt was carried through and the gold again was caught on cleats and sometimes in a piece of sheepskin or Brussels carpet placed at the end of the trough. This aptly named device—some were thirty feet long—required at least six and usually eight or more men to gather and shovel in the gravel, clear the riddle, and keep the water flowing and the trough clear. The

French consul Jacques Antoine Moerenhout described a long tom that washed a ton of dirt every few hours.

With more work and wider cooperation, other elaborations were possible. To open the bed of an active stream men built a diversion dam and dug drainage canals. Several prospectors would pool their resources and labor for at least days and sometimes weeks, then divide the income by shares. A finished dam still had to be maintained and repaired, and a heavy rain sent teams of men into the water, frantically shoring up the crumbling construction. He and his fellows looked "par-boiled," one man wrote after wrinkling up from struggling waist-deep in a stream from three in the morning to until past dark that night. All this effort, furthermore, might come to nothing, for until the dam and ditches were finished there was no way to tell whether gold was waiting under the water. William McFarlin wrote from California:

> In the spring of [18]50 I had about a thousand dollars, but I left the place [I was working] and went to dam the river (and by the way I have damd it often) where everybody thought we would make a pile that summer and go home in the fall but we spent all we had & five months hard labour & never got one dollar & when we settled I owed $155.00 and had but seven dollars in my pocket—one of the company took a razor & cut his throat the same night.[21]

After a week of construction, W. T. Parker and friends had a claim that paid two dollars a day, hardly enough for a plate of beans. Yet, on another dam a year later, Parker cleared nearly seventeen hundred dollars over a few weeks. Another miner's careful accounting showed his daily share ranging from forty to a hundred dollars. One glorious day he made nearly three hundred.

Some hillsides were deep beds of gravel laid down by ancient rivers. Teams of miners turned to "undercutting"—digging broad caverns into the hills, shoring up the ceilings, then causing the cavity to collapse to loosen the rock above, which was then washed. Where bedrock was deep, placer miners dug shafts up to forty-feet down and burrowed off to the sides, a technique called "coyoting." These diggings were a worming of timbered tunnels topped by horse-powered winches. Once the pay dirt was exhausted, coyoters scoured the bedrock for any missed crevices or pockets before abandoning the operation. During winter and exceptional dry spells, when little or no water was available for washing the dirt, some miners continued to dig and stockpile material, pulling it out of coyote holes and trenches, in hopes of jumping the competition at the return of the rains. As much as anything on the mining frontier, this last strategy—storing dirt—testified of the gold seeker's boundless optimism.

At this stage the basics of labor would have looked familiar anywhere in mid-century rural America—or for that matter on any colonial farmstead or medieval village. Men hacked at the earth with picks, moved it with shovels and buckets, and washed the gravel in equipment slapped together with simple tools and elemental carpentry. Hillsides were dug away, thousands of tons of rock moved around, streams diverted into new beds, and pits sunk deep into the earth. A significant portion of the western landscape was reshaped, and except for some help from draft animals and the flow of water, it was all done with human muscle power.

The work was brutal. Squatting for hours in icy streams to test for sign turned out to be the easiest step. Pay dirt often had to be hauled a considerable distance to the water needed to wash it, or ditches dug and wooden channels, or flumes, built to carry water to the dirt. It was "the hardest work I ever did," a miner wrote (with "badly blistered" hands) after three days of shoveling and tossing dirt eight feet out of a ditch to feed a long tom. For their efforts he and his friends together made about fifteen dollars, "so we Bolted."[22] On a typical day another man and seven others washed 275 barrow loads and carried away an equal amount of stone.[23] Another wrote his father that "I would not stay & work in the mines for one year for as much money as Billey Gray ever had," apparently referring to a wealthy neighbor: "It would kill me."[24] Plenty of others chose not to take any chances. "It is very hard work," Samuel Curtis explained to his brother of the Colorado diggings, "and after I had washed one pan full I concluded [gold] was here, but that I was not adapted to digging it."[25]

Catastrophic accidents were rare at this stage, except when miners moved into technologically chancier terrain. Coyoting was a far reach beyond the skills of a Philadelphia boot salesman or Vermont farmer, and when inexperienced miners burrowed deep into loose, alluvial soil, some were crushed or suffocated in cave-ins. Using blasting powder was even riskier. "Oh the awful condition," a miner wrote of a victim of an explosion: "One arm completely Cucked [cooked] . . . the other arm burnt worse, Hand torn to pieces. . . . His face burnt as black as a negro [and] filled with powder and rock . . . and eye blowed out."[26] Most injuries, however, were the common ones of heavy labor—crushed fingers, lacerations, broken bones. The heaviest toll was in extreme fatigue and in chronic wear of backs, arms, shoulders, and legs. Hundreds of hours in icy water brought on early rheumatism; hundreds more in blistering sun left faces leathery and lined. Men worried about the return home. "I am getting very old mother; you would hardly know me," Albert Francisco wrote, "This country wears a man out very fast."[27]

The most extreme expansion of placering—hydraulic mining—reduced the backbreaking tasks of earlier forms, but it introduced problems of its own. When a Connecticut forty-niner was nearly crushed while undercutting a gravel bank, the near miss inspired him to wonder about using the power of water, illustrated in so many ways around the placers, against the hill to break the rock from its bed. His first experiments in 1853 were such a success that the new method (actually the rediscovery of a very old European technique) quickly spread through northern California. At the highest practical point above a placer bed, a creek was diverted into a great metal funnel and fed into a canvas hose fitted at the other end with a large nozzle on a pivot. Compressed through the nozzle's small opening, the water shot out with astounding power. As an operator swiveled the nozzle to blast at a hillside, the gravel flushed into a sluice that filtered the largest debris, then into others that extracted the gold through the same principle of the long tom.

Hillsides would "melt like ice under the midsummer sun," San Francisco's *Daily Alta* wrote of the new technique. Hydraulickers could process as much gravel in an hour as old-style placer miners worked in a week, and with much less human effort. This made poor claims suddenly profitable—and expanded vastly the mining frontier's corrosive impact on the environment. For miners, however, the consequences were ironic, even paradoxical. Harnessing waterpower so effectively, and increasing hugely the amount of mining done, might seem to offer everyone more opportunity. The cost of building a system, however, was far beyond the reach of ordinary gold seekers. Once a hydraulic was in place, the men who bankrolled it needed only a handful of workers to match the labor of a hundred others swinging picks and bending to shovels. This technological advance, that is, tended to throw many out of work while concentrating the profits and control of a goldfield into far fewer hands.

Hydraulic mining was a kind of transition zone in the world of work. Strictly in terms of what was done—washing eroded gold from its surrounding effluvia—it was no different from a lone miner working a rocker. Yet almost every particular showed how the mining frontier was merging with the America of factories and mass production. The scale was industrial. A company on California's Yuba River used three giant nozzles to blast away at gravel banks up to a hundred feet tall. One and a quarter million gallons of water were used each ten-hour workday.[28] Water was carried through large pipes, sometimes for miles. It issued with a thunderous roar, a vivid expression of industrial might and "a weapon of appalling force." Should the stream strike a man, wrote a journalist, "it would not stun him, or simply kill him with the shock and suffocation, but it would rend him limb from limb, as an explosion would." Operations looked even more factory-like as pits deepened and owners turned to drills, blasting powder and other heavier technology to loosen rock for the hoses.

The economic position of workers also changed, and with it the West's meaning for them. As chances to open small-scale operations narrowed rapidly, wage labor came to be used almost exclusively in even modest-sized hydraulics, with "no more spirit in the work . . . [than] in a granite-quarry," one writer thought: "The same weary lifting of the feet, the same languid blows, the same non-communication. . . ."[29] Gouging of labor could be as extreme, and the income gap as wide, as in any eastern sweatshop. The Yuba River company noted above reportedly took out an average of twenty thousand dollars in gold a month. Its entire labor force consisted of six men, each paid four dollars a day.[30]

Here, on the cusp between the frontier's individual entrepreneurship and the rise of industrial mining, is a good point to recall that much of the work in the camps had no direct connection with mining at all. For every hour devoted to prospecting and extracting gold and silver, more were spent feeding, clothing, housing, amusing, and supporting the miners.

A lot of this vital labor was done by women and children. Women could put their minority status to good use. Mining frontiersmen had grown up with work divided between men and women, and when they waved good-bye to their families and left for the gold and silver fields, they suddenly faced a wide range of hopelessly alien jobs. Many were baffled by the simplest chores, especially cooking. "Burnt the beans—burnt the apples—burnt our hands. Had a general burning time," one wrote on the trail to Colorado, and another echoed his frustration: "Burned my hand on the spider [a skillet]—got mad at the potatoes and wouldn't eat them."[31] Men like these continued to flounder in the diggings. Tattered and thin, they would pay plenty to any woman willing to reclaim such toil. Cooking biscuits soon after she arrived, the forty-niner Luzena Wilson was offered five, then ten dollars for the batch by a man longing for any "bread baked by a woman," suggesting not only a growling stomach but a sentimental tug toward home. Women sold pies for one to five dollars each, cooked in restaurants for $30 a day, and kept house for $150 a month, incomes that put them ahead of all but skilled male laborers and the more successful miners. Early Californians were so determined to avoid washing clothes that they sent dirty laundry on regular shuttles to Hawaii. A local laundress was paid the highest rates for bending and scrubbing over steaming tubs. Rumor had it that some seamstresses charged a dollar per button sewn on a shirt. The obvious extension of these opportunities was the boarding or lodging house. For a hefty price women offered a place at the table, an empty bed (or perhaps one shared with one or two lodgers), cleaning, minimal nursing, and often some domestic exchange and ambience—in short, a surrogate home.

Single women supported themselves nicely with such pay, and wives contributed much, and often most, of their family's income. Mining was, to say the least, an erratic business, and the steady demand for home cooked meals and laundered clothes carried many families through dry spells and layoffs. Dame Shirley told of a neighbor's glowing praise of a "magnificent woman" who at sixty-eight pounds "earnt her *old man* . . . nine hundred dollars in nine weeks, clear of expenses, by washing!" With someone like that, he thought, "a man might marry, and make some money by the operation."[32]

Children, too, found plenty of chances to make money. They delivered messages and goods, including their mothers' pies and bread, ran errands, hawked newspapers, and gathered and sold berries and edible greens from the countryside. Young boys staged boxing matches on the streets, one more chance for men to gamble. As with women, customers paid extra for the sentimental satisfaction of some brief contact with this rare commodity, a child, reminding them of others back home. Drawing on the mining frontier's imbalance of age and sex, its hunger for certain services, and its peculiar emotional supply and demand, women and children took on crucial economic roles. They often profited handsomely in the process.

The relentless demand also took its toll. Some wives faced a pace and weight of work in their kitchens at least as exhausting as the men's in the diggings. In her California boarding house, one woman wrote,

> somtimes I am washing and Ironing sometimes I am making mince pie and Apple pie and squash pies. Sometimes frying mince turnover and Donuts. I make Buiscuit and now and then Indian jonny cake and then again I am making minute puding filled with rasons and Indian Bake puddings and then again a nice Plum Puding and then again I am Stuffing a Ham of Pork . . . Somtimes I am . . . making guel for the sick now and then cooking oisters sometimes making coffee for the French people strong enough for a man to walk on that has Faith as Peter had. Three times a day I set my Table which is about thirty feet in length and do all the little fixings about it such as filling pepper boxes and vinegar cruits and mustard pots and butter cups. Somtimes I am feeding my chickens and then again I am scareing the Hogs out of my kitchen and Driving the mules out of my Dining room . . . sometimes I take my fan and try to fan myself but I work so hard that my Arms pain me so severely that I kneed someone to fan me so I do not find much comfort anywhere.[33]

Ellen Hunt, recently arrived in Colorado, told her diary of "Weary days of labor and pain . . . have made 175 loaves of bread and 450 pies. Taken all the care of the children and done all the house work but the washing." And soon afterwards: "All through August nearly worked to death." She would, in fact, die at forty-four, after becoming the state's first lady.[34]

In sexual services women found another voracious demand to play the wife. Prostitution appeared on every mining frontier almost as early as the first gold pans. Women came to their commercial beds by various routes. Despite widespread charges of a "white slave traffic," few if any seem to have been forcibly imported, although whoring probably was often a desperate option. Chinese women signed indenture contracts promising their bodies, usually for about four years, in exchange for passage and board in America.[35] The non-Chinese were a mixed lot, usually with a small majority native-born and others from Ireland, Germany, Latin America, France and a smattering of other nations. Most were between fifteen and thirty. A surprising number were mothers caring for children. In most cases a woman probably entered the trade when economic difficulty coincided with a chance to sell her favors quickly and at a good price. Once in the business, it was not always easy to back out.[36]

To a great extent the sex trade was shrouded—this was, after all, the Victorian era—but one historian estimates that San Francisco's four hundred Chinese prostitutes averaged seven couplings a day, six days a week. This would total nearly seventeen thousand transactions weekly.[37] Assuming prostitutes in the mining camps worked at a similar pace, harlotry was quite an enterprise. If each of the Comstock's 161 prostitutes in 1870 managed forty-two liaisons a week, they would have serviced men 6,762 times. The population of males fifteen years and older was 6,576.[38] Women who could control and keep part of that income could make a comfortable living. In a close study of Helena, Montana, Paula Petrik found that most prostitutes worked independently out of their own small houses from the town's first boom in 1865 until the 1880s, when a handful of madams consolidated operations in several bordellos. Six out of ten white prostitutes owned real or personal property or both in 1870—an economically healthy profile in such a place. During the 1880s, however, the women's independence and income began to slip, and by the turn of the century male pimps controlled the property and management of the city's red light district.

Romantic notions to the contrary, the flesh trade was strictly business—and a rough one. Any advantage over the exhausting labor of laundering or running a boarding house was offset by frequent violence, disease, and the debilitation of drink and drugs. From the start life was degraded and impoverished for many girls of the line, and when control and profits shifted to male managers, as in Helena, virtually all prostitutes sank into the grim, exploited condition common in every American city. Frequent notices of suicides underscored the brutal long-term consequences for most who chose the crib or whorehouse as their working world.

One of the frontier's defining conditions—too few people trying to do too much work—made for other opportunities for women. They were fully capable of the simpler forms of placering. A woman advertised for a husband in 1849 by boasting she could "rock the cradle (gold-rocker, I thank you, Sir!)."[39] Housewives panned the dirt under boardwalks, others worked beside their husbands, and a few rose to oversee a collection of mining claims.[40] This early involvement grew into a considerable number of women prospectors and miners in the twentieth-century West.[41] Wives and single women also ran dry goods stores, liveries, saloons and other businesses normally reserved for men. "Truckee has a female barber," a woman wrote from California: "She is fat, fair, forty and a success. . . . Much praise is due the woman who dare do a legitimate business, notwithstanding the barbarous opinions of so-called civilized society."[42]

Ironically, the frontier may have expanded opportunities more for women who stayed behind. When tens of thousands of husbands launched off for the gold and silver fields, an equal number of wives suddenly found themselves faced with new challenges and the chance to try on new roles. Like the men out West who had to cook and darn socks for the first time, women back home had to shoulder tasks normally left to their spouses. They directed the work of farms and shops, dealt with bankers and recalcitrant hired hands, and made the tough decisions expected of a head of a household. Most took on this double burden reluctantly, but many discovered capabilities they had never suspected. The result was a legacy among these "women in waiting" of new confidence and expanded responsibilities. Some—those who were left widowed, or were abandoned by men who stayed in the camps, or lost patience and ended their marriages—continued their more independent lives. Among reunited couples the balance between the spouses often was closer to even, and in some cases it tilted far in the other direction. When a Wisconsin gold seeker returned broken and deranged, his wife continued in charge of the family. He spent the rest of his years panning for gold beside a creek inside an insane asylum.[43]

Out in the mining towns, despite some unconventional jobs open to them, most women made money by fulfilling men's domestic needs and by keeping them amused—one more example of the powerful urge to carry westward an eastern order, in this case the usual arrangement of labor by gender. As in prostitution, furthermore, the control of laundries, bakeries, and restaurants ended up mostly in men's hands. Like Lydia Burns, earning forty to fifty dollars a month by working in a California public house, in poor health and lonely, most working-class women then were little different from wage miners on the maturing frontier. They worked long and difficult hours for barely enough to meet expenses.[44]

Mining almost instantly spun off a vast range of other work. Once again the mining frontier's developmental pattern—not a continuous advancing line only slightly ahead of the society sending it forth but rather, as Rodman Paul explains, a series of flashes across the mountain West—is essential to understanding its impact. The instant clusters of population had all the usual needs, but they were typically far from their mother cultures and widely separated from each other. This combination of isolation and rapid growth, in Duane Smith's term, made gold and silver rushes "magnets in the mountains." Men on the sniff for profit quickly found ways to meet the sudden demand. Within months enterprises and activities appeared that otherwise would have been decades in coming.

California, the nation's most distant mining frontier, had the advantage of some farming and considerable ranching already underway. Thousands of head of cattle were driven from the southern ranchos up the central valley, many to be devoured and others to begin seed herds close to the mines. Agrarian entrepreneurs like John Horner were planting potatoes, onions, and cabbages by 1850. He grossed $150,000 that year, bought a steamboat for shipping produce and in 1851 nearly doubled his income. Other farmers operated by the score, then by the hundreds. These businessmen, the *Sacramento Transcript* noted, "have been more universally fortunate than those who have engaged in mining."[45] A Colorado booster agreed that "the plow and the scythe will yield a better return . . . than the pan and the pick," a prediction supported by the farms spreading along the South Platte, Arkansas and Cache la Poudre Rivers by the 1860s.[46] Ranches soon expanded out of those valleys onto Colorado's eastern plains; the number of Colorado cattle increased by 1000 percent in the decade after 1870.[47] In Montana a nascent ranching industry expanded hugely as strike followed strike in the northern Rockies.

These endeavors encouraged others—marketing operations, slaughterhouses, freighting, storage facilities, the first light manufacturing. Haying, essentially the middle ground of farming and ranching, provided fuel for the movement of goods and for the heavy work of mining done by animals. One of Colorado's first ranchers turned increasingly to what had started as a sidelight. Eventually he sold more than 4,000 tons of hay each season.[48] Especially in California cultivators found the conditions superb for growing fruit, which had a double appeal: it helped combat scurvy, an early plague of vitamin-starved immigrants, and the sweetness and tartness of a peach or apple offered a powerful sensual reminder of distant homes.

From the hammering together of the first shanties, mining towns demanded vast amounts of timber. Houses and stores were only the start. Mining itself was the hungriest consumer. The flumes and long toms of placering required hillsides of lumber, and far more was needed to timber and shore up tunnels. A single mine in the Comstock, the Ophir, held more wood than in all structures above ground. An estimated 600 million board feet were used in Comstock mines, enough, according to an early historian, to build thirty thousand two-story, six-room houses. Then there was the need for firewood in mills, mines, and homes. Nearly six hundred cords were burned daily in the Virginia City area, or more than two hundred thousand annually and more than two million cords between 1861 and 1878. The Comstock mines—they "might truthfully be said to be the tomb of the forests of the Sierras," Dan DeQuille wrote—were unusual, but no mining region could operate unless fed by enormous numbers of harvested trees.[49]

The work force fanned out into these developing areas of labor. The change was most pronounced in market and governmental centers. In Silver City, the hub of Idaho's isolated southwestern corner, seven out of ten adults earned their pay outside mining-related jobs in 1880. Professionals, merchants, and clerks made up 40 percent of workers.[50] When the regions slightly farther away from the mines are brought to the picture, the non-mining laborers usually outnumbered those in the diggings and the shafts within a few years on each frontier. In 1870 miners made up 30 percent of the Nevada work force, 15 percent of California's, and in the latter state miners were outnumbered by persons in professional and personal services two-to-one. There were variations among the frontiers. Just as diversification was greatest in market towns, so states like Colorado and California had a wider occupational spread than territories like Montana and Idaho that drew heavily on them for outside services.

Nonetheless the overall pattern held. Domestic servants, lawyers, and barbers jostled on the streets of maturing towns with brick makers, carpenters, wagon makers, and liverymen. All gathered in saloons and bellied up to buy from one of the most numerous occupational categories, bartenders. They visited prostitutes, who patronized milliners and bought pies from housewives and opium, morphine and cocaine from narcotics dealers. Wood-choppers gathered what they could from the surrounding hills and ravines to feed the stoves in homes and stores, and when Comstock's stunted growth was gone scores of Chinese moved in to dig the roots and sell them at up to sixty dollars a cord in deep winter.[51] Over the connecting roads and trails a vigorous commerce ebbed and flowed. Colorado's census showed just over thirty-four thousand non-Indians in 1860; by 1865 plains freighting firms alone employed that many men.[52] Large numbers of unskilled laborers performed the grunt work attendant to the growing mercantile and service economy.

The economic connections settled over the country. The result was a working world that precluded all others. It largely set the terms of living. While this way of life had its unique twists and traits left by the frontier, by now it testified that eastern America had insinuated itself into the mining West. In how they labored, and with whom and for what, these westerners expressed the contours and ascendant values of the nation. And like that nation, their working world itself was changing.

IN MANY PARTS of the mining West placer mining was replaced by lode mining, or lode mining was practiced from the start. A placer mine gathered in gold that had been washed out of its original deposit; lode mining captured precious metals before they were eroded, while they were still hidden away as veins in the earth. In California and some other areas, most gold had long been dispersed into placer beds, so extensive lode mining never developed. But elsewhere, as in Colorado, a different geologic history had left most gold sealed in granitic formations. Silver, which does not have gold's trait of remaining relatively pure after it leaves its original home, was never available by placering. Eroded silver was lost. Paying deposits were found only in lodes.

The labor of lode mining was essentially different from placering. Prospectors had to find where a vein or concentration of ore had broken to the surface, or they had to push a shaft into the earth in search of one. Miners then had to pursue the deposit, extract the silver or gold with its surrounding rock, and separate it into its pure form through methods of varying elaboration. This process was progressively more expensive and required greater technical expertise. Everything after the discovery of a deposit—extending and maintaining the underground work, pulling and transporting the ore, processing and smelting—demanded both a huge investment and financial risk. No one could tell when even a healthy vein might suddenly stop or a paying mine run into insurmountable difficulties, leaving the owner with little to show for his massive up-front costs.

It all conspired toward one point: Miners of modest means were in no position to plunge fully into lode mining. Developing even a sure bonanza took thousands of times all the money they could scrape into a pile. Rich lode discoveries, it's true, were made by sourdoughs digging in a minor way. Probably the most famous case was that of Patrick McLaughlin and Peter O'Riley, who stumbled into a deposit of rich silver sulphurets when digging a shallow reservoir to collect water for their gold placer operation. Their find was the first of the Comstock silver strikes. Leadville's rush was set off by George Fryer finding a silver outcropping, Goldfield's by Henry Stimler and William Marsh following an Indian to a spot where rich rock was close to the surface. All these sold out almost immediately, however, and were smart to do so.

A developing lode mine had considerable construction up top, at the least a means of loading and carrying away the ore and, if the shaft were vertical, a large headframe and engine to lower and raise men and rock from deep in the earth. In the mine itself was the elaborate underground town of shafts, adits, drifts, tracks, carts, and other machinery, the vast undertaking described elsewhere by Rodman Paul. Where the water table was breached, huge pumps or great drainage systems were needed. All but the shallowest mines required aid in ventilation, from man-powered bellows to giant blowers as well as shafts devoted to the movement of air. These were only the basics for getting to the ore and getting it out. Operations almost as elaborate were needed to crush and reduce the ore and smelt the desired metal. Supportive activities—for storage, maintenance, fueling, and freighting—further expanded an already sprawling enterprise.

Operations of that size had to be funded through combinations of wealthy individuals or, most often, by forming corporations and offering stock. Unless an investor chose to come close, ownership was far removed from mining itself—and certainly from its workers. Those men now labored under systems essentially no different from other industries in the East. Their income did not depend on their luck and on how well they tricked wealth out of the earth; they were paid wages. They worked on shifts and in teams according to function. They were organized into layers of management and of skills.

A workday in a lode did have one thing in common with the placering era. It was nasty, brutish, and long. Some of the labor was an elaboration from the earliest diggings. Muckers shoveled and hauled rock and dirt shaken loose by drilling and blasting, and although this was more mechanized, with debris wheeled away in carts and lifted to the surface in a skip, it remained, like digging in the placer beds, the movement of thousands of tons of the earth by backbreaking human effort. Much of the underground work, however, demanded specialized skills and experience. The task of tunneling began with drilling holes for blasting. Until the mid-1870s this was done by single- and double-jacking. In the former a man swung a four-pound sledge to strike a round or octagonal chisel-tipped rod, called a steel, which he held against the appointed spot and rotated slightly after each blow. In double-jacking one man held and rotated the steel while another did the hammering with a long-handled eight-pound sledge. Sometimes two men swung at the steel with alternating blows. Often an entire shift was spent drilling several carefully spaced holes in the wall meant to go. A blaster then moved in and filled each hole with its charge of black powder. Fuses were cut so the charges would blow in the right order (and allow the blaster to exit in time), then each was lit with a modified fuse, or spitter. After the blast, miners moved in, pulled out the rubble and placed it where the next shift could muck it away and begin the process again. Around 1875 pneumatic drills dramatically reduced drilling time—as well as throwing double-jacking teams out of work and introducing new hazards to workers.

Miners also installed timber supports to shore up the newly dug tunnels. These were less necessary in the granitic depths of the Rocky Mountains, but in crumbly formations, notably that of the Comstock, installing supports was a major part of mining labor. Typically a tunnel was lined with sets, each made from three timbers eight feet long and eight inches square and formed into an arch. Sets were placed about every five feet, with braces between each for further stability. Cutting and fitting the timbers, deciding their placement, and keeping them vertical and steady were practiced jobs that (literally) supported the work and lives of every-one who went into the hole. Many others labored in subsidiary roles. Young boys handled the mules used to pull the carts, picked up tools, and kept track of who was at work by hanging up and removing brass rings on a tally board. Men worked at the various machinery pumping fresh air into the depths for breathing and compressed air for the drills. Others manned the pumps that kept the shafts from flooding.

Some work demanded special skills and acuity. In places where the ore was of marginal quality or where rock was taken from the edges of a lode, a quick assay was to decide what would be sent to the waste dump and what to the ore bin. Hoisting rock from the mine and raising and low-ering people was done through three jobs. A cage tender, or cager, rode up and down on the lift, stopping on the way down to roll off empty carts and to take full ones onboard. The top lander received the loaded carts and replaced them with empty ones or with supplies. The central figure, per-forming one of the most sensitive jobs of the mine, was the hoist operator. His was the responsibility to set the lift into motion, move it at the proper speed (usually as fast as possible to save time), and stop it at the right place—all from his post up top. Those below communicated with him through a bell, and he with them by jiggling the cage with his controls or moving it a foot or two. Bell signals were adapted from traditional codes brought from Cornwall. If a cage was in motion, for instance, a single ring meant to stop immediately; if it were at rest, a ring meant to raise a load of rock. Three bells, followed by a pause and one more ring told the operator he was bring-ing men up. The potential dangers were obvious. The operator had to be finely attuned to the location of the cages. Lifting too soon, failing to slow as the cage neared the top, jerking the lift while men were boarding, or any other miscalculation could have the most ghastly results. Concentration was critical; a prohibition against talking with or distracting the operator was firmly enforced.

A mine with muckers, drillers, blasters, shift bosses, timbermen, mule boys, cagers, and hoist operators was a sophisticated industrial operation on a par with many advanced eastern factories. Two things set it apart, how-ever. Its purpose was the extraction of natural resources rather than the shaping of raw materials into finished products. And its elaborate labors took place underground, in some cases three thousand feet deep in the earth.

That second difference had obvious implications for these working worlds. Below ground the discomforts and dangers common to all indus-trial workplaces were exaggerated and new ones were created. In any mine deeper than a hundred feet air quickly became stagnant and polluted. As rock dust, the exhalations of workers, and smoke from powder blasts filled the cramped tunnels, men first became woozy and even more fatigued than usual. At the least they were prone to dangerous errors; at worst they collapsed and sometimes died. The long-term effects were obvious to a Colorado editor who noted the "pallid countenance and haggard expression" of men who labored "where the pure air above never penetrates."[53] The most effective strategy was to create a draft and continuous flow of fresh air. If a mine's uppermost opening was high enough on a slope, horizontal tunnels, or adits, were dug from the lowest levels out to the flanks of the hill or mountain. By a natural draw fresh air was pulled in and foul air pushed up and out. Deep in the Comstock owners put aside their bitter competitions and used each other's shafts to maintain a flow of fresh air. Even so the oxygen in dead-end tunnels was so thin that matches sputtered and would not light, candles flickered and went out, and miners worked on the edge of consciousness. The best ventilation systems, furthermore, could turn against those relying on them. If a fire broke out underground, feeding on the millions of board feet of lumber, airshafts became gigantic flues and the mines deadly furnaces.

Terrific heat, in fact, was common under normal conditions in the deeper reaches. At modest depths the temperature was cool, as in a cave, but below a certain point it rose steadily. A systematic study in a Comstock operation found a reading of 50.5 degrees Fahrenheit at 100 feet and 81.5 degrees at 1,000. Over the next 500 feet the temperature rose to 101 degrees. At 2,100 feet it was 119.5 degrees. At those depths miners encountered pockets of water, some as hot as 170 degrees. In the Crown Point mine men used one such reservoir to cook eggs. When a water pocket was punctured unexpectedly while drilling, the scalding water burst out with a terrible force; even when controlled it left the tunnels excruciatingly hot and sodden. So high were air temperatures at the lower depths that metal tools had to be handled with water-soaked cloths. A visitor recalled a "sense of horrible confinement" in stifling heat at 1,300 feet. Workers at that level rested in "cooling rooms" where air was piped in from the surface. As she descended further "the heat seemed to come fairly out of the rock on all sides." Here workers held pieces of ice to their pulses and to their mouths when the air threatened to singe their lungs. At 2,100 feet "a stratum of heat was entered, such as might come from hell itself. The sensation was no longer that of general oppression, but of the danger of being absolutely burned. . . . When the level was entered, the breath was for an instant taken away."[54] Besides drinking gallons of water during a shift, workers cooled themselves as best they could with enormous amounts of ice supplied from above. At the hottest levels of the Comstock's Consolidated Virginia each miner consumed an average of ninety-five pounds daily.

Compounding the difficulties inherent below ground were the dangers of an increasingly mechanized industry. As Rodman Paul emphasizes, the West in effect was the great laboratory of global mining. Mines were sunk deeper than ever in history and were bedeviled with problems no one had ever imagined. New equipment and techniques were devised to meet the challenges. On the positive side the western mines revolutionized an ancient enterprise. But on the negative the men who did the work faced all the ill effects and unforeseen hazards that inevitably come with innovation.

The perils began literally when a miner went to work. Descent into shallower mines might be by ladders or in a large iron bucket lowered by a simple windlass turned by two men. In larger and deeper operations, however, men and equipment were raised and lowered by a lift powered by animals, steam or electricity. With improvements in gearing the speed of the lifts increased steadily until men were sent up and down at a thousand feet per minute, an obvious benefit as the mines were pushed deeper and deeper. The device to carry the men was called a cage—a misnomer, for it was only a platform with a top, or bonnet, but no sides. Only a few inches separated passengers from the walls of the shaft. A typical platform was about four feet square, and up to nine men rode it at a time. Each person, that is, was crammed into less than two square feet of standing room on an open lift while the shaft walls rocketed by at fifteen feet or more per second. If the cage lurched, or if an exhausted man grew dizzy and stumbled, or if a pick or other tool in a miner's grip caught on the shaft wall, or if an incautious hoist operator misheard a signal and engaged the power before the passengers were ready, men would be swept off the speeding platform against the walls, smeared like butter along the shaft. A mine carpenter wrote of recovering one victim: "We took the cage and came on slowly up and gathered up remains or what parts we could find of them—pieces of skull and brains and old clothes." The cables used in the hoists, first developed by John A. Roebling, designer of the Brooklyn Bridge, were remarkably strong, but under enough pressure or if poorly maintained they broke, sending men plunging hundreds of feet to their deaths.

For the work below, one of the great technological breakthroughs was the mechanical drill, first used in the 1870s. With the power of steam or compressed air it could sink holes for blasting far more rapidly than single- or double-jacking while using far less manpower. Tunnels were driven through a mountain five times faster than before. But while it certainly reduced the workload, the pneumatic drill was in other ways the miner's enemy. Besides the obvious economic threat of displacing the skilled labor of hand-drilling, it posed a terrible danger that was only gradually understood. A mechanical drill pulverized the rock with hundreds of blows per minute. This powerful hammering produced a dust that was much finer than that from hand drills or from blasting—so fine that it passed through the close mesh of filtering hairs in the human nose. Some of this dust could be absorbed through the lungs and eliminated, but the silicate matter, a common component, could not. Uncountable numbers of these infinitesimal sharp-edged particles accumulated in a worker's lungs. At the microscopic level each breath taken by this man now stirred up within his chest a great roiling cloud of stones. The result was silicosis, more commonly called miner's consumption, or "miner's con." The symptoms became all too common in all lode mining regions: persistent hacking cough, shortness of breath, and an increasing tendency toward pulmonary infections. The shredding of the lungs invited other illnesses, and full debilitation and death often came from pneumonia, bronchitis, or tuberculosis. Once the connection was understood, a tiny stream of water during drilling reduced the release of dust. Although not eliminated, the danger was lessened, but the damage already done was enormous. A study of a Colorado district showed that respiratory problems accounted for 56 percent of all deaths among miners.

Into the holes in the rock, now drilled more efficiently, was placed the revolutionary blasting power of dynamite. Cheaper and more powerful than black powder, dynamite was being used in western mines within a few years of its invention by Alfred Nobel. Like most innovations, it was first hailed as a godsend to workers. If kept cool it was far more stable than black powder. It did not require close and precise packing in the hole. And with full combustion it did not produce dangerous gases. New dangers soon presented themselves, however. When not stored properly dynamite could be exceptionally volatile—and its accidental detonation of course far more lethal. Charges sometimes held their fire, up to a few hours, then exploded as workers were mucking the rock. If it failed to detonate, a stick could still explode if struck by a pick or drill or even by a piece of dropped debris. And an explosion was gas-free only if dynamite's combustion was total. If incomplete, it left poisonous nitrous gases and carbon monoxide. These were especially insidious because they were much more difficult to detect than gases produced by black powder. A seemingly safe tunnel could be a deathtrap. In Montana three men were found drowned, facedown in puddled water. They had passed out almost immediately upon entering a chamber after a blast.

Over and over the pattern was repeated. An innovation breached some thorny technological barrier. The science and craft of mining took a stride forward. The implementers pointed out (with some truth and some exaggeration) that safety was enhanced as well. Then each new device and method showed its grimmer side. Owners sometimes were guilty of glossing over dangers and refusing to do anything about them. In other cases they and their workers were equally ignorant until experience revealed the threat. Electricity illuminated the miner's working world and reduced the hazards and discomforts of steam power, but its rapid introduction, and the mysteries of its operation, left managers and workers dangerously unaware of what might happen. Before, standing in water and leaning shirtless against a wet wall posed no threat. Now it could bring instant death.

The nature of laboring far into the earth created a radically different working world for miners. Although it kept some of its frontier heritage, its setting was increasingly similar to what was found elsewhere in industrial America. The same was true of relations of worker to worker.

MINERS' COMMUNITIES IN some ways remained much like the camps of the first rushes. Men formed bonds out of their common sweat and difficulties. As in the messes and instant neighborhoods of the placer camps, men established their public characters out of working roles and the quirks and special talents of rough labor. This man was known for what he could do with a fuse, that one for handling a windlass. Drilling contests now were a highlight of holiday celebrations, with the winners heroes equal to the victors in the hose company races. Fraternal lodges remained enormously popular. Nightlife was just as rowdy and, if anything, more persistent. Placer miners who worked all day eventually ran out of steam in a night of carousing, but the more vigorous lode mining centers ran shifts twenty-four hours a day, so as the last of one group was reeling off to bed, the first of another was crowding to the bar. In the categories of both unashamed vice and social coalescence, mining town saloons, gambling dens and whorehouses retained their lofty ranking among American institutions.

In other ways communities and social relations differed markedly from the early days. Men were far more likely to live with their own families; they were pulled equally by the bonds of the home and the mineshaft loyalties and fraternities of vice. Traditionally respectable institutions—churches, women's clubs, literary societies—flourished with a confidence never there in the boom time. The general air of a town was one of permanence and the prevailing assumption was that people were there, if not for good, at least for a longish haul.

The most fundamental change was in how workers saw themselves and each other. The first working communities had grown from a fierce individual competition. Men cooperated when they needed to, but always they thought of themselves as independent operators who were ultimately aligned against everyone else and Lady Luck. That made no sense in lode mining. Miners underground felt the usual human divisions, but when a miner looked for opposition, it was in the man who set his wages, not the one working at his shoulder or those above him in the mills. And those fellow workers were more than helping hands. Inside the intricate machine of an underground mine sloppiness or inattention could mean disaster for everyone. Dependability and mutual reliance became absolute values. In contrast to placer miners, who were called ferociously competitive and impulsive, Charles Howard Shinn wrote that an underground miner's life made him "sane, thoughtful, responsible. . . . He knows himself responsible for the lives of his fellow work-men; his own life hangs upon the honesty of another's work, and that other's life hangs upon the honesty of his own work."[55]

The normal tendency next was toward a wider unity in the face of common threats and difficulties. Workers joined together to support injured miners and to help the families of those killed on the job. The first such programs often grew out of those institutions of brotherhood that had taken root in the early camps, the fraternal lodges. The Masons or Odd Fellows would create a fund from regular dues to tide over a family of an injured miner or to pay for the funeral of one lost in the mine. Their collective beneficence bubbled occasionally up to higher levels, as when voters of Owyhee County, Idaho, petitioned the state (unsuccessfully) to found a home for "old and broken-down mining prospectors."[56]

This impulse—men cooperating to fix a problem they shared because they all worked for somebody else—naturally evolved toward a miner's union. The first two appeared in 1863 where they might have been predicted, Central City, Colorado and Virginia City, Nevada, two of the first major gold and silver lode mining districts. Both were dedicated to the most obvious concern of wageworkers—wages. In April the Colorado workers organized to try to push sagging wages up to three dollars a day for miners and four dollars for blasters. The next month, amid rumors of a pay cut, a Miners' Protective Association appeared on the Comstock, dedicated to keeping wages at four dollars a day.

Neither lasted long, but in 1867 on the Comstock another appeared that was longer-lived and greatly influential. Conditions were encouraging. Workers had an excellent bargaining position because the depth and complexities of mining placed a premium on their skills. Local officials and businessmen mostly sympathized with the miners. There was some common ground of workers and owners because miners took a genuine pride in the lode's wealth and accomplishments, including the introduction of new technologies, despite the new dangers that came with them. Union organizers were moderate in their goals and owners generally willing to work with them. On the key issue of wages, miners reasonably defended the four-dollar day as fair, given the high cost of living and the companies' high profits, while owners recognized that good pay attracted the best labor and kept the work force stable.

By the late 1870s this union and others in the Sierra counted three thousand members. By then others had appeared across the lode mining West, most of them organized by Comstock veterans and many of them adopting almost to the word the constitutions and by-laws from Nevada. They, too, took wages as their most pressing issue. Their histories, however, were often more contentious and not always so successful.

In Nevada's White Pine district, in Silver Reef and Eureka in Utah, in Central City, Colorado and in Tombstone, Arizona, for instance, miners organized and struck during the 1870s and 1880s to keep wages up. All failed. Strikes were more successful in two other Colorado towns, Silverton and Telluride, and in the Dakota Black Hills. The Colorado state government reported that nine out of ten miners (coal as well as gold and silver) went on strike at some time between 1881 and 1888. The union scorecard showed eleven defeats and thirty-five victories.[57] Several factors explain the mixed results. Union leaders were simply shrewder in some places. Violence by workers almost invariably turned the public against them and led to failure. Some owners used strikebreakers to great effect or played on ethnic divisions. The Central City strike collapsed when Irish miners were used against the Cornish-dominated strikers. Strikers who avoided physical confrontations and cultivated local opinion, on the other hand, were much more likely to be rewarded.

Behind these variants was something more basic. The unions' checkered record shows the mountain West in transition from a frontier social order and mindset into a full integration with an emerging industrial nation. Behind the particulars of failure usually was the persistent frontier notion that every man was there for himself, that cooperation was a temporary expedient on the way to private gain, and that when things went sour, one could always move on to another town and new opportunities. Success, by contrast, typically came when miners and others in the town adopted the Comstock perspective. Workers presumed they were there for the long haul. They identified with the extraordinary industrial enterprise of the mines and found their pride and sense of place in the skills, dangers, and mutual reliance of workingmen whose interests were, and would remain, in common.

Community, continually reinvented from the days of those first scramblings, once again was expressing its people's notions of themselves and where they lived. When unions took root and endured, it was because they were supported by a net of assumptions wholly different from those of gold and silver rushes: permanence, mutual responsibility, commitment to a particular place, identification with work and with a rank in society that weren't going to change. Unions failed when there were holes in that net.

Developments in the West and in the nation late in the century encouraged that new perspective, and so cultivated support for unions. Most obvious was the growing realization that the richest deposits had been found. There were some surprises. In the 1890s gold was found at Cripple Creek, just west of Colorado Springs, and in the southwestern part of the state at Creede. In 1901 there was a strike at Thunder Mountain in Idaho and soon afterwards at Tonopah, Nevada. Clearly, however, the bloom was off the rose. A miner understood that odds were dwindling that some new strike would give him a true shot at quick money and a chance to vault among the financially comfortable. Now when he moved around the West it was only to find another job doing the usual work for the usual wages.

At the same time many mining centers were consolidated and controlled more by distant concentrations of wealth. This tended to heighten a worker's sense of natural opposition to owners, who were now far away and faceless, while those owners had little sense of the human implications of their decisions. The gap between labor and capital widened and deepened. Making matters much worse was a glut of silver on the world market because of the spectacular finds of the 1880s and 1890s. As the market price sagged sickeningly owners cut wages and closed less productive mines. This in turn sent many miners looking for work in gold camps, which weakened labor's bargaining position in those places. The cumulative effect was toward that feel of common condition, including common antagonists, that lay beneath the union impulse.

This process culminated in organizations that were more radical in perspective and region-wide in scope. The year after a strike in the Coeur d'Alene region of Idaho in 1892 was broken with unusual brutality and by government intervention, representatives of several unions formed the Western Federation of Miners. The W.F.M., based on the idea that the interests of labor and capital were starkly and unbridgeably opposed, was an umbrella organization uniting miners' locals across the region. W.F.M. leaders later played prominent roles in forming the Industrial Workers of the World (IWW), which reached even more broadly to embrace all labor, regardless of industry or level of skill.

Strikes associated with the W.F.M. were most notable for their militance, the intensity of rhetoric and feelings, and the violence that sometimes came with both. In an early effort, against the vast Sullivan and Bunker Hill silver mines in the embattled Coeur d'Alene country, a steadily escalating confrontation led to the destruction of the company's processing facility, followed by intervention by federal troops. Especially ugly was a strike among gold miners and mill workers in Cripple Creek, Colorado and nearby Colorado City in 1903–4. After a union operative dynamited a railroad station, killing thirteen strikebreakers, the companies cracked down brutally, rounding up strikers and confining them to "bullpens" and transporting some out of the state. This strike, like Idaho's, was broken. Within a few years the W.F.M. softened its militant position and its most charismatic figure, William D. "Big Bill" Haywood, gravitated to the IWW.

The W.F.M.'s confrontational style and its strikes' violence make it easy to miss more stable realities beneath the turbulence. A typical union local was still concerned mostly with conditions in its own mines, ordinary benefits for its members, daily relations with bosses and mayors and sheriffs, the social life in meeting halls, saloons, dances and picnics, and above all the issue that had always topped the list—wages. A local's attention, that is, remained local. Beyond that, a member likely felt some kinship with all the others who mined in the peculiar conditions of the West, where the shafts were deeper, the technology slicker, the dangers sharper, the results more marvelous, and the line starker between the many men who sweated and the few who pocketed the profits. Wider still, that member probably recognized a unity, however vague, among industrial workers generally.

Such a man, in other words, pictured himself at the center of concentric circles. Inside the closest and tightest were his greatest worries—paychecks and shift bosses and how his family would eat if he broke his back. In circles farther out his concerns were less insistent and his identification dimmer. He was a western miner and a worker of the world, true enough, and the lessons of being those things had a claim on him, but their hold was looser.

A more fundamental point is even easier to miss. A man centered in those circles presumed his present and future were mostly set, like it or not. He was firmly placed. His communities were not so much ones he was making as ones he fit into—his town, his union local, his neighborhood, his family's acquaintances, his region, his craft, his class.

For anyone looking for a sign that the frontier had passed, this will do. The frontier was, if nothing else, unsettled possibility. Men and women were drawn to mining camps because their future there was less predictable, which they took to mean more likely to be better. Then came a gradual emergence of order—architectural, political, cultural, ethnic, economic, and moral—and with that the possibilities narrowed. Before, in a mining rush, the work that might be done, the station that work might achieve, and the reward that work might put into the pocket all were deliciously unclear. Now, by the time a miner's working world had room for unions, that earlier bleariness had focused sharply. The new society had found its shape.

*H*ISTORIANS HAVE FUSSED a lot about frontiers—what they did to and for North Americans, the values they embodied, their legacies, and what exactly they were. Once we wave away the dust of disagreement, however, two things seem clear enough. On a frontier previously separate cultures jarred against each other. And when they did, every imaginable kind of change suddenly shot forward. Strangers with wildly different histories were tossed together with a rare suddenness, face-to-face and thought-to-thought. The resulting jolt eventually affected just about everyone and everything involved.

Mining frontiers were arguably the most convulsive of all. A mining boom, as Rodman Paul emphasizes, came as a burst of development far out in some great swatch of the West where, up to that point, the forces making over the nation had barely been felt. Quickly the effects were spiraling away in all directions. Imagined simply as a geometry of change, the scope of impact was far greater than what happened along any advancing line of, say, a farming frontier.

A mining rush brought people from throughout the nation and the world converging with dozens of Native American cultures. All met in cross-fertilization and conflict. They exchanged goods and customs. Their views of reality bumped into one another: the mechanics of the world, rules of conduct, where spirits lived, the meaning of magpies. Invading economies put resources to new uses through technologies imported from a score of nations. The environment shed its skin and took on new shapes with a speed resembling modern time-lapse photography. No other frontiers, except at aberrant moments like the Oklahoma land rushes, came close to mining booms as mixers of cultures and forces of change.

For Indian peoples, these changes were unmatched catastrophes. In California and parts of the Southwest mining frontiers spawned campaigns against natives that were genuinely genocidal. Elsewhere virtually every Indian war began with a mining boom and its consequences. As the fabric of their communities was ripped apart and the basic means of living cut from under them, Indian peoples had no choice but to abandon a preferred way of life for another that placed them at the bottom of every category of power and respect.

The societies that displaced the Indians were unique in what they told about the evolving nation. The most famous statement on the frontier's role in American change, of course, is Frederick Jackson Turner's. A distinctive American people emerged, he wrote, when those moving West had to abandon the traditions, skills, institutions, and values that had evolved in their mother cultures but no longer worked in the vastly different conditions of the frontier. Pioneers innovated. They scrapped much of what their past had given them and devised new answers. The resulting changes were radical in the word's first sense—reaching down to the roots of things. And the first vital step was cutting an older society back to those roots. The frontier, that is, blocked and reversed the history that was brought to it. It undid an accumulated past.

There was plenty in the gold and silver rushes that fit his vision of history reversed and redirected. Human relations were reduced to emotional and social fundamentals: greed, distrust, curiosity, and elemental cooperation. Law and government were trimmed to essentials. Culture seemed suddenly back to its knucklewalking stage. People tried on new roles that suddenly were possible because of the frontier's unsettling power. They found fresh, occasionally bizarre answers to an ancient striving for community. Turner was partly right. In some ways mining frontiers knocked history off its track and shoved it in a new direction.

But in many other ways mining frontiers did just the opposite. They seemed to seize the most transformative changes abroad in America and, rather than blunting or reversing them, carried them forward more rapidly than ever. Seen this way, a mining town was no throwback to an earlier time and no radical departure. It was the distilled essence of America's newly established course—urban, industrial, acquisitive and materialistic, on the move, "a living polyglot" of cultures that collided and converged. Nowhere did capital show more dramatically its growing power to transform American places and to consolidate its control over their resources. A lode mine was a display of the wonders of a new technological age—and a waking nightmare of its horrors. Its workers anticipated how labor throughout the nation would grapple with the new industrial world. Native Americans, marginalized and confined, stood as stark examples of the government's lengthening reach and its hardening insistence that peoples outside the mainstream be absorbed or pushed aside.

The contradictions multiply and deepen the more we look for them. A gold or silver camp was primitive and alien; it was strikingly familiar. It was unlike any city or town of its day; it was a fabulous overstatement of every trait and trend pulling an earlier America toward the one we know.

Maybe this is why mining frontiers hold so many of us in fascination. We look back and marvel at American history's true Land of Odd—men grubbing for meal money and then eating like anacondas, towns consuming themselves in the name of progress, families searching for structure in times of dizzying flux—and something nags at the edge of our awareness. Then we see it. This artifact of strangeness was as well a grand anticipation. Goggling at this distant and exotic past, we realize with a shock that we are looking at ourselves.

NOTES

Chapter 1: Gold and Silver Regions as Frontiers

[1] Cf. Frederick J. Turner, *The Frontier in American History* (New York, 1920), pp. 1–38.

[2] Wallace W. Atwood, *The Physiographic Provinces of North America* (Boston, 1940), p. 281, and maps facing p. 12.

[3] The classic study of mineral deposits is Waldemar Lindgren's *Mineral Deposits* (4th ed., New York, 1933), but see also Alan M. Bateman's *Economic Mineral Deposits* (2d ed., New York, 1950).

[4] See Waldemar Lindgren's "Geologic Introduction" to James M. Hill, *The Mining Districts of the Western United States* (U.S. Geological Survey, "Bulletin," no. 507, Washington, 1912). The location of gold and silver areas is shown in Hill's numerous maps and in those of the more recent study by C. Wayne Burnham, *Metallogenic Provinces of the Southwestern United States and Northern Mexico* (New Mexico State Bureau of Mines and Mineral Resources, "Bulletin," no. 65, Socorro, New Mexico, 1959).

[5] Daniel S. Tuttle, *Reminiscences of a Missionary Bishop* (New York, 1906), p. 77, quoting letter from Tuttle to his wife, Denver, June 14, 1867.

[6] Hiram D. Pierce, *A Forty-Niner Speaks*. Sarah W. Meyer, ed. (Oakland, 1930), p. 9.

[7] Robert E. Strahorn, *To the Rockies and Beyond, or a Summer on the Union Pacific Railway and Branches. Saunterings in the Popular Health, Pleasure, and Hunting Resorts . . .* (Omaha, 1878), pp. 27–28.

[8] Arthur Lakes, *Prospecting for Gold and Silver* (Scranton, 1895), p. 173.

Chapter 2: California, 1848–1858

[1] Walter Colton, *Three Years in California* (New York, 1850), p. 358.

[2] The best study of the circumstances surrounding the gold discovery is that sponsored by the California Historical Society, *California Gold Discovery: Centennial Papers on the Time, the Site and Artifacts* (California Historical Society, "Special Publication" no. 21, San Francisco, 1947). See also James P. Zollinger, *Sutter: the Man and his Empire* (New York, 1939). The spread of the gold fever in California and throughout the United States has been best examined by Ralph P. Bieber in "California Gold Mania," *Mississippi Valley Historical Review*, XXXV (June 1948), pp. 3–28.

[3] Hubert H. Bancroft, *Works* (39 vols., San Francisco, 1882–1890), XXIII, p. 54.

[4] *Ibid.*, XXIII, p. 57, quoting the San Francisco *California Star*, May 20, 1848.

[5] As quoted in Edward C. Kemble, "The History of California Newspapers," Sacramento *Daily Union*, December 25, 1858.

[6] Richard B. Mason, Monterey, to Thomas O. Larkin, June 1, 1848, in George P. Hammond, ed., *The Larkin Papers. Personal, Business, and Official Correspondence*

of Thomas Oliver Larkin, Merchant and United States Consul in California (7 vols., Berkley and Los Angeles, 1951–1960) VII, p. 289.

[7] New York *California Herald-Extra,* January 16, 1849.

[8] The figures are analyzed in Rodman W. Paul, *California Gold: The Beginning of Mining in the Far West* (Cambridge, Mass., 1947), pp. 23–25.

[9] Bancroft, *Works,* XXVI, 328; U.S. Census, *Seventh Census* (1850), p. 993, and *Eighth Census* (1860), "Population," p. 575.

[10] Bancroft, *Works,* XXX, 1; U.S. Census, *Seventh Census* (1850), p. 993, and *Eighth Census* (1860), "Population," p. 401.

[11] John S. Hittell, *Mining in the Pacific States of North America* (San Francisco, 1861), pp. 17–18

[12] Paul, *California Gold,* p. 43, discusses contemporary estimates.

[13] Pringle Shaw, *Ramblings in California; Containing a Description of the Country, Life at the Mines, State of Society, &c. Interspersed with Characteristic Anecdotes, and Sketches from Life, Being the Five Years' Experience of a Gold Digger* (Toronto, n.d.), p. 130. From internal evidence, Shaw was in California until late in 1856 or early in 1857. His book must have been written soon thereafter.

[14] *Ibid.,* p. 15

[15] The role of experienced miners and the evolution of mining techniques are discussed in detail by the present writer in *California Gold,* pp. 44–170.

[16] Shaw, *Ramblings in California,* p. 58

[17] Louise A. K. S. Clappe (Dame Shirley, pseud.), *The Shirley Letters from the California Mines, 1851–1852,* Carl I. Wheat, ed. (New York, 1949), p. 131, letter dated April 10, 1852.

[18] For a review of the different attempts to compile gold statistics, see Paul, *California Gold,* pp. 345–348. An excellent table entitled "California Gold Product," that prints in parallel columns ten different versions of the annual statistics, as compiled by varying authorities, was published by the California State Mining Bureau, apparently in 1904, and is ordinarily appended to the bound volume that contains "Bulletins" nos. 39, 40, and 41 of that Bureau.

[19] San Francisco *Weekly Alta California,* February 15, 1851.

[20] San Francisco *Daily Alta California,* July 17, 1851.

[21] *Ibid.,* September 15; September 23, 1851.

[22] Sacramento *Weekly Union,* May 15, 1852.

[23] For illustrated contemporary descriptions of the different types of mining, see *The Miners' Own Book: Containing Correct Illustrations and Descriptions of the Various Modes of California Mining. Reprinted from the Original Edition of 1858,* Rodman W. Paul, ed. (San Francisco, 1949).

[24] A superb annotated translation was prepared by former President and Mrs. Herbert C. Hoover: Georgius Agricola, *De Re Metallica, Translated from the First Latin Edition of 1556, with Biographical Introduction . . . ,* Herbert C. and Lou H. Hoover, trans. (London, 1912; reprinted New York, 1950).

[25] W. S. Newman, Hangtown [Placerville] January 10, 1854, to James R. De Long, in Carl I. Wheat, ed., " 'California's Bantam Cock,' The Journals of Charles E. De Long, 1854–1863," California Historical Society, *Quarterly,* XI (March 1932), p. 58. The Sacramento *Daily Union,* December 4, 1857, explained that this indirect extension of credit to miners was universal.

[26] John S. Hittell, "The Mining Excitements of California," *Overland Monthly,* 1st ser., II (May 1869), p. 415.

Chapter 3: Opening the Far West, 1858–1868.

[1] Frederick W. Howay, Walter N. Sage, and Henry F. Angus, *British Columbia and the United States: the North Pacific Slope from Fur Trade to Aviation* (Toronto, 1942), p. 141; Margaret A. Ormsby, *British Columbia: a History* (Toronto, 1958), p. 140.

[2] Hittell, *Mining in the Pacific States of North America*, pp. 33–34.

[3] LeRoy R. Hafen, ed., *Colorado and its People. A Narrative and Topical History of the Centennial State* (4 vols., New York, 1948), I, p. 177.

[4] Frank Fossett, *Colorado: its Gold and Silver Mines, Farms and Stock Ranges, and Health and Pleasure Resorts* (New York, 1879), p. 120.

[5] U.S. Census, *Eighth Census*, (1860), "Population," p. 547.

[6] Comparing Charles H. Shinn, *The Story of the Mine, as Illustrated by the Great Comstock Lode of Nevada* (Ripley Hitchcock, ed., *The Story of the West Series*, New York, 1896), p. 59; with Grant H. Smith, *The History of the Comstock Lode, 1850–1920* (University of Nevada, "Bulletin," XXXVII, no. 3, Geology and Mining Series no. 37, Reno, 1943), p. 23.

[7] U.S. Census, *Eighth Census* (1860), "Population," p. 564. The local census is cited in Myron Angel, *History of Nevada, with Illustrations and Biographical Sketches of its Prominent Men and Pioneers* (Oakland, 1881), p. 78.

[8] Bancroft, *Works*, XXXI, pp. 406; 413, fn. 16; 728, fn. 8; U.S. Census, *Ninth Census* (1870), vol. I, "Population," pp. 23, 46.

[9] George W. Van Vleck, *The Panic of 1857, an Analytical Study* (New York, 1943), p. 83. Cf. Frederick Merk, *Economic History of Wisconsin during the Civil War Decade* (State Historical Society of Wisconsin, *Publications*, I, Madison, 1916), *passim*.

[10] U.S. Census, *Eighth Census* (1860), "Population," p. 549.

[11] Fossett, *Colorado*, p. 120.

[12] Eliot Lord, *Comstock Mining and Miners* (U.S. Geological Survey, "Monographs," IV, Washington, 1883), pp. 74–75.

[13] William J. Trimble, *The Mining Advance into the Inland Empire. A Comparative Study of the Beginnings of the Mining Industry in Idaho and Montana, Eastern Washington and Oregon, and the Southern Interior of British Columbia; and . . .* (University of Wisconsin, "Bulletin" no. 638, History Series, vol. III, no. 2, Madison, 1914), p. 141.

[14] Hittell, *Mining in the Pacific States*, pp. 34–35.

[15] *Ibid.*, p. 35.

[16] Statistics for all including California are given in: U.S. Census, *Seventh Census* (1850), pp. 972, 982; *Eighth Census* (1860), "Population," pp. 33–34, 549, 564–565; *Ninth Census* (1870), vol. I, "Population," pp. 299, 328–342, 345–377.

[17] Prentice Mulford, *Prentice Mulford's Story. Life by Land and Sea* (The White Cross Library, New York, 1889), pp. 118–119.

[18] *Ibid.*, pp. 99–100.

[19] *Mining and Scientific Press* (San Francisco), January 19, 1863.

[20] San Francisco *Daily Alta California*, January 9, 1854.

[21] Titus F. Cronise, *The Natural Wealth of California, Comprising Early History; Geography, Topography, and Scenery; Climate; Agriculture and Commercial Products . . .* (San Francisco, 1868), p. 600.

[22] John S. Hittell, *A History of the City of San Francisco and Incidentally of the State of California* (San Francisco, 1878), p. 277.

[23] Cronise, *Natural Wealth*, pp. 609–610.

[24] *Ibid.*, pp. 648–655.

[25] *Mining and Scientific Press,* December 28, 1861.

[26] James W. Watt, "Experiences of a Packer in Washington Territory Mining Camps during the Sixties," William S. Lewis, ed., *Washington Historical Quarterly,* XX (January 1929), p. 51.

[27] Of the several contemporary and modern books that discuss this intricate subject, see especially Oscar O. Winther, *The Old Oregon Country, a History of Frontier Trade, Transportation, and Travel* (Stanford, 1950), pp. 173–245.

[28] Alton B. Oviatt, "Fort Benton, River Capital," in Merrill G. Burlingame and K. Ross Toole, *A History of Montana* (3 vols., New York, 1957), I, pp. 137–155. On Fort Benton's merchants, see Paul F. Sharp's excellent *Whoop-Up Country: The Canadian-American West, 1865–1885* (Minneapolis, 1955), pp. 207–228.

[29] On Colorado's ties, see the present writer's "Colorado as a Pioneer of Science in the Mining West," *Mississippi Valley Historical Review,* XLVII (June 1960), pp. 36–38.

Chapter 4: The Comstock Lode, 1859–1880

[1] San Francisco, *Daily Alta California,* February 3, 1872.

[2] Joseph L. King, *History of the San Francisco Stock and Exchange Board* (San Francisco, 1910), pp. 256–257. King was a broker during the Comstock days, and was president of the Exchange for many years.

[3] For the early history of the diggings on Mt. Davidson, contrast the somewhat differing accounts in Smith, *The History of the Comstock Lode, 1850–1920;* Lord, *Comstock Mining and Miners;* Angel, *History of Nevada;* and William Wright (Dan De Quille, pseud.), *History of the Big Bonanza: an Authentic Account of the Discovery, History, and Working of the World Renowned Comstock Silver Lode of Nevada, Including . . .* (Hartford, 1876).

[4] De Quille, *History of the Big Bonanza,* p. 60.

[5] Compare Lindgren, *Mineral Deposits,* 4th ed., p. 488, with a contemporary classic, James D. Dana, *Manual of Geology, Treating of the Principles of the Science with Special Reference to American Geological History* (4th ed., New York, 1894), p. 339.

[6] J. Ross Browne, "A Peep at Washoe," *Harper's New Monthly Magazine,* XXII (January 1861), p. 156.

[7] Lord, *Comstock Mining and Miners,* p. 415, gives a table of claims. Smith, *History of the Comstock Lode,* pp. 292–293, gives a table of production by individual mines, including dividends and assessments.

[8] Cf. individual biographies in Alonzo Phelps, ed., *Contemporary Biography of California's Representative Men. With Contributions from Distinguished Scholars and Scientists* (2 vols., San Francisco, 1881–1882).

[9] Fremont Older and Cora M. Older, *The Life of George Hearst, California Pioneer* (San Francisco, 1933), pp. 12–91, discuss Hearst's early mining career, but the details as to the first shipment from the Ophir mine are taken from Smith, *History of the Comstock Lode,* p. 16, which is confirmed by Max Crowell, *A Technical Review of Early Comstock Mining Methods* (W.P.A. Project, mimeographed, Reno, 1941), p. 19.

[10] Smith, *History of the Comstock,* pp. 23–24; Lord, *Comstock Mining,* pp. 89–90; De Quille, *History of the Big Bonanza,* pp. 134–136.

[11] In addition to Smith, *History of the Comstock*, pp. 41–43, and Lord, *Comstock Mining*, pp. 84–88, see Almarin Paul's own account in *Mining and Scientific Press*, March 13, 20, 27; April 3, 1869; and the account of the builder of the rival mill in Angel, *History of Nevada*, p. 68. On the whole subject see Almon D. Hodges, Jr., "Amalgamation at the Comstock Lode, Nevada: A Historical Sketch of Milling Operations at Washoe, and an Account of the Treatment of Tailings at the Lyon Mill, Dayton," American Institute of Mining Engineers, *Transactions*, XIX, (1890–1891), pp. 185–231.

[12] As quoted in Smith, *History of the Comstock*, p. 42.

[13] Cf. Henry G. Ferguson, *The Mining Districts of Nevada* (University of Nevada, "Bulletin," vol. XXXVIII, no. 4, Geology and Mining Series no. 40, Reno, 1944), pp. 82–89.

[14] George F. Becker, *Geology of the Comstock Lode and the Washoe District* (U.S. Geological Survey, "Monographs," III, Washington, 1882), p. 7.

[15] Thomas A. Rickard, *A History of American Mining* (A. I. M. E. Series, New York and London, 1932), p. 100.

[16] De Quille, *History of the Big Bonanza*, p. 139.

[17] Becker, *Geology of the Comstock Lode*, p. 3.

[18] The evolution of the diamond drill and Burleigh compressed-air drill are traced in *Mining and Scientific Press*, February 4, 1865; January 8, January 22, May 7, November 5, 1870; June 3, 1871; June 22, 1872; May 16, 1874. A similar evolution in explosives can be traced in *Mining and Scientific Press*, December 23, December 30, 1865; April 28, June 9, 1866; April 6, June 22, 1867; February 22, 1868; February 6, 1869; January 22, April 23, 1870.

[19] Becker, *Geology of the Comstock*, p. 1

[20] John S. Hittell, *The Commerce and Industries of the Pacific Coast of North America; Comprising the Rise, Progress, Products, Present Condition, and Prospects of the Useful Arts on the Western Side of Our Continent* . . . (San Francisco, 1882), p. 299.

[21] Becker, *Geology of the Comstock*, p. 4, Lord, *Comstock Mining*, pp. 385–386, gives a table of occupations, but note that it is for employment both in the mines and the Sutro Tunnel. De Quille, *History of the Big Bonanza*, p. 326.

[22] U.S. Census, *Ninth Census* (1870), vol. I, "Population," p. 199; *Tenth Census* (1880), "Population," p. 452; Lord, *Comstock Mining*, tables on pp. 383–386. Figures include the Sutro Tunnel. On the Cornishmen, see A. K. Hamilton Jenkin, *The Cornish Miner. An Account of his Life Above and Underground from Early Times* (London, 1927), pp. 302, 321–323.

[23] Lord, *Comstock Mining*, pp. 182–190, 266–268, 355–359; Angel, *History of Nevada*, p. 261; De Quille, *History of the Big Bonanza*, p. 440.

[24] Excerpts from it are printed in John D. Galloway, *Early Engineering Works Contributory to the Comstock* (University of Nevada, "Bulletin," vol. XLI, no. 5, Geology and Mining Series no. 45, Reno, 1947), pp. 13–21.

[25] This theme has been developed more fully in the present writer's introduction to the paper-covered edition of *Roughing It* (Rinehart Editions, Holt, Rinehart and Winston, New York, 1953). Subsequent citations are from this edition.

[26] *Ibid.*, p. 219.

[27] George T. Marye, Jr., *From '49 to '83 in California and Nevada. Chapters from the Life of Thomas Marye, a Pioneer of '49* (San Francisco, 1923), pp. 61–63. A state census showed a population of 19,528 in Storey County in 1875.

[28] Oscar Lewis, *Silver Kings: The Lives and Times of Mackay, Fair, Flood, and O'Brien, Lords of the Nevada Comstock Lode* (New York, 1947), p. 4.

²⁹ Bertrand F. Couch and Jay A. Carpenter, *Nevada's Metal and Mineral Production (1859–1940, Inclusive)*, (University of Nevada, "Bulletin," vol. XXXVII, no. 4, Geology and Mining Series no. 38, Reno, 1943), pp. 132–133.

³⁰ Lord, *Comstock Mining*, p. 181.

³¹ *Mining and Scientific Press*, January 30, 1864.

³² Ralston's career and that of his associates is described in Cecil G. Tilton, *William Chapman Ralston, Courageous Builder* (Boston, 1935), and George D. Lyman, *Ralston's Ring: California Plunders the Comstock Lode* (New York and London, 1937). A corresponding group biography of the four "bonanza kings" is Oscar Lewis's *Silver Kings*. See also detailed discussion in Smith, *History of the Comstock*, and Lord, *Comstock Mining*.

³³ On Jones and Hayward, see the reminiscences of Jones' nephew, Harry M. Gorham, *My Memories of the Comstock* (Los Angeles, 1939), pp. 99–122; King, *History of the San Francisco Stock and Exchange Board*, pp. 47–48, 185–186; and Smith, *History of the Comstock*, pp. 128–130, 134–135.

³⁴ *Mining and Scientific Press*, February 3, 1872.

³⁵ *Ibid.*, October 18, 1873.

³⁶ *Ibid.*, December 26, 1874. The first dividend was reported in the *Press*, May 16, 1874.

³⁷ Lord, *Comstock Mining*, p. 315.

³⁸ De Quille, *History of the Big Bonanza*, p. 487.

³⁹ Smith, *History of the Comstock*, p. 259.

⁴⁰ Couch and Carpenter, *Nevada's Metal and Mineral Production*, p. 133.

⁴¹ The best analysis of the bank's failure is that by Tilton, *William Chapman Ralston*, pp. 324–424. But see also the version of one who was a participant in those exciting events: King, *History of the San Francisco Stock and Exchange Board*, pp. 101–113. Ralston's death is a striking example of historical paradox: we have a highly detailed knowledge of Ralston's physical movements on that last day, but we do not know what was in Ralston's mind when he dived into the water for his regular afternoon swim.

⁴² On Sutro's controversial career, compare the differing versions in Smith, *History of the Comstock*, pp. 107–115, Lord, *Comstock Mining*, pp. 216, 230–243, 297–300, 333–346, and Angel, *History of Nevada*, pp. 504–512. The several brief sketches of his life do not always agree on details: Eugenia K. Holmes, *Adolph Sutro. A Brief Story of a Brilliant Life* (San Francisco, 1895); and articles in *Jewish Encyclopedia* (12 vols., New York, 1901–1906), XI, pp. 604–606; *Dictionary of American Biography* (22 vols. and index, New York, 1928–1958), XVIII, p. 223; and *Appleton's Cyclopaedia of American Biography* (8 vols., New York, 1887–1918), VI, p. 2.

⁴³ Smith, *History of the Comstock*, pp. 292–293, gives the statistical table.

⁴⁴ James D. Hague, *Mining Industry* (Clarence King, geologist-in-charge, *United States Geological Exploration of the Fortieth Parallel*, III, Washington, 1870), p. 238.

⁴⁵ *Ibid.*, pp. 238–246; Rossiter W. Raymond, *Mineral Resources of the States and Territories West of the Rocky Mountains* (Washington, 1869), pp. 53–54. Hereinafter cited as Raymond, *Mineral Resources*, 1st rpt., covering 1868. Subsequent reports in this same series (all by Raymond) will be cited in similar fashion.

⁴⁶ Becker, *Geology of the Comstock*, p. 6. Becker felt that over the Comstock's whole history, "it is improbable that more than 75 per cent of the bullion contained in the ore has been recovered." Smith, *History of the Comstock*, p. 256, argues that an estimate of a loss of 25 per cent "appears to be excessive."

⁴⁷ Hittell, *Commerce and Industries*, pp. 298–299.

[48] *Mining and Scientific Press,* March 9, 1872.

Chapter 5: A Study in Contrasts: California and Nevada, 1859–1880

[1] J. Ross Browne and James W. Taylor, *Reports upon the Mineral Resources of the United States* (Washington, 1867), p. 66. This was the first of Browne's two reports and covers 1866.

[2] Cronise, *Natural Wealth of California,* p. 206.

[3] William H. Brewer, *Up and Down California in 1860–1864: The Journal of William H. Brewer, Professor of Agriculture in the Sheffield Scientific School from 1864 to 1903,* Francis P. Farquhar, ed. (New Haven, Conn., 1930), pp. 329–330. Brewer was a member of the survey.

[4] Rossiter W. Raymond, *Statistics of Mines and Mining in the States and Territories West of the Rocky Mountains: being the Seventh Annual Report* (Washington, 1875), p. 171. Covering 1874.

[5] *Ibid.,* p. 165.

[6] G. Chester Brown, "Mines and Mineral Resources of Shasta County, Siskiyou County, Trinity County," California State Mining Bureau, *Chapters of State Mineralogist's Report, Biennial Period 1913–1914* (Sacramento, 1915), pp. 7, 130.

[7] *Mining and Scientific Press,* December 7, 1872, clipping from the San Francisco *Bulletin.*

[8] North San Juan *Hydraulic Press,* April 2, 1859.

[9] Grass Valley *National,* August 22, 1863.

[10] Rossiter W. Raymond, *Statistics of Mines and Mining in the States and Territories West of the Rocky Mountains* (Washington, 1872), 3d rpt., covering 1870, p. 55. This section of the report was from material contributed by W. A. Skidmore of San Francisco.

[11] Raymond, *Statistics of Mines and Mining,* 7th rpt., covering 1874, pp. 115–117, 148–150.

[12] Henry De Groot, "Hydraulic and Drift Mining," California State Mineralogist, *Second Report, from December 1, 1880, to October 1, 1882* (Sacramento, 1882), pp. 159–161.

[13] California State Mineralogist, *Second Report,* p. 115.

[14] Samuel F. Emmons and George F. Becker, *Statistics and Technology of the Precious Metals,* in Clarence King, director of special volume, U.S. Census, *Tenth Census* (1880), vol. XIII (Washington, 1885), p. 200. This section of the report was largely by Albert Williams, Jr.

[15] Cf. Robert L. Kelley, "The Mining Debris Controversy in the Sacramento Valley," *Pacific Historical Review,* XXV (November 1956), pp. 331–346, and the same author's *Gold vs. Grain: The Hydraulic Mining Controversy in California's Sacramento Valley, A Chapter in the Decline of the Concept of Laissez Faire* (Glendale, California, 1959).

[16] Judson Farley, "The Yuba Hydraulic Mines," *Overland Monthly,* 1st ser., V (September 1870), pp. 216–217.

[17] As quoted in Paul, *California Gold,* pp. 286–287.

[18] *Ibid.,* pp. 287–293.

[19] Clarence A. Logan, *Mother Lode Gold Belt of California* (California State Division of Mines, "Bulletin," no. 108, Sacramento, 1935), p. 9.

[20] Paul, *California Gold,* pp. 322–332.

[21] Hittell, *Mining in the Pacific States*, p. 211.

[22] U.S. Census, *Ninth Census* (1870), vol. I, "Population," pp. 682–683, 722.

[23] Couch and Carpenter, *Nevada's Metal and Mineral Production*, pp. 13, 133.

[24] *Roughing It*, pp. viii, 108.

[25] William O. Vanderburg, *Placer Mining in Nevada* (University of Nevada "Bulletin," vol. XXX, no. 4, Reno, 1936), pp. 16–18.

[26] Rossiter W. Raymond, *Statistics of Mines and Mining in the States and Territories West of the Rocky Mountains* (Washington, 1870), 2d rpt., covering 1869, p. 117.

[27] Quotation is from Richard M. Pearl, *Rocks and Minerals* (New York, 1956), p. 185. See also Alan M. Bateman, *Economic Mineral Deposits* (2d ed., New York, 1950), pp. 421–422, 454–456.

[28] The quotations in this and the following paragraph are from this survey: O. H. Hahn, Anton Eilers, and Rossiter W. Raymond, "The Smelting of Argentiferous Lead Ores in Nevada, Utah, and Montana," American Institute of Mining Engineers, *Transactions*, I (1871–1873), pp. 91–131.

[29] Bateman, *Economic Mineral Deposits*, 2d ed., pp. 245–246, 274–289.

[30] Ferguson, *Mining Districts of Nevada*, p. 102. Cf. Bernard York, *The Geology of Nevada Ore Deposits* (University of Nevada "Bulletin," vol. XXXVIII, no. 4, Geology and Mining Series no. 40, Reno, 1944), p. 54.

[31] Selby's career is sketched in Phelps, *Contemporary Biography*, I, pp. 420–423, and Oscar Shuck, ed., *Representative and Leading Men of the Pacific: Being Original Sketches of the Lives and Characters . . .* (San Francisco, 1870), pp. 411–413; see also the *Mining and Scientific Press*, May 4, 1867; November 21, 1868; and January 7, 1871.

[32] For Oreana's brief history, see the *Mining and Scientific Press*, February 23, 1867; Hague, *Mining Industry*, pp. 297–301; Raymond, *Mineral Resources*, 1st rpt., covering 1868, pp. 129–132; Angel, *History of Nevada*, p. 453; and Frederick L. Ransome, *Notes on Some Mining Districts in Humboldt County, Nevada* (U.S. Geological Survey "Bulletin," no. 414, Washington, 1909), p. 10. The quotations are from Raymond's first report, covering 1868, p. 130, and his third report, covering 1870, p. 137.

[33] Winfield S. Keyes, "Notes on Western Lead Smelting," California State Mineralogist, *Eighth Annual Report, for the Year Ending October 1, 1888* (Sacramento, 1888), pp. 804, 809.

[34] On Eureka, see Francis C. Lincoln, *Mining Districts and Mineral Resources of Nevada* (Reno, 1923), pp. 88–89; Joseph S. Curtis, *Silver-Lead Deposits of Eureka, Nevada* (U.S. Geological Survey, "Monographs," VII, Washington, 1884); Arnold Hague, *Geology of the Eureka District, Nevada* (U.S. Geological Survey, "Monographs," XX, Washington, 1892); and Angel, *History of Nevada*, pp. 425–432.

[35] Curtis, *Silver-Lead Deposits of Eureka*, pp. 64, 70.

[36] Keyes, "Notes on Western Lead Smelting," California State Mineralogist, *Eighth Annual Rept.*, pp. 809–813.

[37] The quotation is from Hague, *Geology of Eureka*, p. 7.

[38] Curtis, *Silver-Lead Ores*, p. 4; Couch and Carpenter, *Nevada's Metal and Mineral Production*, pp. 56–57.

[39] On Pioche, see Lincoln, *Mining Districts*, pp. 124–125; Lewis G. Westgate and Adolph Knopf, *Geology and Ore Deposits of the Pioche District, Nevada* (U.S. Geological Survey, "Professional Paper," no. 171, Washington, 1932); and Angel, *History of Nevada*, pp. 477–488.

⁴⁰ Hague, *Mining Industry*, p. 425; Raymond, *Mineral Resources*, 1st rpt., covering 1868, p. 87.

⁴¹ Raymond, *Statistics of Mines*, 2d rpt., covering 1869, p. 117. The White Pine affair has been carefully examined in a modern article: Russell R. Elliott, "The Early History of White Pine County, Nevada, 1865–1887," *Pacific Northwest Quarterly*, XXX (April 1939), pp. 145–168; and in a contemporary one written by a participant: Angel, *History of Nevada*, pp. 648–652. See also Bancroft, *Works*, XXV, pp. 277–281. Production figures are given in Couch and Carpenter.

⁴² Raymond, *Statistics of Mines*, 2d rpt., covering 1869, p. 181; Raymond, *Mineral Resources*, 1st rpt., covering 1868, p. 88.

⁴³ *Mining and Scientific Press*, April 16, 1870.

⁴⁴ Raymond, *Mineral Resources*, 1st rpt., covering 1868, p. 118.

⁴⁵ *Ibid.*, p. 127.

Chapter 6: Colorado, 1859–1880

¹ Tables of production and a chronological outline are given in Charles W. Henderson, *Mining in Colorado. A History of Discovery, Development and Production* (U.S. Geological Survey, "Professional Paper," no. 138, Washington, 1926), pp. 8–17, 69.

² Correspondence printed in the St. Louis *Missouri Republican*, May 11, 1859, as given in LeRoy R. Hafen, ed., *Colorado Gold Rush: Contemporary Letters and Reports, 1858–1859* (LeRoy R. Hafen, ed., *The Southwest Historical Series*, X, Glendale, California, 1941), pp. 310–311.

³ Of the many accounts, one of the best is Jerome C. Smiley, ed., *History of Denver, with Outlines of the Earlier History of the Rocky Mountain Country* (Denver, 1901), pp. 253–268. But see also Percy S. Fritz, *Colorado, The Centennial State* (New York, 1941), pp. 105–118.

⁴ The quotation is from Ransome's preface to Edson S. Bastin and James M. Hill, *Economic Geology of Gilpin County and Adjacent Parts of Clear Creek and Boulder Counties, Colorado* (U.S. Geological Survey, "Professional Paper," no. 94, Washington, 1917), p. 14. For a similar statement concerning this same area, see Russell D. George, *Geology and Natural Resources of Colorado* (Boulder, Colo., 1927), p. 91.

⁵ Smiley, *History of Denver*, p. 269.

⁶ Henderson, *Mining in Colorado*, p. 69 (table).

⁷ Fossett, *Colorado*, p. 246; Henderson, *Mining in Colorado*, p. 69.

⁸ Fossett, *Colorado*, p. 147; U.S. Census, *Eighth Census* (1860), "Population," p. 547; *Ninth Census* (1870), vol. I, "Population," p. 16.

⁹ Fossett, *Colorado*, p. 138. On the placers see Fossett's account, pp. 120–141, 245; and Ovando J. Hollister, *The Mines of Colorado* (Springfield, Mass., 1867), pp. 69–74, 122.

¹⁰ Wolfe Londoner, "Western Experiences and Colorado Mining Camps," *Colorado Magazine*, VI (March 1929), p. 69 (transcription of an interview in 1884).

¹¹ Hollister, *The Mines of Colorado*, pp. 64–69, 74, 103–122; Hague, *Mining Industry*, pp. 497, 506.

¹² Hollister, *The Mines of Colorado*, p. 134; Fossett, *Colorado*, pp. 143, 226.

¹³ Pearl, *Rocks and Minerals*, p. 193.

¹⁴ Hollister, *The Mines of Colorado*, p. 131.

¹⁵ *Ibid.*, pp. 131–140; Fossett, *Colorado*, pp. 133–136.

16 Henderson, *Mining in Colorado*, p. 69.

17 Bayard Taylor, *Colorado: A Summer Trip* (New York, 1867), p. 61.

18 *Ibid.*, pp. 56–57.

19 Lynn I. Perrigo, "The Cornish Miners of Early Gilpin County," *Colorado Magazine*, XIV (May 1937), pp. 92–101; C. H. Hanington, "Early Days of Central City," *Colorado Magazine*, XIX (January 1942), p. 8.

20 Hague, *Mining Industry*, pp. 560, 567; Raymond, *Statistics of Mines*, 2d rpt., covering 1869, p. 364. Hague specifically excludes from his estimate any subsequent product from the tailings. Raymond warns that his is only an educated guess.

21 Raymond, *Statistics*, 2d rpt., covering 1869, p. 347.

22 Bastin and Hill, *Economic Geology of Gilpin*, p. 155.

23 *Mining and Scientific Press*, February 26; March 12; April 9; April 16, 1870.

24 *Ibid.*, March 8, 1873, clipping from *Colorado Mining Review*.

25 For Hill's career, see *Dictionary of American Biography*, IX, pp. 43–44; Smiley, *History of Denver*, p. 552. His correspondence has been published under varying titles in the *Colorado Magazine*, XXXIII (October 1956), pp. 241–276; XXXIV (January 1957), pp. 22–47; XXXIV (April 1957), pp. 121–134; XXXIV (July 1957), pp. 184–202.

26 For Pearce's career, see *Dictionary of American Biography*, XIV, pp. 353–354; Smiley, *History of Denver*, p. 568. A very useful article on Hill and Pearce is that by Jesse D. Hale, Hill's brother-in-law and employee, "The First Successful Smelter in Colorado," *Colorado Magazine*, XIII (September 1936), pp. 161–167.

27 Henderson, *Mining in Colorado*, p. 69.

28 Smiley, *History of Denver*, pp. 579–631.

29 *Ibid.*, p. 579.

30 Rev. William Crawford to the American Home Missionary Society, Denver, July 13, 1863, as printed in Colin B. Goodykoontz, "Colorado as Seen by a Home Missionary, 1863–1868," *Colorado Magazine*, XII (March 1935), p. 62.

31 Louis L. Simonin, "Colorado in 1867 as Seen by a Frenchman," Wilson O. Clough, trans., *Colorado Magazine*, XIV (March 1937), p. 57.

32 Fossett, *Colorado*, p. 33.

33 Ellsworth C. Mitick, "A History of Mining Machinery Manufacture in Colorado," *Colorado Magazine*, XXIV (November 1947), pp. 225–241; XXV (January 1948), pp. 34–44; XXV (March 1948), pp. 75–92; XXV, (May 1948), pp. 136–142.

34 Smiley, *History of Denver*, pp. 551–556.

35 Rodman Wilson Paul, "Colorado as a Pioneer of Science in the Mining West," *Mississippi Valley Historical Review*, XLVII (June 1960), p. 45.

36 The quotations and details are from the reminiscences of Carlyle C. Davis, *Olden Times in Colorado* (Los Angeles, 1916), pp. 112–118, 124.

37 U.S. Census, *Tenth Census* (1880), "Population," pp. 447, 499.

38 Paul, "Colorado as a Pioneer of Science," *Mississippi Valley Historical Review*, XLVII, p. 45.

39 Henderson, *Mining in Colorado*, pp. 132–133, 176. Note that these statistics are for Lake County rather than for Leadville exclusively. Note also that the whole question of stating silver output in this era is complicated by the increasing gap between the commercial price for silver and the coinage value.

40 First quotation from Samuel F. Emmons, "Lead Smelting at Leadville, Colorado," in Samuel F. Emmons and George F. Becker, *Statistics and Technology of the Precious Metals* (U.S. Census, *Tenth Census*, 1880, XIII, Washington, 1885),

p. 288; second quotation from C. H. Hanington, "Smelting in Colorado," *Colorado Magazine*, XXIII (March 1946), p. 83.

⁴¹ Emmons, "Lead Smelting at Leadville," Emmons and Becker, *Statistics and Technology*, p. 289.

⁴² *Ibid.*, p. 295.

⁴³ Samuel F. Emmons, *Geology and Mining Industry of Leadville, Colorado* (U.S. Geological Survey, "Monographs," XII, Washington, 1886), p. 367. For Emmons' career, see *Dictionary of American Biography*, VI, pp. 151–152.

⁴⁴ U.S. Geological Survey, *Second Annual Report, 1880–1881* (Washington, 1882), p. xx.

⁴⁵ Davis, *Olden Times in Colorado*, pp. 190–191.

⁴⁶ U.S. Geological Survey, *Second Annual Report*, p. xxiii.

⁴⁷ As quoted in Thomas G. Manning, "The Influence of Clarence King and John Wesley Powell on the Early History of the United States Geological Survey," *Interim Proceedings of the Geological Society of America*, part 2 (May 1947), pp. 25–26.

⁴⁸ Colorado Scientific Society, *Proceedings*, I (1883 and 1884), pp. xi–xxi.

⁴⁹ Peter H. Van Diest, "Address of the Retiring President," Colorado Scientific Society, *Proceedings*, II, part III (1887), p. 284.

⁵⁰ Whitman Cross and Richard A. F. Penrose, Jr., "Geology and Mining Industries of the Cripple Creek District, Colorado," U.S. Geological Survey, *Sixteenth Annual Report, 1894–1895* (4 vols., Washington, 1895–1896), Part II, p. 113.

⁵¹ *Ibid.*, p. 117.

⁵² The quotations and details are from Paul, "Colorado as a Pioneer of Science," *Mississippi Valley Historical Review*, XLVII, pp. 49–50.

Chapter 7: Northwest and Southwest, 1860–1880

¹ *Mining and Scientific Press*, January 28, 1882.

² *Ibid.*, January 29, 1881.

³ For an excellent discussion of the early Idaho mining community, see Merrill D. Beal and Merle W. Wells, *History of Idaho* (3 vols., New York, 1959), I, pp. 266–324.

⁴ Bancroft, *Works*, XXXI, p. 427.

⁵ John Hailey, *The History of Idaho* (Boise, 1910), p. 107.

⁶ Waldemar Lindgren, "The Mining Districts of the Idaho Basin and the Boise Ridge, Idaho," U.S. Geological Survey, *Eighteenth Annual Report, 1896–1897*, part III (Washington, 1898), p. 655.

⁷ Hailey, *History of Idaho*, pp. 66, 92. Hailey was one of the first to operate pack trains over this route.

⁸ *Ibid.*, p. 107.

⁹ William J. McConnell, *Early History of Idaho* (Caldwell, Ida., 1913), p. 56.

¹⁰ C. Aubrey Angelo (Chaos, pseud.), *Idaho: A Descriptive Tour, and Review of its Resources and Route* (San Francisco, 1865), pp. 48–50.

¹¹ Raymond, *Statistics of Mines and Mining*, 2d rpt., covering 1869, p. 253.

¹² Tuttle, *Reminiscences of a Missionary Bishop*, p. 216.

¹³ *Ibid.*, pp. 132–133, 140–141.

¹⁴ Browne, *Report on the Mineral Resources*, 2d rpt., covering 1867, p. 517.

¹⁵ A. K. Eaton and others, "Notes on Montana," in Raymond, *Mineral Resources*, 1st rpt., covering 1868, p. 139.

[16] Raymond, *Statistics of Mines and Mining*, 4th rpt., covering 1871, p. 258.

[17] Robert E. Strahorn, *The Resources of Montana Territory and Attractions of Yellowstone National Park: Facts and Experiences on the Farming, Stock Raising, Mining, Lumbering, and other Industries of Montana* . . . (Helena, 1879), p. 43.

[18] For mutually contradictory tables of Idaho production, see Beal and Wells, *History of Idaho*, I, p. 298; August C. Bolino, "The Role of Mining in the Economic Development of Idaho Territory," *Oregon Historical Quarterly*, LIX (June 1958), p. 141; Lindgren, "Mining Districts of the Idaho Basin," U.S. Geological Survey, *Eighteenth Ann. Report*, pp. 652–653; and W. W. Staley, *Gold in Idaho*, (Idaho Bureau of Mines and Geology, "Pamphlet" No. 68, Moscow, Ida., 1946), pp. 8–9. For Montana there is a modern table that is largely a duplicate of contemporary figures, in Merrill G. Burlingame and K. Ross Toole, *A History of Montana* (3 vols., New York, 1957), I, pp. 358–359. Such figures need editing.

[19] For population estimates, see Hailey, *History*, pp. 92, 116, 138, 142; Merle W. Wells, "Territorial Government in the Inland Empire," *Pacific Northwest Quarterly*, XLIV (April 1953), p. 80, fn. 1; Browne, *Report on Mineral Resources*, 2d rpt. covering 1867, p. 512; H. N. Elliott, ed., *History of Idaho Territory, Showing Its Resources and Advantages* . . . (San Francisco, 1884), p. 83.

[20] U.S. Census, *Ninth Census*, (1870), vol. I, "Population," pp. 8, 719–756.

[21] Raymond, *Statistics of Mines and Mining*, 6th rpt., covering 1873, p. 243.

[22] U.S. Census, *Tenth Census* (1880), "Population," p. xxxix.

[23] Winfield S. Keyes, "Mineral Resources of the Territory of Montana," in James W. Taylor, *Report on the Mineral Resources of the United States East of the Rocky Mountains*, 2d rpt., covering 1867 (Washington, 1868), p. 40. But for an estimate that 75,000 to 100,000 people visited Montana in 1864, see Trimble, *Mining Advance*, p. 130, fn. 41.

[24] U.S. Census, *Ninth Census* (1870), vol. I, "Population," pp. 8, 719–765.

[25] A good modern study of quartz mining troubles in one Idaho area is: Robert L. Romig, "Stamp Mills in Trouble," *Pacific Northwest Quarterly*, XLIV (October 1953), pp. 166–176.

[26] Raymond, *Statistics of Mines*, 4th rpt., covering 1871, p. 281.

[27] *Ibid.*, 6th rpt., covering 1873, p. 353.

[28] Cf. an address delivered in 1876 by Charles S. Warren, "Historical Address 'The Territory of Montana,'" Historical Society of Montana, *Contributions*, II (1896), p. 70, and Walter H. Weed, *Geology and Ore Deposits of the Butte District, Montana* (U.S. Geological Survey, "Professional Paper," no. 74, Washington, 1912), p. 18.

[29] For an illuminating discussion of this, see K. Ross Toole, "When Big Money Came to Butte," *Pacific Northwest Quarterly*, XLIV (January 1953), pp. 23–29. Individual biographies are given in *Progressive Men of the State of Montana* (Chicago, c. 1902).

[30] On the beginnings of copper, see Weed, *Geology and Ore Deposits of Butte*, pp. 19–20, and the excellent article by K. Ross Toole, "The Anaconda Copper Mining Company: A Price War and a Copper Corner," *Pacific Northwest Quarterly*, XLI (October 1950), pp. 312–329.

[31] Weed, *Geology and Ore Deposits of Butte*, p. 22.

[32] Beal and Wells, *History of Idaho*, I, p. 418, 494–552.

[33] *Ibid.*, pp. 571–574.

[34] On the Coeur d'Alene region in general, see W. Earl Greenough, *First 100 Years, Coeur d'Alene Mining Region, 1846–1946* (Mullan, Ida., 1947). On the principal mine developed in the rush, see T. A. Rickard's essay on "The Bunker Hill

Enterprise" in his *History of American Mining*, pp. 318–340. On labor, see Robert W. Smith's *The Coeur d'Alene Mining War of 1892: A Case Study of an Industrial Dispute* (Oregon State Monographs, *Studies in History*, no. 2, Corvallis, Oreg., 1961).

[35] Albert Burch, "Development of Metal Mining in Oregon," *Oregon Historical Quarterly*, XLIII (June 1941), pp. 105–128; *Oregon Metal Mines Handbook* (Oregon State Department of Geology and Mineral Industries, "Bulletin," no. 14-A, Portland, 1939), pp. 8–9; *The Oregonian's Handbook of the Pacific Northwest* (Portland, 1894), pp. 67–71.

[36] Marshall T. Huntting, *Gold in Washington* (Washington State Division of Mines and Geology, "Bulletin," no. 42, Olympia, 1955), p. 29. See also George A. Bethune, *Mines and Minerals of Washington. Annual Report of First State Geologist* (Olympia, 1891), pp. 5–27.

[37] The whole question of the Mormons and mining has been splendidly analyzed in Leonard J. Arrington's *Great Basin Kingdom, an Economic History of the Latter-Day Saints, 1830–1900* (Cambridge, Mass., 1958), pp. 64–95, 240–244, 473–474.

[38] Leonard J. Arrington, "Taxable Income in Utah, 1862–1872," *Utah Historical Quarterly*, XXIV (January 1956), pp. 21–47.

[39] Raymond, *Statistics of Mines*, 3d rpt., covering 1870, pp. 2, 218; *Mining and Scientific Press*, March 9, 1872.

[40] Raymond, *Statistics of Mines*, 4th rpt., covering 1871, p. 300.

[41] *Ibid.*, p. 301.

[42] Bert S. Butler, Gerald F. Loughlin, Victor Heikes, and others, *The Ore Deposits of Utah* (U.S. Geological Survey, "Professional Paper," no. 111, Washington, 1920), p. 127.

[43] The Emma's spectacular history has been well examined in two essays: W. Turrentine Jackson, "The Infamous Emma Mine: a British Interest in the Little Cottonwood District, Utah Territory," *Utah Historical Quarterly*, XXIII (October 1955), pp. 339–362; and Clark C. Spence, *British Investments and the American Mining Frontier, 1860–1901* (Ithaca, 1958), pp. 139–182. For the comment on Silliman, see John F. Fulton and Elizabeth H. Thomson, *Benjamin Silliman, 1779–1864, Pathfinder in American Science* (New York, 1947), pp. 240–241.

[44] D. B. Huntley, "The Mining Industries of Utah," in Emmons and Becker, *Statistics and Technology of the Precious Metals* (U.S. Census, *Tenth Census*, XIII), p. 406.

[45] Godfrey Sykes, *The Colorado Delta* (American Geographical Society, "Special Publication" no. 19, Washington and New York, 1937), pp. 8–34.

[46] Fayette A. Jones, *The Mineral Resources of New Mexico* (New Mexico State School of Mines, Mineral Resources Survey, "Bulletin" no. 1, Socorro, N. Mex., 1915), pp. 9–10.

[47] The early history of New Mexico mining is outlined in Fayette A. Jones, *New Mexico Mines and Minerals. World's Fair Edition, 1904. Being an Epitome of the Early Mining History and Resources of New Mexican Mines, in the Various Districts . . .* (Santa Fe, 1904); and Waldemar Lindgren, Louis C. Graton, and Charles H. Gordon, *The Ore Deposits of New Mexico* (U.S. Geological Survey, "Professional Paper" no. 68, Washington, 1910), pp. 17–20.

[48] The early history of Arizona mining is indicated in Rufus K. Wyllys, *Arizona: the History of a Frontier State* (Phoenix, 1950), pp. 117–122, 219–225; Frederick L. Ransome, "Historical Sketch," in Kirk Bryan, *The Papago Country, Arizona* (U.S. Geological Survey, "Water-Supply Paper" no. 499, Washington, 1925), pp. 3–23; and J. B. Tenney, "History of Arizona Gold Mining," in Eldred D. Wilson, J. B. Cunningham, and G. M. Butler, *Arizona Lode Gold Mines and Gold Mining* (Arizona

Bureau of Mines, Mineral Technology Series no. 37, "Bulletin" no. 137, Tucson, 1934), pp. 16–17.

[49] Raymond, *Statistics of Mines,* 8th rpt., covering 1875, p. 337.

[50] *Ibid.,* p. 341.

[51] Richard P. Rothwell, "Gold and Silver," in David T. Day, *Report on Mineral Industries* (U.S. Census, *Eleventh Census* [1890], Washington, 1892), p. 40.

[52] James K. Hastings, "A Boy's Eye View of the Old Southwest," *New Mexico Historical Review,* XXVI (October 1951), pp. 287–301.

[53] Frank C. Lockwood, *Pioneer Days in Arizona, from the Spanish Occupation to Statehood* (New York, 1932), pp. 191–217; John M. Myers, *The Last Chance: Tombstone's Early Years* (New York, 1950), pp. 25 ff.; James H. McClintock, *Arizona, Prehistoric—Aboriginal—Pioneer—Modern* (3 vols., Chicago, 1916), II, pp. 410–412. In general, see Arthur L. Walker, "Recollections of Early Day Mining in Arizona," *Arizona Historical Review,* VI (April 1935), pp. 14–43.

[54] In addition to Walker's article, pp. 37–40, see Robert G. Cleland, *A History of Phelps Dodge, 1834–1950* (New York, 1952).

Chapter 8: First Attempts at Self-government

[1] The statutes organizing the Western territories are conveniently collected in 56th Cong., 1st Sess. S. Doc. No. 148, *Organic Acts for the Territories of the United States with Notes Thereon, Compiled from Statutes at Large of the United States; also, Appendixes* (Washington, 1900). The government of the territories has been well studied in Earl S. Pomeroy's *The Territories and the United States, 1861–1890, Studies in Colonial Administration* (Philadelphia, 1947).

[2] *Mining and Scientific Press,* September 25, 1869.

[3] William J. McConnell, *Early History of Idaho* (Caldwell, Ida., 1913), p. 254.

[4] James Fergus, "A Leaf from the Diary of James Fergus Relative to the Fisk Emigration Party of 1862, and Early Mining Life at Bannack, 1863," Historical Society of Montana, *Contributions,* II (1896), p. 254.

[5] C. Aubrey Angelo (Chaos, pseud.), *Idaho: A Descriptive Tour and Review of its Resources and Route* (San Francisco, 1865), pp. 51–52.

[6] *Roughing It,* p. 250.

[7] Sarah E. Royce, *A. Frontier Lady. Recollections of the Gold Rush and Early California.* Ralph H. Gabriel, ed. (New Haven, 1932).

[8] Richard G. Lillard, ed., "A Literate Woman in the Mines: the Diary of Rachel Haskell," *Mississippi Valley Historical Review,* XXXI (June 1944), pp. 81–98.

[9] Louise M. Palmer, "How We Live in Nevada," *Overland Monthly,* 1st ser., II (May 1869), pp. 457–462. See also the recollections of a very ill-tempered woman: Mrs. Mary M. Mathews, *Ten Years in Nevada: or, Life on the Pacific Coast* (Buffalo, 1880).

[10] R. S. Lawrence, ed., *Pacific Coast Annual Mining Review and Stock Ledger, Containing Detailed Official Reports . . .* (San Francisco, 1878), p. 157.

[11] Angelo, *Idaho,* p. 50.

[12] John Hailey, *The History of Idaho* (Boise, 1910), p. 91.

[13] McConnell, *Early History,* p. 20.

[14] Granville Stuart, *Forty Years on the Frontier, as Seen in the Journals and Reminiscences of Granville Stuart, Gold-Miner, Trader, Merchant, Rancher and Politician,* Paul C. Phillips, ed. (2 vols., Cleveland, 1925), I, p. 237.

[15] W. A. Goulder, *Reminiscences: Incidents in the Life of a Pioneer in Oregon and Idaho* (Boise, 1909), p. 232.

[16] The classic contemporary account, from which all subsequent narratives have borrowed heavily, is Thomas J. Dimsdale's *The Vigilantes of Montana, or Popular Justice in the Rocky Mountains*, originally published at Virginia City, Montana, 1866.

[17] The present writer has discussed this at greater length in "'Old Californians' in British Gold Fields," *Huntington Library Quarterly*, XVII (February 1954), pp. 161–172. But see also the fine pioneer research on this subject in Trimble, *Mining Advance into the Inland Empire*, pp. 187 ff.

[18] *The Statutes of California, Passed at the Second Session of the Legislature: Begun on the Sixth Day of January, 1851, and Ended on the First Day of May, 1851, at the City of San Jose* (n.p., 1851), p. 149 (section 621 of Civil Practice act).

[19] Public Lands Commission, "Report of the Public Lands Commission Created by the Act of March 3, 1879, Relating to Public Lands in the Western Portion of the United States and to the Operation of Existing Land Laws," 46th Cong., 2d Sess., H.R. Exec. Doc. No. 46 (Ser. No. 1923), p. xxxiv.

[20] Curtis H. Lindley, *A Treatise on the American Law Relating to Mines and Mineral Lands within the Public Land States and Territories and Governing the Acquisition and Enjoyment of Mining Rights in Lands of the Public Domain* (2 vols., San Francisco, 1897), I, p. 49.

[21] Gregory Yale, *Legal Titles to Mining Claims and Water Rights, in California, under the Mining Law of Congress, of July, 1866* (San Francisco, 1867), pp. 84–85; cf. Winfield S. Keyes, "Remarks on the Operation in Montana of the United States Mineral Land Act of July 26, 1866," in Rossiter W. Raymond, *Mineral Resources of the States and Territories west of the Rocky Mountains* (Washington, 1869), pp. 152–154. The quotation is from the *Mining and Scientific Press*, December 24, 1864.

[22] Morton v. Solambo Copper Mining Co., 26 Cal. 533.

[23] Sparrow v. Strong, 3 Wallace (70 U.S.), 104.

[24] Stewart's life is summarized in the *Dictionary of American Biography*, XVIII, pp. 13–14; in James L. Harrison, comp., *Biographical Directory of the American Congress, 1779–1949* (Washington, 1950), p. 1867; and in Effie M. Mack, "William Morris Stewart, Empire Builder, 1827–1909," American Historical Association, Pacific Coast Branch, *Proceedings*, 1930, pp. 185–192. His autobiography was entitled *Reminiscences of Senator William M. Stewart of Nevada*, George R. Brown, ed. (New York and Washington, 1908). Note that Stewart was attorney for the plaintiff in *Sparrow* v. *Strong*, cited above, and that Chase's decision drew heavily upon Stewart's argument. Effie M. Mack, *Nevada, a History of the State from the Earliest Times through the Civil War* (Glendale, 1936), p. 431.

[25] The legislative history of the statute is given in Yale, *Legal Titles*, pp. 10–12. Nominally Senator John Conness of California, chairman of the committee on mines, and senior to Stewart, was in charge of the bill. The background of this legislation has been well analyzed in Joseph Ellison, "The Mineral Land Question in California, 1848–1866," *Southwestern Historical Quarterly*, XXX (July 1926), pp. 34–55; and in Beulah Hershiser, "The Influence of Nevada on the National Mining Legislation of 1866," Nevada Historical Society, *Third Biennial Report*, 1911–1912, pp. 127–167.

[26] For text, see 14 U.S. Statutes at Large (1865–1867), p. 251.

[27] Lindley, *A Treatise on the American Law Relating to Mines*, 3d ed., III, p. 1814.

[28] *Mining and Scientific Press*, July 14, 1866.

[29] Lindley, *A Treatise*, 1st ed., I, pp. 74–78.

[30] *Ibid.*, I, pp. 75–77.

[31] Curtis, *Silver-Lead Deposits of Eureka*, pp. 111–113, gives a good summary of the case. But see also an analysis of the key definitions established in the case, by Robert S. Morrison, *Digest of the Law of Mines and Minerals and of All Controversies Incident to the Subject-Matter of Mining . . .* (San Francisco, 1878), especially pp. 218–219.

[32] Sewell Thomas, *Silhouettes of Charles S. Thomas, Colorado Governor and United States Senator* (Caldwell, Idaho, 1959), pp. 30–31.

[33] *Mining and Scientific Press*, October 25, 1879.

[34] Public Lands Commission, "Report," 46th Cong., 2d Sess. H.R. Exec. Doc. No. 46, pp. xxxiv–xl.

[35] Robert S. Morrison, *Mining Rights in Colorado. Lode and Placer Claims, Possessory and Patented, from the District Organizations to the Present Time* (4th ed., Denver, 1880), p. 11.

Chapter 9: Culmination in the Black Hills

[1] Richard I. Dodge, *The Black Hills. A Minute Description of the Routes, Scenery, Soil, Climate, Timber, Gold, Geology, Zoology, Etc.* (New York, 1876), p. 11

[2] For a well illustrated survey of the Black Hills rush, see Hyman Palais, "A Survey of Early Black Hills History," *The Black Hills Engineer*, XXVII (April 1941), pp. 1–101.

[3] Charles Collins, *Collins' History and Directory of the Black Hills, Containing Historical Sketches Pertaining to the First Settlement . . .* (Central City, Dak. Terr., 1878), p. 23.

[4] Jesse Brown and A. M. Willard, *The Black Hills Trails. A History of the Struggles of the Pioneers in the Winning of the Black Hills*, John T. Milek, ed. (Rapid City, S. Dak., 1924), pp. 419–421. Brown and Willard were themselves Black Hills pioneers. Their book is in part reminiscences; in part an anthology of material from local sources.

[5] The popularity of this song, especially as sung by Brown, is recalled by Richard B. Hughes, *Pioneer Years in the Black Hills*, Agnes W. Spring, ed. (Glendale, 1957), p. 113. Hughes was a pioneer newspaper editor in the Black Hills.

[6] A contemporary description of Deadwood, from the Sidney, Nebraska, *Telegraph*, May 22, 1877, is printed in Brown and Willard, *Black Hills Trails*, pp. 468–473. For the lawyer's comment, see Brown and Willard, p. 349. On pioneer newspapers, see *ibid.*, pp. 485–489, and also Hughes, *Pioneer Years*, pp. 172 ff. On local politics, see description from the Sidney *Telegraph*, printed in Brown and Willard, pp. 361–365.

[7] Langrishe was a remarkably well-liked figure. All the reminiscent accounts speak of him, and with affection. His career is best described in Melvin Schoberlin's *From Candles to Footlights: A Biography of the Pike's Peak Theatre, 1859–1876* (Denver, 1941).

[8] Details concerning religion and education can be found in Mildred Fielder, ed., *Lawrence County, for the Dakota Territory Centennial* (Lead, S. Dak., 1960).

[9] Louis Janin, *Report on Some of the Leading Mining Claims of the Whitewood Mining District in the Black Hills, Lawrence County, Dakota. Printed for the Shareholders of the Homestake, Giant and Old Abe, Highland, Golden Terra, and Deadwood Mining Claims* (n.p., 1879), pp. 5–6. Typescript copy in the possession of

James A. Noble, Pasadena. The preface is dated San Francisco, July 25, 1878. Pagination is that of the typed copy, not the printed original.

¹⁰ *Ibid.*, p. 6.

¹¹ *Ibid.*, pp. 5, 18–19.

¹² U.S. Census, *Tenth Census* (1880), "Population," pp. 735, 814.

¹³ Annie D. Tallent, *The Black Hills; or, the Last Hunting Ground of the Dakotahs. A Complete History of the Black Hills of Dakota from their First Invasion in 1874 . . .* (St. Louis, 1899), pp. 520–523; Janin, *Report on Some Leading Mining Claims*, p. 14.

¹⁴ U.S. Census, *Tenth Census* (1880), "Population," p. xxxviii. On their life in Deadwood, see Bennett, *Old Deadwood Days*, pp. 7, 15, 27–32.

¹⁵ Dodge, *The Black Hills*, pp. 107–108.

¹⁶ Jerry Bryan, *An Illinois Gold Hunter in the Black Hills. The Diary of Jerry Bryan, March 13 to August 20, 1876*, Clyde C. Walton, ed., (Illinois Historical Society, "Pamphlet Series," no. 2, Springfield, Ill., 1960). All quotations and details are from this little pamphlet.

¹⁷ Moses Manuel, "Forty-Eight Years in the West. Autobiography of Moses Manuel, as dictated to his nephew P. A. Gushurst." Typescript in possession of James A. Noble, Pasadena. Except where otherwise indicated, quotations and details are from this transcript. Another version of this transcript is in the possession of the Homestake Mining Company, Lead, South Dakota. The Homestake Company's version is a typescript that bears the title "Forty-Eight Years in the West. Dictated to Miss Mary Sheriff by Moses Manuel, Helena, Montana, 1903." A covering letter from Moses Manuel's daughter, Edna Manuel Adamson, Edmonton, Alberta, October 3, 1951, states that she has made this copy from "the original" in her possession. But the Noble version contains sections that are missing from the Homestake Company text.

¹⁸ A running commentary on the rush to Fort Wrangel, Dease Lake, and the Stikine River mines is given in the *Mining and Scientific Press*, September 20, 1873; April 18, May 16, May 30, 1874.

¹⁹ Mrs. Tallent, *The Black Hills*, p. 510, says that the Hearst interests paid a total of $105,000 for the claims that together ultimately made up Homestake Mine No. 1.

²⁰ "Appendage by Edna Manuel Adamson, daughter of Moses Manuel," October 3, 1951, to the copy of Moses Manuel's narrative in the possession of the Homestake Mining Company, Lead, S. Dak.

²¹ Information about Simmons is scarce. A long obituary article from an unspecified local newspaper, dated December 24, 1920 (the day after Simmons' death), is printed in Brown and Willard, *Black Hills Trails*, pp. 539–541. Except where otherwise indicated, quotations and details are from this article.

²² Bancroft, *Works*, XXV, pp. 177–178, fn. 4; Angel, *History of Nevada*, p. 447, shows that Simmons was elected in 1862, 1863, and January 1864.

²³ Walter W. Johnson, "List of Officers of the Territory of Montana to 1876," Historical Society of Montana, *Contributions*, I (1876), p. 292. And cf. reference to Simmons as Indian agent in "Affairs at Fort Benton from 1831 to 1869. From Lieut. Bradley's Journal," Historical Society of Montana, *Contributions*, III (1900), p. 282.

²⁴ Black Hills Mining Men's Association, *Papers Read before the Black Hills Mining Men's Association at their Regular Monthly Meetings, on the Mining and Metallurgy of Black Hills Ores, together with a Brief Outline . . .* (Omaha, 1904).

²⁵ Except where otherwise indicated, quotations and details are from W. W.

Dixon, "Sketch of the Life and Character of William H. Clagett," Historical Society of Montana, *Contributions*, IV (1904), pp. 249–257. See also summary of Clagett's life in James L. Harrison, comp., *Biographical Directory of the American Congress, 1774–1949* (Washington, 1950), p. 977.

[26] *Roughing It*, chaps. XXVII–XXX.

[27] Bancroft, *Works*, XXV, pp. 177–178, fn. 4, and p. 185. fn. 24; Angel, *History of Nevada*, pp. 8, 88–89, 447, 606.

[28] Hiram M. Chittenden, *The Yellowstone National Park, Historical and Descriptive* (Cincinnati, 1895), pp. 92–96.

[29] Bancroft, *Works*, XXXI, p. 676, which also summarizes Clagett's legislative accomplishments.

[30] Brown and Willard, *Black Hills Trails*, p. 373, quoting W. H. Bonham of the Deadwood *Pioneer-Times*. For a very similar comment on the early Deadwood bar, see Hughes, *Pioneer Years*, p. 121. Hughes speaks of "Clagett of the silver tongue." Collins, *Collins' History and Directory of the Black Hills* (1878), pp. 41, 53, lists Clagett and his partner, W. C. Kingsley, in "lawyer's row."

[31] In addition to the description in Dixon's reminiscent essay, see the vivid (though, unfortunately, ghost-written) description in William T. Stoll, *Silver Strike. The True Story of Silver Mining in the Coeur d'Alenes*, "As told to H. W. Whicker" (Boston, 1932).

[32] Stoll, *Silver Strike*, pp. 14–16. Stoll himself was the young attorney.

[33] McConnell, *Early History of Idaho*, pp. 369–384, prints the text of the documents.

[34] James F. Wardner, *Jim Wardner, of Wardner, Idaho. By Himself* (New York, 1900). Except where otherwise noted, quotations and details are taken (with reservations) from this book.

[35] As a corrective to Wardner's exaggerations, note the description of Wardner's role in T. A. Rickard's essay, "The Bunker Hill Enterprise," *History of American Mining*, especially pp. 321–323.

[36] Information about Gushurst has been derived from Tallent, *The Black Hills*, pp. 518, 599–602, and from Mr. Albert F. Gushurst of Golden, Colorado, son of P. A. Gushurst. Additional details and a photograph of P. A. Gushurst and his wife may be found in the Lead *Daily Call*, May 17, 1953.

[37] Tuttle, *Reminiscences of a Missionary Bishop*, p. 172.

[38] Samuel H. Willey, *Thirty Years in California. A Contribution to the History of the State, from 1849–1879* (San Francisco, 1879), p. 70.

Chapter 10: Breaking and Building Communities

[1] Giacomo Puccini, *La Fanciulla del West* (Milan: G. Ricordi, 1974), pp. 1–35. Puccini's opera is based on David Belasco's melodrama, *Girl of the Golden West*. Readers might identify the opening song as Puccini's variation on the familiar folk tune, "Old Dog Tray," which in turn is full of echoes of earlier folk and literary traditions.

[2] Quoted in Robert V. Hine, *Community on the American Frontier: Separate but Not Alone* (Norman: University of Oklahoma Press, 1980), p. 15.

[3] Robert H. Lowie, *Myths and Traditions of the Crow Indians* (Lincoln: University of Nebraska Press, 1993), pp. 99–102, 115–17, 119–28.

[4] Morris Edward Opler, *Myths and Tales of the Chiricahua Apache Indians* (Lincoln: University of Nebraska Press, 1994), p. 78.

[5] Robert F. Heizer and Albert B. Elsasser, *The Natural World of the California Indians* (Berkeley: University of California Press, 1980), p. 210.

[6] Finley McDiarmid, "Daily Remarks," September 10, 1850, Finley McDiarmid Letters, Bancroft Library.

[7] Although both the Southern Cheyennes and Kiowas suffered from epidemics during several years of the great overland expansion, both took their heaviest losses in 1849.

[8] Howard Stansbury, *An Expedition to the Valley of the Great Salt Lake of Utah. . . .* (Philadelphia: Lippincott, Grambo and Co., 1855), pp. 43–46.

[9] Garrick Mallery, *Picture-Writing of the American Indians,* (New York: Dover Publications, 1972), vol. 1, p. 323; Russell Thornton, *American Indian Holocaust and Survival: A Population History Since 1492,* (Norman: University of Oklahoma Press, 1987), pp. 99–100.

[10] Dr. H. T. Ketchum to William P. Dole, September 30, 1863, Letters Received, Colorado Agency, Bureau of Indian Affairs. Ketchum was visiting Cheyennes, Kiowas and Comanches along the Arkansas River.

[11] Albert Barnitz to wife, Jennie, August 13, 1867, September 3, 1867, Albert Barnitz Papers, Beinecke Rare Book and Manuscript Library, Yale University.

[12] James Mason Hutchings diary, December 10, 1855, Bancroft Library.

[13] W. M. Gardner to Miss. S. M. Gardner, June 12, 1850, William M. Gardner Papers, Special Collections, University of North Carolina Library.

[14] W. M. Gardner to Miss. S. M. Gardner, June 12, 1850; William M. Gardner, "Army Life at Camp Far West," both in William M. Gardner Papers, Special Collections, University of North Carolina Library; H. C. Bailey, "California in '53. From the Reminiscences of H. C. Bailey," Bancroft Library.

[15] Helen M. Carpenter, "Among the Diggers of Thirty Years Ago," *Overland Monthly,* 21:124 (April 1893): p. 391.

[16] Robert F. Heizer, ed., *They Were Only Diggers: A Collection of Articles from California Newspapers, 1851–1866, On Indian and White Relations* (Ramona, Calif.: Ballena Press, 1974), pp. 29, 37, 44–45.

[17] Albert H. Hurtado, *Indian Survival on the California Frontier* (New Haven: Yale University Press, 1988), pp. 201–7.

[18] Israel Lord journal, August 10, 1850, Henry E. Huntington Library.

[19] Henry Lansford, "Rocky Mountain Highs . . . and Lows," *Colorado, Rocky Mountain West,* 14:4 (January–February, 1979): R22–R25, R36. Mark Wyman, *Hard Rock Epic: Western Miners and the Industrial Revolution, 1860–1910* (Berkeley: University of California Press, 1979), p. 182.

[20] Harry Faulkner diary, June 14, 1859, Western History Collections, Denver Public Library.

[21] [Virginia City, Montana] *Territorial Enterprise,* April 26, 1866.

[22] William Benemann, ed., *A Year of Mud and Gold: San Francisco in Letters and Diaries, 1849–1850* (Lincoln: University of Nebraska Press, 1999), pp. 64, 70.

[23] Louise Amelia Knapp Clappe, *The Shirley Letters from California Mines in 1851–52* (San Francisco: T. C. Russell, 1922), p. 7; John Eagle to Margaret Eagle, June 10, 1853, June 20, 1853, John Eagle Letters, Henry E. Huntington Library; Timothy Osborn journal, March 5, 1851, Bancroft Library, University of California, Berkeley.

[24] J. Ross Browne, *J. Ross Browne: His Letters, Journals, and Writings*, ed. Linn Fergusson Browne (Albuquerque: University of New Mexico Press, 1969), pp. 234–35.

[25] Theodore Taylor Johnson, *Sights in the Gold Region, and Scenes by the Way* (New York: Baker and Scribner, 1849), p. 177.

[26] W. Augustus Knapp, "An Old Californian's Pioneer Story," *Overland Monthly*, 10:58 (October 1887): p. 404.

[27] Shoshone County Commissioners Book A, September, 1861-August, 1862, Shoshone County Courthouse, Wallace, Idaho.

[28] George A. Lawrence, *Silverland* (London: Chapman and Hall, 1873), pp. 173, 174–75.

[29] John J. Powell, *Nevada: The Land of Silver* (San Francisco: Bacon & Company, 1876), pp. 1, 246–47.

[30] Mrs. M. M. Mathews, *Ten Years in Nevada: Or, Life on the Pacific Coast* (Buffalo: Baker, Jones, and Co., 1880), p. 168.

[31] Joseph Milner diary, 1850, typescript, pp. 10–11, University of North Carolina Library; Aylett R. Cotton, "Across the Plains to California in 1849 and After: An Autobiography," typescript, pp. 42–43, Bancroft Library. W. T. Parker's diary shows him joining in a series of companies to build diversion facilities, with members paid in shares. W. T. Parker diary, October 25, June 15, 1850, October 12, November 8, 1851, Henry E. Huntington Library.

[32] Malcolm J. Rohrbough, *Days of Gold: The California Gold Rush and the American Nation* (Berkeley: University of California Press, 1999), p. 76; Ralph Mann, *After the Gold Rush: Society in Grass Valley and Nevada City, California, 1849–1870* (Stanford: Stanford University Press, 1982), p. 225.

[33] Sally Zanjani, *Goldfield: The Last Gold Rush on the Western Frontier* (Athens: Swallow Press/Ohio University Press, 1992), p. 99.

[34] Gerstaecker, "Narrative," pp. 236–37, 251, quoted in Susan Lee Johnson, *Roaring Camp: The Social World of the California Gold Rush* (New York: W. W. Norton and Company, 2000), p. 169.

[35] Hubert Howe Bancroft, *The Works of Hubert Howe Bancroft. Vol. XXIII. History of California* (San Francisco: The History Company, 1888), p. 228.

[36] For the case of a miner moving often among several working companies, most of them engaged in building diversion dams, see W. T. Parker diary, Henry E. Huntington Library. And for a dramatic account of men working together to save their dams and claims during a flood, see John Eagle to Margaret Eagle, May 27, 1853, John H. Eagle Letters, Henry E. Huntington Library.

[37] Mathews, *Ten Years*, p. 181.

[38] Johnson, *Roaring Camp*, p. 173; Benemann, *Year of Mud and Gold*, p. 152.

[39] George Kinney to Elizabeth Mitchell, April 5, 1863, Mitchell Family papers, Henry E. Huntington Library; W. T. Parker diary, September 16, 1850, Henry E. Huntington Library; Shirley Letters, pp. 203–4.

[40] J. Dell Carson to Ana Lloyd, March 13, 1892, Samuel H. Steelman papers, Special Collections, University of North Carolina Library.

[41] W. Augustus Knapp, "An Old Californian's Pioneer Story," *Overland Monthly*, 10:58 (October 1887): p. 405.

[42] Zanjani, *Goldfield*, p. 134.

[43] Mathews, *Ten Years in Nevada*, p. 171.

[44] LeRoy R. Hafen, ed., *Colorado Gold Rush: Contemporary Letters and Reports, 1858–1859* (Glendale, Calif.: Arthur H. Clark Company, 1941), pp. 193–94.

[45] Israel Lord journal, August 4, 1850, Henry E. Huntington Library.

[46] Adams's diary is quoted in Robert G. Athearn, "A Brahmin in Buffaloland," *Western Historical Quarterly*, 1:1 (January 1970): p. 30.

[47] Edward Austin to sister, September 21, 1849, Edward Austin Papers, Bancroft Library.

[48] Eliot Lord, *Comstock Mining and Miners*, United States Geological Survey Monographs, vol. IV (Washington, D.C.: Government Printing Office, 1883), p. 377; (Silver City, Idaho) *Owyhee Avalanche*, February 3, 1866.

[49] Zanjani, *Goldfield*, p. 137.

[50] For a recent persuasive argument that California camps were less disorderly than usually described, see Martin Ridge, "Disorder, Crime and Punishment in the California Gold Rush," *Montana, The Magazine of Western History*, 49:3 (autumn, 1999): pp. 12–27.

[51] David T. Courtwright, *Violent Land: Single Men and Social Disorder from the Frontier to the Inner City* (Cambridge: Harvard University Press, 1996), pp. 81–82; John Boessenecker, *Gold Dust and Gunsmoke: Tales of Gold Rush Outlaws, Gunfighters, Lawmen, and Vigilantes* (New York: John Wiley and Sons, Inc., 1999), p. 324.

[52] Wyman, *Hard Rock Epic*, p. 153.

[53] Clappe, *Shirley Letters*, p. 38.

[54] Thomas J. Farrell reminiscence, Box 50, Works Progress Administration Oral Histories, Special Collections, Montana State University Library.

[55] Israel Lord journal, December 23, 1850, Henry E. Huntington Library.

[56] William Perkins, "El Campo de los Sonoraenses, or Three Years Residence in California," p. 25, Bancroft Library.

[57] Howard L. Scamehorn, ed., *The Buckeye Rovers in the Gold Rush* (Athens: Ohio University Press, 1965), p. 105; Nelle Frances Minnick, "A Cultural History of Central City, From 1859 to 1880, In Terms of Books and Libraries" (Master's thesis, University of Chicago, pp. 50–51.

[58] Andrew F. Rotter, "'Matilda, For Gods Sake Write': Women and Families in the Argonaut Mind," *California History*, 58:2 (summer 1979): pp. 128–41. Charles Brown, in the mining fields of Colorado, wrote his wife, Maggie, in terms unusually explicit for that time. "Ahh wont it be bliss to be together once more? then nothing but death will part us. I feel that I could kiss that little 'tater hole' if it would do any good. . . ." And: "Darling I am beginning to think that I have nothing like the passion that I used to have, altho every night, I have that old pain . . ." And: "My virtue is all right and I think that it will remain so for I do not care to meddle with any of the women that I see here but I look forward to something nice soon. I know that it will be the best in the world. . . ." Lillian Schlissel, Byrd Gibbens, and Elizabeth Hampsten, *Far From Home: Families of the Westward Journey* (New York: Schocken Books, 1989), pp. 126, 128. A woman wrote to her lover in the camps: "If you was here, I suppose we should do some tall fucking." Quoted in Albert L. Hurtado, *Intimate Frontiers: Sex, Gender and Culture in Old California* (Albuquerque: University of New Mexico Press, 1999), p. xxv.

[59] Perkins, "El Campo," p. 183; Hinton H. Helper, *The Land of Gold: Reality versus Fiction* (Baltimore: H. Taylor, 1855), pp. 43, 44.

[60] Rodman W. Paul, *A Victorian Gentlewoman in the Far West: The Reminiscences of Mary Hallock Foote* (San Marino: The Huntington Library, 1972), pp. 175–78.

[61] Julia Stone diary, July 30, 1865, Frank L. Stone Collection, Special Collections, Montana State University Library.

[62] *Silverton Democrat*, December 6, 1884, quoted in Allan G. Bird, *Silverton Gold: The Story of Silverton's Largest Gold Mine* (N.p.: By the author, 1995), pp. 24–25; Ward, *Prairie Schooner*, p. 169; W. T. Parker diary, October 28, 1850, Henry E. Huntington Library; Robert G. Lillard, ed., "A Literate Woman in the Mines," *Mississippi Valley Historical Review*, 31:1 (June 1944): p. 86, 88, 90–91, 95; Sue H. Summers reminiscence, pp. 5–6, 10, Arizona Historical Society.

[63] Odie B. Faulk, *Tombstone: Myth and Reality* (New York: Oxford University Press, 1972), pp. 104–6.

[64] For a discussion of this relationship in American cities generally, see Neil Larry Shumsky, "Tacit Acceptance: Respectable Americans and Segregated Prostitution, 1870–1910," *Journal of Social History*, 19:4 (summer 1986): 665–79. For its perceptive application to Virginia City, Nevada, see Marion S. Goldman, *Gold Diggers and Silver Miners: Prostitution and Social Life on the Comstock Lode* (Ann Arbor: University of Michigan Press, 1981).

[65] Walter Van Tilburg Clark, ed., *The Journals of Alfred Doten, 1849–1903* (Reno: University of Nevada Press, 1973), vol. 2, pp. 858, 867. Entries for August 21 and October 4, 1865.

[66] October 13 [1867] . . . 9 PM OK 113 Shz mjcndzt mz & vcuket dlii shz gjd cs pjdh jvv–Vlrsd dlmz L zfzr gjd mw gcn jvv ln dhxd yxw ln mw ilvz–pciiw gjjt vcuk–[She mounted me & fucked till she got us both off–First time I ever got my gun off in that way in my life–bully good fuck].

[67] Ibid., p. 926. Entry for May 10, 1867.

[68] Daniel Pidgeon, *An Engineer's Holiday* (London: Kegan Paul, Trench, and Co., 1883), p. 155.

Chapter 11: The World's Convention

[1] Louise Amelia Knapp Clappe, *The Shirley Letters from California Mines in 1851–52* (San Francisco: T. C. Russell, 1922), p. 121.

[2] William J. Trimble, *The Mining Advance in the Inland Empire* (Madison: University of Wisconsin, 1914), p. 140; Paula Mitchell Marks, *Precious Dust: The American Gold Rush Era: 1848–1900* (New York: William Morrow and Company, Inc., 1994), p. 278; William P. Daingerfield to "J," August 18, 1850, William P. Daingerfield Letters, Bancroft Library.

[3] George Harwood Phillips, *Indians and Intruders in Central California, 1769–1849* (Norman: University of Oklahoma Press, 1993), pp. 107–16.

[4] Donald Jackson and Mary Lee Spence, eds., *The Expeditions of John Charles Fremont* (Urbana: University of Illinois Press, 1970), vol. 1, pp. 687–88; Walter Van Tilburg Clark, ed., *The Journals of Alfred Doten, 1849–1903* (Reno: University of Nevada Press, 1973), vol. 1, p. 67.

[5] Isidora Filomena de Solano, "Autobiography," Bancroft Library.

[6] From J. S. Holliday, *The World Rushed In: The California Gold Rush Experience* (New York: Simon and Schuster, 1981). The reference here was to Oregonians, many of whom had recently arrived from Missouri and the middle border, an especially turbulent part of the country.

[7] Elijah Renshaw Potter, "Reminiscences of the Early History of Northern California and of the Indian Troubles," Bancroft Library.

[8] A. G. Tassin, "Chronicles of Camp Wright," *Overland Monthly*, 10:55 (July 1887): p. 27.

[9] The most accessible summary of the Yana and Yani extermination is in Theodora Kroeber, *Ishi in Two Worlds: A Biography of the Last Wild Indian in North America* (Berkeley: University of California Press, 1961), although her account is taken mostly from a more detailed but less accessible source: T. Waterman, *The Yana Indians*, University of California Publications in American Archaeology and Ethnology, 13: 2 (1918): pp. 35–102.

[10] James R. Grossman, ed., *The Frontier in American Culture: Essays by Richard White and Patricia Nelson Limerick* (Chicago and Berkeley: The Newberry Library and University of California Press, 1994), p. 27.

[11] *Report of the Commission Appointed Under Act of Congress Approved June 1, 1872 to Negotiate With the Shoshone Indians in Wyoming Territory* (Washington, D.C.: GPO, 1873), pp. 12–14.

[12] *Missouri Republican*, March 27, 1859, in LeRoy R. Hafen, ed., *Colorado Gold Rush: Contemporary Letters and Reports, 1858–1859* (Glendale, Calif.: Arthur H. Clark Company, 1941), p. 17.

[13] Thomas O. Larkin to James Buchanan, June 28, 1848, in *Documents Accompanying the President's Message at the Second Session of the Thirtieth Congress,* House Ex. Doc. 1, 30th Cong., 2nd sess. 1848, p. 54.

[14] Friedrich Gerstaecker, *Narrative of a Journey Round the World* (London: Hurst and Blackett, 1853), p. 116.

[15] Jacques Antoine Moerenhout, *The Inside Story of the Gold Rush* (San Francisco: California Historical Society, 1935), pp. 22, 25.

[16] A. P. Nasatir, *The French in the California Gold Rush* (New York: American Society of the French Legion of Honor, 1934; Franco-American Pamphlet Series, No. 3), p. 13 and passim.

[17] J. S. Holliday, *Rush for Riches: Gold Fever and the Making of California* (Berkeley: University of California Press, 1999), p. 13.

[18] Quintard Taylor, *In Search of the Racial Frontier: African Americans in the American West, 1528-1990* (New York: W. W. Norton, 1998), p. 84.

[19] W. T. Parker diary, November 15, 1851, Henry E. Huntington Library.

[20] Taylor, *In Search of the Racial Frontier,* p. 85; Rudolph M. Lapp, *Blacks in Gold Rush California* (New Haven: Yale University Press, 1977), pp. 50–55.

[21] Taylor, *In Search of the Racial Frontier,* p. 84.

[22] Henry Sheldon Anable diary, September 13, 1852, Bancroft Library; James Mason Hutchings diary, April 4, 1855, Bancroft Library.

[23] Israel Lord journal, August 10, 1850, Henry E. Huntington Library.

[24] Taylor, *In Search of the Racial Frontier,* pp. 86–87; Reuben Murrell to Sam Murrell, October 4, 1849, Henry E. Huntington Library.

[25] Ralph Mann, *After the Gold Rush: Society in Grass Valley and Nevada City, California, 1849-1870,* (Stanford: Stanford University Press, 1982), p. 86.

[26] Mark Wyman, *Hard Rock Epic: Western Miners and the Industrial Revolution, 1860-1910* (Berkeley: University of California, 1979), p. 42.

[27] Jay Monaghan, *Chile, Peru, and the California Gold Rush of 1849* (Berkeley: University of California Press, 1973), p. 135.

[28] Joseph R. Conlin, *Bacon, Beans, and Galantines: Food and Foodways on the Western Mining Frontier,* (Reno: University of Nevada Press, 1986), pp. 182, 184, 192.

[29] Mrs. C. M. Churchill, *"Little Sheaves" Gathered While Gleaning after Reapers. Being Letters of Travel Commencing in 1870, and ending in 1873* (San Francisco: by the author, 1874), pp. 89–90.

[30] Liping Zhu, *A Chinaman's Chance: The Chinese on the Rocky Mountain Mining Frontier* (Niwot: University Press of Colorado, 1997), pp. 172–73. Conversion sometimes was complete—an Idaho editor described a derby-wearing salesman for a Chinese cigar firm as having "a dudish appearance and the gab and glib tongue of a thoroughbred U.S. drummer."

[31] David T. Courtwright, *Violent Land: Single Men and Social Disorder from the Frontier to the Inner City* (Cambridge: Harvard University Press, 1996), p. 166.

[32] Otis E. Young, Jr., *Western Mining* (Norman: University of Oklahoma Press, 1970), pp. 221–23.

[33] Ronald M. James, "Knockers, Knackers, and Ghosts: Immigrant Folklore in the Western Mines," *Western Folklore,* 51 (April, 1992): pp. 153–77.

[34] Henry Valentine, *California; or the Feast of Gold* (London: R. MacDonald, ca. 1849).

[35] Clappe, *Shirley Letters,* p. 129.

[36] Nasatir, *French in the California Gold Rush,* pp. 12–13.

[37] James Mason Hutchings diary, May 10, 1855, Bancroft Library.

[38] Walter Van Tilburg Clark, ed., *The Journals of Alfred Doten, 1849-1903* (Reno: University of Nevada Press, 1973), vol. 1, pp. 65–66.

[39] John Hovey, "Account of the Troubles Between the American Miners and the Frenchmen of the Garde Mobile at Mokelumne Hill," Henry E. Huntington Library.

[40] Malcolm J. Rohrbough, *Days of Gold: The California Gold Rush and the American Nation,* (Berkeley: University of California Press, 1999), pp. 224–25; P. Hugo Reid to Abel Stearns, July 18, 1849, Henry E. Huntington Library.

[41] Susan Lee Johnson, *Roaring Camp: The Social World of the California Gold Rush* (New York: W. W. Norton and Company, 2000), p. 216.

[42] John Hovey, "Historical Account of the Troubles Between the Chilean and American Miners in the Calevaros Mining District," Henry E. Huntington Library.

[43] Henry H. Mason to sister, November 22, 187[4?], Henry H. Mason Letters, Bancroft Library.

[44] Wyman, *Hard Rock Epic,* pp. 32–33.

[45] Fiorello H. La Guardia, *The Making of an Insurgent: An Autobiography, 1882–1919* (New York: Capricorn Books, 1948), p. 27.

[46] Alfred Barstow, "Statement of Alfred Barstow, a Pioneer of 1849," Bancroft Library; W. T. Parker diary, May 16, 1852, Henry E. Huntington Library.

[47] Liping Zhu, *A Chinaman's Chance: The Chinese on the Rocky Mountain Mining Frontier* (Niwot: University Press of Colorado), 1997); Liping Zhu "No Need To Rush: The Chinese, Placer Mining, and the Western Environment," *Montana, The Magazine of Western History,* 49:3 (autumn, 1999): p. 51.

[48] *Dutch Flat Forum,* March 27, 1877, quoted in Russell Towle, comp., *The Dutch Flat Chronicles* (Dutch Flat, Calif.: Giant Gap Press, 1994), p. 287.

[49] Samuel Bowles, *Across the Continent: A Summer's Journey to the Rocky Mountains, the Mormons, and the Pacific States, with Speaker Colfax* (Springfield, Mass.: Samuel Bowles and Company, 1865), p. 242.

[50] Carl I. Wheat, ed., "'California's Bantam Cock': The Journals of Charles E. De Long, 1854–1863," *California Historical Society Quarterly,* 8:4 (December, 1929): pp. 337–63.

[51] Sam Wong and Assistants, *An English-Chinese Phrase Book Together with the Vocabulary of Trade, Law, etc.* . . . (San Francisco: Cubery and Co., 1875); Benoni Lanctot, *Chinese and English Phrase Book, With the Chinese Pronunciation Indicated in English, Specially Adapted for the Use of Merchants, Travelers and Families* (San Francisco: A. Roman and Company, 1867). Both in Bancroft Library, University of California, Berkeley.

[52] Mary Roberts Coolidge, *Chinese Immigration* (New York: Henry Holt and Company, 1909), pp. 21–22.

[53] For a summary of the number of Chinese emigrants and their estimated numbers in California and on the Pacific coast, see Coolidge, *Chinese Immigration,* p. 498.

[54] Virginia City, Nevada *Territorial Enterprise,* June 23, 1877.

[55] Coolidge, *Chinese Immigration,* p. 32.

[56] C. C. Goodwin, "The Early Comstock Miners," in *Virginia City Miners' Union* (Reno, Nevada: 1912).

[57] John Fall to Henry Blasdel, January 10, 1869, telegram, Henry E. Huntington Library; Virginia City, Nevada *Territorial Enterprise,* May 23, 1867.

[58] Charles J. McClain, *In Search of Equality: The Chinese Struggle Against Discrimination in Nineteenth-Century America* (Berkeley: University of California Press, 1994), pp. 82–83.

[59] William Carroll to Ann [Carroll] Buck, September 8, 1860, Henry E. Huntington Library.

[60] Stuart Creighton Miller, *The Unwelcome Immigrant: The American Image of the Chinese, 1785–1882* (Berkeley: University of California Press, 1969), p. 162.

[61] Diana Ahmad, "Opium Smoking, Anti-Chinese Attitudes, and the American Medical Community, 1850–1890," *American Nineteenth Century History,* 1:2 (summer 2000): p. 57.

[62] George A. Lawrence, *Silverland* (London: Chapman and Hall, 1873), p. 136.

[63] Ibid.

[64] Mrs. M. M. Mathews, *Ten Years in Nevada: Or, Life on the Pacific Coast* (Buffalo: Baker, Jones, and Co., 1880), pp. 254, 257, 260.

[65] Timothy Osborn journal, December 26, 1850, Bancroft Library; Thomas Forbes to "Dear Sir," March 15, 1850, Gold Rush Letters, Bancroft Library; Geo[rge] M[cKinley] Murrell to Eliza F. Murrell, 1851 or 1852, Henry E. Huntington Library.

[66] M[atthew] G[ilbert] Upton, "Etchings in El Dorado, or the Wags and Waggeries of the Argonauts of '49," especially chapter 4, "The Celestial as Man and Brother," manuscript reminiscence, Henry E. Huntington Library. For a recent study emphasizing the accomplishments and relative acceptance of Chinese in the Boise River basin of Idaho, see Liping Zhu, *A Chinaman's Chance.*

Chapter 12: Worlds of Work

[1] Timothy Osborne journal, Bancroft Library. This undated poem is at the conclusion of the journal.

[2] James J. Rawls, "Gold Diggers: Indian Miners in the California Gold Rush," *California Historical Quarterly,* 55:1 (spring 1976): 28.

[3] J. S. Holliday, *The World Rushed In: The California Gold Rush Experience* (New York: Simon and Schuster, 1981), p. 327.

[4] E. W. Gifford and Stanislaw Klimek, *Cultural Element Distributions: II. Yana,* University of California Publications in American Archaeology and Ethnology, 37:2 (1936): pp. 71–100.

[5] Julian Steward, "Two Paiute Autobiographies," *University of California Publications in American Archeology and Ethnology,* 33:5 (1934): pp. 423–38.

[6] William Bent to Superintendent for Indian Affairs, December 17, 1858, letters received, Upper Arkansas Agency, Office of Indian Affairs. This letter is reprinted in Leroy R. Hafen and Ann W. Hafen, eds., *Relations with the Indians of the Plains, 1857–1861* (Glendale, Calif.: Arthur H. Clark Company, 1959), pp. 173–74.

[7] George Harwood Phillips, *Indians and Intruders in Central California, 1769–1849* (Norman: University of Oklahoma Press, 1993), pp. 119–123.

[8] Jacques Antoine Moerenhout, *The Inside Story of the Gold Rush* (San Francisco: California Historical Society, 1935), p. 27.

[9] Aylett Cotton, "Across the Plains to California in 1849 and After: An Autobiography," typescript, Bancroft Library; Richard Barnes Mason to Brig. Gen. R. Jones, August 17, 1848, *Documents Accompanying the President's Message at the Second Session of the Thirtieth Congress,* House Ex. Doc. 1, 30th Cong., 2nd sess. 1848; Susan Lee Johnson, *Roaring Camp: The Social World of the California Gold Rush* (New York: W. W. Norton and Company, 2000), pp. 220–21.

[10] Timothy Coffin Osborn journal, October 20, 1850, Bancroft Library.

[11] Mrs. C. M. Churchill, *"Little Sheaves" Gathered While Gleaning after Reapers. Being Letters of Travel Commencing in 1870, and ending in 1873* (San Francisco: by the author, 1874), p. 47; W. T. Parker diary, October 28, 1850, Henry E. Huntington Library.

[12] Steward, "Two Paiute Autobiographies," p. 436.

[13] Elijah Renshaw Potter, "Reminiscences of the Early History of Northern California and of the Indian Troubles," Bancroft Library.

[14] Potter, "Reminiscences;" W. T. Parker diary, July 22, 1850, Henry E. Huntington Library.

[15] For specific mention of this connection, see J. Ross Brown to J. W. Denver, December 19, 1858, J. Ross Browne Letters, Bancroft Library and John E. Ross, "Narrative of an Indian Fighter," Bancroft Library.

[16] James J. Rawls, *Indians of California: The Changing Image* (Norman: University of Oklahoma Press, 1984), pp. 88–93.

[17] Johnson, *Roaring Camp,* p. 221.

[18] Moerenhout, *Inside Story,* p. 22.

¹⁹ Churchill, *"Little Sheaves,"* pp. 47, 50; George A. Lawrence, *Silverland* (London: Chapman and Hall, 1873), p. 95.

²⁰ John H. Eagle to Margaret Eagle, February 10, 1853, John H. Eagle Letters, Henry E. Huntington Library.

²¹ Quoted in David T. Courtwright, *Violent Land: Single Men and Social Disorder from the Frontier to the Inner City* (Cambridge: Harvard University Press, 1966), p. 71.

²² Benjamin Baxter journal, May 23, 1850, Henry E. Huntington Library.

²³ Ibid.; W. T. Parker diary, June 22, 1851, Henry E. Huntington Library.

²⁴ Quoted in Malcolm J. Rohrbough, *Days of Gold: The California Gold Rush and the American Nation* (Berkeley: University of California Press, 1999) p. 190.

²⁵ Samuel S. Curtis to Henry Curtis, November 22, 1858, Samuel S. Curtis Letters, Kansas Collection, Spencer Library, University of Kansas.

²⁶ J. C. Coates to Jane S. Coates, Letter, August 6, 1852, Henry E. Huntington Library.

²⁷ Quoted in Rohrbough, *Days of Gold,* p. 192.

²⁸ J. S. Holliday, *Rush for Riches: Gold Fever and the Making of California* (Berkeley: University of California Press and Oakland Museum of California, 1999), p. 210.

²⁹ Albert Webster, "A Day at Dutch Flat," *Appleton's Journal,* 1:4 (October 1876): pp. 302–5.

³⁰ Holliday, *Rush for Riches,* p. 210.

³¹ Daniel Witter diary, July 3, 1859, Colorado State Historical Society; Anonymous, "Overland Journey to Colorado," May 29, 1863, Western History Collections, Denver Public Library.

³² Louise Amelia Knapp Smith Clappe, *The Shirley Letters From the California Mines, 1851–1852* (Berkeley: Heyday Books, 1998), p. 36.

³³ Quoted in Rohrbough, *Days of Gold,* p. 179.

³⁴ LeRoy R. Hafen, ed., "Diary of Mrs. A. C. Hunt, 1859," *Colorado Magazine* 21:15 (September 1944): pp. 169–70.

³⁵ For two examples of such contracts, see George Anthony Peffer, *If They Don't Bring Their Women With Them: Chinese Female Immigration Before Exclusion* (Urbana: University of Illinois Press, 1999), p. 117.

³⁶ For two excellent studies of western prostitution, one set in a prominent mining region, see Anne M. Butler, *Daughters of Joy, Sisters of Misery: Prostitutes in the American West, 1865–90* (Urbana: University of Illinois Press, 1985) and Marion S. Goldman, *Gold Diggers and Silver Miners: Prostitution and Social Life on the Comstock Lode* (Ann Arbor: University of Michigan Press, 1981).

³⁷ Lucie Cheng Hirata, "Free, Indentured, Enslaved: Chinese Prostitutes in Nineteenth Century America," *Signs* 5 (1979): pp. 3–29.

³⁸ Ronald James, *The Roar and the Silence: A History of Virginia City and the Comstock Lode* (Reno: University of Nevada Press, 1998), p. 94. The figure for the number of prostitutes is taken from the federal census for Storey County; they made up 7.3 percent of women listed with occupations, including those keeping house.

³⁹ Paula Mitchell Marks, *Precious Dust: The American Gold Rush Era: 1848–1900* (New York: William Morrow and Company, Inc., 1994), p. 338.

⁴⁰ Ibid., pp. 338–40.

⁴¹ For a fine study of women in mining, especially after 1900, see Sally Zanjani, *A Mine of Her Own: Women Prospectors in the American West, 1850–1950* (Lincoln: University of Nebraska Press, 1997).

⁴² Churchill, *"Little Sheaves,"* p. 48.

⁴³ The revealing study on this important chapter in social history is Linda Peavy and Ursala Smith, *Women in Waiting in the Westward Movement: Life on the Home Frontier* (Norman: University of Oklahoma Press, 1994). The case of the deranged gold seeker is mentioned on page 39. See also Rohrbough, *Days of Gold,* pp. 106–18.

[44] Lydia Burns to Polly Burns, September 18, 1853, June 1854, Lydia Burns Letters, Henry E. Huntington Library.

[45] Holliday, *Rush for Riches,* pp. 194–95.

[46] Parker and Huyett, *The Illustrated Miners' Hand-Book and Guide to Pike's Peak. With a New and Reliable Map, Showing All the Routes, and the Gold Regions of Western Kansas and Nebraska* (St. Louis: Parker and Huyett, 1859), p. 17.

[47] Ibid.; Alvin T. Steinel, *History of Agriculture in Colorado* (Fort Collins: State Agricultural College, 1926), pp. 32, 50–51; William Wyckoff, *Creating Colorado: The Making of a Western American Landscape, 1860–1940* (New Haven: Yale University Press, 1999), pp. 157–64.

[48] Elliott West, *The Contested Plains: Indians, Goldseekers and the Rush to Colorado* (Lawerence: University Press of Kansas, 1998), p. 243.

[49] Dan De Quille [William Wright], *The Big Bonanza* (New York: Alfred A. Knopf, 1967), p. 174.

[50] Elliott West, "Five Idaho Mining Towns: A Computer Profile," *Pacific Northwest Quarterly,* 73:3 (July 1982): pp. 111–12.

[51] Eliot Lord, *Comstock Mining and Miners,* United States Geological Survey Monographs, vol. IV (Washington, D.C.: Government Printing Office, 1883), pp. 202–5.

[52] West, *Contested Plains,* p. 224. The number of freighters refers to those working the routes from Missouri valley towns to Colorado and is based on reports of employment by firms based in the Missouri valley.

[53] Mark Wyman, *Hard Rock Epic: Western Miners and the Industrial Revolution, 1860–1910* (Berkeley: University of California Press, 1979), p. 107.

[54] Mrs. M. M. Mathews, *Ten Years in Nevada: Or, Life on the Pacific Coast* (Buffalo: Baker, Jones, and Co., 1880). pp. 304–6.

[55] Charles Howard Shinn, *The Story of the Mine, As Illustrated by the Great Comstock Lode of Nevada* (New York: D. Appleton and Company, 1903), p. 242.

[56] Wyman, *Hard Rock Epic,* p. 185.

[57] Wyman, *Hard Rock Epic,* pp. 157–58.

A NOTE ON STATISTICS

Superlatives come easily—too easily—to any one who is writing about the mining West. Contemporary accounts are so strewn with inflationary phrases that the adjectives lose their force. A critical reader soon finds himself seeking statistics that can be used as a quantitative test of verbal evidence. When a contemporary observer proclaims Forlorn Hope Gulch "the biggest camp of all time," the reader asks, How many people? How much gold (or silver)? There are other economic and social phenomena that one would like to measure, but the number of people and the amount of treasure seem to be the two basic indexes and also the two categories for which approximate data can be most frequently supplied.

Obviously, no precise figures are possible when dealing with so volatile a subject as the mining West. The federal census must, of course, be used as the primary reliance for population statistics, even though the decennial periods so often came at the wrong time to catch a gold or silver rush at its peak, and even though the census probably had additional faults. Indignant local editors claimed that the census underrepresented their communities, because it did not catch all the footloose prospectors and miners. On the other hand, local amateur estimates of population tended to exaggerate. Enough research has been done to show that census reports of the latter half of the nineteenth century sometimes made significant errors in classification and computation, but until better figures are available, the historian must use the census and be grateful.

For mineral production the situation is more indefinite than for population. Until 1866 the federal government did not collect statistics. In the meantime many private individuals and agencies made estimates based on one or another body of evidence. Local journalists and mining men attempted to estimate production, on the basis of personal observation, interviews, and press reports. Wells, Fargo & Co. kept accounts of the treasure shipped in their care. The customs house at San Francisco maintained records of bullion and coin passing through that port, which handled most of the Far West's exports during the 1850s. The United States Mint's several offices kept books that showed the quantity and approximate origins of deposits received by them. Private refiners had similar accounts.

In 1866 J. Ross Browne and James W. Taylor were appointed special commissioners of the Treasury Department to compile facts and figures on mineral resources. Taylor's work, covering the Rockies and Eastern states, was inconsequential, but Browne published useful reports covering the rest of the Far West during 1866 and 1867. Browne's successor was Rossiter W. Raymond, a mining engineer of high ability and integrity. Raymond stretched his instructions so as to include the Rockies. Despite inadequate appropriations by Congress, Raymond continued to publish careful annual volumes until Congress discontinued his office after the report covering 1875. The year 1876 was a complete blank. In the following year the director of the Mint began preparing annual reports that continued until the task was taken over by the United States Geological Survey, and later by the Bureau of Mines.

Federal statistics thus start with 1866, but both Browne and Raymond, lacking funds to employ agents in the different local areas, were dependent on existing sources, such as the express companies, and on information supplied by people whom they could persuade to help them. When the director of the Mint assumed responsibility in 1877, he had better statistical resources at his command. He recalculated Browne's and Raymond's national totals in the light of the Mint's records of bullion actually received by the Mint offices, private refiners, and jewelers, plus the amount exported independently. The director concluded that in the case of gold a "very accurate determination" could be made on this basis; in regard to silver, he felt much less confidence.

The director's revisions indicated that Browne's national totals for 1866 were a gross exaggeration, that the national totals for 1867, 1868, and 1875 were also distinctly in excess, although not to so drastic a degree, while those for 1874 were above the mark by a very moderate amount. Most unfortunately, the Mint statisticians did not attempt to recalculate Browne's and Raymond's figures for individual states and territories. In connection with the census of 1890, Richard P. Rothwell, a distinguished mining editor, republished this whole body of federal statistics in convenient form, but without attempting to reconcile the Mint's revised national totals with Browne's and Raymond's statistics for the several states and territories whose joint product supposedly made up those totals. See Richard P. Rothwell, "Gold and Silver," in David T. Day, special agent, *Report on Mineral Industries in the United States at the Eleventh Census: 1890* (Washington, 1892), pp. 33–152, also republished in Volume I of Rothwell's annual volumes, *The Mineral Industry, Its Statistics, Technology and Trade, in the United States and Other Countries from the Earliest Times to the End of 1892* (New York, 1893), pp. 171–232. For a modern discussion of the shortcomings of the national totals, see *Historical Statistics of the United States, 1789–1945: A Supplement to the* Statistical Abstract of the United States (Washington, 1949), pp. 137–138.

This means that out of the whole era prior to 1877, reasonably acceptable federal estimates are available only for the years 1869–1874, inclusive. For some of the individual states, however, modern recalculations have been made through the efforts of varying authorities who have, unfortunately, based their highly technical work upon several quite different hypotheses. Such reappraisals have usually resulted in a distinct reduction in the figures formerly accepted for the early years. The reduction is especially sharp in the case of California. See detailed comments in the footnotes to the pertinent chapters of this book.

ESSAY ON BIBLIOGRAPHY

Brief general surveys of the Far West in this period include Ray Allen Billington's *The Far Western Frontier, 1830–1860* (Henry S. Commager and Richard B. Morris, eds., *The New American Nation Series*, New York, 1956); the same author's *Westward Expansion, a History of the American Frontier* (2d ed., New York, 1960); and LeRoy R. Hafen and Carl C. Rister, *Western America: The Exploration, Settlement, and Development of the Region beyond the Mississippi* (2d ed., New York, 1950).

Any study of the Far West in the nineteenth century must pay respectful attention to Hubert Howe Bancroft's encyclopedic histories of individual states, published as his *Works* (39 vols., San Francisco, 1882–1890). In both his text and his incredibly long footnotes Bancroft preserved a vast amount of significant material that would otherwise have been lost. Much additional fugitive material can be found in the numerous and often elaborate histories that have been written about all of the Western states and many of the counties. Some of the states have had energetic local historical societies that have collected and published in their quarterlies and annuals important diaries, reminiscences, letters, and business papers.

There are no satisfactory general histories of either mining or mining rushes in the Far West. But one can hardly praise too highly the pioneering study of the Northwest by William J. Trimble, *The Mining Advance into the Inland Empire: A Comparative Study of the Beginnings of the Mining Industry in Idaho and Montana, Eastern Washington and Oregon, and the Southern Interior of British Columbia; and of Institutions and Laws Based upon that Industry* (University of Wisconsin, "Bulletin" No. 638, History Series, vol. III, no. 2, Madison, 1914). Trimble's interpretive comments and conclusions do much to illumine the history of the whole mining West. W. P. Morrell's *The Gold Rushes* (V. T. Harlow and J. A. Williamson, eds., *The Pioneer Histories,* London, 1940; New York, 1941) is a very good introduction to gold rushes throughout the world and has three highly competent chapters on North America. Glenn C. Quiett's *Pay Dirt, a Panorama of American Gold-Rushes* (New York, 1936) stresses the dramatic.

Thomas A. Rickard's *A History of American Mining* (*A.I.M.E. Series,* New York and London, 1932) is really a series of separate essays, written at widely varying times, about particular episodes. Rickard was the most noted editor of mining trade journals of his day. See also his *Man and Metals, A History of Mining in Relation to the Development of Civilization* (2 vols., New York and London, 1932) and *The Romance of Mining* (Toronto, 1945). A most helpful guidebook is Muriel S. Wolle's *The Bonanza Trail: Ghost Towns and Mining Camps of the West* (Bloomington, 1953). Mrs. Wolle, a teacher of fine arts, has drawn a picture of each town, written up its history and anecdotes, and supplied generalized maps, an introductory essay, and a glossary of mining terms. One aspect of Western mining has been well studied by Clark C. Spence, *British Investments and the American Mining Frontier, 1860–1901* (Ithaca, 1958), and the same subject has been treated by both W. Turrentine Jackson and Roger V. Clements in a series of articles scattered through historical journals (References to some of these articles will be found in the footnotes and the bibliography below).

Brief but good select bibliographies of the history of the mining West are given in Oscar Handlin and others, *Harvard Guide to American History* (Cambridge, 1954), pp. 368–369, 411–412, and in Billington, *Westward Expansion,* 2d ed., pp. 835–838.

More than fifty years ago Walter R. Crane made a devoted but awkward attempt to exploit what was then a rapidly growing body of technological writing about mining. By clipping and pasting together long excerpts from technical journals, he compiled a massive volume that has been little used because it is so ill-organized, difficult to read, and uneven in historical accuracy: *Gold and Silver, Comprising an Economic History of Mining in the United States, the Geographical and Geological Occurrence of the Precious Metals, with their Mineralogical Associations* . . . (New York, 1908). The raw materials that went into this book were included in Crane's elaborate *Index of Mining Engineering Literature, Comprising an Index of Mining, Metallurgical, Civil, Mechanical, Electrical and Chemical Engineering Subjects as Related to Mining Engineering* (2 vols., New York, 1909–1912).

Of fundamental importance for this study has been the series of reports published by the United States mining commissioners and covering the years 1866–1875, inclusive. For an additional discussion of this series see the "Note on Statistics" that precedes this bibliography. There were ten of these annual reports, the first two prepared by J. Ross Browne and James W. Taylor, the others by Rossiter W. Raymond. Titles vary. Simultaneous with these annual volumes were notable reports by the great government-subsidized expeditions to study the West. For this study the most significant was James D. Hague's large volume, *Mining Industry,* which was published as volume III of Clarence King's *United States Geological Exploration of the Fortieth Parallel* (7 vols. plus atlas, Washington, 1870–1880). Where these expeditions left off, the United States Geological Survey began (in 1879, under King's leadership). References to the survey's many useful reports appear in the appropriate sections below. Access to the vast body of technical literature published by federal, state, and private agencies may be gained by using the massive bibliographies and indexes that the United States Geological Survey has long sponsored: John M. Nickles, *Geologic Literature on North America, 1785–1918* (U.S. Geological Survey, "Bulletin" nos. 746, 747, 2 vols., Washington, 1922, 1924); the same author's *Bibliography of North American Geology, 1919–1928* (U.S. Geological Survey, "Bulletin" no. 823, Washington, 1931); Emma M. Thom, *Bibliography of North American Geology, 1929–1939* (U.S. Geological Survey, "Bulletin" no. 937, Washington, 1944); Ruth R. King, Emma M. Thom, and others, *Bibliography of North American Geology, 1940–1949* (U.S. Geological Survey,

"Bulletin" no. 1049, 2 vols., Washington, 1957); and annual volumes since that date.

As a part of the census of 1880 Clarence King was asked to supervise the compilation of a special volume on gold and silver. He obtained the services of some of the ablest men who were then beginning work with the new United States Geological Survey: Samuel F. Emmons and George F. Becker, *Statistics and Technology of the Precious Metals* (Clarence King, director of special volume, *Tenth Census*, 1880, XIII, Washington, 1885).

The *Mining and Scientific Press*, a trade journal published at San Francisco from 1860 to 1922, had a unique position in Western mining circles and is today a repository of all kinds of information essential to the historian. Its title varied at times.

In using these technical materials it is important to start with an understanding of the natural environment. Two good studies of the physiography of Western America are: Wallace W. Atwood, *The Physiographic Provinces of North America* (Boston, 1940); and Nevin M. Fenneman, *Physiography of Western United States* (New York, 1931). Descriptions of many mining districts are given in a classic textbook by a great geologist, Waldemar Lindgren, *Mineral Deposits* (4th ed., New York, 1933); and in the more recent volume by Alan M. Bateman, *Economic Mineral Deposits* (2d ed., New York, 1950). Two important ventures into mapping and classifying the mining areas are James M. Hill's *The Mining Districts of the Western United States* (U.S. Geological Survey, "Bulletin" no. 507, Washington, 1912), and C. Wayne Burnham's *Metallogenic Provinces of the Southwestern United States and Northern Mexico* (State Bureau of Mines and Mineral Resources, New Mexico Institute of Mining and Technology, "Bulletin" no. 65, Socorro, N. Mex., 1959).

California, 1848–1858

Almost as much has been written about the Gold Rush as about Abraham Lincoln. A good select guide to the literature on the subject is Carl I. Wheat's *Books of the California Gold Rush* (San Francisco, 1949). A good general survey is John W. Caughey's *Gold is the Cornerstone* (Berkeley and Los Angeles, 1948). Oscar Lewis has studied the maritime phase in *Sea Routes to the Gold Fields: The Migration by Water to California in 1849–1852* (New York, 1949); but see also the older study by Octavius T. Howe, *Argonauts of '49: History and Adventures of the Emigrant Companies from Massachusetts, 1849–1850* (Cambridge, Mass., 1923). The overland route has been best examined by two highly competent historians who were nominally editing overland diaries: David M. Potter, ed., *Trial to California. The Overland Journal of Vincent Geiger and Wakeman Bryarly* (New Haven, 1945); and Dale L. Morgan, ed., *The Overland Diary of James Pritchard from Kentucky to California in 1849* (Denver, 1959).

The present writer has discussed the evolution of the mining industry and the life of the miner in *California Gold: The Beginning of Mining in the Far West* (Cambridge, Mass., 1947). An excellent guidebook not only to the geology but also to all physical survivals, such as buildings, is that for which Olaf P. Jenkins was the director, *Geologic Guidebook along Highway 49—*

Sierran Gold Belt, the Mother Lode Country, Centennial Edition (California State Division of Mines, "Bulletin" no. 141, San Francisco, 1948). Illustrated contemporary descriptions of mining may be found in *The Miners' Own Book, Containing Correct Illustrations and Descriptions of the Various Modes of California Mining* (San Francisco, 1858; reprinted, Rodman W. Paul, ed., San Francisco, 1949). An excellent contemporary handbook on mining and mining life is John S. Hittell's *Mining in the Pacific States of North America* (San Francisco, 1861). Contemporary travel accounts are so numerous that any selection must be arbitrary. A few of the best that have been made available by modern reprints are: E. Gould Buffum, *Six Months in the Gold Mines: From a Journal of Three Years' Residence in Upper and Lower California, 1847–1848–1849* (Philadelphia, 1850; reprinted, John W. Caughey, ed., Los Angeles, 1959); Bayard Taylor, *Eldorado, or, Adventures in the Path of Empire: Comprising a Voyage to California, via Panama; Life in San Francisco . . .* (2 vols., New York, 1850; reprinted in one volume in *Bayard Taylor's Works,* Household Edition, New York, 1882; and reprinted, Robert G. Cleland, ed., New York, 1949); J. D. Borthwick, *Three Years in California* (Edinburgh and London, 1857; reprinted as *The Gold Hunters* in Horace Kephart, ed., *Outing Adventure Library,* Oyster Bay, N. Y., 1917); and Louise A. K. S. Clappe (Dame Shirley, pseud.), *The Shirley Letters from the California Mines, 1851–1852,* Carl I. Wheat, ed. (New York, 1949).

Mrs. Clappe's letters have the especial value of being the observations of a well-educated woman who became a surprisingly understanding observer of life in two small mining camps. A woman's narrative of quite a different but equally valuable kind is Sarah E. Royce's *A Frontier Lady: Recollections of the Gold Rush and Early California,* Ralph H. Gabriel, ed. (New Haven, 1932).

Several special topics connected with mining deserve mention. Quicksilver mining, so important to gold mining, is excellently described by Henry W. Splitter in "Quicksilver at New Almaden," *Pacific Historical Review,* XXVI (February 1957), pp. 33–49. A divisive political dispute developed out of the damage done to farm land by debris washed down from the hydraulic mines. It has been studied by Robert L. Kelley in *Gold vs. Grain: The Hydraulic Mining Controversy in California's Sacramento Valley, A Chapter in the Decline of the Concept of Laissez Faire* (Glendale, 1959). See also the same author's "The Mining Debris Controversy in the Sacramento Valley," *Pacific Historical Review,* XXV (November 1956), pp. 331–346. Insight into the channels through which British money found its way into California mines is given in W. Turrentine Jackson's "Lewis Richard Price, British Mining Entrepreneur and Traveler in California," *Pacific Historical Review,* XXIX (November 1960), pp. 331–348.

Opening the Far West, 1858–1868

The most important single book is Trimble's *Mining Advance into the Inland Empire.* The present writer has discussed the subject in chapter xi of *California Gold.* Hittell's *Mining in the Pacific States* contains a great deal of useful information and comment, as does the same author's *History of the City of San Francisco and Incidentally of the State of California* (San Francisco,

1878). A stimulating modern interpretation is given in Robert G. Athearn's *High Country Empire: the High Plains and Rockies* (New York, 1960), pp. 69–98.

On the key factor of transportation, see Oscar O. Winther's *The Old Oregon Country, a History of Frontier Trade, Transportation, and Travel* (Stanford, 1950), and the same author's articles: "The Place of Transportation in the Early History of the Pacific Northwest," *Pacific Historical Review*, XI (December 1942), pp. 383–396, and "Pack Animals for Transportation in the Pacific Northwest," *Pacific Northwest Quarterly*, XXXIV (April 1943), pp. 131–146. Randall V. Mills has discussed the Columbia River route in *Stern-Wheelers up Columbia: A Century of Steamboating in the Oregon Country* (Palo Alto, 1947); and Earle K. Stewart has written on the same subject in "Steamboats on the Columbia: the Pioneer Period," *Oregon Historical Quarterly*, LI (March 1950), pp. 20–42. On steamboating on California rivers, including the Colorado, see Jerry MacMullen's *Paddle-Wheel Days in California* (Stanford, 1944). Much additional information on navigation on the Colorado is given in Godfrey Sykes, *The Colorado Delta* (American Geographical Society, "Special Publication" no. 19, Washington and New York, 1937). Donald Sage has written about the Fraser River in "Gold Rush Days on the Fraser River," *Pacific Northwest Quarterly*, XLIV (October 1953), pp. 161–165.

A good deal can be learned about trade with the Rocky Mountain region from Paul F. Sharp's excellent *Whoop-Up Country: The Canadian-American West, 1865–1885* (Minneapolis, 1955), and from Alton B. Oviatt's "Fort Benton, River Capital," in Merrill G. Burlingame and K. Ross Toole, *A History of Montana* (3 vols., New York, 1957), I, pp. 137–155.

The Comstock Lode, 1859–1880

One could fill a good-sized library with books about the Comstock Lode, but to do so would involve a great deal of repetition. Most of the writing has been based upon the material contained in a few notable contemporary books and a still smaller number of good modern ones. The essential modern reappraisal is Grant H. Smith's *The History of the Comstock Lode, 1850–1920* (University of Nevada, "Bulletin," XXXVII, no. 3, Geology and Mining Series, no. 37, Reno, 1943). Smith devotes much time to correcting Eliot Lord's excellent contemporary history, *Comstock Mining and Miners* (U.S. Geological Survey, "Monographs," IV, Washington, 1883), which has recently been reprinted with an introduction by David F. Myrick and a wealth of excellent illustrations (Berkeley, 1959). Another major contemporary history is that by William Wright (Dan De Quille, pseud.), *History of the Big Bonanza: An Authentic Account of the Discovery, History, and Working of the World Renowned Comstock Silver Lode of Nevada, including* . . . (Hartford, 1876). This was reprinted under the title *The Big Bonanza*, Oscar Lewis, ed. (New York, 1947).

A contemporary general history that contains much on mining is that edited by Myron Angel, *History of Nevada, with Illustrations and Biographical Sketches of its Prominent Men and Pioneers* (Oakland, 1881). This has been reprinted with an introduction by David F. Myrick (Berkeley, 1958).

A well-known history that draws heavily upon Eliot Lord's book is Charles H. Shinn's *The Story of the Mine, as Illustrated by the Great Comstock Lode of Nevada* (Ripley Hitchcock, ed., *The Story of the West Series*, New York, 1896).

Of contemporary descriptive accounts, Mark Twain's *Roughing It* (Hartford, 1872) is in a class by itself. It has been reprinted, with the present writer as editor, as a Rinehart Edition (New York, 1953). A similar but less successful narrative by J. Ross Browne was published originally in two separate units: *Crusoe's Island: a Ramble in the Footsteps of Alexander Selkirk. With Sketches of Adventure in California and Washoe* (New York, 1864); and *Adventures in the Apache Country: A Tour through Arizona and Sonora, with Notes on the Silver Regions of Nevada* (New York, 1869). Recently the two pieces have been republished in a single volume, with alien material excluded, as *A Peep at Washoe and Washoe Revisited* (Balboa Island, California, 1959).

A narrative that is worth mentioning chiefly because it is one of the few by a woman is Mary M. Mathews' *Ten Years in Nevada: or, Life on the Pacific Coast* (Buffalo, 1880). Mrs. Mathews must have been a very difficult woman. A less censorious female sketch is Louise M. Palmer's "How We Live in Nevada," *Overland Monthly, II* (May 1869), pp. 457–462.

Two technical papers of importance are Almon D. Hodges, Jr., "Amalgamation at the Comstock Lode, Nevada: A Historical Sketch of Milling Operations at Washoe, and an Account of the Treatment of Tailings at the Lyon Mill, Dayton," American Institute of Mining Engineers, *Transactions*, XIX (1890–1891), pp. 195–231; and Max Crowell's mimeographed *A Technical Review of Early Comstock Mining Methods* (W.P.A. Project, Reno, 1941). The basic geological study is George F. Becker's *Geology of the Comstock Lode and the Washoe District* (U.S. Geological Survey, "Monographs," III, Washington, 1882).

Several biographies and autobiographies offer important insights. Especially significant is Oscar Lewis's *Silver Kings, the Lives and Times of Mackay, Fair, Flood, and O'Brien, Lords of the Nevada Comstock Lode* (New York, 1947). Ethel Manter has covered some of the same ground in *Rocket of the Comstock: The Story of John William Mackay* (Caldwell, Idaho, 1950). Cecil G. Tilton has made a careful analysis of Ralston's career in *William Chapman Ralston, Courageous Builder* (Boston, 1935); while George D. Lyman has made an absorbing drama out of the same episodes in *Ralston's Ring: California Plunders the Comstock Lode* (New York, 1937). William M. Stewart's colorful but often unreliable autobiography has been published as *Reminiscences of Senator William M. Stewart of Nevada*, George R. Brown, ed. (New York and Washington, 1908). See also Effie M. Mack, "William Morris Stewart, Empire Builder, 1827–1909," American Historical Association, Pacific Coast Branch, *Proceedings*, 1930, pp. 185–192.

A Study in Contrast: California and Nevada, 1859–1880

Materials for this topic are thin and badly scattered. Much factual information can be found in the several great encyclopedic volumes compiled during this era: John S. Hittell, *The Resources of California, Comprising the Society,*

Climate, Salubrity, Scenery, Commerce and Industry of the State (6th ed., San Francisco, 1874); the same author's *The Commerce and Industries of the Pacific Coast of North America; Comprising the Rise, Progress, Products, Present Condition* . . . (San Francisco, 1882); and Titus F. Cronise's *The Natural Wealth of California, Comprising Early History; Geography, Topography,* . . . *Mines and Mining Processes* . . . (San Francisco, 1868).

The present writer has studied California mining after 1860 in chapters xiv–xviii of *California Gold.* Richard G. Lillard has provided a suggestive and informative introduction to Nevada mining in *Desert Challenge: An Interpretation of Nevada* (New York, 1942), pp. 170–306.

Myron Angel's *History of Nevada* is an essential source for information about individual Nevada towns. It should be used in conjunction with Francis C. Lincoln's *Mining Districts and Mineral Resources of Nevada* (Reno, 1923) and Henry G. Ferguson's *The Mining Districts of Nevada* (University of Nevada, "Bulletin," XXXVIII, no. 4, Geology and Mining Series no. 40, Reno, 1944). Very helpful is Bernard York's *The Geology of Nevada Ore Deposits* (University of Nevada, "Bulletin," XXXVIII, no. 4, Geology and Mining Series, no. 40, Reno, 1944). Ferguson's and York's monographs were published as twin studies and complement each other nicely.

Russell R. Elliott has made a highly competent sampling of Nevada local history in "The Early History of White Pine County, Nevada, 1865–1887," *Pacific Northwest Quarterly,* XXX (April 1939), pp. 145–168. W. Turrentine Jackson has prepared a book-length manuscript on the same subject. See also the reminiscences of B. F. Miller, "Nevada in the Making, Being Pioneer Stories of White Pine County and Elsewhere," Nevada State Historical Society, "Papers," IV (1923–1924), pp. 255–474.

Geological monographs on particular localities include: Clarence A. Logan, *Mother Lode Gold Belt of California* (California State Division of Mines, "Bulletin," no. 108, Sacramento, 1934); William D. Johnston, Jr., *The Gold Quartz Veins of Grass Valley, California* (U.S. Geological Survey, "Professional Paper," no. 194, Washington, 1940); Waldemar Lindgren, *The Tertiary Gravels of the Sierra Nevada of California* (U.S. Geological Survey, "Professional Paper," no. 73, Washington, 1911); Joseph S. Curtis, *Silver-Lead Deposits of Eureka, Nevada* (U.S. Geological Survey, "Monographs," VII, Washington, 1884); Lewis G. Westgate and Adolph Knopf, *Geology and Ore Deposits of the Pioche District, Nevada* (U.S. Geological Survey, "Professional Paper," no. 171, Washington, 1932); and Frederick L. Ransome, *Notes on Some Mining Districts in Humboldt County, Nevada* (U.S. Geological Survey, "Bulletin," no. 414, Washington, 1909).

Colorado, 1859–1880

Perhaps the best way to start a study of Colorado is to consult Virginia L. Wilcox's *Colorado: A Selected Bibliography of Its Literature 1858–1952* (Denver, 1954). Percy S. Fritz has supplied a convenient modern history that has much on mining: *Colorado, the Centennial State* (New York, 1941). An excellent local history is that edited by Jerome C. Smiley, *History of Denver, with*

Outlines of the Earlier History of the Rocky Mountain Country (Denver, 1901).

Two very good contemporary books studied the mines in detail: Ovando J. Hollister, *The Mines of Colorado* (Springfield, Mass., 1867); and Frank Fossett, *Colorado, its Gold and Silver Mines, Farms and Stock Ranges, and Health and Pleasure Resorts. Tourist's Guide to the Rocky Mountains* (New York, 1879). The information given in these contemporary handbooks may be checked against Charles W. Henderson, *Mining in Colorado. A History of Discovery, Development and Production* (U.S. Geological Survey, "Professional Paper" no. 138, Washington, 1926). See also Muriel S. Wolle, *Stampede to Timberline: the Ghost Towns and Mining Camps of Colorado* (Boulder, 1949).

The present writer has tried to evaluate Colorado mining in "Colorado as a Pioneer of Science in the Mining West," *Mississippi Valley Historical Review*, XLVII (June 1960), pp. 34–50. Since Colorado is blessed with an energetic state historical society, quantities of useful local material have been collected for publication in the *Colorado Magazine*. LeRoy R. Hafen has been associated with much of this notable effort. A few of the many good articles in it include: C. H. Hanington, "Early Days of Central City," XIX (January 1942), pp. 3–14, and "Smelting in Colorado," XXIII (March 1946), pp. 80–84; Lynn I. Perrigo, "The Cornish Miners of Early Gilpin County," XIV (May 1937), pp. 92–101; J. T. Thompson, "Cousin Jack Stories," XXXV (July 1958), pp. 187–192; Joseph Kingsbury, "The Pike's Peak Rush, 1859," IV (January 1927), pp. 1–6; Clark C. Spence, "The British and Colorado Mining Bureau," XXXIII (April 1956), pp. 81–92, and "Colorado's Terrible Mine: A Study in British Investment," XXXIV (January 1957), pp. 48–61.

Professor Spence has used again some of this Colorado material in his excellent monograph, *British Investments and the American Mining Frontier*.

Contemporary directories of Colorado mines are numerous. See especially Thomas B. Corbett, comp., *The Colorado Directory of Mines, Containing a Description of the Mines and Mills, and the Mining and Milling Corporations of Colorado . . .* (Denver, 1879); and Robert A. Corregan and David F. Lingane, comps., *Colorado Mining Directory; Containing an Accurate Description of the Mines, Mining Properties and Mills, and . . .* (Denver, 1883).

Material descriptive of Leadville is plentiful. Frank Fossett's book is very good on this subject. See also Carlyle C. Davis, *Olden Times in Colorado* (Los Angeles, 1916); Sewell Thomas, *Silhouettes of Charles S. Thomas, Colorado Governor and United States Senator* (Caldwell, Ida., 1959); and Lewis A. Kent, *Leadville: The City, Mines and Bullion Product, Personal Histories of Prominent Citizens . . .* (Denver, 1880). Don L. and Jean H. Griswold have written a detailed modern account in *The Carbonate Camp Called Leadville* (Denver, 1951).

A few of the more important geological reports on individual localities include: Samuel F. Emmons, *Geology and Mining Industry of Leadville, Colorado* (U.S. Geological Survey, "Monographs," XII, Washington, 1886); Whitman Cross and Richard A. F. Penrose, Jr., "Geology and Mining Industries of the Cripple Creek District, Colorado," U.S. Geological Survey, *Sixteenth Annual Report, 1894–1895,* part II (Washington, 1895), pp. 1–209; Josiah E.

Spurr, *Geology of the Aspen Mining District, Colorado* (U.S. Geological Survey, "Monographs," XXXI, Washington, 1898); William H. Emmons and Esper S. Larsen, *A Preliminary Report on the Geology and Ore Deposits of Creede, Colorado* (U.S. Geological Survey, "Bulletin," no. 530, Washington, 1913); and Edson S. Bastin and James M. Hill, *Economic Geology of Gilpin County and Adjacent Parts of Clear Creek and Boulder Counties, Colorado* (U.S. Geological Survey, "Professional Paper, "no. 94, Washington, 1917).

Northwest and Southwest, 1860–1880

Because of the great geographical scope of this topic, material relating to it is scattered through a large number of books and articles.

Starting with the Northwest, a good place to begin is Herman J. Deutsch's essay, in two installments, "Geographic Setting for the Recent History of the Inland Empire," *Pacific Northwest Quarterly*, XLIX (October 1958), pp. 150–161, and L (January 1959), pp. 14–25. A very good general history of the whole area is Dorothy O. Johansen and Charles M. Gates, *Empire of the Columbia: A History of the Pacific Northwest* (New York, 1957). An alternative general history that is particularly good on transportation is Oscar O. Winther's *The Great Northwest, a History* (New York, 1947). Both of these books devote a section to mining. So does Harold E. Briggs in *Frontiers of the Northwest: A History of the Upper Missouri Valley* (New York, 1940). But Trimble's *Mining Advance into the Inland Empire* is the pioneering historical study of the region to which all subsequent scholars owe much.

Two articles that are pertinent to the whole Northwest are: Leslie M. Scott, "The Pioneer Stimulus of Gold," *Oregon Historical Quarterly*, XVIII (September 1917), pp. 147–166; and W. Turrentine Jackson, "British Capital in Northwest Mines," *Pacific Northwest Quarterly*, XLVII (July 1956), pp. 75–85.

Turning to individual Northwestern states, Merrill D. Beal and Merle W. Wells have written an excellent *History of Idaho* (3 vols., New York, 1959), which includes good chapters on mining life. August C. Bolino has discussed "The Role of Mining in the Economic Development of Idaho Territory," *Oregon Historical Quarterly*, LIX (June 1958), pp. 116–151. Robert L. Romig has given a good picture of local troubles in "Stamp Mills in Trouble," *Pacific Northwest Quarterly*, XLIV (October 1953), pp. 166–176. Joseph K. Howard has written an illuminating interpretation on "The Coeur d'Alene: Vulnerable Valley," in *Rocky Mountain Cities*, Ray B. West, Jr., ed. (New York, 1949), pp. 55–77.

Good reminiscent accounts by pioneers tell a great deal about mining life in Idaho: Thomas Donaldson, *Idaho of Yesterday*. Thomas B. Donaldson, ed. (Caldwell, Ida., 1941); John Hailey, *The History of Idaho* (Boise, 1910); William J. McConnell, *Early History of Idaho, by W. J. McConnell, who was Present and Cognizant of the Events Narrated* (Caldwell, Ida., 1913); and W. A. Goulder, *Reminiscences. Incidents in the Life of a Pioneer in Oregon and Idaho* (Boise, 1909).

Of the numerous pamphlets published by the state, particular mention should be made of W. W. Staley, *Gold in Idaho* (Idaho Bureau of Mines and Geology, "Pamphlet," no. 68, Moscow, Ida., 1946).

Montana, like Idaho, has been the subject of some very good recent historical writing. The best general history is that by Merrill G. Burlingame and K. Ross Toole, *A History of Montana* (3 vols., New York, 1957). But see also Merrill G. Burlingame, *The Montana Frontier* (Helena, 1942). See also K. Ross Toole's really notable interpretation, *Montana: An Uncommon Land* (Norman, Okla., 1959). Toole's predecessor as a free-ranging critic was Joseph K. Howard, *Montana: High, Wide, and Handsome* (New Haven, 1943). Toole has made a further contribution in two illuminating articles in the *Pacific Northwest Quarterly:* "When Big Money Came to Butte," XLIV (January 1953), pp. 23–29, and "The Anaconda Copper Mining Company: A Price War and a Copper Corner," XLI (October 1950), pp. 312–329. The information about Butte in these two articles has been supplemented recently by a sketch of one of the principal figures by James High, "William Andrews Clark, Westerner: an Interpretative Vignette," *Arizona and the West,* II (Autumn, 1960), pp. 245–264.

There is also an older history of Butte and copper, but it contributes little: Robert G. Raymer, *A History of Copper Mining in Montana* (Chicago and New York, 1930).

Important for an understanding of the silver and copper of Butte is also Walter H. Weed's *Geology and Ore Deposits of the Butte District, Montana* (U.S. Geological Survey, "Professional Paper," no. 74, Washington, 1912).

Oregon's mining history is best approached by way of several articles that together suggest the principal episodes: Albert Burch, "Development of Metal Mining in Oregon," *Oregon Historical Quarterly,* XLIII (June 1941), pp. 105–128; Wallace D. Farnham, "The Development of an Oregon County, 1852–1890: Mines, Farms, and a Railroad," *Pacific Historical Review,* XXV (February 1956), pp. 29–45; Loretta Louis, "History of Ruby City: the Life and Death of a Mining Town," *Pacific Northwest Quarterly,* XXXII (January 1941), pp. 61–78; and Clark G. Spence, "British Investment and Oregon Mining, 1860–1900," *Oregon Historical Quarterly,* LVIII (June 1957), pp. 101–112. See also *The Oregonian's Handbook of the Pacific Northwest* (Portland, 1894).

Washington's mining districts are described in George A. Bethune's *Mines and Minerals of Washington: Annual Report of First State Geologist* (Olympia, 1891), and Marshall T. Huntting, *Gold In Washington* (Washington State Division of Mines and Geology, "Bulletin," no. 42, Olympia, 1955).

Leonard J. Arrington has written an excellent analysis of Mormon Utah: *Great Basin Kingdom: An Economic History of the Latter-day Saints* (Cambridge, Mass., 1958). His book should be read in conjunction with a geological and historical study by Bert S. Butler, Gerald F. Loughlin, Victor C. Heikes, and others, *The Ore Deposits of Utah* (U.S. Geological Survey, "Professional Paper," no. 111, Washington, 1920). A detailed contemporary description of "The Mines of Utah" is printed as chapter LVII of T. B. H. Stenhouse's *The Rocky Mountain Saints: a Full and Complete History of the Mormons, . . . including . . . the Development of the Great Mineral Wealth of the Territory* (New York, 1873). Mark A. Pendleton recalled his boyhood in a Utah mining town in "Memories of Silver Reef," *Utah Historical Quarterly*, III (October 1930), pp. 99–118. The Emma mine is discussed in both Clark Spence's *British Investments and the American Mining Frontier*, and W. Turrentine Jackson's "The Infamous Emma Mine: A British Interest in the Little Cottonwood District, Utah Territory," *Utah Historical Quarterly*, XXIII (October 1955), pp. 339–362.

In rather disorganized fashion, Fayette A. Jones performed the very useful service of drawing together the scraps of information about New Mexico's early mines: *New Mexico Mines and Minerals . . . Being an Epitome of the Early Mining History and Resources of New Mexican Mines . . .* (Santa Fe, 1904). A very important study is that by Waldemar Lindgren, Louis C. Graton, and Charles H. Gordon, *The Ore Deposits of New Mexico* (U.S. Geological Survey, "Professional Paper," no. 68, Washington, 1910). A detailed chronology of mining is included in Stuart A. Northrop's *Minerals of New Mexico* (rev. ed., Albuquerque, 1959). Reminiscences of Silver City are given in James K. Hastings, "A Boy's Eye View of the Old Southwest," *New Mexico Historical Review*, XXVI (October 1951), pp. 287–301. Two contemporary documents are: Richard E. Owen and E. T. Cox, *Report on the Mines of New Mexico* (Washington, 1865), and R. S. Allen, "Pinos Altos, New Mexico," *New Mexico Historical Review*, XXII (October 1948), pp. 302–332 (a reprint of an 1889 pamphlet).

Arizona's struggle to develop mining is described by Rufus K. Wyllys in his general history, *Arizona: The History of a Frontier State* (Phoenix, 1950). See also an almost contemporary history for a discussion of mining in some detail: *History of Arizona Territory, Showing its Resources and Advantages; with Illustrations Descriptive of its Scenery, Residences, Farms, Mines, Mills* (San Francisco, 1884), pp. 189–206. A contemporary handbook does the same thing, but with no perspective and an excess of detail: Richard J. Hinton, *The Hand-Book to Arizona: its Resources, History, Towns, Mines, Ruins and Scenery* (San Francisco, 1878). Very interesting are Arthur L. Walker's "Recollections of Early Day Mining in Arizona," *Arizona Historical Review*, VI (April 1935), pp. 14–23. The early years are described by Sylvester Mowry, *Arizona and Sonora: the Geography, History, and Resources of the Silver Region of North America* (3d ed., New York, 1864); and Daniel E. Conner, *Joseph Reddeford Walker and the Arizona Adventure*, Donald J. Berthrong and Odessa Davenport, eds. (Norman, Okla., 1956). Tombstone is presented in colorful fashion by John M. Myers, *The Last Chance. Tombstone's Early Years* (New York, 1950); and by John P. Clum, "It All Happened in Tombstone," *Arizona Historical Review*, II (October 1929), pp. 46–72. The latter article was reprinted in *Arizona and the West*, I (August 1959), pp. 232–247. A helpful general picture is given by Frank C. Lockwood in *Pioneer Days in Arizona, from the Spanish Occupation to Statehood* (New York, 1932). Of the several technical papers, see especially Morris J. Elsing and Robert E. S. Heineman, *Arizona Metal Production* (Arizona Bureau of Mines, Economic Series, no. 19, University of Arizona, "Bulletin," VII, no. 2, Tucson, 1936).

First Attempts at Self-government

The literature dealing with this subject is voluminous. No more can be attempted here than to indicate a few of the more important books and articles.

On territorial government, the best work is Earl S. Pomeroy's *The Territories and the United States, 1861–1890: Studies in Colonial Administration* (Philadelphia, 1947). There have been many studies of individual governments, such as Clark C. Spence's "The Territorial Officers of Montana, 1864–1889," *Pacific Historical Review*, XXX (May 1961), pp. 123–136; and Merle W. Wells's "Territorial Government in the Inland Empire," *Pacific Northwest Quarterly*, XLIV (April 1953), pp. 8–87. The Federal statutes are conveniently compiled in *Organic Acts for the Territories of the United States with Notes Thereon, Compiled from Statutes at Large of the United States; also, Appendixes . . .* , 56th Cong., 1st Sess., S. Doc. No. 148 (1900).

The classic book on self-government by the miners is Charles H. Shinn's *Mining Camps, a Study in American Frontier Government* (New York, 1885), reprinted, intro. Joseph H. Jackson, New York, 1948. See also Shinn's *Land Laws of Mining Districts* (Johns Hopkins University, *Studies in Historical and Political Science*, 2d ser., II, no. 12, Baltimore, 1884). Shinn has been much criticized in recent years because of his undiscriminating enthusiasm for self-constituted local government and because of his naïve faith in the inherent capacity of the Germanic race for ruling themselves, but if read critically his books still form an illuminating and even exciting introduction to the subject. Since Shinn's acquaintance was largely with the Pacific Coast, it is well to read also Thomas M. Marshall's "The Miners' Laws of Colorado," *American Historical Review*, XXV (April 1920), pp. 426–439, and the accompanying documents that Marshall edited as *Early Records of Gilpin County, Colorado, 1859–1861* (University of Colorado, *Historical Collections*, II, Boulder, Colo., 1920). A comparable case-study of Arizona, which shows how the original locators tried to use the local codes to monopolize all promising ground, is Harwood Hinton's excellent "Frontier Speculation: A Study of the Walker Mining District," *Pacific Historical Review*, XXIX (August 1960), pp. 245–255.

On the question of law and order, there are a few contemporary classics and a vast number of subsequent works. The most important contemporary book is Thomas J. Dimsdale, *The Vigilantes of Montana, or Popular Justice in the Rocky Mountains. Being a Correct and Impartial Narrative of the Chase, Trial, Capture and Execution of Henry Plummer's Road Agent Band, together with . . .* (Virginia City, Mont., 1866), reprinted many times at Virginia City, Helena, and Butte, Montana, and recently at Norman, Okla., 1953. Nathaniel P. Langford, who was a participant, has covered much of the same ground in his *Vigilante Days and Ways, The Pioneers of the Rockies: The Makers and Making of Montana, Idaho, Oregon, Washington, and Wyoming* (2 vols., Boston, 1890).

Under the title of *Popular Tribunals*, Bancroft devoted two whole volumes of his *Works* (XXXVI and XXXVII) to the subject. Theodore H. Hittell likewise spent a full volume (III) on the subject in his *History of California* (4 vols., San Francisco, 1885–1897). Josiah Royce was preoccupied with this question throughout his *California, from the Conquest in 1846 to the Second Vigilance Committee in San Francisco: A study of American Character* (Horace E. Scudder, ed., *American Commonwealths*, Boston and New York, 1886), reprinted, Robert G. Cleland, ed., New York, 1948.

Modern studies include: Mary F. Williams, *History of the San Francisco Committee of Vigilance of 1851: A Study of Social Control on the California Frontier in the Days of the Gold Rush* (Berkeley, 1921); James A. B. Scherer, *"The Lion of the Vigilantes": William T. Coleman and the Life of Old San Francisco* (Indianapolis, 1939); Lynn I. Perrigo, "Law and Order in Early Colorado Camps," *Mississippi Valley Historical Review*, XXVIII (June 1941), pp. 41–62; Wayne Gard, *Frontier Justice* (Norman, Okla., 1949); and George D. Hendricks, *The Bad Man of the West* (rev. ed., San Antonio, 1959).

In recent years a more skeptical attitude has characterized some of the writing about the handling of early law and order. The present writer has compared experience in the United States with that in Britain's overseas possessions in " 'Old Californians' in British Gold Fields," *Huntington Library Quarterly*, XVII (February 1954), pp. 161–172. In reaction against modern-day vigilanteism, John W. Caughey has written critically in "Their Majesties the Mob: Vigilantes Past and Present," *Pacific Historical Review*, XXVI (August 1957), pp. 217–234, reprinted with an extensive set of documents as *Their Majesties, the Mob* (Chicago, 1960). John W. Smurr has similarly been led to "Afterthoughts on the Vigilantes," *Montana, the Magazine of Western History*, VIII (April 1958), pp. 8–20.

On mining law there are some notable treatises written by lawyers for lawyers. The pioneer, which dealt primarily with California, was Gregory Yale, *Legal Titles to Mining Claims and Water Rights, in California, under the Mining Law of Congress, of July, 1866* (San Francisco, 1867). A comparable Colorado study was Robert S. Morrison's *Mining Rights in Colorado: Lode and Placer Claims, Possessory and Patented, from the District Organizations to the Present Time* (4th ed., Denver, 1880). Subsequently the scope of Morrison's manual was broadened and it was reissued as *Mining Rights on the Public Domain*, with other attorneys as coauthors. The classic treatise has long been Curtis H. Lindley, *A Treatise on the American Law Relating to Mines and Mineral Lands within the Public Land States and Territories and Governing the Acquisition and Enjoyment of Mining Rights in Lands of the Public Domain* (2 vols., San Francisco, 1897; expanded into three volumes in later editions).

In regard to the first federal statute, Beulah Hershiser has done a very careful piece of research in "The Influence of Nevada on the National Mining Legislation of 1866," *Nevada Historical Society, Third Biennial Report, 1911–1912*, pp. 127–167; and Joseph Ellison has made a parallel study in "The Mineral Land Question in California, 1848–1866," *Southwestern Historical Quarterly*, XXX (July 1926), pp. 34–55, and in his *California and the Nation, 1850–1869, A Study of the Relations of a Frontier Community with the Federal Government* (University of California, *Publications in History*, XVI, Berkeley, 1927), pp. 54–78.

Culmination in the Black Hills

Several modern works tell the story. Harold E. Briggs wrote of it in "The Settlement and Economic Development of the Territory of Dakota," *South Dakota Historical Review*, I (April 1936), pp. 151–166. Hyman Palais focused more directly on the Black Hills in "A Survey of Early Black Hills History," *The Black Hills Engineer*, XXVII (April 1941), as did Cleophas C. O'Harra, "Custer's Black Hills Expedition of 1874" and "The Discovery of Gold in the Black Hills," *The Black Hills Engineer*, XVII (November 1929). These were special numbers of *The Black Hills Engineer*, devoted entirely to the articles indicated. Much historical material was presented in Joseph P. Connolly and Cleophas C. O'Harra, *The Mineral Wealth of the Black Hills* (South Dakota School of Mines, "Bulletin," no. 16, Rapid City, S. Dak., 1929). Useful but not free from factual errors is the chapter on the Black Hills in Howard R. Lamar's *Dakota Territory, 1861–1889: A Study of Frontier Politics* (Yale Historical Publications, "Miscellany" no. 64, New Haven, 1956).

Contemporaries wrote some good accounts that are part history, part reminiscence. All kinds of useful information may be found in Annie D. Tallent, *The Black Hills; or, the Last Hunting Ground of the Dacotahs: A Complete History of the Black Hills of Dakota from their First Invasion in 1874 to the Present, Comprising . . .* (St. Louis, 1899). A similar comment could be made concerning the curious assortment of materials collected by Jesse Brown and A.M. Willard, *The Black Hills Trails. A History of the Struggles of the Pioneers in the Winning of the Black Hills*, John T. Milek, ed. (Rapid City, S. Dak., 1924). A newspaperman's recollections have been published as Richard B. Hughes, *Pioneer Years in the Black Hills*, Agnes W. Spring, ed. (Glendale, 1957). A lady who grew up in Deadwood has written a colorful story in Estelline Bennett, *Old Deadwood Days* (New York, 1928).

The county in which Deadwood, Lead, and the other chief mining towns are located has had its history recorded in a very useful recent volume, Mildred Fielder ed., *Lawrence County, for the Dakota Territory Centennial* (Lead, S. Dak., 1960). James A. Noble has given a clear picture of the geology of the great Homestake Mine's deposits in "Ore Mineralization in the Homestake Gold Mine, Lead, South Dakota," *Bulletin of the Geological Society of America*, LX (March 1950), pp. 221–252. An introductory sketch of the mine itself is given in *The Homestake Story, a South Dakota Enterprise* (5th ed., n.p., 1960).

Addendum

While this book has been in press, several publications of special significance have appeared: Doyce B. Nunis, Jr., has edited a remarkable account of the Northwestern mines, *The Golden Frontier, The Recollections of Herman Francis Reinhart, 1851–1869* (Austin, 1962); Frank C. Robertson and Beth Kay Harris have written *Boom Towns of the Great Basin* (Denver, 1962); John E. Baur has published "Early Days and California Years of John Percival Jones, 1849–1867," *Southern California Quarterly*, XLIV (June 1962), pp. 97–131; and Merle W. Wells has prepared *Rush to Idaho* (Idaho Bureau of Mines and Geology, "Bulletin," no. 19, Moscow, Ida., n.d.).

Breaking and Building Communities

Readers curious about the social life of the mining frontier should begin by consulting Rodman Paul's bibliographical essays in this volume. Sources he cites on mining regions and mining towns often contain social descriptions. Certainly a fruitful work is Paul's earlier work, the splendid *California Gold: The Beginning of Mining in the Far West* (Cambridge, 1947). The question of community has been discussed masterfully in a context much broader than that of mining towns in Robert V. Hine, *Community on the American Frontier: Separate but Not Alone* (Norman, 1980). Although not addressed directly as such, community making is also a major theme in most books dealing with the social history of mining towns. Some of the most revealing of these will be mentioned below.

There is a large anthropological literature on the many tribes directly affected by mining rushes. Three examples from California will give the reader a taste: Stephen Powers, *Tribes of California* (Berkeley, 1977; originally published among *Contributions to North American Ethnology* by the U.S. Geographical and Geological Survey, 1877), Robert F. Heizer and Albert B. Elsasser, *The Natural World of the California Indians* (Berkeley, 1980) and Malcolm Margolin, ed., *The Way We Lived: California Indian Reminiscences, Stories and Songs* (Berkeley, 1981). Historians can fruitfully apply such sources to help them in reconstructing the history of Indians in mining regions. A few examples are James J. Rawls, *Indians of California: The Changing Image* (Norman, 1984), James L. Haley, *Apaches: A History and Culture Portrait* (Norman, 1981), John H. Moore, *The Cheyenne Nation: A Social and Demographic History* (Lincoln, 1987), and Alvin M. Josephy, Jr., *The Nez Perce Indians and the Opening of the Northwest* (New Haven, 1965).

Because of the especially devastating impact of the gold rush on California native peoples, historians have given that region unusual attention. Among the basic works are Rawls, *Indians of California* (cited above), Sherburne Cook, *The Conflict Between the California Indians and White Civilization* (Berkeley, 1976), Albert L. Hurtado, *Indian Survival on the California Frontier* (New Haven, 1988), George Harwood Phillips, *Indians and Intruders in Central California, 1879–1849* (Norman, 1993) and by the same author, *Indians and Indian Agents: The Origins of the Reservation System in California, 1849–1842,* and two collections of documents, Robert F. Heizer, ed., *The Destruction of California Indians* (Santa Barbara, 1974) and Clifford E. Trafzer and Joel R. Hyer, eds., *Exterminate Them!* (East Lansing, 1999).

There have been several excellent recent works on the social history of the mining frontier. The sesquicentennial of the California rush inspired two of the best: Malcolm J. Rohrbough, *Days of Gold: The California Gold Rush and the American Nation* (Berkeley, 1997) and J. S. Holliday, *Rush for Riches: Gold Fever and the Making of California* (Berkeley, 1999). Holliday's earlier work, *The World Rushed In: An Eyewitness Account of a Nation Heading West* (New York, 1981), employs the extraordinary diary of the New Yorker William Swain, interspersed with observations from other forty-niners, to provide a superb composite portrait of the great rush. Paula Mitchell Marks takes a broader look at mining rushes across the West, including Alaska, in *Precious Dust: The American Gold Rush Era, 1848–1900* (New York, 1994). Analytical and provocative, Susan Johnson's *Roaring Camp: The Social World of the*

California Gold Rush (New York, 2000) stresses the fluidity of gender and ethnic relations and the tensions that resulted. Duane Smith's *Rocky Mountain Mining Camps: The Urban Frontier* (Bloomington, 1967) teaches us plenty about a region far less studied than the Pacific coast, and Ronald M. James, *The Roar and the Silence: A History of Virginia City and the Comstock Lode* (Reno, 1998) takes a fresh look at one of the most famous and revealing western boomtowns.

Students interested in pursuing particular aspects of the rushes similarly have a smorgasbord of choices. Ralph Mann's *After the Gold Rush: Society in Grass Valley and Nevada City, California, 1849–1870* (Stanford, 1982) is the best on the changing demography of a camp. Joann Levy, *They Saw the Elephant: Women in the California Gold Rush* (Hamden, Connecticut, 1990) and Paula Petrik, *No Step Backward: Women and Family on the Rocky Mountain Mining Frontier, Helena Montana 1865–1900* (Helena, 1987) are especially good on women's experiences, while children in the camps are included in Elliott West's *Growing Up With the Country: Childhood on the Far-Western Frontier* (Albuquerque, 1989). Joseph R. Conlin pursues the surprisingly revealing question of eating habits in *Bacon, Beans, and Galantines: Food and Foodways on the Western Mining Frontier* (Reno, 1986). For a study of one moveable institution, see Elliott West, *The Saloon on the Rocky Mountain Mining Frontier* (Lincoln, 1979). It is one of several works that stress the tension between, on the one hand, the conservative impulse to transplant eastern culture into this new setting and, on the other, the frontier's power to shape society and to bring out the contradictions in the values brought to it. For an important study of this tension in the spiritual life of the frontier, see Laurie F. Maffly-Kipp, *Religion and Society in Frontier California* (New Haven, 1994). Brian Roberts, *American Alchemy: The California Gold Rush and Middle-Class Culture* (Chapel Hill, 2000) takes a broader—and exceptionally intelligent—look at the same phenomenon.

Finally, interested readers will find a host of republished diaries, letters, and reminiscences that portray life in the camps more vividly than any historian could hope to do. Among the best are Louise Amelia Knapp Smith Clappe, who wrote as Dame Shirley, *The Shirley Letters From the California Mines, 1851–1852* (Berkeley, 1998), Chauncey L. Canfield, ed., *The Diary of a Forty-Niner* (New York, 1992), Rodman W. Paul, ed., *A Victorian Gentlewoman in the Far West: The Reminiscences of Mary Hallock Foote* (San Marino, 1972), Andrew F. Rolle, ed., *The Road to Virginia City: The Diary of James Knox Polk Miller* (Norman, 1960), Anne Ellis, *The Life of an Ordinary Woman* (Lincoln, 1980), Walter Van Tilburg Clark, ed., *The Journals of Alfred Doten, 1849–1903,* 3 vols., (Reno, 1973), and James L. Thane, Jr., ed., *A Governor's Wife on the Mining Frontier: Letters of Mary Edgerton from Montana, 1863–1865* (Salt Lake, 1976).

The World's Convention

Direct assaults on Indian peoples triggered by California mining rushes are treated in some detail in Rawls, *Indians of California* and documented in Heizer, *The Destruction of California Indians,* both cited in the previous bibliographical essay. For examples of accounts of conflicts elsewhere in the West with roots in gold and silver discoveries, see Dan L. Thrapp, *The Conquest of Apacheria* (Norman, 1967),

Jerome A. Greene, *Nez Perce Summer, 1877: The U.S. Army and the Nee-Me-Poo Crisis* (Helena, 2000), E. A. Schwartz, *The Rogue River Indian War and Its Aftermath, 1850–1980* (Norman, 1997), and Elliott West, *The Contested Plains: Indians, Gold-seekers and the Rush to Colorado* (Lawrence, 1998). The Great Sioux War of 1876 has inspired long shelves of books, one of which considers the precipitating event in the Black Hills: Donald Jackson, *Custer's Gold: The United States Cavalry Expedition of 1874* (New Haven, 1966).

Most general sources on mining town society, and certainly all those mentioned for the preceding chapter, discuss the ethnic and cultural variety of mining frontiers. Some discuss the subject in more detail and with greater analytical energy. James, *The Roar and the Silence,* is especially good on the human stew that was the Comstock. Rohrbough, *Days of Gold,* has an excellent account of the French in California. Johnson, *Roaring Camp,* offers some fascinating arguments regarding the dynamic and often troubled relations between whites and miners from Mexico and South America as well as the sexual maneuverings among those groups. That latter topic is the focus of a particularly insightful study: Albert L. Hurtado, *Intimate Frontiers: Sex, Gender, and Culture in Old California* (Albuquerque, 1999).

Other works focus on particular ethnic and national groups. Jay Monaghan considers early English-speaking arrivals in California whose great distance from their mother country gave them a jump on the competition: *Australians and the Gold Rush: California and Down Under, 1849–1854* (Berkeley, 1966). Abraham P. Nasatir's *The French in the California Gold Rush* (New York, 1934) is the best account of this controversial group in the mother lode; on others who met serious opposition from late-arriving forty-niners from the states, see Jay Monaghan, *Chile, Peru, and the California Gold Rush of 1849* (Berkeley, 1973). Miners from Cornwall, especially important as skilled workers, have inspired two fine studies, John Rowe, *The Hard-Rock Men: Cornish Immigrants and the North American Mining Frontier* (New York, 1974) and A. L. Rowse, *The Cousin Jacks: The Cornish in America* (New York, 1969). On a prominent group defined both ethnically and religiously, there is Robert E. Levinson, *The Jews in the California Gold Rush* (Berkeley, 1978).

The unusual experience—and the unusually harsh response to—Chinese immigrants have inspired the most extensive study of any ethnic group of the mining West. Two outstanding works analyzing that hostility are Stuart Creighton Miller, *The Unwelcome Immigrant: The American Image of the Chinese, 1785–1882* (Berkeley, 1969), which concentrates on the rhetoric of discrimination, and Alexander Saxton, *The Indispensable Enemy: Labor and the Anti-Chinese Movement in California* (Berkeley, 1971), with an emphasis on the economic roots of the hostility. A recent book taking a fresh look at Chinese women immigrants is George Anthony Peffer, *If They Don't Bring Their Women Here: Chinese Female Immigration before Exclusion* (Urbana, 1999). Something of an antidote to the large literature on oppression and hostility, Liping Zhu's *A Chinaman's Chance: The Chinese on the Rocky Mountain Mining Frontier* (Niwot, 1997) emphasizes the relatively friendly relations between whites and Chinese in the Idaho camps, the assertiveness of Chinese in defending themselves, and their relatively high degree of success.

Worlds of Work

Much remains to be written about the impact of the mining frontiers, and frontiers generally, on the working worlds of Indian peoples, but a vigorous interest in environmental history has begun to direct historians' attention in that direction. Once again Rawls, *Indians of California,* is an admirable example of what can be learned from studying this topic. West, *The Contested Plains,* takes as its theme the clash of visions of Colorado's native peoples and its mining frontiersmen, including their means of working the land. The devastating impact of overland gold rushes on the economic environments of Great Basin peoples is the backdrop of Brigham D. Madsen's *The Shoshoni Frontier and the Bear River Massacre* (Salt Lake City, 1985).

Work was so central to life on the mining frontier that most histories include descriptions. Two recent works already cited—Rohrbough, *Days of Gold* and Holliday, *Rush to Riches*—offer especially detailed accounts as well as the reactions of gold seekers to the backbreaking labor. One essential book, wonderfully detailed, on the workaday lives of miners, their equipment and the perils of their jobs is Otis E. Young, Jr., *Western Mining* (Norman, 1970). It includes a useful glossary of terms and phrases. The best study of the history of the environmental impact of mining work is Duane A. Smith, *Mining America: The Industry and the Environment, 1800–1980* (Lawrence, 1987). Accounts of specific mining towns often describe working life and give a reader insight into how work might differ from place to place. James's *The Roar and the Silence* on the Comstock and Terry Cox, *Inside the Mountains: A History of Mining Around Central City, Colorado* (Boulder, 1989) are good examples. Many older classics cited by Rodman Paul deal with the techniques and accomplishments of labor; DeQuille's *The Big Bonanza* and Lord's *Comstock Mining and Miners* are notable in this regard.

In case readers are tempted to assume the process of finding and working strikes was an entirely male enterprise, there is Sally Zanjani, *A Mine of Her Own: Women Prospectors in the American West, 1850–1950* (Lincoln, 1997). Levy, *They Saw the Elephant* and Marks, *Precious Dust* offer considerable material on women's contribution to the economic life of mining towns. West, *Growing Up With the Country,* does the same for children. Given its lurid fascination, prostitution not surprisingly has drawn plenty of attention. The best book on the general subject of western harlotry is Anne Butler, *Daughters of Joy, Sisters of Misery: Prostitutes in the American West, 1865–90* (Urbana, 1985). For perceptive analyses of the flesh trade and what it revealed about the mining frontier in two particular settings, see Marion S. Goldman, *Gold Diggers and Silver Miners: Prostitution and Social Life on the Comstock Lode* (Ann Arbor, 1981) and Petrik, *No Step Backwards*. The frontier seems to have had as much an effect on the lives, including the labors and responsibilities, of women left back home as it did on more direct participants. On this subject we have a fine book: Linda Peavy and Ursula Smith, *Women in Waiting in the Westward Movement: Life on the Home Frontier* (Norman, 1994).

The transition from placer to lode mining transformed not only the miner's working world but his relationship to his fellow laborers as well. Two fine works explore this transition and provide especially useful descriptions of life underground: Ronald C. Brown, *Hard-Rock Miners: the Intermountain West, 1860–1920* (College Station, 1979) and Mark Wyman, *Hard Rock Epic: Western Miners and the Industrial*

Revolution, 1860–1910 (Berkeley, 1979). The change in laboring environments was intimately related to the rise of labor unions in western mines, so both of these books deal in some detail with unions, their origins and conflicts. Two books that focus more sharply on unionization are Richard E. Lingenfelter, *The Hardrock Miners: A History of the Mining Labor Movement in the American West, 1863–1893* (Berkeley, 1974) and Alan Derickson, *Workers' Health, Workers' Democracy: The Western Miners' Struggle, 1891–1925* (Ithaca, 1988).

INDEX